FELLOWSHIP IN A RING

A Guide for Science Fiction and Fantasy Book Groups

Neil Hollands

LIBRARIES UNLIMITED

An Imprint of ABC-CLIO, LLC

A B C ● C L I O

Santa Barbara, Califc   Oxford, England

Copyright 2010 by Libraries Unlimited

Library of Congress Cataloging-in-Publication Data

Hollands, Neil.
  Fellowship in a ring : a guide for science fiction and fantasy book groups / Neil Hollands.
       p. cm.
  Includes bibliographical references and index.
  ISBN 978-1-59158-703-3 (alk. paper)
1. Fantasy fiction—Appreciation—Handbooks, manuals, etc. 2. Science fiction—Appreciation—Handbooks, manuals, etc. 3. Book clubs (Discussion groups)—Handbooks, manuals, etc. 4. Group reading—Handbooks, manuals, etc. 5. Fantasy fiction—Themes, motives. 6. Science fiction—Themes, motives. I. Title.
  PN3435.H63 2010
  809.3'8766—dc22   2009046456

14 13 12 11 10   1 2 3 4 5

This book is also available on the World Wide Web as an eBook.
Visit www.abc-clio.com for details.

ABC-CLIO, LLC
130 Cremona Drive, P.O. Box 1911
Santa Barbara, California 93116-1911

This book is printed on acid-free paper ∞
Manufactured in the United States of America

To Sharon, who may find fantastic worlds difficult to enter,
but who makes my world fantastic every day.

Contents

Acknowledgments

Successful book groups require collaboration. Putting together a handbook about them took even more. Several groups of people deserve acknowledgment.

Several other book group leaders were kind enough to share their experiences and perspectives with me. Thanks to Georgine Olsen of Fairbanks, Alaska's Noel Wien Library; Steven Torres-Roman of DeKalb Public Library; A. T. Campbell, III, of Austin's FACT SF/F Group; Christine Mitchamore of San Antonio Public Library; Mac Moyer of Eugene, Oregon; Marnie Oakes of Ruben Hoar Library in Littleton, Massachusetts; and Phil De Parto of the Science Fiction Association of Bergen County, New Jersey.

The support and wisdom of my librarian colleagues make my writing projects possible. Williamsburg Regional Library is the best readers' advisory library anywhere. Thanks to our fearless division leader, Barry Trott; my colleagues, Amy Bunn, Charlotte Burcher, Janet Curtis, Cheryl Edwards, Penelope Hamblin, Rebekah Hartberger, Avery Hicks, Jennifer Kuncken, Gail Mann, Barbara Riebe, Andrew Smith, Marion Sullivan, Dwight Woodward, and Jessica Zellers; and our directors, John Moorman and Genevieve Owens.

The people at Libraries Unlimited support their writers graciously and make knowledge available that might otherwise go uncollected. Special thanks to my editor, Barbara Ittner.

Finally, I'd like to thanks my fellow fans in Hampton Roads, the whole crew at MarsCon, and, most important to this volume, the members of the Williamsburg Science Fiction and Fantasy Book Group, from whom I learn more about the genres than I teach. I'd especially like to thank my co-leader Bob Snare, who got the group off the ground and keeps us all in line, and our other founding members and regulars (or should I say irregulars?): Crystal Bertoncini, Brian and Rachel Bevins, Catherine and Terry Bond, Kathryn Dickerson, Mary Horton, Deb King, Jim Kladder, Jim Michie, Cathy Morrison, Don Noble, Andrea Norfolk, Dan Norfolk, Gary Robertson, Carolyn Snare, Vittorio Treppo, and Bud Webster. Your knowledge about and enthusiasm for the genre are bottomless, and your friendship and support cannot be topped.

Preface

On a rainy Tuesday evening, members of the Williamsburg Area Science Fiction and Fantasy Book Group begin to arrive at the library. As with many science fiction/fantasy groups, some members had known each other from local fandom for decades. A few discovered their shared interest back in their school days. Some participated in a group that called it quits after suffering through disagreements about which books to read and undue pressure from their bookstore host to buy new hardbacks. With the introduction of a thematic format and help from the local library, they quickly reconstituted and added new members.

They're a diverse bunch: young readers and old, men and women in equal numbers. There are students, retirees, laborers, and professionals, the expected information technology workers and scientists, sure, but also educators, homemakers, writers, and other artistic types. Some read voraciously; others struggle to finish a book each month. Some read only speculative fiction; others also enjoy nonfiction, literary fiction, or other genres. A core group never misses a meeting, but new faces, visitors, or occasional members join the fray each month. It's a disparate group, but they share an enthusiasm for science fiction and fantasy and a common pleasure in discussing these genres.

In any month, there are 15 to 20 attendees. It's a good size; there are plenty of viewpoints to hear, but enough time to get around the table in the two allotted hours. As the group filters in, members pass around used books or look through advance reader copies sent by Baen, Tor, and other publishers. Several group members love crafts and share tips or even work on projects during the meeting. The group's writers exchange ideas and feedback or happily publicize new publications. Upcoming conventions, author events, gaming opportunities, and library programs are announced.

This group uses themes instead of reading a common book. A list of books that fit the topic and some thematic discussion questions were distributed at the end of last month's meeting. Readers return with the books they chose to read, selected either from the list or discovered independently in bookstores or from their own collections. One member is usually asked to prepare a 5- to 10-minute introduction of the topic that kicks off the meeting. After that, discussion proceeds around the table, with readers introducing one or two books each.

As discussion proceeds, any topic can become part of the conversation (and usually does). This group tolerates more distractions than most: discussion of new movies or television series, a riff of atrocious puns, debate on the merits of cover art, an anecdote about a favorite author, or even fascination with self-heating hot chocolate or a spray can of pancake batter. As one of two co-leaders, I gently steer us back to the books when I must, but usually discussion circles back without prompting. Most of our readers select books on the theme, but sometimes a reader ignores the theme to introduce a great book that he or she just can't wait to talk about, and that's tolerated too. There is a mix of new books, classics, short stories, graphic novels, and even the occasional film or music album. By the time we finish, almost everyone has discovered more books that they want to read and marked several titles on next month's list, getting ready for the next go-around.

For this group, the evening isn't over. Each meeting is followed by a late meal at nearby Tequila Rose, an event often joined by latecomers or family members who are not genre readers. Group members form the core of the staff for MarsCon, a local convention. They gather for seasonal parties, game nights, and coffee talk in weeks when the book group doesn't meet. They attend each other's special occasions. They come to each other's aid when someone needs help or gets sick. The group has become a family—a dysfunctional family perhaps, but a family nonetheless.

My Williamsburg group is just one of hundreds that meet around the world to enjoy and discuss the literature of science fiction and fantasy. Whether your fellowship (to borrow a term from one of our greats) of readers has already begun its quest or is just beginning the journey, this book can help.

Introduction

Although the advice contained in this handbook can benefit any book group, this is the first book aimed specifically at speculative fiction readers: fans of science fiction and fantasy. These genres have their own literature, with readers whose demography and lifestyles create advantages and challenges that differ from those of other reading groups.

I've taken lessons learned from my own group and my experiences as a librarian, supplemented them by talking to leaders of other speculative fiction groups, and scoured the shelves for the most discussable titles and ideas in the speculative fiction realm. The book provides counseling for the moments when your fellowship becomes unruly, threatening to fracture or fall into the book group equivalent of the Crack of Doom. It identifies the books and themes that get the best results, inspiring successful discussions. You'll be equipped with discussion questions, facilitation hints, and resources to make the most of each meeting.

It is hoped that this book will be especially useful to libraries. In addition to providing advice, discussion materials, and examples for book groups, the book includes basic, genre-specific readers' advisory information. Careful perusal of its contents provides a guide for collection development in science fiction and fantasy. The lists in Chapters 2 and 5 can easily be converted into booklists to be distributed at your library or into topical displays.

This book is divided into five chapters. In Chapter 1 you'll learn everything you need to start a group and facilitate it successfully. I'll explain why science fiction and fantasy are good genres to discuss and why a book group is the format in which to discuss them. Advice is given about how to find members and select the time, place, and format for meetings. The chapter explores the roles of group leaders and some techniques for selecting titles. Methods of facilitating discussion are considered, as are suggestions for helping readers talk about books with success. Special consideration is given to the question of whether meetings should center on a common book or a broader theme. There are hints for working with science fiction and fantasy readers and best practices that help these two camps get along. A lighthearted section examines how to work with common science fiction and fantasy reader types. Chapter 1 concludes with ideas for adding extra fun to group meetings.

Chapter 2 is a crash course in the science fiction and fantasy genres. It begins with definitions of 16 major subgenres in each genre, identifying excellent examples of each of those 32 areas of speculative fiction. A glossary of 50 terms adds depth to any book group discussion. Two lists of general discussion questions—one for fantasy, the other for science fiction—complete the chapter, providing tools to discuss any work of speculative fiction.

Chapters 3 and 4 examine 50 of speculative fiction's most discussable books in depth—25 each for fantasy and science fiction. Analysis includes bibliographic details for each book, a biography of the author, links to the author's Web site and other online resources, a plot synopsis, enumeration of the book's appeal points, discussion questions, and suggestions for further reading for those who enjoy the book. For additional scope, I've added lists of 100 more authors in each genre, including a suggested work to discuss first for each.

Chapter 5 details over 40 themes upon which a successful genre discussion can be conducted. Clever quotes and a short introduction get your thoughts percolating about the theme. A generous list of good books that fit each theme is provided, as are thematic discussion questions and links to online resources. A list of 100 more themes that your group can explore closes the chapter.

Throughout this book, I've attempted to represent the full scope of these wonderful genres. I've included books marketed for adults and those marketed for young adults; series and stand-alone works; story anthologies and single-author collections; speculative works marketed as literary fiction side by side with pulse-pounding pulp novels. But despite this inclusive spirit, these are large genres with a long publishing history, and, inevitably, some wonderful works await my discovery and yours. Because the subject at hand is reading for book groups, my selections lean toward the kind of substantial writing that can support group discussion.

In particular, I've made one decision that may be controversial: the works listed throughout this volume are almost entirely books that are in print at the time of this writing. Although this may displease some readers and critics and excludes hundreds of strong books and authors that groups might enjoy, the fact remains that book groups need selections that are easy to obtain quickly. So my apologies to fans of the classics; I, too, would like to see many works back in print. If your group would like to focus on the genre's history, I encourage you to use the appendix of print and online resources that concludes this work. It includes both resources for book groups and resources for genre study.

More groups are discussing this fascinating, diverse literature all the time. There are readers of these genres in every community, and, with just a little encouragement and organization, you can form a ring of fellowship around the table of your choice.

Chapter 1
Starting and Facilitating Your Group

WHY START A SCIENCE FICTION/FANTASY BOOK GROUP?

Long sequestered in the ghettoes of genre fiction, science fiction and fantasy have been sneered at by snooty readers, largely ignored by critics, and ill-serviced by publishers who insist on using covers that embarrass adult readers and reinforce the impression that these are genres for children. Even those who love the genres sometimes avoid suggesting their discussion in book groups, believing them too plot-driven to incite good discussion or simply avoiding a confrontation with the uninformed stereotypes held by other group members.

The truth is that science fiction and fantasy contains hundreds of excellent books for discussion. Yes, many works of speculative fiction are plot-driven, but science fiction and fantasy often mix complex characters, detailed settings, and a full gamut of writing styles with those strong stories, giving groups plenty to discuss. Yes, there is great reading for young people (and their families) in these genres, but that's no reason for adult groups to avoid them. There are plenty of serious adult works too. Libraries, in particular, should factor the all-ages appeal of speculative fiction into their decision making as they choose which kinds of book groups to support.

The biggest knock against these genres is that, because they are works of imagination and not realism, that they are only good for escapism. Although a few are looking for escape, the large majority of speculative fiction readers know that these books speak to both their minds and their emotions. Science fiction is a literature of ideas, concepts that have strong implications for how we should conduct our world. Fantasy fiction brims with complex moral dilemmas and uses its imagined settings to explore concepts such as loyalty, bigotry, violence, revenge, courage, and justice. In the end, only readers with limited skills of inference and imagination find these genres lacking in worthwhile content and emotional impact.

Not only does this literature merit attention, the book group is the ideal place to have that discussion. Sometimes teased or dismissed by "realist" readers, whose favorite works often feature unbelievable plots despite their "real world" settings, science fiction and fantasy readers are looking for an outlet to talk about the books they love. Ostracized by some as geeks or nerds, many science fiction and fantasy (**hereafter abbreviated SF and F**) fans flourish in a supportive environment where they can socialize without being made self-conscious.

Joining a group helps readers validate the time they spend on books, time that some—individuals who feel little compunction to reduce hours that they themselves spend on telephones, television, or their own leisure activities—tell them is frivolously spent. Group members finish more books as they concentrate to finish books in time for upcoming meetings. Discussion groups expand literary horizons, help readers find writers they otherwise would not have chosen, provide a chance to compare interpretations, and encourage deeper understanding of what one reads.

For libraries, support of book groups should be fundamental. Groups build a bridge between the library and its reading community. While spending time in book groups, staff members have a chance to explain library policies, highlight collections, and listen directly to the needs of the library's core group of readers. My hours with book groups have provided the inspiration for dozens of displays and provided the knowledge I've needed to build a fantastic speculative fiction collection. Book group participants attend other library programs and become some of our most valued volunteers. For a small investment of staff time and money, libraries gain much from book groups.

And now is a better time than ever to talk about science fiction and fantasy. Diversity among both the writers and the writing are at all-time highs. Science fiction continues to expand its scope beyond the base material of space travel and alien encounters to include the full range of future possibilities. No longer can it be stigmatized as wonky literature with strong ideas but cardboard characters, with good science but little insight into human nature. Fantasy has also broadened its purview, looking to the contemporary world and historical places and times beyond medieval Europe for its settings. It continues to probe the nature of good and evil, but instead of portraying these concepts as clashing armies, good and evil often battle in the heart of each major character. These are just a few reasons why right now is a great time for your science fiction/fantasy book group.

FORMING A SCIENCE FICTION/FANTASY BOOK GROUP

Finding Members

To start your speculative fiction group, you'll have to overcome bias often held by F & SF readers: the idea that book groups are only for snobby literary types. Degraded by a few literary readers, SF & F readers have developed their own wrongheaded misconceptions as a means of self-defense. Those who haven't participated in book groups may picture them as stuffy events, where academic types blow hot air about critical theories and deconstruction, finding ways to take all of the fun out of reading. They may imagine gaggles of charming grandmothers, using books as an excuse for pastry, gossip, and an afternoon outing. Or they may envisage Stepford wives and glad-handing Babbitts, pasting on phony smiles to join in a well-coiffed, grim battle to determine the neighborhood social hierarchy. A few, trying to protect the vicarious foothold they have gained in the social mainstream, may be reluctant to gather with genre readers, preferring to keep their jones for Terry Pratchett, Mercedes Lackey, or Harry Turtledove as a shameful secret.

To conquer these fears and gather your group, you must prepare to seek out the dark, strange, or hidden places where the fans go. Convince them to embrace their geekiness, overcome their social phobias, and moderate their most extreme behaviors. Most important, you'll have to show them that book groups are fun and rewarding—neither the dreary, preachy lecture hall that one kind of imagination fears, nor the droning prattle and clinking cups of meaningless tea parties that the other suspects. Use white lies, use trickery, use bribes of books or chocolate, whatever it takes to get them out. They'll thank you for it later.

Three or four dedicated readers can make a functional book group, but aim to find 10 to 20, depending on the format you plan to use and the space where you plan to meet. This may seem like a lot of people, but you will probably lose one-quarter of your starting members in the first few meetings. Even when the group becomes established, it is not unusual to lose another quarter of the group to other commitments at any given meeting. Ultimately, a group that grows too large is a problem, but as you get started, it's a luxury. An overlarge group can always split, but more likely, any overcrowding will help whittle away less dedicated readers.

Start with word of mouth. You probably know at least one or two science fiction/fantasy readers, but if you don't, try asking people who read other kinds of books or people who enjoy science fiction and fantasy films and television. Even if your first contacts aren't interested in a book group, they may know others who are. At this stage, emphasize that no commitment is implied, that you're simply going to assemble science fiction/fantasy fans and see whether you can find common ground for a reading group. Ask each new contact to try to find another reader or two. Collect contact information as you go.

If the group is based at a library or bookstore, don't settle for a single mode of publicity for the book group. One poster on the bulletin board isn't going to cut it. You may already be familiar with some of your core readers of speculative fiction. Start by trying to recruit them. Make up bookmarks with a contact and a meeting date. Distribute them at public service desks. If science fiction and fantasy are shelved separately, put fliers or bookmarks in those spaces. Stuff bookmarks in science fiction/fantasy works that are on the library's new bookshelf or hold shelf. Advertise the organizational meeting in your newsletter and on your website.

When five or six recruits have been located, it's time to get serious: set a firm first meeting date two months hence and work hard in the intervening time to find a full quota of readers. Make your best guess about when the group might meet and spend those hours searching the science fiction/fantasy section of local bookstores and libraries. These "right-time, right-place" readers make excellent potential members.

If word-of-mouth and personal contacts don't produce enough members, expand the search. See whether nearby libraries and bookstores will advertise the group. Use eye-catching graphics and provide contact information on strips that can be pulled off the bottom of the announcement. Make bookmarks that announce the group and ask if they can be distributed or even inserted in science fiction and fantasy novels. Colleges, community centers, restaurants, coffeehouses, and supermarkets are among many locations that may provide notice boards or allow posters in windows. Colleges may have science fiction, fantasy, anime, or manga clubs that nonstudents can attend or funds that can be tapped for new groups if you can attract some student members.

If you're not a librarian, make sure to consult with local librarians or those who work in bookstores. They may know if another science fiction/fantasy group meets in your area or be able to connect you with more genre readers. They might even be potential group members themselves. Later, they might aid your group in tracking down a room to meet in or in getting enough copies of a particular book.

Another key method of finding F & SF readers is to check local fandom activities. You may or may not consider yourself a likely candidate to wear Star Wars costumes, pitch battle royale in the local park, watch anime until your eyes bleed, or twirl with the local chapter of the Society for Creative Anachronism (SCA) in the annual May dances, but many insightful readers participate in such activities. Local conventions (call them "Cons") attract people from all walks of life and do not require you to wear costumes or do anything else you find embarrassing. Spending Saturday at a Con passing out fliers, attending panels likely to attract readers, or lurking around book vendor tables may produce a good yield of potential members. And you'll have fun in the process!

Look to create synergy by connecting your group with other SF & F themed groups. For instance, the Science Fiction Association of Bergen County New Jersey (http://sfabc.org) offers television and video viewing and discussion groups, guest speakers, topical discussions, and a writer's group, along with book groups. Gaming groups are another place to recruit. Check in with any local shops that support role-playing or other table gaming. Leave fliers or ask for contact information for local games. Some occupations and hobbies draw a high number of genre readers. Try large computer- or science-related businesses for science fiction readers or explore crafting groups or pet lovers for fantasy fans. If the SCA, other medieval groups, or re-enactors of any kind are locally active, they may also yield participants.

Don't forget advertising in other media. Consider taking classified ads in local newspaper or local cable television channels that have public events calendars. The Internet is full of resources to help people with common interests get together. Try announcing your organizational meeting on Google Base (http://base.google.com), Craigslist (http://www.craigslist.org), backpage (http://www.backpage.com), or any well-used community calendar. Websites for local radio and television stations often have bulletin boards and calendars. Look for readers in your area on social networking sites aimed at book lovers, such as LibraryThing (http://www.librarything.com), GoodReads (http://www.goodreads.com), or Shelfari (http://www.shelfari.com). If you live in a place that is isolated from other readers, work a shift that makes physical meetings with others difficult, or are in some way homebound, these sites also provide means for participating in an online book group.

The Organizational Meeting

If a meeting place is not already decided, choose a location for your group's organizational meeting the same way you would choose the location for a blind date: central, public, and inexpensive—with a casual, noncommittal atmosphere. Remember, this blind date may draw a crowd, so make sure there is a room or table big enough for the group and that noise—created both by your group and by the rest of the establishment—won't be disruptive.

At the organizational meeting, you'll have eight major goals:

- Energize readers about the potential of the group.
- Introduce yourselves to one another.
- Establish a group management model.
- Determine any limits on subject matter or membership.
- Decide what kind of books to read and select the first few books or themes.
- Set the time and date of future meetings.
- Select the permanent location (or locations) for meetings.
- Select a preliminary format for the group.

Most of these tasks are addressed in detail later in this chapter, but let's tackle the first four now. Just because you convince a suitable number of people to turn up for an organizational meeting doesn't mean that your group has left the launch pad. Continue using the model of the blind date: be friendly but don't come on too strong. Emphasize your common interest by bringing book lists or copies of books by popular genre authors to pass around. Don't overdo it with jargon, costuming, gaming gear, or other science fiction/fantasy paraphernalia until you know how interested other readers are in these things. Avoid swearing, off-color remarks, or any behavior that might suggest sexism or other bigotry.

Above all, don't do all of the talking yourself. Other members become invested in the group more quickly if they think of it as our group, not just your group. Encourage everyone to introduce themselves, their occupation, their interest in the science fiction and fantasy genres, and their favorite genre writers. Listen actively to what they say. Take a few notes. Collect contact information and follow up quickly after the group meeting to send out a group message. Strongly consider selecting a book or theme for one of the first meetings that caters to common interests of members, particularly those whose membership you most want to retain.

Although the social awkwardness of SF & F fans is vastly overemphasized by media stereotypes, fans may seem eccentric to the general population. Fans share an interest for which some might ostracize or, at least, tease them. The SF & F reading population is analyzed more thoroughly later in this chapter, but, for now, suffice it to say that SF/F book group members may hope to fulfill social needs beyond book discussion. At the organizational meeting, don't come on too strong, but don't be afraid to suggest going for drinks, appetizers, or desserts, or for a browsing session in the library or at a bookstore when the organizational business is done. It's okay to hint that other social activities might follow. Just don't corner anyone in the parking lot, pass out your business card, plan dates, or try to start a live-action role-playing session before you know your new friends or have priority number one—the book group—up and running.

If you've done the work to organize the group and have strong plans for how it should be organized, establish this immediately. If it's important to you, establish your benign dictatorship from the start by limiting the options for the meeting place, time, and early book selections. With such control comes responsibility, so plan to offer to do further advertising work and notification reminders of the first meetings. This strong style works for many book groups, if the leader doesn't get too controlling and does a good job of organizing. However, adopting a more democratic style may be less likely to scare people away, allowing full discussion of when and where the group should meet and which books to read.

If you intend to place any limits on subject matter, now is the time to do it. Do you want to read only fantasy, only science fiction, or both? If both, should the mix be balanced or lean toward one of the genres? Do your tastes tend toward classics or contemporary works? Do they tend toward pulpier works, the mainstream of the genre, or more literary authors? Do you want to read related genres, such as horror, thrillers, paranormal romance, or nonfiction about the genre? Do you want to read graphic novels or young adult material on occasion? If anyone objects strongly to extreme violence, sexuality, obscenity, or other kinds of content, now is the time to put those objections on the table. Unless your group is in strong agreement over subject matter limits, it is best to leave possibilities open to any book that the readers select. Remind everyone that a great value of book groups is to stretch reader horizons, which sometimes includes new authors and diverse styles. If there are conflicting tastes, themed meetings keep your group together best—but more on that later.

Some reading groups decide to restrict membership through means other than the reading material. Members might have to meet a minimum age; come from a particular age range; be single or of a particular gender; or live, work, or go to school in a common area. Because of the difficulty in finding enough readers devoted to particular genres, it's usually best to avoid such restrictions when forming a science fiction/fantasy group. Unless some critical secondary goal is also intended for the group—to provide a place for singles to mix, a boys' or girls' night out, or a haven for teens or seniors, for instance—you'll do better with open membership. Over time, you'll probably come to appreciate as much diversity in perspective as you can get.

In my experience, science fiction/fantasy groups are more likely to attract male readers than book groups as a whole. Although wide-scale numbers are difficult to find, Elizabeth Long reported, in 2003 in *Book Clubs*, that of 121 Houston-area groups, 64% were all female, 33% were co-ed, and 3% had only male members. Nobody has done a survey of speculative fiction groups, but anecdotal evidence suggests that the large majority are co-ed, with some all-male groups, and only a few all-female groups. Even though diversity among science fiction/fantasy fans continues to improve, you may want to make special efforts to encourage the recruitment and retention of women, readers of color, or younger readers. This is not for the purpose of social activism or creating a dating pool: readers from different backgrounds bring different insights to discussion.

At minimum, leave your organizational meeting with the time, place, and choice of books for three meetings established. Showing that much commitment provides a solid base on which your group can build. Decide who will lead discussion or provide an introduction to the books or theme in each of these meetings. If there is no obvious reason to fear overcrowding, encourage everyone to continue to recruit more members. If the group is at risk of becoming too large, establish a policy for inviting new members. Make sure that someone summarizes what was decided, posts it on the Internet if possible, and sends this summary over email or other means to both those who attended and anyone who could not make the organizational session.

If your organizational meeting doesn't attract enough readers, or common ground for a long-term book group isn't clear, consider forming a short-term genre study group. This method can be especially useful if you have active readers who are not sure about the depth of their interest in the science fiction/and fantasy genres. Pick a theme, an author of common interest, or a defined set of three or four books and agree to a short schedule of meetings. This gives you time to test the waters and recruit more readers. If the group hasn't gelled at the end of the defined period, you can let it go without hard feelings.

THE MEETING: TIME, PLACE, AND FORMAT

The questions of where, when, how, and for how long are crucial to the success of book groups. The first step to determining the answers is to establish the intent of your group, because this may help decide other factors. Is your main intent a fun night out with friends, careful study of the genres, or something in between? Do you want to focus on certain authors, topics, or books, or do you want to survey the breadth of speculative fiction? Most groups look for balance in all of these matters, but some are more focused, particularly if the membership is small. Regardless, it's worth discussing, because it shapes and may even decide how much time you need, which meeting places are appropriate, which format to choose, and what kinds of discussions and comments are most apt.

Because they appeal to a broad range of ages, most speculative fiction groups choose weeknight meetings. This is the time when the greatest numbers of readers are available. Older groups often prefer daytime hours, and some groups find success on weekend afternoons, but these meeting times are more likely to restrict attendance. If your group can only meet for one hour, you either need to restrict the number of members or limit discussion to a single book at each meeting. There just won't be time for other approaches. Most groups find a two-hour meeting most effective, leaving time for a variety of formats and allowing for a good discussion that is neither rushed nor endurance-testing. Longer meetings work for some groups, but if you go longer, make sure to break in the middle and offer refreshments.

How often should your group meet? Most book groups prefer monthly meetings, which allow enough time to read most books, but not so much time that members begin to forget the book or the upcoming meeting dates. This is not set in stone. Groups can succeed with more or less frequent meetings, based on their intent and the amount of time that members can devote to reading. Monthly meetings, however, make a good default for groups that are getting started. If the day of the week, time, and place are consistent, monthly meetings are easy to remember.

Where should you meet? Sometimes this choice is limited to one or two possibilities, but look for options, because your choice of venue affects the discussion. Meetings in public places are less intimidating to new members, keep hosting pressures to a minimum, and generally have better parking. Meetings in private homes may be harder to locate and make newcomers uncomfortable, but, for established groups, they provide a sense of friendship and intimacy. A dedicated room enhances concentration, keeps the group focused, and allows the comforts of privacy, but an open space, such as a bookstore or restaurant, may be more genial or provide access to refreshments, copies of books, or other welcome distractions. A library that allows food in meeting rooms may meet every criteria, although one downside can be early closing times that force the group to rush. Many locations can work, but think in advance about how each possibility might affect your group.

Consider costs, noise levels, access to parking and restrooms, pet or smoking allergies, comfort of chairs, temperature control, access to telephones and Internet, and options to bring in outside food and drink. Make sure there is enough space: enough chairs that readers can face each other and see and hear the other participants. Can the space accommodate a reader with disabilities or one who needs an extra large chair? Would you have to rush to finish at a particular time? Are other occupants friendly to science fiction/fantasy fans? Can books be passed around without getting lost or dirty? A location that can guarantee a scheduled space and time is highly preferable. If you cannot get such guarantees, make sure the management is friendly to your group and allows necessary rearrangements. Consider sending someone early to stake out space and have a nearby fallback planned for emergencies.

One factor that many groups fail to consider is the format of the meeting. This is not necessarily disastrous: sometimes the best way to decide a format is to leave the discussion open and see what develops organically. However, if your meetings are not satisfying in any way, be aware that format can make a big difference. Here are some formatting questions to consider:

- How will books be selected?
- Will your group read one shared work, read a particular author, read on a theme, leave selections completely open, or vary methods from meeting to meeting?
- How will new members be introduced? Are guests allowed? Is membership open, or is there a formal process for adding new members? Can membership be revoked?

- If the meeting is held in a private home, what is expected of the host?
- Will you have a permanent discussion leader, rotate this role from meeting to meeting, or go without?
- How will you begin discussion? Will someone introduce the work or the topic? If so, how much time should this introduction take?
- Will each member talk about the reading in turn, will talk be controlled in some way, or will the floor be open?
- Will background on the author be provided? If so, who will obtain it?
- Will anyone look into reviews of works in question or the history of the theme?
- Will the group address particular discussion questions? If so, will these be created by the group or by one person? Provided to the group in advance or at the meeting?
- When discussing authors, subgenres, or other themes, will participants be limited to introducing one book, or can they bring more?
- Will any time be saved for talking about books outside of the meeting's official topic?
- Is time needed to select future reading? To introduce next month's book or theme?
- Will refreshment be allowed? Encouraged? If so, will they be eaten during a break or throughout the meeting? Who will provide them? Or will the group go out for food and drinks after the meeting?

For the group's early meetings, consistency in time, place, and format are important. Don't make many shifts until you've given your original plans a good trial run. When your membership is more established, if flaws to your methods become obvious, or if your membership changes over time, then you can tinker with structure. In the early stages, it is more important that your members know what to expect.

THE ROLES OF GROUP LEADERS

To borrow a metaphor from the literature, leading a book group is like leading a motley crew of characters on a quest. It requires motivating the group to attend and participate, deciding the group format, delegating roles appropriately, communicating basic rules and methods, facilitating discussion, and occasionally dealing with problem personalities. Even if your group is a participatory democracy, somebody should keep organized and remind them when decisions need to be made. Group leaders may delegate these tasks, but someone needs to undertake them. If you remember *The Hobbit* or *The Lord of the Rings*, you have a good example of how not to organize your group. Gandalf, as beloved a character as he is, does not lead groups well. He withholds key information, disappears without notice, and only delegates duties vaguely.

If you have the beginnings of a group, but no one willing to take on leadership, consider approaching a local library. They may be able to provide a leader, recruit an interested staff member, or at least support one of your members in fulfilling the leadership role. Here are a few hints for success in each of a book group leader's major roles.

Basic Communications

After selecting time, place, and format, the next step is to follow through over time, maintaining the group's schedule and communicating it to members. Book groups have failed because of simple mistakes, such as forgetting to schedule meeting space or failing to remind members consistently of upcoming meetings. Communication duties can be assigned to a secretary, shared through Internet tools, or controlled entirely by the group leader. There are many options, but it falls on the group leader to make sure that at least one of these is working.

Keep a membership notebook or devise a form for new members to complete. Bring these to each meeting. A little attention goes a long way toward keeping readers coming back. The subject, time, and location should be confirmed and advertised to members at least one month before each meeting and once again shortly before the meeting. Messages can be passed through telephone calls, email messages, or some kind of communications tree. Websites such as Meetup (http://www.meetup.com) and Yahoo Groups (http://groups.yahoo.com) provide a means to advertise your group, collect contact information, send meeting reminders, and post announcements and digital files. Schedules can be composed in many kinds of software and should include directions to the meeting place (or a link to the address in Google Maps, Yahoo Maps, or Mapquest). Include any parking instructions, food or drink limitations, important information about format, and a contact number.

Managing and Leading the Discussion

Techniques for managing discussion are addressed in detail later. For now, take note that someone has to guide discussion. Your group may even choose a *laissez-faire* approach, letting conversation flow where it will, but even this low-maintenance approach should be decided upon, not simply left to chance. Otherwise, you might find it difficult to respond if a strong-willed member tries to force a different structure on the group at a later time.

The group leader is not required to lead discussions, but the group leader should either decide or lead the group in deciding which roles (if any) a discussion leader will play. Discussion-leading duties—such as introducing the book, researching the author, finding reviews, or writing discussion questions—were listed in the section on selecting the time, place, and format of the group. Even when these roles are delegated to other individuals, the group leader should remain aware of the overall quality of discussion and help guide it to success.

Resolving Controversies and Problems

Perhaps the most difficult role of the group leader is to resolve controversies. Nobody joins or starts a book group with the goal of practicing dispute mediation. Most groups function happily for long periods without major problems, but every group eventually encounters a difficult member, a clash of wills, or fundamental disagreement over group objectives or format. Whether you decide matters yourself, as a powerful but kind king or queen, or resolve disputes by calling the galactic federation to order, you need to be prepared for crisis. One group I read about, upon encountering an extremely problematic member, decided to pretend to disband the group but then started it again in a new location. This was creative, but not functional problem solving (and the excluded member probably found out about the new group anyway).

Real leadership requires subtlety and finesse: catching most problems before they begin, nudging the group gently back on course when it wanders, and artfully resolving conflicts without seeming to take sides. When subtlety fails, leadership requires strong decisions on difficult matters: standing behind a necessary ruling that leaves some members unhappy, making major revisions to the group's subject or format, quietly asking a member to change behaviors, even deciding to exclude someone from participation or guiding the group through a split into two parts. Most problems can be avoided or resolved through planning and use of the methods described in this book, but as you take the responsibility of leading a group, understand that the day may come when you must act to protect the life of your group. There Gandalf is a good model: Be prepared for the day when you must stand up to your group's Balrog and say, "You shall not pass."

Motivating and Energizing

One oft-neglected role of the group leader deserves special mention—that of motivator and energizer. More groups fail or underachieve as a result of ennui and mediocrity, not major disputes or disasters. Even the conflicts and ill feelings that bring some groups to a bickering end can be reduced or prevented by a combination of comic relief, back patting, and cheerleading. Motivation is the job of every member of the group, but it starts with the group leader. Here's a sampling of small, well-placed actions that keep your quest moving forward:

- Thanking members for coming.
- Recalling something said well by a member in a previous meeting.
- Remembering the favorite books of another reader.
- Making connections to previous successful discussions.
- Jump-starting the conversation when it lags.
- Discovering interesting angles on books that are difficult to discuss.
- Finding bright spots when the book or topic is disappointing.
- Returning discussion to a member who is interrupted or a lead left unexplored.
- Motivating the group to tackle new subjects and challenging books as needed .
- Drawing comments from quieter participants.
- Diffusing conflict with a well-timed joke or distraction.
- Digging deeper when the discussion is superficial.
- Encouraging members (with subtlety) to attend more consistently, find new readers, or finish the book.
- Building excitement for next month's book or topic.
- Sending the group away on a positive note: "Thanks for your ideas and participation," "I'm looking forward to next month's meeting," or "It was fun to hear you defend your views of the book so vigorously."

SELECTING TITLES

The most debated matter in your book group is likely to be which books to read next—and with good reason—selecting the right titles goes a long way toward discussion success. A little bit of forethought can greatly aid your results. Here are the advantages and disadvantages of the five selection methods most often used by groups:

Benevolent monarchies leave book selection to one person or to a small elite. This method succeeds or fails according to the skill and knowledge of the selectors. For some groups it works very well, but with the strong-willed, opinionated readers of science fiction and fantasy, it can be a tough sell. In a full group, the average reader may not have the book knowledge to make great selections, and necessary compromises may further dilute the results. A few well-read selectors may make better selections, but whenever a selection fails, watch out! The rest of the group may be quick to gripe or even stage a revolt. If you prefer selection by benevolent monarch, elicit feedback occasionally so that the other readers feel included.

Annual/biannual group selection is sort of like Tolkien's Ent moots. In one or two meetings a year, everyone gets together and makes the case for the books they want. Compromises are made and a calendar is set. This has the advantages of involving the group and enabling discussion of the proposed titles; however, the debate can result in smoldering hurt feelings. To get the best results, encourage everyone to research the books that they advocate and to bring reviews. Formalize the voting method, allow limited vetoes, or guarantee that every reader selects at least one book to help the process along. This method takes time away from book discussion, which can be a curse if your group hates to miss a month or a blessing if December or the summer months find members too busy to finish a book. One disadvantage of this and other methods that select books far in advance is that opportunities for spontaneity or for matching the group mood can be lost.

Rotation is a low-maintenance, democratic selection method. Captain Kirk picks for January, Spock for February, Bones in March, Uhura in April, and so on. The selector is generally responsible for leading discussion that month. It's simple, and everyone gets a turn. This method is, however, the most haphazard and open to personal opinion. You'll get great surprises that other methods might not find, but also a larger proportion of duds. Warning: Book group members have been shut outside the ship's airlock for frequent unpopular selections. If you use this method, make sure that the selector knows when his or her turn is near and comes to group with a choice ready (or, preferably, a few choices that can be briefly discussed). Otherwise, you'll lose precious reading time waiting for a selection after the fact. Under no circumstances should you allow someone to select a book for a meeting that he or she is not planning to attend.

Formal nominations and voting are a particular variation of the group selection method. It takes organization, but with **email** or paper ballots, this method can be implemented in a way that doesn't use precious meeting time. It's hard to argue with the fairness of putting the results to a vote. This method most often results in mainstream selections on which everyone can agree, which may not suit readers looking for edgier fare or little-known authors. For best results, make sure that fair-minded annotations of similar length accompany each of the candidate books.

The thematic approach allows each member to bring any book that fits a theme. In each meeting, several books are discussed instead of just one. It's an underused approach to talking about books that is a great fit for many SF/F groups. There is a trade-off: Breadth of discussion is gained, but some depth lost. Thematic meetings also take more time. This method allows the greatest free choice, a quality that is often in high demand among science fiction/fantasy readers. Chapter 5 of this book is devoted to support materials for thematic meetings.

BOOK CHARACTERISTICS THAT LEAD TO GOOD DISCUSSIONS

No matter which approach is taken, the group needs books that are easy to obtain and interesting to discuss. Here are some factors to consider in book selection.

In Print and Easy to Find

When a common book is read, SF/F groups rarely find that local libraries and bookstores carry enough copies so that some mail ordering isn't necessary, making it especially important that books are selected at least one month in advance. Unless your members are wealthy, choose books published in paperback.

Length

Many excellent fantasy and science fiction books are over 500 pages. Many readers find long books difficult to complete in time for a monthly meeting (but this can vary, so poll your group). Books under 400 pages that still have solid content are preferable. Some groups have experimented successfully with splitting large books or series over two meetings.

Stand-Alones vs. Series

The many series of genre fiction, especially series that need to be read in order, challenge book groups. It just isn't very satisfying to leave the series incomplete, and some readers resent starting long series that they feel compelled to finish. When you choose a series work, go with the first book, allow members to read any book by the author, or utilize a theme in which the series fits instead.

Character-Driven, Idea-Driven, Plot-Driven, or Style-Driven

There are many ways to write a book, but authors usually emphasize one or two of the preceding categories. Books with interesting characters are easy to discuss because readers can debate the characters' choices, consider their success in relationships, or highlight their various quirks. Idea-driven books also work well in groups: simply discuss those ideas. These are generalizations, but good fantasy writing often has strong characters, and good science fiction often has strong ideas. The third type of book, one that has a substantial plot but thin characters and few ideas, is challenging for groups. Plot-driven books make for fun, page-turning reading, a quality prized by many speculative readers, but after a few remarks about plot twists and plausibility, conversation can taper off quickly. Style-driven books are rare in speculative fiction, although the artier corners of the genre—literary crossovers, slipstream, and the New Weird, for instance—are dominated by style. These books work well for experienced, eloquent book groupers with some background in literary analysis, less well for others. Choose them only if they are a good fit for your group

Established Writers vs. Newer Writers

Although I'd like to advocate exploration of new writers, the truth is that established writers often make a better choice for groups. It's easier to find support information about them, and it's likely that some of your readers are familiar with their other work, two factors that aid discussion.

Political, Ethical, and Philosophical Choices

Conflicts may not be fun in real life, but they're the guts of fiction, and the more those guts get twisted, the more impact the book has on readers. Books brimming with dilemmas work well for book groups. Science fiction and fantasy are loaded with such books. Seek them out.

Genre Ideas with Real-World Analogs

Can you compare the war in the book to one in the real world? Would a similar degree of oppression result in a real-world revolution? Do the burdens and costs of doing magic compare with the burdens created by other talents or responsibilities? Is the sociology of fantasy and alien worlds similar to that of Earth? Do uses of technology and science, degradation of the environment, or decisions about health and genetics in the book suggest courses of action for Earth's future? Such comparisons provide grist for your discussion.

Strong Settings and Frames

Another quality of good science fiction and fantasy that translates well to discussion is world building. Does the book have a strong connection to history? Does it invite comparisons to the geography and society of the real world? Is the setting original, but drawn with excellent detail? Do the qualities of the natural world or created environments have an impact on the events of the book or on the behavior of the people who live there? Is there a well-designed system of magic? How about exploration of a science, an art, a craft, an occupation, or some other field of endeavor? Reading with these qualities provides an opportunity for armchair travel. You'll want to talk with others about your trip when it's over.

Young Adult and Children's Books

Don't forget books for younger readers when selecting books for genre readers. The choices in fantasy and science fiction are simply too good to ignore. These books invite happy nostalgia, bring memorable stories to mind, or invite discussion of family or loved ones.

Controversial Books

Controversy can stem from many elements in science fiction and fantasy. Does the book have extreme violence, sex, or language? Does it feature antiheroes or unreliable narrators? Is it written in an unusual style that may aggravate some readers but fascinate others? Does it describe societies or behaviors that would be found abhorrent in our own world? Does it take strong political stances? Is it dripping with dark humor and irony? You'll have to measure your group's response to such controversial material. Some thrive on debate, but others become offended, depressed, or turn the book's conflicts into interpersonal conflicts.

Seasonal Appropriateness and Recurring Topics

Many speculative reading groups enjoy romance crossovers in February, horror books in October, or short, easy books in December or in the summer, when there may be less time to read. If you find a popular author or a topic that works especially well for your group, consider making an annual return.

Award Winners and Classics

When in doubt, time-tested books make good choices. So do books for which discussion materials and reviews are readily available. Use the resources provided in the rest of this book, including the appendices, to help your group make some easy and satisfying selections.

Balance

To keep everyone in your group happy, maintain balance. Alternate between easy reads and more challenging work. Be aware of the preferences of individual readers and balance old work and new, science fiction and fantasy, stories and long works accordingly.

No matter which books your group selects, it's a good idea to keep a log of your group's history. At minimum, keep a list of which books or topics were read and when. Even better, make a few notes after each meeting about how well the discussion went. This log will prove **invaluable** as your group ages and as you add new members who want to know what books and topics have already been addressed.

TALKING ABOUT BOOKS SUCCESSFULLY

Dreary minutes spent listening to the long-winded, the awkward silence or sputtering talk of those who don't know what to say, readers who quit because of frustration with the format—these are just a few of the problems that groups can encounter. A newly formed group can talk about expectations for the discussion with a blank slate. If your group has been around a while, this talk is trickier: some may take criticism of the discussion personally, dominant members may hijack the discussion, or complaints that need to be aired may be left out to avoid hurt feelings. In the latter case, consider passing around a blind survey and then compiling the results. Here are a few of the questions you might ask:

- On a scale from 1 (listen) to 7 (talk), do you prefer to listen to others or make sure your own opinions are voiced in the book group?
- On a scale from 1 (stick to the book or theme at hand) to 7 (any topic that interests the group should be fair game), how much would you like the group to concentrate discussion?
- On a scale from 1 (I prefer deep analysis of one book) to 7 (I prefer to hear a little about a broad range of books), what are your goals for the book group?
- On a scale from 1 (focus discussion on questions) to 7 (use discussion questions only if conversation lags), how much do you like to focus on discussion questions?
- Is the flow of discussion in our group good, or are a few individuals dominating inappropriately?
- Is there enough interaction and debate in our group?
- Are there too many interruptions?
- Do you get to say as much as you would like?
- What would be your preferred balance of science fiction and fantasy titles (or topics)? From what you know of our readers, how should our group balance selections?
- How would you prefer to balance the selection of classic and recent books (or topics)? What balance would our whole group like best?
- Should we place limits on the amount of time that one individual talks, or on the number of books that one individual introduces? If so, what would you suggest?
- Any other concerns about the method or direction of our discussion?

Emphasize that the goal of such a survey is not to censure individuals or necessarily to change group behavior, only to determine general intent and to make everyone aware of perceived problems. If no major problems surface, it is probably sufficient to share the compiled results. If shared frustrations are identified, adjustments to the format can be considered.

MANAGING DISCUSSION

A book group discussion is like HAL in *2001: A Space Odyssey*: once it gets running, it takes on a life of its own. You can't really stop it from going where it goes, but you can use little programming nudges and logic tricks to improve the results and to keep it from getting out of control. If the conversation degrades too much, you might have to shut down a few of the modules in the array before trouble results. Here are a few pieces of advice for preventing an unruly discussion from turning off the life support for your group.

Introduce the Book, Author, and Topic Clearly

Bring a short author biography and read a few highlights from it aloud, and then pass the rest around the group. You might also bring reviews; author interviews; pictures or maps of people, places, and things included in the book; or other related materials. You don't need to recap the plot, although it won't hurt to describe briefly how the book begins and who the narrators are. Then introduce a few key questions or make a few remarks about what makes the book exceptional. After that, let the conversation begin; don't steal everyone's thunder by overdoing your introduction.

Prepare and Use Discussion Questions Wisely

Prepare a few good discussion questions or topics and distribute them before the meeting to help readers think about the novel as they read. When the actual meeting begins, let readers have their say, and then use questions that have not been addressed to stoke the conversation judiciously when it starts to lose heat. Don't become so obsessed in getting through all of your questions that you stop listening to the answers or following other discussion paths in which the group is more interested.

Find Out What Your Readers Want to Discuss

Encourage your readers to bring their own short lists of talking points to the group. This gets them thinking about the book in advance and takes pressure off the discussion leader. If the size of your group allows, you might even take a minute and go around the circle before discussion begins, asking each reader to identify one or two of the points that they would like the discussion to address.

Select a Few Short Passages to Read Aloud in a Pinch

Don't overdo it: this approach is dull if overused. No one wants a discussion leader who is in love with the sound of his or her own voice. But reading a well-chosen passage can help bring a conversational point to life. This technique is especially worth pursuing when the author's use of language is a strong point.

Once the Conversation Gets Rolling, Stay out of the Way

A discussion leader is not a teacher, so don't lecture. The group will quickly come to resent a leader (or any reader) who talks too much. Once a conversation gains momentum, don't stop it by pursuing new points. Instead, be a role model for good listening skills. Focus on asking good questions that encourage readers to enhance their own comments. Rephrase comments if they are unclear.

Watch Out for Signs of Trouble

If one of the readers seems to misunderstand another, clarify. Ask for definitions of jargon and further explanation of unclear references. Steer the discussion away from combativeness, especially if it starts to get personal. If someone is interrupted, cut off the interrupter politely, ask the person to hold his or her thought, and return conversation to the person who was interrupted. Solicit alternatives to highly negative comments by asking if anyone has a different point of view.

One Thing at a Time

When too many balls of discussion are in the air at once, your group may not be able to juggle them all. Some get dropped and lost. A discussion leader can avert this problem by politely jumping in and steering the conversation away from too many sidetracks. Even better, "signpost" the discussion as it goes along with comments such as, "I think we've said enough about the lead characters, let's look at the setting now," or "Your comment introduces us to the whole idea of pacing in this book: let's talk about that," or "Before we move on, does anybody else have any different responses to the last question?"

Don't Let Generalizations Kill the Discussion

If a quick consensus is reached that everyone loves or hates the book, discussion is likely to dry up quickly. Don't settle for bland agreement, which probably isn't indicative of the range of opinions that your readers secretly hold. If someone loves the book, ask him or her to identify one or two aspects of it that were exceptional and talk about why this was the case, then consider following up by asking if there were any aspects of the book that were not as strong. Dig deeper to find out why a book was "well written" or "terrible." Why is it better than average books? What could have been done to improve it?

In a Pinch, Use Formal Means to Combat Recurring Problems

Generally it's best to use subtle means to quiet a reader who dominates the group too much, stop interruptions that run amok, or remedy chronic time management problems, but if these problems persist, address them more directly. Ask a quiet reader to serve as timekeeper. He or she can start a timer to allow a speaker a minimum amount of time before being interrupted or hold up a flag to indicate that someone has gone on too long. Assign someone a gatekeeper role, monitoring that turns at discussion proceed equally around the circle. Pass an object to the speaker who has the floor. Require raising of hands before comments, and set an order for comments when hands are raised. These measures may feel awkward and should not be a permanent solution, but they help everyone realize when violations occur. If a few readers still won't moderate their behavior, the group leader needs to have a private conversation with them, asking them nicely to control themselves. It's a rare case when someone actually has to be asked not to come to a group.

SUGGESTIONS FOR TALKING ABOUT A SHARED BOOK

Many who join groups have no experience in discussing literature. To that end, it's a good idea to put together a short list of suggestions on how to talk about a book. These suggestions can be discussed by the group, distributed to new members, or recommunicated if the group needs minor repair. Here's a sample:

- Finish the book whenever possible. When you cannot finish, please attend, but don't expect others to avoid discussion of the ending or other plot points.
- Prepare for the book group as you read: take a few summary notes, mark passages, or make a list noting key sections. Write down three to five talking points—questions or ideas—and bring them to the meeting.
- Research the book. Reading short biographies of the author, summaries of his or her other books, or reviews greatly enhances both your understanding and the quality of discussion. If you find information, bring it to share with the group.
- If you don't have much to say, your participation is still crucial to the group. Ask questions. Encourage others to expand on some of their more interesting comments.
- Be careful about expressing absolute opinions. If you love or hate the book, we want you to say so, but don't assume that everyone agrees. If you are specific about what you like or what bothers you about the book, instead of absolute in your judgments, it leaves room for others to voice a different opinion.

Here are some general points to consider when preparing for the discussion:

General Reactions

On a scale from 1 to 10, how much did you like the book? What are its major strengths and flaws? Who is the ideal reader for this book? What questions are you left asking? What emotional reactions does the book provoke? What surprised you about the book?

Author

What is the author's background? How is this background reflected in the book? If you have read other works by this author, how do they compare?

Time and Place of Origin

How are the place and the historical period in which the book was written reflected in the results? Is it typical of where and when it came from? Which parts stand the test of time? How would the book be different if it were written now?

Point of View

From whose point of view is the story told? How does this point of view affect what is said? Would the book be significantly different if related from a different point of view? Do you find the narrator(s) believable? Trustworthy? Likeable? Interesting?

Characters

Which characters most catch your interest? Do you relate to the lead characters? Do you find them believable? Interesting? Who is your favorite secondary character? Are any of them superfluous, indistinct, or annoying? Do characters change and grow over the course of the book or remain static? If some characters are static, are they good examples of their type?

Pacing

Do you find the book quick moving or slow? Does the pacing change over the course of the book? Does it fit the scope of the book's story? Is the ending or some other part of the book rushed or underdeveloped? Do any particular sections drag?

Settings and Frames

How good is world building in the book? Is it believable? Would you like to live in or visit the book's setting? Does it remind you of other real or fictional places? What role do geography, weather, architecture, and landscape play in how characters behave or the plot develops? Are particular skills, hobbies, occupations, or fields of endeavor well or poorly used or described? What topics does the book make you want to explore further?

Central and Secondary Conflicts

What are the central conflicts in the book? Do you find the way that they are resolved believable? Likeable? Do characters behave in a moral way?

Plotting

Is the plot predictable, or are some of its events surprising? Do you find any side plots distracting? Are any of them more interesting than the central plot? How does the author build suspense?

Genre

Is this book typical of the genre or anomalous? In which subgenres does it fit? Would the genre be better or worse if more of the books were like this?

Style

Is there anything unusual about the author's style? Do you like the amount and style of description? Would you describe the book as easy to follow or challenging?

Connections

Does this book remind you of other books? Of films? Do any other authors have a similar style? What books do you recommend to someone who enjoys this book? Will you seek out other books by this author? Would this book make a good film? If so, who should star?

The Ending

Did you like the way the book ends, or would you somehow change it? Do you like the way the plot is resolved? Is there important unfinished business? What might happen after the book is over? Would you welcome a sequel or series?

DARE TO THEME: AN ALTERNATIVE TO READING THE SAME BOOK

Problems of the One-Book Group

The model for book groups ensconced in contemporary practice is one in which every participant reads the same book. This solid approach suits many book groups and results in a discussion of good depth when the book is right for the group and the right questions are considered. It's not, however, the only approach to book grouping. Many groups, in fact, would do better with a different approach. That approach is the thematic discussion.

Consider: it's difficult in any group to find a book that fits the tastes of every reader. One size does not fit all. One reader's golden ring is another's deadly burden. One reader's spice is another's noxious drug. Although some difference of opinion expands horizons and promotes discussion, too much discord eventually leads to skipped meetings, readers who quit coming altogether, and book groups that crumble. This problem is aggravated when dealing with SF and fantasy readers, who are opinionated and self-directed in their reading preferences. Put together 10 readers who love speculative fiction and you may still find little agreement about what they'd prefer to read.

Even when you find common ground, or at least come to a reluctant compromise on which titles to read, problems with the same-title book group don't end. Now you've got to find enough copies of the selections. Even larger libraries rarely carry more than two or three copies of the same science fiction or fantasy title. The same is true for bookstores. Personal libraries may yield a few more copies, but chances are that at least some of your readers will have to wait until another reader finishes or order a copy of the book through the mail. That means less time to finish and more readers who either skip the meeting or come but are unable to discuss the book fully.

One-book discussions are also tricky. They may achieve good debate and good depth, but they can also sputter to a halt if there is either collective pleasure or dislike for the book. Some readers are suited to a hearty debate, but others get offended easily, protect the feelings of a strong-willed reader who speaks more readily, or are simply shy. Their voices get lost in the hubbub. Science fiction/fantasy readers, in particular, are likely to cluster on one end of the spectrum—extrovert or introvert. If your book group tends to be dominated by a few voices, it's a good indication that one-book discussions aren't working for you. SF/F discussions also tend to follow even more tangents than those of the average book group. If your readers are trying to spread the discussion anyway, why fight it? A thematic discussion may fit their temperament.

The last problem with the single-book model for science fiction/fantasy readers is that many of the best genre books don't work in it. Plot-heavy books—neither short books driven by action and plot twists, nor long books with large casts of characters and interwoven stories—are difficult to discuss. This does not mean that they aren't great books; in fact, many speculative fiction readers prefer the genres precisely because of their great plots. But collectively recapping a plot simply isn't rewarding for a group.

The Thematic Group: Methods and Benefits

In comparison, consider the thematic book group. For each meeting, a theme is selected. This theme might be the work of a particular author; the output of a school of authors; books written in a particular period, a shared subject matter, a subgenre, a format; or nominees or winners of a particular award. Within that theme, each reader selects a work of his or her choice. To aid less knowledgeable readers in selection, it's a good idea to provide, a month in advance, a list of sample works that fit the theme.

At the meeting, someone introduces the theme and asks a few questions that are crucial to understanding it. These questions help other readers focus their comments. Discussion proceeds around the table, with each reader introducing the title that he or she selected and connecting it to the broader theme. Books are passed around the table. Although everyone will not be equally interested in every book, everyone gets along, interesting ideas within the theme are explored, interesting veins of conversation are mined, and everyone goes home with more knowledge of the genres and a few more books on his or her personal "to read" list. In my experience, readers in science fiction and fantasy are always grateful for exposure to new authors.

Because one potential challenge of science fiction/fantasy groups is to locate enough dedicated readers to sustain meetings, it's especially important to avoid erosion of the membership base. Thematic meetings allow readers of fantasy and readers of science fiction, who, in some cases, are wired very differently, to play nicely together. It allows older readers, who in these genres often focus on short stories and classic authors, and younger readers, who tend to prefer novels and a different list of authors, to coexist and learn from each other. Readers who have a difficult time completing a book can still attend, drawing connections from the selections of others or introducing a book read in the past. Readers who won't attend if they don't like the monthly selection are more likely to find an interesting book within the broader scope of a theme.

With a wider playing field, there is less competition for common titles. Even small-town libraries and bookstores can usually support thematic groups. Because readers can find books quickly, they are more likely to finish in time. In a pinch, they can read short works or graphic novels. And those plot-driven books? No problem. In the thematic format, where emphasis is more on introducing the book than on debating its merits, plot-driven novels work perfectly well.

Finally, the thematic meeting has structural advantages. Boredom is unlikely: If you're not interested in one book, the next may be something very different. Perhaps best of all, every reader is encouraged to speak, as extroverts and introverts alike can be allotted the same amount of time to introduce their books. Groups that prefer to spread leadership instead of focusing it on one person—often the case among speculative fiction fans—find that it's less demanding for an inexperienced group leader to introduce a theme than to manage the complex group dynamics of a one-book discussion. SF/F fans frequently have a highly developed visual sense, are interested in collecting books, or focus on minutiae only discovered by examining the book in question, so the steady stream of books around the table is a big plus.

Chapter 5 of this book is devoted to specific themes for science fiction/fantasy book groups. You'll find over 40 complete themes—with book lists, discussion questions, and thematic resources, plus ideas for another 50 themes.

Preventing and Combating the Downsides of Themes

The most obvious flaw with the thematic model is that it sacrifices some of the depth of discussing one book. To mitigate this problem, use a few thematic questions to focus comments.

Instead of exploring a particular book deeply, your group's goal is to plumb the depths of the theme. Try to follow the presentation of each book with a few questions. Give and take are still encouraged.

Meetings in this format may take longer than shared-book groups: plan accordingly. The thematic group requires careful time management. Allow 15 minutes for opening business and introduction of the theme, 3 to 10 minutes (depending on group size) for each participant, and a few minutes at the end to introduce the next theme. With gentle reminders, most groups adjust to these parameters. If your group doesn't, bring an egg timer or appoint a timekeeper. If everyone follows the same rules, nobody should get offended by being told that it's time to move on. You might have to set limits on how many books each participant may introduce or allow multiple books only after everyone has presented his or her first book.

Because readers are not familiar with every theme, it helps if a facilitator can prepare a list of potential book choices. This is a role that someone in the group may relish or a task that suits the skills of librarians and bookstore workers looking for a support role. Stick to the theme, but select themes that allow diversity of selection when possible. Balance science fiction themes with fantasy themes and choose as many as possible that allow selection from both genres. Alternate histories, time-travel books, apocalyptic novels, award winners, humorous titles, antiheroes, strong female lead characters, coming-of-age stories, graphic novels, young adult books, and horror, mystery, and literary crossovers are available in both genres.

As in any book group, readers possess various levels of verbal skill. There are plenty of suggestions in the next section about how to help those who initially find participating in a book group difficult. Prepare a sheet of advice that can be given to new participants and periodically redistributed to members as a gentle reminder. In particular, remind readers that they should not assume that others have read the book; that their goal is to encourage others to seek out the book if they would like it. Because of this, it's important that they don't spoil the ending or give away too many plot twists. In the thematic format, you will see consistent improvement among almost all of your readers in their ability to introduce their books.

Advice for Discussion: Thematic Groups

Discussion of themes differs slightly. Here is advice for participants in this kind of group:

- Don't depend on off-the-cuff description of your book. Think about what to say in advance; even consider practicing your remarks aloud. It's okay to bring notes. Unless you know the group is small, keep comments to less than five minutes.
- When possible, bring your book and pass it around the group.
- State the title of the book and its author's name clearly. Tell the group when it was published, how many pages long it is, and whether or not it won any major awards. If the author is well-known, place the book within the scope of his or her career.
- Your first goal is to provide a teaser of information, not a description of every detail of the book. It is good to set the plot up by describing events from the first few chapters or by revealing a few significant events, but under no circumstances should you spoil the ending or other major plot twists.
- Include a brief description of the setting, the main characters, and your favorite secondary characters. If it is unusual in some way, describe the author's style or the narrative voice.

- A second goal is to provide information that entices those who would like the book and warns away those who won't like it. If you love the book say so, but be careful about absolute pans. Are there readers who might enjoy the book, even if you didn't?

- Besides briefly introducing and reviewing your book, your third goal is to connect it to the theme of the discussion. How does your book fit within that theme? What does it have to say about the subject? Is it typical or atypical of books on this theme? If thematic questions are asked, be prepared to answer them, but only when your book is relevant to that question.

- Draw comparisons when possible. Does the book share qualities with others you've read? Does the author have a familiar style? Conversely, what sets this book apart? Does it address the same subject as another book but draw different conclusions?

- What was your favorite scene? Your favorite character? Can you provide an example of the book's humor? Don't read long passages aloud, but a well-chosen page or good paraphrasing can serve as a good summary when you aren't sure what else to say.

If the book was part of a series, place it within that series. Do the books need to be read in order? Will you continue to later books?

SUCCESS WITH FANTASY AND SCIENCE FICTION READERS

Although it is easy to stereotype science fiction/fantasy fans too much, working with them is sometimes different than working with other readers. Although it can become counterproductive to assume too much about how particular readers will behave in a given situation, some general observations may help group leaders in planning meetings and guiding discussion. If you are a librarian or other book group organizer who reads some science fiction and fantasy but doesn't spend much time with the readers of these genres, you may want to give this section extra thought.

The demographics of speculative fiction readership are changing. For many years, the core market of science fiction readers got older, without enough new young fans to counter the aging of first-wave fans. Recent popularity of fantasy fiction and a new trend of popularity in young adult science fiction are beginning to change these numbers, but the organizer of a speculative fiction group should still expect to see plenty of readers over 40. Female fans are also on the rise. Although your group is likely to have more men than women (a fact which likely makes it different than book groups of any other kind), the average group is likely to have at least a few dedicated female readers. Racial diversity is another matter. Even though the percentages of writers and readers of color are slowly growing, their numbers are still low. If your group is lucky enough to recruit minority readers, nurture their point of view and make sure that they feel comfortable.

The science fiction/fantasy fan is unlikely to be shocked by any particular kind of content. On the whole, their interest in speculative fiction makes them more likely to be open to a wide range of behaviors and belief systems. Politically, there are more liberals than conservatives, but there is also a long-standing tradition of libertarian beliefs among science fiction readers. There are also many science fiction/fantasy readers with a military background or an interest in military strategy.

Science fiction and fantasy are even more diverse than other genres. Speculative fiction includes short, light books and long, complex, philosophical or scientific tomes. It includes everything from pulpy action to obscure literary work. It includes historical, contemporary, and futuristic settings. It appeals to young readers and old readers, men and women. To complicate matters even more, there was a distinct period, which many readers remember, when short stories dominated speculative fiction, and some older readers prefer that format strongly. In sum, these genres draw a diverse crew of readers, and often their tastes don't match. That can make finding a book that everyone in your group wants to read even more difficult than it is for other book groups. Still, everyone will get along if there is input into the selection process. Keep the tastes of your specific group of readers in mind as you make selections, not just books touted by contemporary critics. If your group is especially diverse, choose the thematic approach to meetings instead of trying to force everyone to read the same book.

Sometimes labeled as geeks or nerds, many SF and F readers have come to resent being looked down upon by readers of "serious" literary fiction. Avoid any hint of pretentiousness when working with them. Their counter-reactions to the snobbery they have faced may extend beyond adverse feelings toward a few elitist critics and on to the books that literary readers recommend, so unless you know your audience well, don't try to sell a title to them by saying that it's of "high literary quality" or was written by a literary author. Just describe the plot and let the book succeed or fail on its own merits. In your group, cultivate an atmosphere of respect for all tastes, whether they are for the literary or pulpy ends of the genre. Graphic novels and manga, light serial fiction, media tie-ins, and young adult and children's books can be read side by side with complex literary blends, doorstop-sized series entries, and books laden with mythic allusions or theoretical science.

The distribution of conversation in speculative groups varies even more than in other groups—with extreme variance between readers who talk easily and freely and readers who say very little at all. The challenge for discussion leaders in such an environment is to encourage quiet members to gain confidence in speaking their opinions while not suppressing the energy that more extroverted members bring to discussion or discouraging them from sharing their knowledge or stories. A good strategy is to enlist talkative readers, who are probably aware of their tendencies, in trying to draw out those who talk less. Thematic meetings also help in this regard, because each reader is given time in this format to introduce a book. Just make sure to ask follow-up questions when quiet readers don't provide enough information about their selected titles.

Conversation may be less guarded, more lighthearted than in other book groups. Overstatements and superlatives can be abundant, whether in praise or condemnation of books. This happens for many reasons, most often because of simple enthusiasm for the genres. Go with it as much as you can, because the upside is honest, frank, and funny discussion. If a participant is made uncomfortable by confrontation, intercede with some humor or add a voice to his or hers in favor of the title in question. When extreme opinions surface, ask those who make them to clarify or ask if they really mean to be taken so strongly. Don't take comments personally; they're usually meant as an expression of personal taste, not a judgment of the taste of others. Besides, the person who disagrees with you in one meeting is likely to support you in the next.

Science fiction/fantasy fans are often hobbyists, collectors, and enthusiasts. Many love all media forms: film, television, music, and graphic arts, especially. Expect diversions and sidetracks in discussion. Unless your group has decided that it wants a focused discussion, allow them to pursue tangents. Build time for them into your meeting format. If such comments start to overwhelm book discussion, consider encouraging a spin-off group or extra time before or after your meeting devoted to other subjects of interest. A big upside of this diversity is that references to other books or media will often be recognized by at least some of your participants. When they aren't, simply ask the person who made the reference to explain more about it.

Because they may have had difficulty in finding others who share their passion for the genres, science fiction/fantasy book groupers may look to extend the social scope of the group beyond the meeting. Don't be surprised to see a bit of costuming, enthusiastic sharing of action figures, or other genre-related activities. Consider going out for dinner after meetings, planning game or movie nights, spinning off an informal gathering in off weeks, or organizing car pools or shared rooms at conventions. Instead of skipping holiday months, plan parties. Allow members to celebrate birthdays and other special occasions with each other during book group time. More suggestions for adding variety and fun to meetings are at the end of this chapter.

As with any diverse group, the best method for promoting great interactions among your collection of fans is to learn to understand and appreciate each of them as individual readers. One of the best things you can do as a group leader (or participant) is to keep a notebook at each meeting, noting books that excite each reader. Refer to these preferences in discussion; let readers know when new books by their A-list authors are published, or try these favorites yourself and share your reactions.

WIZARDS VS. ANDROIDS: HELPING FANTASY AND SCIENCE FICTION READERS GET ALONG

It's something that every speculative fiction reader understands, but those who don't read the genres just don't get. Science fiction and fantasy are two different beasts. Fans wince when they see one term used to describe both genres, a crime to which libraries and bookstores must often plead guilty. Many fans don't even like the term "speculative fiction," which makes a convenient catch-all phrase but smacks of academic hoodoo to the average fan. (You might earn points with such fans by noting that Robert Heinlein was the term's original proponent.) Although there are many of us who like both genres or have joined forces in an effort to promote the literature or keep the peace, there are many others who prefer one of the genres over the other.

Orson Scott Card once wrote semiseriously that the way to tell the difference between the genres was to note whether the cover had rivets or trees, but the real divide is deeper. This difference of opinion stems from the writing styles that are prevalent in each genre. Although both genres are often packed with action, feature imaginative settings, and speculate about alternate realities, in other aspects of appeal they split. Science fiction tends to be a literature of ideas: hard science or philosophy. Some of its writers sacrifice character development or stylistic flourishes in pursuit of some corner of the truth. Fantasy tends to be more character- or style-driven. An obvious difference between the two genres is that fantasy tends to appeal to those interested in cultures of the past (although contemporary fantasies are hot), and science fiction, of course, focuses on the future. There is also a gender split (albeit a decreasing one). Particularly among young readers, boys gravitate toward science fiction and girls toward fantasy.

These are generalizations, but they are prevalent enough to affect book groups. Some fans simply don't read the "other" genre. You can pick your favorite or the majority's favorite and read only from that genre, but because science fiction/fantasy groups often struggle to find an adequate number of regular readers, such a choice may be self-defeating. It may also prove highly controversial in the future as the membership of your group changes.

A better solution is to compromise, selecting books in proportion to your membership's preferences: "We'll read two science fiction titles each season, as long as the rest of you agree to try one fantasy." Pick books by authors who write in both genres. Lois McMaster Bujold, Stephen R. Donaldson, Poul Anderson, Elizabeth Bear, John C. Wright, and Scott Westerfeld are good examples. Look to authors whose work straddles the divide, such as Gene Wolfe, C. S. Friedman, Anne McCaffrey, or Kage Baker. Humor and action translate well for readers of both genres. Many themes can be used that allow readers to select from either genre.

Beyond book selection, you can promote peace with humor and understanding. Acknowledge preference differences and celebrate common ground. As a group leader or facilitator, try not to betray your preferences. Find fantasy books with a heavy dose of logic and science fiction with complete character portrayals, and use these as counterexamples if genre bashing begins. It's okay—in fact, it's interesting—to compare the genres and learn to understand why different books appeal to different readers. You know you're cultivating the proper atmosphere when Miss Moonbeam speaks glowingly of a book suggested by Mr. Rivets or when Diane Database acknowledges that, even though this isn't the book for her, she can see why William DeWizz likes it.

BESTIARY: CARE AND FEEDING OF COMMON SCIENCE FICTION/FANTASY READER TYPES

This section is lovingly dedicated to the fine specimens who collect together in my book group. Speaking as one beast on behalf of the rest, it's a zoo in there! Family, genus, and species, one can classify common SF and fantasy reader types. Such classifications do not bring absolute understanding of any individual; each has his or her own combination of quirks. But here are some species that you might find in your bestiary. This tongue-in-cheek look at some of their familiar traits is intended to help you keep the whole menagerie coexisting happily.

The species of genus *Crock-o-style* are recognizable by their prevailing preference for particular styles, periods, and subgenres. Notable species include *Baen barfly,* interested mainly in works from its namesake press. *Barfly* has a strange fascination with electronic books and hyperbolic chat sessions. Its obsessions with military tactics, libertarian political causes, and the individualist ethic make it difficult to distinguish from *Pulpful badass,* a species that venerates Conan and his ilk. To distinguish the two, present a specimen with cheap, dog-eared paperbacks with the most tawdry cover art available. If this results in declarations of literary merit, the species at hand is most likely *Pulpful.* If the ebook version is requested instead, it is *Barfly.*

Crock-o-style is a diverse genus, in which subtle pheromone differences create intermittent interspecies antagonisms. For instance, *Pagan lovechild,* which feeds on depictions of Wiccan magic, goddess worship, and tofu, may exhibit uncharacteristic ferociousness when left in proximity with *Barfly* or *Pulpful.* The same is true for *Paranormal palpititious* and *Vlad inhaler,* who read, respectively, paranormal romance and vampire fiction. To avoid bared canines, splashing of holy water, or flourishing of stakes, it's best to alternate the books selected for the group between the species present. Find books that cater to common interests, or allow time at the end of one-book discussions in which *Crock-o-styles* can rhapsodize about favorites.

The oldest species of *Crock-o-style* is *Warhorse auriferous.* These Golden Age warriors bandy the names, publication dates, and magazines of origin for obscure stories, recount romanticized versions of early Con adventures, and bicker about the earliest example of each subgenre. *Warhorses* are known to squirm, squawk, and cry out when confronted with contemporary works. As with all *Crock-o-styles,* it is best to work with the interests of *warhorses* instead of fighting them. Take benefit from their considerable topical knowledge instead of inducing the convulsions, frothing at the mouth, and ejaculation of epithets evoked by ongoing ignorance of their preferences.

Of the same order as *Crock-o-style* is genus *Hobbyhorse.* Like *Crock-o-style, Hobbyhorse* species are unnaturally fascinated with particular topics, but, in this case, the topics are only partially connected to the interests of a book group. Species definitely descended from *Hobbyhorse* include *Manga-niac maladaptus, Comic-kaze pilotus,* the *Redeyed videophile, Artsy craftastic,* and *Hector collector.* Dispute continues as to whether single-author species, such as *Heinlein heroicus* and *Pterry-dact terrible* are properly classified as *Crock-o-style* or *Hobbyhorse.* Despite tendencies to worship iconic objects and compulsively twist topics into ritualistic chants on preferred subjects, *Hobbyhorses* can make happy, healthy members of your group. Their specialized knowledge can be both educational and mesmerizing in a fetishistic way. Consider occasionally allotting 15 minutes of meeting time for them to display the colorful objects they so earnestly hoard.

A particularly challenging *Hobbyhorse* species are *Writers rohanica,* who may attempt to turn book groups into writer's groups. Although you may answer their queries about markets and encourage their analysis of books from a writer's perspective, under no circumstance allow them to read aloud from their work. When encouraged in this way, they become overexcited, reading longer passages and pleading for increasingly vigorous and harsh applications of critique. Fortunately, in SF/F groups, *Writers* are common and can often form their own herds. This basic strategy is essential for working with all the *Hobbyhorses:* Make it clear that they are welcome to indulge their interests in context, but that the group is primarily oriented to book discussion. If their interest in books wanes, or it becomes apparent that they are mistakenly trying to breed with other species in a desperate play for the "next best thing," it may be time to help them find a closer match through the local fandom extension service.

Genus *Opin-upine* is notoriously prickly. Species such as *Noncomputus mentis* (emulators of Vulcan logic as applied to plot holes), the *Inquisitor anachronous* (sticklers for historical accuracy in even the most fantastic of fiction), and *Hardscience vainglorious* (who believe the genre is SCIENCE fiction, and that the fiction part is a nuisance) are highly volatile. All may exhibit puffing of the breast, hissing, head-butting, or other unseemly behaviors when confronted with that which they categorize as mistakes. They are capable of speed-reading through large portions of beautifully executed text without comment before zeroing in on a damning detail.

Although book groups need *Opin-upines* to verify scientific and historical data, the key is to extract the benefits of their kind while learning to calm them when they encounter the most egregious examples of fancified facts and poetic license. Encourage *Opin-upines* to broaden their vigilance to other areas of literary endeavor: complexity of character, believability in world building, and reach of imagination, for instance. Over time, this expanding sense of the goals of literature may help quell their most extreme fits. If that doesn't work, keep them occupied by examining the output of *Writers rohanica.*

Less tractable, and often at cross purposes with other SF/F readers are species *Raisa highbrow* and *Ass-thete alexandrian.* The triggers for their vitriolic spasms are more esoteric, harder to identify than those of other *Opin-upines.* They tend to enjoy a kind of writing that, through its difficulty, promotes equivalent demonstrations of grief in the common SF/F reader. If they become particularly distressed by a simple, pulpy action novel, you might quiet them by sending them questing for symbols, allegory, or hints of postmodern irony. In dire emergencies, suggest that the author in question has "deconstructed the subject to a primitive level, invoking Jungian archetypes at a primordial, fabulist level." If their aggressive posturing can be kept from frightening others, *Highbrow* and *Ass-thete* will prove invaluable assets in improving the quality of discussion. Or you can just giggle every time they say "onomatopoeia."

Our final major genus is the ironically named *Ela-quant,* made fascinating by the range of bizarre behaviors that its species exhibit when verbal activity is required. *Blushalot rosatica* has difficulty speaking even one sentence aloud before lapsing into embarrassed silence. Despite this lack of social exposure, *Blushalot* can make worthwhile contributions to the group with a little prodding. Ask follow-up questions after her or his brief comments to encourage the full story. If this fails, don't worry too much; *Blushalot* is often capable of enjoying the group in silence.

At the other end of the *Ela-quant* spectrum are several more challenging species. *Raconteur regurgitatus* never met a story he didn't like and want to embellish, which would be more troublesome if his tales weren't so damn good. Just let him know clearly when he is exceeding time limits. *Babbling filterfree,* which has the unique property of speaking aloud every thought that enters its mind, and *Derailer deviatus,* capable of inserting fascinating but largely unrelated comments in faster-than-light intervals, are entertaining but difficult to control. Try a mixture of firm admonishments to return to topic, continuations of the original topic as if nothing had been said, and indulgence of some of the more entertaining tangents these species produce.

Every speculative book group is required by bylaws to include at least one specimen of the species *Strangelove angelica. Strangelove* is capable of a full analysis of a book, complete with plot recap, readalike references, dramatic pauses, and knowing raises of the left eyebrow. Unfortunately, this analysis remains stubbornly impenetrable to other species. There is little one can do with *Strangelove,* but as with other *Ela-quant* species, exposure to other species may lead to its gradual improvement in communication. All *Ela-quant* behaviors are exacerbated by nervousness and lack of social experience. As the demands of a group become clearer, their identifying characteristics become camouflaged.

Last, consider the controversial species *Phandom menace.* This may be a distinct species or may simply be a clever mimic of the characteristics of other species. Reported sightings are frequent but difficult to document. *Phandom,* as witness accounts purport, has almost omniscient knowledge of the science fiction and fantasy genres and unwavering enthusiasm for every aspect of them. Because of this, it is often mistaken for the *Common Know-It-All,* but if *Phandom* is bluffing, witnesses have been unable to detect it.

IDEAS FOR EXTRA FUN

Over time, every book group may require variations in practice to remain fresh. Here are a few great ideas for extra fun that have been culled from the best practices of existing groups.

Answer a Reading Question

Which book has been on your shelf the longest? What's the first book you remember reading? What book did everyone like that you hated? Do you ever read the ending of a book before you finish it? Who is the most overrated or underrated writer? If you could visit the world of one genre book, what would it be? For an icebreaker, take a question like this and go quickly around the room with your answers.

Invite an Author

Most science fiction/fantasy authors are familiar with speaking to groups of fans on the Con circuit. They know the value of building an audience a few readers at a time. It's likely that your members have connections to some of these writers. Stage a reading, a talk, or invite the author to a discussion of his or her book.

Watch a Movie or Television Program Together

This activity can take place in lieu of book discussion one month or be used in conjunction with reading the book from which the film was adapted. Many SF & F readers are videophiles as well. Watch for upcoming release dates, and join other fans in catching a film on opening night.

Bring Thematic Food and Drink

Although food is not frequently featured in fantasy and science fiction, it does make an occasional appearance. Why not build a little foodie fun into a meeting? Drain a mug of mead or cider. Have reader-chefs bring their interpretation of the food of the future, a fantasy feast, or, getting more specific, Tolkien's Lembas bread or Harry Harrison's Soylent Green. Yum.

Design Games and Puzzles

These can vary from the simple to the elaborate. Have each reader compose a trivia question about the book or theme. Match a list of authors with a disordered list of their titles or famous characters. Print pictures of famous SF/F authors from the Internet and see whether readers can identify them. Compose haiku about the discussion book. See who can write down the most titles by an author, the most books that include a particular plot element, or the most authors whose name begins with a particular letter in a two-minute period. Variations are limited only by creativity and provide an excellent icebreaker, diversion, or discussion starter.

Have a Book or Toy Exchange

F/SF readers tend to be incorrigible collectors. Why not start a paperback exchange, have a group yard sale, or trade genre-related toys or memorabilia? Check to see if your favorite publishers will provide advanced reader copies or if the library that serves you can hold aside fantasy and science fiction from its Friends sale for your group's first perusal.

Change the Location

Something as simple as a one-meeting change of venue can breathe fresh life into your group. Go out to dinner, spread blankets in a park, or see whether one of your members would like to host a party from his or her home.

Read outside Your Usual Parameters

Read horror for Halloween. Have members bring their favorite books that are not fantasy or science fiction. Talk about books that introduced you to the genre. Try children's books. Try poetry. Try a screenplay. Let your writer members have one evening to share some work. If you normally read a common book, try a theme, or if you read themes, read a common book. Variety may be all that a stale group needs to shake off the funk.

Rate the Book

A clever practice of Denver's long-running Science Fiction and Fantasy Book Club is to have each member rate the book on a scale from 1 to 10. They cap each meeting with these ratings and post them on their Club website. Over time, such a practice can help group members understand one another's preferences and document their history.

Stage a Group Reading

Break out a screenplay, an old radio script, or a story with lots of dialogue and try reading it aloud. Or simply take turns reading from a classic story. It's a simple tactic guaranteed to generate a few laughs and a memorable meeting.

Try a Service Project

Collect a donation of genre books for a local school, library, or prison. Serve food at a homeless shelter. Stage talks, a reading, or screen a film at a nursing home. Hold a charity auction for the local animal shelter. Field a team for a charity walk. Volunteer at the library where you meet. People feel good when they take some time to give something back to the community.

Celebrate or Remember Together

Keep a birthday calendar and bring treats. Share remembrances on the event of a great author's passing. Throw a holiday party or celebrate your group anniversary. Have a game night or a barbecue. Whether you're trying to get used to each other or open new trails in a long-running acquaintance, a few celebrations may be just the ticket.

Invite Guests

One night a year, encourage members to bring a friend or family member to the discussion. It's a great way to get to know one another better. More important, it's good to help loved ones understand what you're doing and why you spend precious time on a book group.

Compile Your Favorites

Collectively build a list of your favorite authors, books, stories, characters, genre films, or examples of a theme. Put the list in a nice format: a booklet, a bookmark, or a Web page, for instance. Donate the list to your local library or bookstore. Read selections from the list for your next group meeting.

Start a Group Scrapbook, Website, or Blog

Your group has knowledge that other readers covet and a history that is worth documenting over time. Why not collect or compile the date and subject of your meetings, your booklists, small summaries, favorite comments, short reviews or essays, discussion questions, pictures, and other materials into a book, website, or blog?

Make Reading Resolutions

Once a year, perhaps in January, share your reading resolutions for the coming year. What would you like to read more of? What would you like to avoid? Which classic will you finally attempt? Which monster series will you finally finish? For extra fun, review the resolutions a year later.

Chapter 2
Understanding the Genres

One of the great joys of participating in a science fiction/fantasy book group is placing each book in the context of the genre's history. The materials in this chapter are meant to start and enhance that discussion. Compact definitions of fantasy and science fiction have been constructed by dozens of important genre writers and thinkers. The results are controversial and more fun to debate than they are conclusive. This book defines my concepts of science fiction/fantasy operationally rather than trying to crystallize them into one sentence. I'm leaving your book group an open field to define the genres for yourselves.

This chapter does, however, contain a thorough categorization of the two genres, a glossary of useful terminology, and discussion questions applicable to any work of science fiction or fantasy. Continue to Chapters 3 and 4 for discussion materials on particular books and for lists of other good authors and books in each genre. Chapter 5 contains discussion materials related to major themes in science fiction and fantasy. Resources for further study are in the appendix. Refer to the appendix for a short chronology of science fiction/fantasy history.

CLASSIFYING FANTASY AND SCIENCE FICTION

Some may question the value of sorting speculative fiction works into subcategories. After all, any subgenre can be broken into still smaller categories. Many books fit multiple categories; others fit solidly in none. But debate about the categorization of speculative fiction isn't just idle jaw-flapping or an obsession with pigeonholing. These are diverse genres—with some books that appeal to almost any reader. But there are also books that may appall any kind of reader. Figuring out which books to pair with which readers can make all of the difference in whether those readers grow to love fantasy and science fiction or find the books unsatisfying.

Besides, debate on which categories each book fits into is entertaining, helping readers draw connections between their favorite works. In most speculative fiction book groups, this becomes the most frequent and fruitful topic of discussion. So, for your edification and argumentative pleasure, here are my top subgenres of science fiction/fantasy.

THE SUBGENRES OF FANTASY

Epic/Quest/High Fantasy

Typical Book: A motley collection of heroes band together and go off to find the magical Doohickey, slay the evil Whatzitz, and/or get help from the all-powerful Whozitz. Glorious nail-biting adventures ensue, culminating in the saving of the world (until the next book in the series anyway).

Related to: Coming-of-age fantasy, "realistic" epic fantasy, alternate historical fantasy, hero fantasy, political fantasy.

Trends: Brought to ascendancy by Tolkien's _The Lord of the Rings_, epic high fantasy has ruled the fantasy roost for nearly 50 years, but the field has recently diversified, with urban fantasy and "realistic" epic fantasy, in particular, rising to new heights.

Great Examples:

Peter S. Beagle	_The Last Unicorn_
Stephen R. Donaldson	The Chronicles of Thomas Covenant, starting with _Lord Foul's Bane_
Raymond E. Feist	Riftwar Saga, starting with _Magician: Apprentice_
J. V. Jones	Sword of Shadows, starting with _A Cavern of Black Ice_
Robert Jordan	The Wheel of Time, starting with _The Eye of the World_
Guy Gavriel Kay	_Tigana_
Greg Keyes	Kingdoms of Thorn and Bone, starting with _The Briar King_
J. R. R. Tolkien	_The Lord of the Rings_
Tad Williams	Memory, Sorrow and Thorn, starting with _The Dragonbone Chair_

Coming-of-Age Fantasy

Typical Book: Raised by farmers/wolves/traveling musicians, young Destiny has always felt slightly out of place. Perhaps it is the enormous "chosen one" tattoo on his or her forehead or the bursts of uncontrolled magical power that have destroyed several playmates. But when a crotchety old wizard returns to reveal the truth, Destiny begins an adventure to master skills and combat the Dark Lord.

Related to: Any other type of fantasy can involve a coming-of-age arc, but it's most common in epic high fantasy and fables.

Trends: As long as some readers are young, or young-at-heart, coming-of-age stories will be popular. The success of Harry Potter has proven the powerful draw of this subgenre. Recently, this part of the genre has seen books of greater length and darker subject matter.

Great Examples:

Lloyd Alexander	Chronicles of Prydain, starting with _The Book of Three_
David Eddings	_The Belgariad_ (now available in omnibus)
Ursula K. Le Guin	Earthsea Chronicles, starting with _A Wizard of Earthsea_
C. S. Lewis	Chronicles of Narnia, starting with _The Lion, the Witch, and the Wardrobe_
Garth Nix	Abhorsen trilogy, starting with _Sabriel_
Tamora Pierce	Song of the Lioness, starting with _Alanna: The First Adventure_

Philip Pullman	His Dark Materials, starting with *The Golden Compass*
Patrick Rothfuss	The Kingkiller Chronicles, starting with *The Name of the Wind*
J. K. Rowling	Harry Potter series, beginning with *Harry Potter and the Sorcerer's Stone*

Political Fantasy

Typical Book: It's always taken luck and genius to navigate the politics of (insert name of world, country, city, or nonprofit organization here). But now something really rotten is going on. It falls on the shoulders of our heroes (unlikely, inexperienced, unwanted, or under-estimated) to overcome early missteps, survive treachery and betrayal, and outwit the forces of evil.

Related to: Often lumped together with epic quest fantasy, political fantasy is more about outwitting and outmaneuvering opponents than about battles, quests, or magic. It's also similar to "realistic" fantasy and alternate historical fantasy.

Trends: Political fantasy is on the rise, particularly among adult readers.

Great Examples:

Daniel Abraham	The Long Price Quartet, starting with *A Shadow in Summer*
Lois McMaster Bujold	Chalion series, starting with *The Curse of Chalion*
Jacqueline Carey	Kushiel series, starting with *Kushiel's Dart*
Dave Duncan	The King's Blades, starting with *The Gilded Chain*
Jennifer Fallon	Hythrun Chronicles, starting with *Medalon*
Lian Hearn	Tales of the Otori, starting with *Across the Nightingale Floor*
Robin Hobb	The Farseer Trilogy, starting with *Assassin's Apprentice*
Brandon Sanderson	Mistborn series, starting with *Mistborn: The Final Empire*

Alternate Historical Fantasy

Typical Book: Before academia drove it screaming from the world, magic pervaded medieval/ancient/Victorian life. The authors balance precariously between satisfying the demands of historical verisimilitude from SCA inquisitors and yet still pleasing us with depictions of, for instance, the War of the Roses as a clash between mermaids and centaurs.

Related to: Political fantasy, some "realistic" epic fantasy.

Trends: The trend is away from the history of Europe in the classical and medieval periods and toward other countries and more recent eras and events.

Great Examples:

Emma Bull	*Territory*
Orson Scott Card	The Tales of Alvin Maker, starting with *Seventh Son*
Susanna Clarke	*Jonathan Strange and Mr Norrell*
Harry Harrison	*The Hammer and the Cross*
Guy Gavriel Kay	*The Lions of Al-Rassan*
Guy Gavriel Kay	*A Song for Arbonne*
J. Gregory Keyes	The Age of Unreason, starting with *Newton's Cannon*
Naomi Novik	Temeraire series, starting with *His Majesty's Dragon*

Paul Park   <u>White Tyger</u> series, starting with *A Princess of Roumania*
Harry Turtledove   <u>Videssos</u> series, starting with *The Misplaced Legion*

"Realistic" Epic Fantasy

Typical Book: Our antiheroes (who only rape, pillage, and murder when it meets their . . . ahem . . . "moral code" or is really important) wade hip-deep through muck, gore, moral qualms, and the bodily fluids of especially nasty enemies, using sharp weapons in the same way that a blind man uses a cane. Although several of them die horribly along the way, they ultimately defeat the nasties, thus allowing their putrid world to continue stinking.

Related to: Political fantasy, heroic fantasy, some historic fantasy, some epic high fantasy.

Trends: This part of the genre is hot, thanks to the breakout power of George R. R. Martin's <u>Song of Ice and Fire</u>. Adult fantasy fans, in particular, appreciate the added believability of fantasy with less random magic and more shades of gray in character depiction.

Great Examples:

Joe Abercrombie   <u>First Law</u> trilogy, starting with *The Blade Itself*
David Anthony Durham   <u>Acacia</u>, starting with *The War with the Mein*
Steven Erikson   <u>Malazan Book of the Fallen</u>, starting with *Gardens of the Moon*
George R. R. Martin   <u>A Song of Ice and Fire</u>, starting with *A Game of Thrones*
Sarah Micklem   <u>Firethorn</u> series, starting with *Firethorn*
Elizabeth Moon   *The Deed of Paksenarrion*
Richard K. Morgan   *The Steel Remains*
K. J. Parker   <u>Engineer Trilogy</u>, starting with *Devices and Desires*
Brian Ruckley   <u>The Godless World</u>, starting with *Winterbirth*
Ken Scholes   <u>The Psalms of Isaak</u>, starting with *Lamentation*

Hero Fantasy

Typical Book: What's that on the horizon? Is it a bird? Is it a plane? No! It's Pulp Badass! Accompanied by his sidekick, Comic Relief, and the love of his life, his sword Heartbreaker, he travels the world in search of justice and groovy magical stuff. It's a lonely, difficult life, given variety only by the many fun and exciting ways there are to kill deserving enemies. I'm not using "hero fantasy" in the same sense as "heroic fantasy," an overly generic term loaded with classical literary meanings, sometimes used to describe a style closer to epic high fantasy. This subgenre is sometimes called "sword and sorcery," another catchy, but too-inclusive-to-be-useful term.

Related to: "Realistic" epic fantasy, epic high fantasy, urban fantasy adventure.

Trends: Most of the best work in this subgenre is a few decades old, and it didn't help when its most artful contemporary practitioner, David Gemmell, died in his prime a few years ago. Still, this part of the genre draws in many new readers, particularly young males. Because they are simple but exciting, the classics in this subgenre hold up especially well.

Great Examples:

David Gemmell   <u>Drenai Tales</u>, starting with *Legend*
David Gemmell   <u>The Rigante</u>, starting with *Sword in the Storm*
Terry Goodkind   <u>Sword of Truth</u>, starting with *Wizard's First Rule*

Robert E. Howard	<u>Conan</u>, starting with *The Coming of Conan the Cimmerian*
Fritz Leiber	<u>Fafhrd and the Gray Mouser</u>, starting with *Lankhmar: Swords and Deviltry*
Michael Moorcock	<u>Elric</u> series, starting with *Elric of Melniboné*
R. A. Salvatore	<u>The Legend of Drizzt</u>, starting with *Homeland*
Matthew Woodring Stover	<u>Overworld</u> series, starting with *Heroes Die*
Roger Zelazny	*The Great Book of Amber*

Dark Fantasy

Typical Book: It's a lot like a horror novel except . . . okay, it is a horror novel. It's difficult to draw a clear line between these two genres. Dark fantasy has more fantastic elements in it than the average horror novel. In terms of what appeals to different readers, which is our concern here, the important distinction is that this is the "it's-mainly-supposed-to-scare-you" horror fantasy, as opposed to the "it's-mainly-supposed-to-excite-you" kind of dark fantasy of the next subgenre. The distinction is subjective, but it is important to many readers who prefer one style to the other.

Related to: Urban fantasy adventures, new weird, mythic explorations, some fantasy romance.

Trends: Horror has been in a lull, because many of its readers have turned instead to urban fantasy.

Great Examples:

Clive Barker	*Weaveworld*
Anne Bishop	<u>Dark Jewels</u>, starting with *Daughter of the Blood*
Christopher Golden	<u>The Veil</u>, starting with *The Myth Hunters*
Graham Joyce	*The Tooth Fairy*
Caitlin Kiernan	<u>Deke and Chance</u>, starting with *Threshold*
Stephen King	*The Stand*
Tanith Lee	*The Secret Books of Paradys*
H. P. Lovecraft	*At the Mountains of Madness*
Chelsea Quinn Yarbro	<u>St. Germain</u> series, starting with *Hotel Transylvania*

Urban Fantasy Adventures

Typical Book: Believe it or not, in the big city, strange happenings lurk just below the surface. And it's not just the city's usual freaks, perverts and deviants . . . there are monsters and magic, too! Our hipster hero must battle the beasties and negotiate with magical forces, while leaving plenty of time to pursue the opposite sex, drop clever one-liners, and maintain a suitably cool persona.

Related to: Dark horror fantasy, fantasy romance, some mythic fantasy and hero fantasy.

Trends: Drawing readership from fantasy, romance, and thriller fans, acceptable to both women and men, this is the hottest corner of the fantasy genre.

Great Examples:

Ilona Andrews	<u>Kate Daniels</u> series, starting with *Magic Bites*
Patricia Briggs	<u>Mercy Thompson</u>, starting with *Moon Called*
Jim Butcher	<u>Dresden Files</u>, starting with *Storm Front*

Rachel Caine	<u>Weather Warden</u> series, starting with *Ill Wind*
Simon R. Green	<u>Nightside</u>, starting with *Something from the Nightside*
Charlaine Harris	<u>Southern Vampire</u> series, starting with *Dead until Dark*
Kim Harrison	<u>The Hollows</u>, starting with *Dead Witch Walking*
T. A. Pratt	<u>Marla Mason</u> series, starting with *Blood Engines*
Rob Thurman	<u>Leandros Brothers</u>, starting with *Nightlife*

Fantasy Romance

Typical Book: Headstrong, beautiful, and feisty, our crime-fighting heroine can't choose between the tall, dark, and troubled vampire or the animal heat and flowing chest hair of his werewolf enemy. She's infuriated by, yet strangely attracted to, both. Learning to control her strange magic, surprised to find that she's the chosen one, and overcoming disasters—caused by his pigheadedness, stoic silence, and urges to feed on people—she discovers the good man within, the misunderstood lover who can tame her sassy ways. Between dating, hating, and mating, Muffy the Vampire Player and Vlad Impale-Her must find time in their social calendar to stop the even-more-evil undead from turning the world into Hell.

Related to: Urban fantasy adventure, some fables.

Trends: Fantasy romance has a larger share of the romance market than ever before. A few year's ago, this part of the genre was populated mostly by princesses and men in kilts, but now the undead are more prevalent. Some fantasy fans love this too, but others won't go near it.

Great Examples:

Kresley Cole	<u>The Immortals after Dark</u>, starting with *A Hunger Like No Other*
Mary Janice Davidson	<u>Queen Betsy</u> series, starting with *Undead and Unwed*
Christine Feehan	<u>GhostWalkers</u>, starting with *Shadow Game*
Jeaniene Frost	<u>Night Huntress</u> series, starting with *Halfway to the Grave*
Sherrilyn Kenyon	<u>Dark-Hunter</u> series, starting with *Fantasy Lover*
Marjorie Liu	<u>Dirk and Steele</u>, starting with *Tiger Eye*
Stephenie Meyer	<u>Twilight</u> series, starting with *Twilight*
Nalini Singh	<u>Psy-Changelings</u>, starting with *Slave to Sensation*
J. R. Ward	<u>Black Dagger Brotherhood</u>, starting with *Dark Lover*

Humorous Fantasy

Typical Book: The awkward and horrible nature of reality is rendered very funny by transporting the setting into a thinly disguised fantasy world, but then it is made very horrible and awkward again by the heavy use of atrocious puns.

Related to: Any other kind of fantasy can be given a humorous treatment.

Trends: Pratchett continues to dominate this group, but other writers, such as Jasper Fforde, A. Lee Martinez, and Christopher Moore, are on the rise.

Great Examples:

Piers Anthony	<u>Xanth</u> series, starting with *A Spell for Chameleon*
Peter David	<u>Apropos of Nothing</u>, starting with *Sir Apropos of Nothing*
Jasper Fforde	<u>Thursday Next</u> series, starting with *The Eyre Affair*
William Goldman	*The Princess Bride*
Austin Grossman	*Soon I Will Be Invincible*

Barry Hughart	*Bridge of Birds*
A. Lee Martinez	*Gil's All-Fright Diner*
Walter Moers	*The 13 1/2 Lives of Captain Bluebear*
Terry Pratchett	Discworld, starting with *The Colour of Money* (but readable in almost any order)
Jonathan Stroud	Bartimaeus trilogy, starting with *The Amulet of Samarkand*

Literary Fantasy

Typical Book: With convincing but cryptic characters, dreamlike environments, alliterative in-jokes, droll wordplay, graceful metaphor, nonlinear timelines, and metareferences, the author creates a magical variation on the real world that alternately induces amazement, confusion, ennui, and, ultimately, insanity in the reader. Magical realism, a style using especially small doses of fantasy in otherwise realistic settings and particularly associated with Latin American authors, is a subset of literary fantasy.

Related to: New weird, mythic fantasy, some political and "realistic" epic fantasy.

Trends: A growing number of literary fiction writers are including fantastic elements in their novels. The success of books such as *Jonathan Strange & Mr Norrell*, *The Life of Pi*, *The Historian*, and *The Time Traveler's Wife* suggests that this trend will continue to expand. The acceptance of these books has also opened the fantasy genre as a possibility for more mainstream readers.

Great Examples:

Mikhail Bulgakov	*The Master and Margarita*
Jonathan Carroll	*The Ghost in Love*
John Crowley	*Little, Big*
Keith Donohue	*The Stolen Child*
Gabriel Garcia-Márquez	*One Hundred Years of Solitude*
Mark Helprin	*A Winter's Tale*
Kelly Link	*Stranger Things Happen*; *Magic for Beginners*
Mervyn Peake	Gormenghast, starting with *Titus Groan*
Tim Powers	*The Anubis Gates*

The New Weird

Typical Book: If it's typical, it's not new weird. Books in this subgenre are like drugs, except they're legal and slower acting. What ties this subgenre together is its deliberate subversion of genre conventions. I include authors who are not typically considered new weird, who might have begun writing before the name evolved, but who exhibit the same characteristics. This subgenre can be very similar to literary fantasy, but new weird works are typically marketed primarily to fantasy readers and usually contain more fantasy elements.

Related to: Literary fantasy, dark horror fantasy, some mythic fantasy, and science fantasy.

Trends: The wide variety of approaches to new weird fiction make it difficult for the subgenre to coalesce, and many readers never find such deliberately challenging books appealing. Despite this, as part of speculative fiction's ever-continuing quest to reinvent itself, a growing number of readers and writers are taking up the challenge.

Great Examples:

K. J. Bishop	*The Etched City*
James P. Blaylock	*The Adventures of Langdon St. Ives* omnibus
Hal Duncan	<u>The Book of All Hours</u>, starting with *Ink*
Daryl Gregory	*Pandemonium*
M. John Harrison	*Viriconium*
China Miéville	<u>Bas-Lag (New Crobuzon)</u>, starting with *Perdido Street Station*
Haruki Murakami	*Hard-Boiled Wonderland at the End of the World*
Jeff VanderMeer	*City of Saints and Madmen*
Gene Wolfe	<u>The Book of the New Sun</u>, starting with *Shadow & Claw* omnibus

Fables

Typical Book: In a strange land, a story from the Brothers Grimm happens, but more slowly. Experiencing the tale from the lead character's perspective, readers discover that it's even more twisted than the creepy story that scared them into compliance with parental rules as children.

Related to: Mythic fantasy, coming-of-age fantasy.

Trends: This part of the genre has been quiet recently, but retold fables are an established part of the fantasy canon. They remain popular, especially among younger readers.

Great Examples:

Piers Anthony	<u>Incarnations of Immortality</u>, starting with *On a Pale Horse*
Orson Scott Card	*Enchantment*
Ellen Datlow and Terri Windling, eds.	Story collections, starting with *Snow White, Blood Red*
Pamela Dean	*Tam Lin*
Alex Flinn	*Beastly*
Shannon Hale	*Book of a Thousand Days*
Juliet Marillier	<u>Sevenwaters</u> series, starting with *Daughter of the Forest*
Robin McKinley	*Beauty*
Edith Pattou	*East*

Mythic Fantasy

Typical Book: In dreamlike style, the gods of different cultures clash, and the heroes of mythology move into the house next door. Magic mixes with anthropology lessons and a trickster god or two. If you have to give a report on this subgenre, use words like *mythos*, *allegory*, and *Jungian*. This kind of fantasy shares many traits with fables but is typically more complex and more shrouded in the mists.

Related to: Fables, some new weird, literary fantasy, and dark horror fantasy.

Trends: Before Tolkien changed the genre forever, mythic fantasy and hero fantasy were the largest part of the genre. That role has diminished, but this subset of the genre is still healthy. Contemporary work in mythic fantasy often takes a complex, philosophical approach, searching for the deep resonance of archetypal, mythic ideas.

Great Examples:

Charles de Lint	Newford, starting with *Memory and Dream*
Gregory Frost	*Shadowbridge*; *Lord Tophet*
Neil Gaiman	*American Gods*
Robert Holdstock	Ryhope Wood, starting with *Mythago Wood*
Ursula K. Le Guin	Earthsea, starting with *A Wizard of Earthsea*
Patricia McKillip	*Riddle-Master* omnibus
Catherynne M. Valente	The Orphan's Tales, starting with *In the Night Garden*
John C. Wright	Chaos series, starting with *Orphans of Chaos*

Science Fantasy

Typical Book: Advanced technology and magic meet in tales contrived to torment library cataloguers, who cannot decide whether they should use the rocket sticker or the dragon sticker.

Related to: New weird, some urban fantasy adventures.

Trends: Science fiction is going through a dormant period, but, as fantasy tends toward less emphasis on the medieval period and more frequent use of contemporary settings, science fantasy is on the upswing. Recent works of science fantasy often take a lighter, pulpy approach.

Great Examples:

C. S. Friedman	Coldfire Trilogy, starting with *Black Sun Rising*
Randall Garrett	*Lord Darcy* omnibus
Rosemary Kirstein	Steerswoman, starting with *The Steerswoman's Road* omnibus
Anne McCaffrey	Pern, starting with *Dragonflight*
Andre Norton	Witch World, starting with *The Gates to Witch World* omnibus
Robert Silverberg	Majipoor, starting with *Lord Valentine's Castle*
Dan Simmons	*Ilium*; *Olympos*
S. M. Stirling	The Change, starting with *Dies the Fire*
Charles Stross	Merchant Princes, starting with *The Family Trade*

Of course, the genre has plenty of other corners to play in: mystery crossover, graphic novels, animal fantasy, family sagas, role-playing tie-ins, steampunk, Arthurian, and superhero fantasies, to name just a few. Check the thematic section of this book, Chapter 5, for more coverage.

THE SUBGENRES OF SCIENCE FICTION

Space Opera

Typical Book: Think big—and I'm not talking about statuesque singers. A large cast of characters adventures across multiple solar systems. Along the way, expect elaborate action set pieces bigger than anything onstage at the Met or La Scala. Originally applied derogatorily to SF that wasn't . . . sniff . . . suitably serious, the space opera moniker was embraced by fans.

Related to: Planetary romance, future history, military and adventure SF, some hard SF

Trends: Recent trends should please both highbrows and action fans: the new space opera is big, action-packed, and philosophical, particularly as it's written by the British.

Great Examples:

Iain M. Banks	The Culture, starting with *Consider Phlebas*
Lois McMaster Bujold	Vorkosigan Saga, starting with *Cordelia's Honor* omnibus
Peter F. Hamilton	Night's Dawn, starting with *The Reality Dysfunction*
Larry Niven	Ringworld series, starting with *Ringworld*
Alastair Reynolds	Revelation Space universe, starting with *Revelation Space*
Justina Robson	*Natural History*
Karl Schroeder	Virga, starting with *Sun of Suns*
Allen Steele	Coyote series, starting with *Coyote*
Vernor Vinge	Queng Ho, starting with *A Deepness in the Sky*

Planetary Romance/Up Close with Aliens

Typical Book: Sent in search of the lost colony/investigating reports of a new race/ jettisoning from a damaged space ship, Zap Spacestud, Dr. Felicity Lovegood, and the rest of the away team find themselves on the surface of planet Exotica. They encounter aliens, and that's when the romance starts—no, not that kind of romance, the old-fashioned kind: glamorous, outlandish adventures. After some interspecies misunderstandings and some beautiful but deadly (for minor characters) run-ins with the planet's ecology, weather, flora, and fauna, accommodation is reached between the two species, one that will hold until the next book in the series.

Related to: Space opera, some hard SF future history, and new wave/social science fiction.

Trends: This is an older corner of the genre that is showing recent signs of revival.

Great Examples:

Neal Asher	Spatterjay series, starting with *The Skinner*
Marion Zimmer Bradley	Darkover series, starting with *Darkover: First Contact* omnibus
Tobias S. Buckell	*Crystal Rain*; *Ragamuffin*; *Sly Mongoose*
Alan Dean Foster	Pip & Flinx, starting with *The Tar-Aiym Krang*
Frank Herbert	Dune series, starting with *Dune*
Kay Kenyon	The Entire and the Rose, starting with *Bright of the Sky*
Andre Norton	Hosteen Storm series, starting with *The Beast Master*
Dan Simmons	Hyperion Cantos, starting with *Hyperion*
Sheri S. Tepper	*Grass*
Karen Traviss	Wess'Har series, starting with *City of Pearl*

Hard SF

Typical Book: In a prose style that ought to come with schematics, a calculator, and science texts, the author speculates on the impact of developments that might (but probably won't) happen. Whether the story dives into black holes or ozone holes, queries quarks or quasars, manipulates chromosomes, or bats around Buckyballs, you feel like you've completed an advanced correspondence course, if you can finish the book.

Related to: Future history, some slipstream/literary SF, more recent space opera.

Trends: As science progresses, this decade's hard SF is often viewed as more imaginative later, but hard science always remains a cornerstone of the genre.

Great Examples:

Stephen Baxter	<u>Manifold</u> series, starting with *Manifold: Time*
Greg Bear	*Eon*
Gregory Benford	*Timescape*
David Brin	<u>Uplift Saga</u>, starting with *Sundiver*
Arthur C. Clarke	*Rendezvous with Rama*
Hal Clement	*Heavy Planet: The Classic Mesklin Stories*
David Hartwell and Kathryn Cramer, eds.	*The Ascent of Wonder*; *The Hard SF Renaissance*
Kim Stanley Robinson	<u>Mars</u> series, starting with *Red Mars*
Peter Watts	*Blindsight*

Time Travel/Alternate History

Typical Book: Something happened to change the outcome of World War II, the U.S. Civil War, or the reign of Napoleon or Elizabeth I. (The rest of history, particularly ordinary lives, aren't affected. It's in the by-laws.) Now Stonewall Jackson is fighting Martians or Eleanor Roosevelt loves an artificial intelligence. Our hero from the future battles wardrobe malfunction, anachronisms, and worst of all, the dread paradox that prevents his or her conception in a quest to restore the natural order.

Related to: Utopia/dystopia/political SF, some science fantasy.

Trends: As the science behind time travel has become increasingly questionable, alternate history has become more common. Whether the science is solid or not, there is always a market for these books among history aficionados.

Great Examples:

Kage Baker	<u>The Company</u>, starting with *In the Garden of Iden*
Octavia Butler	*Kindred*
L. Sprague de Camp	*Years in the Making: The Time-Travel Stories of L. Sprague de Camp*
Philip K. Dick	*The Man in the High Castle*
Kathleen Ann Goonan	*In War Times*
Keith Roberts	*Pavane*
Harry Turtledove	*Guns of the South*
Jo Walton	<u>Alternative Britain</u> series, starting with *Farthing*
H. G. Wells	*The Time Machine*
Connie Willis	*The Doomsday Book*

New Wave/Social Science Fiction

Typical Book: There's not a lot that's typical about this part of science fiction, at least not for the typical **SF** fan. The books often work on a smaller scope. They're more introspective and less packed with action. Subjects such as sociology, anthropology, psychology, sexuality, gender roles, racial identity, and even—gasp!—feelings and emotions are explored.

Related to: Slipstream/literary SF, utopia/dystopia/political SF, some future history.

Trends: The official heyday of the new wave was in the 1960s and 1970s, evolving as a response to the Golden Age's adventure focus, and then supposedly eclipsed by a counter-reaction toward hard SF, but strong works of social science never truly go out of style.

Great Examples:

J. G. Ballard	*The Complete Stories of J. G. Ballard*
Thomas Disch	*Camp Concentration*
Harlan Ellison, ed.	*Dangerous Visions*
Robert Heinlein	*Stranger in a Strange Land*
Zenna Henderson	*Ingathering: The Complete People Stories of Zenna Henderson*
Daniel Keyes	*Flowers for Algernon*
Ursula K. Le Guin	*The Left Hand of Darkness*
Marge Piercy	*Women on the Edge of Time*
Robert Silverberg	*Dying Inside*

Future History

Typical Book: After the Have-Not Wars, after the first three Galactic Expansions, after the Psy-Singularity and the Third Sex Protocols, after the Greater Nanoplague, the five Imperial Visitations, and the Invertebrate Expansion—that's when something really interesting happened . . .

Related to: Often combines with other subgenres, such as space opera, utopia/dystopia/political SF, alternate history; some new wave/social science fiction, hard SF, and apocalyptic/post-apocalyptic SF.

Trends: As long as we wonder about civilization in the future, future history SF will be at the core of science fiction.

Great Examples:

Isaac Asimov	Foundation series, starting with *Foundation*
James Blish	*Cities in Flight*
Octavia Butler	Patternist series, in *Seed to Harvest* omnibus
C. J. Cherryh	The Company Wars, starting with *Downbelow Station*
Gordon R. Dickson	Childe Cycle, starting with *Dorsai Spirit* omnibus
Robert Heinlein	Future History, starting with *Revolt in 2100/Methuselah's Children*
Ken MacLeod	The Fall Revolution, starting with *Fractions* omnibus
David Marusek	*Counting Heads*
Ian McDonald	*River of Gods*

Utopia/Dystopia/Political SF

Typical Book: A writer from the past describes how much better the world will be when we have attained current levels of technology, or a writer from the present describes how bad it will be when technology has improved. Either way, it tells you what the author thinks of politics now.

Related to: Future history, slipstream/literary SF, some new wave/social science fiction, cyberpunk/pessimistic futures, alternate history.

Trends: One of the oldest science fiction subgenres, utopias/dystopias are evergreen

Great Examples:

M. T. Anderson	*Feed*
Ray Bradbury	*Fahrenheit 451*

Ernst Callenbach	*Ecotopia*
Cory Doctorow	*Little Brother*
Aldous Huxley	*Brave New World*
Ursula K. Le Guin	*The Dispossessed*
Lois Lowry	*The Giver*
George Orwell	*1984*
Sheri S. Tepper	*The Gate to Women's Country*
Yevgeny Zamyatin	*We*

Apocalypse and Post-Apocalypse

Typical Book: After the bombs, nuclear winter descended on Earth, which wouldn't have been so bad, except that it stopped us from seeing the comet coming our way. When that landed, it set off an ecological disaster! But that's okay, because we mutated to adapt to the new environment. Except then the mutation started a horrible plague. But in the end it's okay after all, because it turns out that it's exciting and rewarding to be one of the random survivors, particularly if you're one of the good ones, who gets to spend his or her days killing the bad ones.

Related to: Future history, utopian/dystopian/political SF, some cyberpunk, adventure science fiction, literary/slipstream science fiction.

Trends: Always popular, there are apparently even more ways for the world to end (or almost end) nowadays. This part of the genre is very popular, with both mainstream and science fiction authors exploring the end.

Great Examples:

David Brin	*The Postman*
Octavia Butler	*Parable of the Sower*; *Parable of the Talents*
Pat Frank	*Alas, Babylon*
Stephen King	*The Stand*
Walter M. Miller, Jr.	*A Canticle for Leibowitz*
Larry Niven and Jerry Pournelle	*Lucifer's Hammer*
Nevil Shute	*On the Beach*
Kate Wilhelm	*Where Late the Sweet Birds Sang*
John Wyndham	*Day of the Triffids*

Cyberpunk/Pessimistic Futures

Typical Book: Rom Driver is into computers. No, he doesn't just like them: he plugs in appendages. On a dull afternoon, he takes designer drugs and hacks into secure databases so that his avatar can have a few adventures. While there, Rom discovers the cable company's sinister plot to foreclose on the national debt or Microsoft's plan to hardcode Vista into the DNA of future children. Only Rom can save the rotten world from absolute monopoly, but then again, Rom's not exactly dependable. This might not turn out so well . . .

Related to: Utopian/dystopian/political SF, mystery and thriller crossovers.

Trends: Cyberpunk isn't as common as it was in its 1980s to 1990s heyday, but it still inspires a style of hip, anticonglomerate, semiparanoid dark followers.

Great Examples:

| Max Barry | *The Company* |

Philip K. Dick	*Do Androids Dream of Electric Sheep?*
William Gibson	<u>The Sprawl</u>, starting with *Neuromancer*
Haruki Murakami	*Hard-Boiled Wonderland and the End of the World*
Neal Stephenson	*Snow Crash*
Bruce Sterling	*Schismatrix Plus*
Charles Stross	*Halting State*
Walter Jon Williams	*Hardwired*
Jack Womack	<u>Ambient</u> series, starting with *Ambient*

Mystery Crossovers and Future Thrillers

Typical Book: It's not rocket science (although that might be involved). These are mysteries and thrillers set in the future. Because the deductions of a detective and the work of the scientist are both based on logical principles, the genres fit together easily.

Related to: Cyberpunk/pessimistic futures, many time-travel/alternate history novels.

Trends: We're in the age of the crossover writer, and this subgenre may be at its zenith.

Great Examples:

Lou Anders, ed.	*Sideways in Crime*
Isaac Asimov	*The Caves of Steel*; *The Naked Sun*
Alfred Bester	*The Demolished Man*
William Gibson	<u>The Bridge</u>, starting with *Virtual Light*
Warren Hammond	*KOP*; *Ex-KOP*
K. W. Jeter	*Noir*
Jonathan Lethem	*Gun, with Occasional Music*
Jack McDevitt	<u>"Hutch" Hutchins</u> series, starting with *The Engines of God*
Richard Morgan	*Thirteen* (published as *Black Man* in the United Kingdom)

Military and Other Adventure Science Fiction

Typical Book: It's the movie version of science fiction—big guns, bigger explosions, fast spaceships—although even the most action-oriented of science fiction's subgenres have more science and sensibility than anything you find at the multiplex.

Related to: Mystery/thriller crossovers, space opera, planetary romance.

Trends: The aging of the Star Wars and Star Trek franchises has actually been good for adventure science fiction, because other series and authors have found larger audiences.

Great Examples:

Taylor Anderson	<u>Destroyermen</u>, starting with *Into the Storm*
David Drake	*The Complete Hammer's Slammers, Volumes 1–3*
Joe Haldeman	*Forever War*; *Forever Peace*
Robert A. Heinlein	*Starship Troopers*
Sandra McDonald	<u>Terry Myell and Jodenny Scott</u>, starting with *The Outback Stars*
John Ringo	<u>Posleen War</u>, starting with *A Hymn before Battle*
John Scalzi	<u>Old Man's War</u> series, starting with *Old Man's War*
John Steakley	*Armor*
David Weber	<u>Honor Harrington</u> series, starting with *On Basilisk Station*

Coming-of-Age Science Fiction

Typical Book: Little Janey (or Jimmy) dreams of going to the stars. So when she (or he) becomes a teenager, and civilization comes to an end (literally, this isn't just angst), she (or he) does! But on arrival, it becomes clear that space is a big place. Little J can't decide whether to be buddies with the aliens, reach for a laser gun, or fly screaming back to the ruins of Earth. After learning some valuable lessons, Little J is ready for adulthood, or perhaps evolution into some higher form.

Related to: Any science fiction subgenre can combine with coming-of-age tales, although it's more common with optimistic, adventure-focused stories, such as space opera.

Trends: Young adult science fiction is still waiting for its *Harry Potter*-level breakout, but hot authors for adults, such as Cory Doctorow and John Scalzi, are becoming aware that there are books to be sold in this market. Expect more soon.

Great Examples:

Orson Scott Card	*Ender's Game*
Suzanne Collins	<u>The Hunger Games</u> series, starting with *The Hunger Games*
Margaret Peterson Haddix	<u>Shadow Children</u>, starting with *Among the Hidden*
Pete Hautman	*Rash*
Robert A. Heinlein	*Have Space-Suit Will Travel*; *Citizen of the Galaxy*; many other juvenile novels
Anne McCaffrey	*The Ship Who Sang*
Linda Nagata	*Memory*
Patrick Ness	*The Knife of Never Letting Go*
Philip Reeve	<u>The Hungry City Chronicles</u>, starting with *Mortal Engines*
Robert Charles Wilson	*Spin*

Slipstream/Literary SF

Typical Book: Some of science fiction's trippiest concepts are married to sophisticated, complex writing styles. Expect nonlinear plots, multiple narrators, descriptive passages, as much philosophy as science, and fewer special effects. You may have to look for it in a different aisle at the bookstore or library, but by all means look for it.

Related to: New wave/social science fiction, utopian/dystopian/political science fiction, apocalyptic SF.

Trends: In the era of crossovers, the literary establishment is more willing to allow science fiction concepts and the science fiction genre is more open to literary trappings, but it's still tricky to match these books with their audience.

Great Examples:

Margaret Atwood	*The Handmaid's Tale*
Samuel R. Delany	*Dhalgren*
Karen Joy Fowler	*Sarah Canary*
Stanislaw Lem	*Solaris*
Elizabeth Moon	*The Speed of Dark*
Thomas Pynchon	*Gravity's Rainbow*
Mary Doria Russell	*The Sparrow*; *Children of God*

| Dan Simmons | *Ilium*; *Olympos* |
| Neal Stephenson | *Anathem* |

Science Fiction Humor

Typical Book: In space, no one can hear you scream, but only because you're laughing too hard.

Related to: Humor can be paired with any of science fiction's other subgenres, taking on different styles as needed: silly humor with the lighter more optimistic genres and satirical dark comedy with the darker subgenres.

Trends: It's hard to sustain laughs over an entire book, particularly in SF, so the high point of science fiction humor may have come back when stories dominated. Still, there are knowing chuckles, silly giggles, and belly laughs to be found in the genre, usually at its fringes.

Great Examples:

Douglas Adams	*The Ultimate Hitchhiker's Guide to the Galaxy*
John Barnes	*Gaudeamus*
Terry Bisson	*Bears Discover Fire and Other Stories*
Austin Grossman	*Soon I Will Be Invincible*
Spider Robinson	<u>Callahan's</u>, starting with *Callahan's Cross-Time Saloon*
John Scalzi	*Agent to the Stars*
Robert Sheckley	*Dimensions of Sheckley: The Selected Novels of Robert Sheckley*
Kurt Vonnegut	*Cat's Cradle*; *Galapagos*
Connie Willis	*To Say Nothing of the Dog*

Short Stories

Typical Book: They're . . . um . . . shorter. Honestly, there's not much more than that to tie this category together, but one just can't overlook how important the short story has been to science fiction and continues to be for many of its readers. Besides, many of the story masters are simply too diverse in their craft to fit into just one of the other subgenres.

Related to: Any subgenre of science fiction can be written in the story format.

Trends: The age of writers making a living from stories is largely past us. Most of the contemporary story magazines struggle to maintain solvency and a subscriber base, but there are enough stories, old and new, to keep readers very busy.

Great Examples:

Single Author Collections

Ray Bradbury	*Bradbury Stories: One Hundred of His Most Celebrated Tales*
Ted Chiang	*Stories of Your Life and Others*
Arthur C. Clarke	*The Collected Stories of Arthur C. Clarke*
Harlan Ellison	*The Essential Ellison*
C. M. Kornbluth	*His Share of the Glory: The Complete Short Science Fiction of C. M. Kornbluth*
Margo Lanagan	*White Time*; *Black Juice*; *Red Spikes*
Robert Silverberg	*Phases of the Moon: Six Decades of Masterpieces*

| Cordwainer Smith | *The Rediscovery of Man: The Complete Short Science Fiction of Cordwainer Smith* |
| James Tiptree, Jr. | *Her Smoke Rose Up Forever* |

Anthologies

Lou Anders, ed.	*Fast Forward 1 and 2*
Orson Scott Card, ed.	*Masterpieces: The Best Science Fiction of the 20th Century*
Gardner Dozois, ed.	*The Year's Best Science Fiction* annual collections
George Mann, ed.	*The Solaris Book of New Science Fiction, Volumes 1–3*
Tom Shippey, ed.	*The Oxford Book of Science Fiction Stories*
Robert Silverberg, ed.	*The Science Fiction Hall of Fame, Volume 1*

Science Fantasy

See the science fantasy section in the breakdown of fantasy subgenres,
Science fiction has many other subgenres: far futures, cosmological SF romance and horror crossover, and superpowers, to name just a few. There are also SF subjects—robots, genetics, and nanotechnology, for instance—that are mined so frequently that they could be considered subgenres. Use the themes in Chapter 5 to further explore science fiction's divisions.

GLOSSARY

Collect 'em all and impress your friends! Here are 50 useful concepts from science fiction and fantasy that are not mentioned elsewhere in this book. They're a great addition to any genre discussion.

Albatross: Thanks to Coleridge's druggy dreams, the permanent symbol of bad luck hanging around the neck of an ancient mariner or, by extension, any other character.

Alien Artifact/ Big Dumb Object: A large object, usually of unknown origin and purpose, and possessing surprising properties, which creates a sense of awe in the science fiction humans who find it. The BDO emphasizes our smallness in the big universe. Also used endearingly for that guy who sits in the corner of book group and rarely talks.

Alien Space Bats: An unlikely intervention in the course of normal events that creates a divergence into an alternate history. As with many terms originally used derisively, alien space bats have been embraced by genre writers, who have included them in some novels as a winking in joke. If nothing else use alien space bats as an excuse for why you didn't finish this month's book.

Artificial Intelligence: Term for machines that gain the ability to think and reason independently. For extra points, shorten this to AI. Development of AI leads to great advances in technology (see Singularity) and raises questions about the rights and emotions of machines. In SF, AI often shows rampancy, overwriting its programming and endangering human creators.

Ansible: A device, given this name by Ursula K. Le Guin, that allows faster-than-light communication over great distances of space. Its availability greatly simplifies the plot tasks of a science fiction writer, but there is no known scientific basis for building an ansible at this time, so do not plan to use it as a way to participate in your book group while on vacation.

Asimov's Laws: Introduced in a 1942 short story, Asimov's laws of robotics are (1) a robot may not injure a human being or, through inaction, allow a human being to come to harm; (2) a robot must obey orders given to it by human beings, except when such orders conflict with the first law; and (3) a robot must protect its own existence as long as such protection does not conflict with the first or second law. Asimov uses these laws as an example of how powerful robots can be tools, designed in a way that precludes a Frankenstein rampage. Of course, there are always loopholes. If your group really wants to geek out, sit around one night and write additional laws and corollaries.

Astral Plane: A spiritual/mystical realm where magicians, the spirits of the dead, or hallucinating fantasy characters may go to wander. This can be used derisively in discussion: "The novel got off to an intriguing start, but then it wandered off onto some astral plane."

Chekhov's Gun: Not Star Trek Chekhov, but Anton Chekhov, who famously said, "One must not put a loaded rifle on the stage if no one is thinking of firing it." This device isn't limited to speculative fiction use, but it certainly crops up there. Can be used to describe any ominous bit of foreshadowing that suggests a likely end to the story.

Chosen One: The character marked by tattoos, birthright, or other prophecy to face off against the Dark Lord. The Chosen One usually has no clue how to use his or her powers at the start of the story. Also makes a good nickname for the reader whose turn it is to pick next month's book.

Clarke's Laws: Established in three essays by the great Arthur C., these laws are the following: (1) When a distinguished but elderly scientist states that something is possible, he is almost certainly right. When he states that something is impossible, he is very probably wrong. (2) The only way of discovering the limits of the possible is to venture a little way past them into the impossible. (3) Any sufficiently advanced technology is indistinguishable from magic. If you learn only one phrase to mutter wisely at book group, learn the third law.

Creatures: Fantasy just can't get along without 'em. At the minimum, SF book group participants should know *centaurs* (half-men, half-horse), *chimeras* (lion head, snake tail, breathes fire), *unicorns* (horse with a horn, favors virgins), *Pegasus* (hard-to-catch winged horse), *griffins* or *gryphons* (lion head, eagle wings and talons), *harpies* (greedy women with bird wings), *basilisks* (lizards that leave venom trails and kill with a glance, *medusas* (snake-haired women, turn those who see them into stone), the *Sphinx* (a lion with a human or bird head that guards something and asks riddles), *sirens* (half-women, half-birds, sing beautifully and lure men to their deaths), and the *minotaur* (bull-headed man who guards a labyrinth.)

Deus ex Machina: A "god from the machine," some unlikely or miraculous force, coincidence, or previously undeveloped power or device dropped into the story at the last minute to resolve conflicts for which the author couldn't find a more convincing resolution. The *deus ex machina* is the source of many unsatisfactory endings.

Dying Earth: A la Jack Vance, a world where the sun is near exhaustion and magic is re-asserting itself as a force. It would make a fine nickname for your favorite geezer book group.

Easter Egg: First applied to computer programming, an Easter egg is a hidden or subtle allusion, sometimes homage, sometimes satire, tucked into a work. In novels, this is usually a clever reference to the work of a favorite author or an earlier book with a similar theme.

Exposition—Infodump: Written material that conveys information that the reader needs in order to appreciate a novel's ideas and plot. A necessary evil in concept-heavy genres such as science fiction and fantasy, awkward use of exposition is given the inelegant name of *infodump*. Also useful when one of your book group companions explains too much: "Quit the infodump and tell us what you thought of the book."

Faerie: Also *sidhe, fairy, fay, fey, fair folk*, or pretty much any combination of vowels following the letter "f." Originating in Celtic mythology, these are beautiful, magical, but tricksy folk whom humans encounter—sometimes to their benefit, but usually to their detriment—in fantasy fiction. The term is also used for the parallel world in which these creatures live. In addition to Tinkerbell and her ilk, faeries include elves, sprites, brownies, pixies, dwarves, goblins, trolls, demons, shapeshifters, and a slew of other magical folk. They can be divided into the human-beneficial or human-neutral folk of the Seelie Court and the evil fey of the Unseelie Court.

Fandom: A subculture and community of people who are science fiction/fantasy enthusiasts. Fans talk in *fanspeak* and attend *Cons*, where they share their hobby through talk, *cosplay* (costuming), *filking* (familiar tunes refitted with fannish lyrics), all kinds of game play, and watching anime and other SF/F video fare. Your SF/F book group should try to tap into local fandom to guarantee a strong base.

Fanfiction: Fiction written by amateurs that reuses characters and settings from favorite works. Fanfiction is most often shared online, but enthusiasts in your book group may look to share their own *fanfic*. Writers of fanfiction have developed a terminology too extensive to include here. The term can also be used derisively, particularly when an author cannibalizes his or her own work with a poor sequel: "This reads like bad *fanfic*."

Faster than Light: Often shortened to FTL, travel or communication at speeds faster than light is of critical interest to science fiction writers. Most scientists do not believe that FTL is possible. If this is true, long-distance space travel—particularly by single individuals of reasonable patience and lifespan—becomes exceedingly difficult, changing the way that space stories are written and making other future technologies a more likely focus. If, however, a writer can convince us that FTL can work, groovy space adventuring and even time travel become possibilities.

Fix-up: A novel created by cobbling together a set of themed stories. Fix-ups were common in the era when stories dominated, less common now. Just as some people enjoy critiquing plastic surgery, your group may enjoy debating whether or not the patching shows on a fix-up.

Generation Ship: A self-sustaining ship that travels slower than light speed, carrying generations of occupants on some kind of intergalactic mission. Energy, food, air, water, and hillbilly genetics are major concerns for science fiction authors who employ a generation ship. Worst question to ask on a generation ship: "Are we there yet?"

Golem: From Jewish folklore, a being made of clay, animated by magic—usually by inscription, inserting magic words on a scroll in its mouth, or using the bodily fluids of the creator. The golem is to fantasy what the robot is to **SF**, a device for exploring subjects such as obedience and control, what it is to be alive, and what it is to be a creator.

Green Man: A mythical being or god who takes the form of a man, usually depicted with a face or hair made from leaves. The Green Man is a symbol of death, rebirth, fertility, and nature. Fantasy fiction writers often employ the Green Man, his surrogates, and minions as living symbols of human communion or battle with nature.

Holy Grail: In Christian mythology, the dish or cup used by Christ at the Last Supper, which can give eternal life but can only be found and drunk from by one who is absolutely pure. In various traditions, it's guarded by Joseph of Arimathea and his line or, more important to fantasy, by the Fisher King. The Grail is the subject of many Arthurian legends among others. The term is also used symbolically for any subject of great desire that motivates people to quest.

Interstitial Fiction: Works that straddle the boundaries of established genres, increasingly the preference of certain writers, publishers, and readers. Interstitial fiction is often a good choice for book groups because it provides a compromise for varying reader tastes, unusual premises, and good fodder for discussion. Also called *crossover* works.

Jumping the Shark; *Somebody Cut the Film*: Two useful phrases for the basic idea that a work or author has lost the thread, passed from plausibility into ridiculousness. "Jumping the shark" derives from an episode late in the run of *Happy Days* in which the Fonz goes to California and must jump a shark pond on water skis to prove himself cool. Because fantasy and SF ask readers to suspend disbelief, it is easy for the genres to become outlandish, thus jumping the shark.

Low Fantasy: Back-formed from the more familiar *high fantasy*, a low fantasy is one told in a pulpy, violent, dark, mud-spattered style. It features characters of low birth and complex morality, talking in everyday street language.

MacGuffin: Alfred Hitchcock introduced this term for the highly desirable object that starts characters on a competitive quest. The MacGuffin is usually not as important in the end as the action of questing itself. In my group, the theme that jumpstarts discussion is often a MacGuffin.

Mary Sue: An annoyingly perfect lead character who can seem to do no wrong. The Mary Sue can be female or male, although the latter may be given other names, such as Prince Charming. Adult readers of fantasy may find the Mary Sue to be unbelievable or a surrogate for author wish fulfillment. Jaded readers may find themselves rooting for the villain and against the Mary Sue.

Metaverse: A virtual world where humans interact through avatars and other software agents or, by extension, the conjunction of many such worlds. In science fiction novels, actions in the metaverse often have real-world implications.

Nanotechnology: Control of matter at the molecular or atomic level, sometimes self-replicating: a recipe for plenty or for disaster, depending on which science fiction novel one reads. Nanotech can be performed by *nanobots*. If it breaks down, it may result in a *gray goo* disaster.

Nibelungenlied: Epic poem of German origin about Siegfried. Based on events of the fifth and sixth centuries, the extensive story contains many events and objects that have fueled fantasy fiction (and Wagner's opera cycle), including fateful predictions, dragon slaying, betrayal of brothers and companions, and a cloak of invisibility.

Niven's Law: The converse of Clarke's third law: "Any sufficiently advanced magic is indistinguishable from technology."

Packing Peanuts: Details thrown into a book that serve as padding between real plot developments. Some packing peanuts prevent a novel from becoming too frantic, but it's no fun to open a package that's all styrofoam and no birthday present.

Parallel Universe: A self-contained world that coexists in parallel with ours. Parallel universes or worlds are used in both science fiction and fantasy. Key questions in regard to parallel universes are how one can pass into or communicate with others in them and how events or rules there compare to the rules here. Also good for droll book group comments: "In a parallel universe, John liked one of the books we read once."

Phildickian: Named after Philip K. Dick, an adjective used to describe writing in which reality and illusion become hard to distinguish. It's an interesting quality, trippy and hypnotic in the hands of some writers, annoying and dreary when used by others. More important, the adjective is vastly fun to say out loud. For more auctorial descriptives, see *Tolkienesque*.

Picaresque: Adjective for fiction in which a rascally character, usually of low social class, engages in humorous adventures, deftly navigating a corrupt and chaotic world, while thumbing his or her nose at the powers that be. It's an important theme to geekdom's perpetual underdogs.

Plot Coupon: A derisive term for a book in which the protagonists must collect a set of objects or complete an arbitrary set of tasks in order to achieve success, in the same way that earlier generations collected green stamps or box tops to obtain magical material goods.

Plot Voucher: A sort of magical get-out-of-jail-free card, given to the protagonist earlier in the novel and used to escape a later dilemma. The plot voucher can be used gracefully or with a heavy hand, but it's a device that all genre readers should know.

Powderpuffing: The author's habit, particularly prevalent in speculative fiction, to be especially kind to sympathetic characters. If the leads continually dodge a hail of bullets while lesser characters die around them, it can ruin the believability of the scenario. See *Redshirt*.

Prose Edda: An epic work of Icelandic verse, written by Snorri Sturluson (probably the best author name ever) around 1220, providing one of the primary sources of Norse mythology. It contains many concepts familiar to fantasy writers and readers: for instance Valhalla—the home of Odin, other Norse gods, and the Valkyries—located in Asgard, accessible only by the Bifrost rainbow bridge and ultimately destroyed in the armageddon Ragnarok.

Recursive Fiction: Fiction that makes use of worlds or characters created by other authors, a popular method in science fiction/fantasy, where so many interesting worlds and memorable characters have been created. Another word for such writing is *pastiche*.

Redshirt: From the original *Star Trek* series, a character (so named for his usual wardrobe) whose only purpose is to fill out the landing party, dying so that none of the developed characters have to be sacrificed. Look around the table at your book group: any redshirts?

Robinsonade: Named after *Robinson Crusoe*, a literary work in which a protagonist or a small group is suddenly separated from civilization and forced to improvise with the materials at hand. Whether by falling into not-so-wonderland, crashing a spaceship, slipping through a wormhole, or sudden apocalyptic degradation, many SF/F books employ similar themes. This would make another really cool name for a book group.

SETI: Pronounced phonetically, rhymes with *yeti*. It's the Search for Extra Terrestrial Intelligence, frequently made in SF novels, not to be confused with SITI, the Search for Intra Textual Intelligence—in the book you shouldn't have read.

Singularity: An evolutionary leap in intelligence and technological development that occurs when intelligent machines surpass human limits and then rapidly augment their own skills and abilities. This might also occur if everyone reads the book and shows up at the next meeting.

Sturgeon's Law: "Ninety percent of everything is crap." It's meant as a defense of science fiction, fantasy, or any other field in which a few weak straw-man examples are used as grounds to attack the whole. You can use Sturgeon's Law as a sort of "same to you" if everyone in your group hates your taste, but you might better spend your time in search of the elusive final ten percent.

Terraforming: Changing the properties of a planet, particularly its atmospheric properties, so as to make it inhabitable for humans. As scientists and science fiction writers have become more aware of the difficulties of long-distance space travel and the rarity of planets that can support life naturally, interest in terraforming has risen.

Tolkienesque: Adjective for writing similar to Tolkien's: usually meaning epic fantasy told in lyrical, somewhat formal language. You can throw around *auctorial descriptives* like this for fun. I propose *heinleinine, leguinian, powersful, bradburial, pohlish, feisty, bujoldfashioned, leibearary, tepperid*, and *o'Kay*. And before you make crude jokes, read the entry for *Phildickian*.

The Wild Hunt: From myth, a pack of supernatural, undead, or fairy hunters, dogs, or horses who give perpetual chase, sometimes to villains, sometimes simply to those who cross their path. In various versions, Odin, Herne the Hunter, or King Arthur leads them. The Wild Hunt or a similar group appears frequently in fantasies. Yet another fine nickname for your book group!

BASIC DISCUSSION QUESTIONS FOR SCIENCE FICTION

In which science fiction subgenres does this book fit?

How does this book differ from the average science fiction novel? In what ways is it exceptional?

Which writers seem to have influenced the author? What other books are similar?

Is the author's vision of the future believable? Are the characters and their actions believable?

What do you think of the book's cover? Is it fitting, or does it lead you to expect something different from the book?

Describe the pacing of the book. How does its pacing affect your appreciation of the story?

Does the author address any contemporary real-world issues or questions in the science fiction context? Does placing them in this context change how you view the issue?

From what point of view is the story told? Is the narrative voice interesting?

Does the book give rise to any emotions in you as a reader?

Which character is your favorite and why? Which is your least favorite?

In the book, how are character behaviors or the structure of society changed by developments in science and technology?

Which scene or chapter is your favorite? Why is it memorable?

Is the future likely to develop in a way similar to the events of this book?

Is the science behind the technologies in this book accurate? Does the author give you enough detail to make that judgment?

Is the author's style appropriate to the story and to the tone that he or she tries to convey? How does this author rate as a stylist?

Which relationship between two characters is the most interesting in the book?

To what kind of readers would you recommend this book? Who should steer away from it?

Is the resolution of the book satisfying? Would you change it in some way?

Will you continue with other books in this series or by the same author? Why?

Would this book make a good film? What would be difficult to show on camera? Who would you cast in the film?

BASIC DISCUSSION QUESTIONS FOR FANTASY FICTION

In which fantasy subgenres does this book fit? How is it different from the typical fantasy book? In what ways is it exceptional?

Which other authors seem to influence this work? What other books are similar?

Are you able to suspend disbelief while reading this book? Do you find the characters and story to be believable despite the fantastic setting?

What do you think of the cover? Is it fitting, or does it lead you to expect something different?

Describe the pacing of the book. How does the pacing affect your appreciation of the story?

Which character is your favorite and why? Which is your least favorite?

How good is the quality of worldbuilding in the book? Which location would you most like to visit? Would the same plot work if it were set in another time or culture?

Does the book give rise to any emotions in you as a reader?

Which scene or chapter is your favorite? Why is it memorable?

Does the author address any real-world issues or questions in the fantasy context? Does placing them in this context change the way in which the issues can be addressed?

Does the author's style seem appropriate to the story and to the tone that he or she tries to convey? How does this author rate as a stylist?

What do you think of how magic is handled in the book? Are there limits or costs to its practice? Is the system of magic unique, or is it similar to that in other works?

From what point of view is the story told? Is the narrative voice interesting?

Which relationship between characters is the most interesting in this book?

Are you satisfied by the book's resolution? Would you change it in some way?

To what kind of readers would you recommend this book? Who should steer away from it?

Will you continue with other books in this series or by the same author? Why or why not?

Would this book make a good film? What would be difficult to show on camera? Who would you cast in the film?

Chapter 3

25 Great Fantasy Novels
for Book Groups

Daniel Abraham

A Shadow in Summer

ABOUT THE AUTHOR

Daniel Abraham is a rising star on the fantasy and science fiction scene. A student of writers George R. R. Martin and Connie Willis, Abraham's short fiction is well known. *A Shadow in Summer*, which opens The Long Price Quartet, is his first novel. The Quartet completes publication in 2009. He has also collaborated with Martin on the Wild Cards series and the novel *Hunter's Run*. Abraham lives in New Mexico with his wife and daughter, where he combines writing with duties as a stay-at-home dad.

PLOT SUMMARY

The city-state of Saraykeht has prospered, not because of its military prowess but because of economic power created by the abilities of *andats*, thoughts brought to life by poet-magicians. Seedless, an andat who can remove seeds from cotton (and babies from wombs), conspires to escape the control of his poet, Heshai, setting off a chain of events with political and personal consequences for Saraykeht and its people. An unlikely set of characters—an aging female overseer, her young assistant, the assistant's laborer boyfriend, and an apprentice poet—are faced with complex choices that will decide their own fates and that of their city.

Publication Date: 2006

331 p.

AUTHOR'S WEBSITE

http://www.danielabraham.com

APPEAL POINTS

Abraham's unusual fantasy features little in the way of traditional action or violence. This is a thinking person's fantasy that appeals to readers interested in moral and political questions. It explores the nature of freedom, control, and how to function when in over one's head. With its unusual magic system, Asian-feeling setting, and nontraditional lead characters (an aging and aching woman overseer and a love triangle of inexperienced young folk with limited powers), this novel works well for experienced readers who like fantasy but are looking for new approaches.

DISCUSSION QUESTIONS

- Most of the characters in this novel are driven by desires to overcome a sense of being trapped and to conduct their lives in the way they see fit. Which are truly limited? Which are finding the right path to autonomy?

- One of the author's goals in writing this novel was to create an alternative to the typical medieval setting of fantasy. Is his attempt to create an Eastern setting successful?
- The characters in this fantasy are unusual in that they lack the military, magical, or political powers typical of leads in fantasy epics. Does this make them more or less interesting to you?
- *A Shadow in Summer* has almost no physical fighting or magical action sequences. Without these elements, does the fantasy remain exciting? Should other writers follow this lead?
- Is Seedless a villain or a hero? What about Heshai? What about Wilson?
- Physical poses are used extensively as a supplement to communication in Abraham's world. What do you think of this device?
- *A Shadow in Summer* shows the difficulties of maintaining a society dependent on the magical abilities of a few individuals. What are these difficulties? Could such a society survive and succeed?
- Is the plot against Heshai designed primarily by the Galts or primarily by Seedless?
- Does anyone behave badly in the love triangle between Itani, Liat, and Maati? How should their relationships be resolved? Should any of them end up together?
- How do you interpret the title *A Shadow in Summer*?
- Does Otah make the right choice when he leaves his training at the start of the novel?
- Years pass between the events of this novel and the second book of <u>The Long Price Quartet</u>. What do you predict will happen to these characters in the years that follow?

SUGGESTED READING IF YOU LIKE *A SHADOW IN SUMMER*

Daniel Abraham	more of the <u>Long Price Quartet</u>, starting with *A Betrayal in Winter*
Lian Hearn	<u>Tales of the Otori</u>, starting with *Across the Nightingale Floor*
Robin Hobb	The <u>Farseer Trilogy</u>, starting with *Assassin's Apprentice*
Laurie J. Marks	*Fire Logic*
Brandon Sanderson	*Elantris*

Richard Adams

Watership Down

ABOUT THE AUTHOR

Richard Adams was born in Berkshire in the Hampshire district of England in 1920. After serving in World War II and receiving a master's degree from Oxford University, he served in Britain's Department of Agriculture and Department of the Environment until 1974, when he was able to switch to writing full-time. Once president of the Royal Society for the Protection of Cruelty to Animals, Adams's reputation comes mostly from his novels about animals, especially *Watership Down*, *Shardik*, and *The Plague Dogs*. He lives with his wife, less than 10 miles from his birthplace.

PLOT SUMMARY

A small, strange, clairvoyant rabbit named Fiver predicts doom for his warren. Convinced of the danger by Hazel, Fiver's confident brother, a small group of rabbits sets off in search of a new home, escaping the military rabbits who rule their warren (and the warren's destruction soon after their departure). Eventually, with help from a seagull, they discover an overcrowded warren called Efrafa, a military state controlled by General Woundwort. Lacking any females, Hazel and a strong rabbit named Bigwig devise a plan to help a group of does escape from Efrafa. The escape succeeds, but it leads to a final battle between Woundwort's army and Hazel's followers on their new home of Watership Down.

    Publication Date: 1972

    448 p.

READER'S GUIDE

http://www.sparknotes.com/lit/watership/study.html

APPEAL POINTS

A book about talking bunnies can be a tough sell to adult readers, but *Watership Down* can be read by all ages and enjoyed on many different levels. Animal lovers and those concerned with the environment are obvious audiences, but *Watership Down* is also a must for those who love good character development, allegory, myth, heroic adventure, or sheer storytelling prowess. Readers who enjoy sociology, psychology, or ethics find plenty to make them ponder. There is one caveat: female rabbits are woefully underrepresented.

DISCUSSION QUESTIONS

- Should *Watership Down* be categorized as fantasy fiction?
- Does this novel appeal more to children or adults?

- Is it important to the novel that rabbits are the protagonists, or would another kind of animal work just as well?
- Which is your favorite of the rabbits?
- Should women be offended by the shortage of female characters in *Watership Down*? By the portrayal of the does?
- Compare the various leadership styles exhibited in *Watership Down*.
- What do you think of El-ahrairah? Do his adventures bear similarity to those of other mythological heroes?
- Is the Black Rabbit of Inlé the equivalent of the Grim Reaper for rabbits, or is his portrayal different in some way?
- What themes does *Watership Down* share with Tolkien's works, *The Hobbit* and *The Lord of the Rings*?
- Is humankind the prime source of evil in the world of *Watership Down*?
- How are Adams's rabbits different from humans?

SUGGESTED READING IF YOU LIKE *WATERSHIP DOWN*

Richard Adams	*Shardik*
Richard Adams	*Tales from Watership Down*
David Clement-Davies	*The Sight*
Brian Jacques	Redwall series, starting with *Redwall*
Kij Johnson	*The Fox Woman*; *Fudoki*
Tad Williams	*Tailchaser's Song*

Lois McMaster Bujold

The Curse of Chalion

ABOUT THE AUTHOR

Bujold was born in Ohio in 1949 and has lived in Minneapolis since 1995. After college at Ohio State, she worked as a pharmacy technician, but quit to raise a family. While staying at home with two small children, she followed a friend's lead and became serious about her writing. Her first novel was published in 1983, and she has since published over 20 more. Her Vorkosigan space operas and Chalion fantasies have produced more Hugo and Nebula wins for best novel than any other writer: six so far.

PLOT SUMMARY

When Cazaril escapes from captivity, he wants only a quiet life in his homeland. Instead, he is given the post of tutor to the Royesse (princess) Iselle. Soon Cazaril finds himself fending off political intrigue, hired assassins, a family curse, religious magic, and the unwanted attentions of the very nobles who betrayed him into slavery. Despite his resourcefulness, his options begin to narrow. Finally, to protect his charge and save the kingdom, Cazaril is faced with the ultimate sacrifice.

Publication Date: 2001

448 p.

AUTHOR'S WEBSITE: THE BUJOLD NEXUS

http://www.dendarii.com

APPEAL POINTS

Bujold may be as close to a sure bet recommendation as any author in speculative fiction. Everyone seems to like her work. *The Curse of Chalion* is part of a loosely connected series, but stands up well on its own. Her focus is on strong, likable characters and exciting, well-paced plots. Her lead character, Cazaril, is modest but capable. He handles pressure well and gets the best out of others. Because Cazaril is that rarity in fantasy, a middle-aged protagonist, this book is an especially good choice for older fantasy fans. Her female characters are also, as always, superb. There's enough romance to satisfy those who like it, but it's subtle enough not to overwhelm those who don't. *Chalion* balances character development, action, and politics. The world of Chalion is distinctive because of low use of magic and an interesting five-god religion, but otherwise it can be compared to medieval Europe. Bujold is a graceful writer, whose straightforward, compact style keeps her books shorter than those of most contemporary speculative fiction authors. She doesn't confuse readers, but her intelligence satisfies adults who might be sensitive about reading a genre that they think is mainly for children.

DISCUSSION QUESTIONS

- Why has Bujold won more major awards for best novel than any other speculative writer?
- In what ways does Cazaril differ from the usual fantasy hero? Do the differences make you enjoy the character more or less?
- Which secondary character do you most enjoy? Which is the most annoying? The most evil?
- How do the five gods of Chalion make this world different from a monotheistic culture?
- How does Iselle's portrayal compare to that of the typical fantasy princess?
- What do you think of the romance between Cazaril and Bertriz?
- Before the <u>Chalion</u> books, Bujold was known for her long series of <u>Vorkosigan</u> space operas. For those who have read both, are there similarities between the author's science fiction and her fantasy? Significant differences?
- Were you surprised by the revelation of Umegat's powers? Does he remind you of any other characters in fantasy fiction?
- Did you guess the nature of the curse of Chalion before it was revealed? Were you surprised by its origins?
- The second book in the <u>Chalion</u> series features Ista as its lead character. Does that surprise you? How do you think Bujold will develop her character in *Paladin of Souls*?

SUGGESTED READING IF YOU LIKE *THE CURSE OF CHALION*

Daniel Abraham	The <u>Long Price Quartet</u>, starting with *A Shadow in Summer*
Patricia Bray	*The First Betrayal*
Lois McMaster Bujold	Other <u>Chalion</u> fantasies, starting with *Paladin of Souls*
Guy Gavriel Kay	*The Lions of Al-Rassan*

Jonathan Carroll

The Ghost in Love

ABOUT THE AUTHOR

The son of a screenwriter and an actress, Jonathan Carroll was born in New York City in 1949. As a teen Carroll drifted into delinquency, but he returned from the verge when a friend was shot dead by police. After taking degrees in English from Rutgers and the University of Virginia, he took up teaching. He has been a resident of Vienna, Austria, since the 1970s, and has published 15 novels and many short stories. Recurrent themes in Carroll's work are the inclusion of bits of his own biography, talking animals (especially dogs), and exploration of the human condition through metaphoric fantasy.

PLOT SUMMARY

When Ben Gould falls, hitting his head on the sidewalk, he's supposed to die, but he doesn't, beginning a series of strange events. The angel of death sends a ghost, Ling, to watch Ben, but the ghost falls in love with Ben's girlfriend, Germany. Ben discovers change in himself. For one, he can talk to his dog Pilot, and second, he finds himself living through the sensations of Danielle Voyles, a woman who cannot see Ben, but like him, has somehow survived a killing accident. Ben and Germany have become estranged because of his odd, uncommunicative behavior, but when he tries to explain the bizarre turns his life has taken, the two instead witness a disturbing killing by a knife-wielding man. Ben, Germany, Pilot, Ling, and Danielle soon find themselves on a twisty, fantastic journey through their own present and past, where they combat death, the frightening man, and their own worst personality traits and fears.

Publication Date: 2008

320 p.

AUTHOR'S WEBSITE

http://www.jonathancarroll.com

APPEAL POINTS

Carroll's writing works on many levels: as twist-filled ghost tale, as love story, as philosophical treatise, and as a visual collection of vignettes full of beautiful sensory details. Romantics, cooks, and animal lovers are especially pleased, because the book caters strongly to those interests. Some readers may be highly interested in Carroll's use of fantastic metaphors to explore a philosophy of life and death, memory and self, love and relationships. Others may find his approach precious or unconvincing, but they are probably not the sort of readers who pick up fantasy in the first place. Carroll's work is different from typical genre fantasy and uses few of the same conventions. Readers who are highly used to those conventions may find this work refreshing or, conversely, too different to please them.

DISCUSSION QUESTIONS

- Who is your favorite character in the novel? Why?
- *The Ghost in Love* is full of memorable scenes. Which is your favorite?
- Are you more likely to recommend this book to a fantasy reader or to a literary fiction reader? Can you identify any comparable works in the mainstream of genre fantasy?
- What do you think of Carroll's characterization and use of Pilot and other animals?
- In the scene where Danielle meets with her past selves, she first spends time reassuring them, then becomes fascinated with asking them questions. What questions would you ask if you could confront your past selves? Do you agree with the idea developed in this scene that we change dramatically and rapidly?
- Are the many plot twists in this book easy or difficult to follow? Do all of its fantastic elements feel organic, or do you find them hard to believe?
- The connection of food to important moments in life is a recurring theme in the novel. Is this true of your life as well? Do you have significant memories of food connected to any important events in your memory?
- What do you think of Danielle's decision to stay in her life's happiest moment? Will it work for her in the long run, or is she stuck?
- What has Ben learned by the end of the novel? What has Germany learned? In what sense do you think that death has been challenged?

SUGGESTED READING IF YOU LIKE *THE GHOST IN LOVE*

Nick Bantock	Griffin & Sabine series, starting with *Griffin & Sabine*
Jonathan Carroll	*The Land of Laughs*
Jonathan Carroll	*The Marriage of Sticks*
John Crowley	*Little, Big*
Charles de Lint	*Memory and Dream*
Kelly Link	*Stranger Things Happen*
Haruki Murakami	*The Wind-Up Bird Chronicle*

Peter David

Tigerheart

ABOUT THE AUTHOR

Although he has never had a true breakout novel, Peter David is a journeyman writer who has pleased an endless stream of readers with over 70 novels, many comic books, and several television series. His novels include works in the <u>Star Trek</u>, <u>Babylon 5,</u> and <u>Battlestar Galactica</u> series; novelizations of many superhero films; a series, beginning with *Knight Life*, that retells the King Arthur story in a modern context; and his own original fantasy series about <u>Sir Apropos of Nothing</u> and <u>The Hidden Earth</u>. Comic work includes stints on <u>The Incredible Hulk</u>, <u>Spider-Man</u>, <u>Wolverine,</u> <u>Aquaman</u>, and the graphic adaptation of Stephen King's <u>The Dark Tower.</u> David lives in Long Island with his wife and three children.

PLOT SUMMARY

Tigerheart follows Paul Dare, a boy growing up in London. When Paul's younger sister disappears, his serious-minded mother rejects his storytelling father, tries to eliminate the fantastic influences from Paul's life, and has a breakdown. Paul, who travels in the Anyplace (Neverland) with a white tiger companion and is fascinated by tales of The Boy (Peter Pan), returns to that dream world with Fiddlefix (Tinkerbell) to find a new little girl to replace his lost sister. There he finds himself caught up in a series of desperate adventures with The Boy, The Vagabonds (Lost Boys), his tiger, Gwenny (Wendy), the evil Mary Slash (a sister of Captain Hack), a gang of pirates, and a tribe of Indians.

    Publication Date: 2008

    304 p.

AUTHOR'S WEBSITE

http://www.peterdavid.net

APPEAL POINTS

David's novel is sure to please fans of the Peter Pan legend. Like J. M. Barrie's book, it features an omniscient narrator whose witty commentary on the action of the novel may be even more important than the book's events. The book has a great deal to say about the nature of childhood (especially of boys) and the process of parenting. It explores the connection of the real world and the fantasy world. This is an easy-to-read book, full of tongue-in-cheek humor that appeals to and is appropriate for a broad age range of readers.

DISCUSSION QUESTIONS

- Would J. M. Barrie be pleased with David's pastiche of his work? Does David manage to capture any part of Barrie's style as a writer? Does he stay true to Barrie's characters? Which book is better?

- In what ways does David make the Peter Pan story more contemporary?
- Do the intrusions of the author add to this tale or distract from it?
- What are the differences between Paul Dear and The Boy?
- Barrie's work is usually placed in the children's section. Should this work join it there, or does it belong in the young adult or adult sections of a library or bookstore?
- Do you agree with the book's treatment of the differences between boys and girls?
- Would you like to have The Boy as a friend or companion? To what extent would you trust him?
- Which of the female characters—Fiddlefix, Gwenny, or Princess Picca—does The Boy need most? Does he need any of them? Which of these three would you choose as a companion?
- Do you like the author's resolution of the clash between Paul, The Boy, and Hack and Slash?
- Will Paul return to the Anyplace? Will his father? If so, what will their role there be?
- What will happen to the Dear family after the events of the novel?

SUGGESTED READING IF YOU LIKE *TIGERHEART*

J. M. Barrie	*Peter Pan*
Dave Barry and Ridley Pearson	*Peter and the Starcatchers; Peter & the Shadow Thieves; Peter & the Secret of Rundoon*
Andrew Birkin	*J. M. Barrie and the Lost Boys: The Real Story behind Peter Pan*
Peter David	*Knight Life; One Knight Only; Fall of Knight*
Keith Donohue	*The Stolen Child*
Cornelia Funke	Inkheart series, starting with *Inkheart*
Geraldine McCaughrean	*Peter Pan in Scarlet*

Stephen R. Donaldson

Lord Foul's Bane

ABOUT THE AUTHOR

Born in Cleveland in 1947, Donaldson is the son of a medical missionary. He lived in India until the age of 16. He served two years as a conscientious objector during the Vietnam War. On his return, he completed a master's degree in English at Kent State, then dropped out of his Ph.D. program to write full-time. The first six books of his <u>Chronicles of Thomas Covenant</u> resulted, followed by five novels in his science fiction epic, <u>The Gap</u>. Donaldson received a doctorate in literature in 1993 and achieved black belt status in Shotokan karate in 1994. After a 21-year gap, he returned to Thomas Covenant in 2004 for <u>The Last Chronicles</u> series.

PLOT SUMMARY

Leprosy brings Thomas Covenant to ruin: divorced by his wife and shunned by his community. Startled by a raving beggar, he walks in front of a car. He wakes in a world called The Land, summoned by Drool Rockworm, a cavewight who derives power from the Staff of Law. Rockworm's master, Lord Foul, prophesies that Covenant will destroy The Land, but that Rockworm will destroy it sooner if not stopped. Covenant is to deliver this taunting message to the Council of Lords, magicians who rule from a rocky fortress called Revelstone. The embittered Covenant thinks that The Land is a delusional dream from which he will awake with his leprosy out of control. Because he believes that his actions in the land are imaginary, he commits heinous acts, in particular the rape of his healer. He refuses to wield the magic available to him through his white gold wedding ring and only reluctantly joins the quest to confront Rockworm. With the aid of a friendly giant, the lore of stone and wood magic, the wild horse Ranyhyn, the powerful Council, and their ageless warrior allies the Bloodguard, Covenant must rise above his sins and disbelief to complete his epic quest and challenge the forces of evil.

    Publication Date: 1977

    369 p.

AUTHOR'S WEBSITE

http://www.stephenrdonaldson.com

APPEAL POINTS

Much has been made of antihero Covenant, and reader tolerance of (or fascination with) him has a large impact on enjoyment of this book. However, the charm and variety of the secondary characters—for the most part unabashedly heroic—may temper Covenant's nastiness. Another draw is The Land, one of the best fantasy worlds ever created. The story dramatizes ethical questions: those who enjoy philosophical thinking find much to ponder, but those who prefer straightforward action may be frustrated. Heavy use of figurative language and unfamiliar words also divides readers. The controversial rape at the start of this book turns some off. The resolution of this novel is not unsatisfying, but most readers continue happily through the three books of The First Chronicles and on to The Second Chronicles of Thomas Covenant.

DISCUSSION QUESTIONS

- Is the reaction of Covenant's community and family to his leprosy realistic? Can you imagine life with such an extreme disease?
- Which secondary characters do you enjoy most? For whom do you feel the most grief?
- Can this book be read as an ecological fable?
- An important theme in this book is choice and free will. What choices do the heroes of the novel have to make? To what extent is Covenant's participation in events forced upon him?
- Do any of the mitigating circumstances begin to justify the Covenant's rape of Lena? Do any of his later actions begin to redeem him?
- Where do Lord Foul and Rockworm rank in comparison to other villains in fantasy fiction?
- How do you feel about life-governing oaths, after reading about those taken by the Loresraat or the Bloodguard?
- Is Covenant's disbelief reasonable? How would you react if thrown into a similar astounding situation? Contrast Covenant's approach to belief with that of the typical fantasy reader.
- If you could visit one location in The Land, where would you go?
- What do you predict will happen next in the series? Will you continue reading?

SUGGESTED READING IF YOU LIKE *LORD FOUL'S BANE*

Stephen R. Donaldson	More from The Chronicles of Thomas Covenant, starting with *The Illearth War*
E. R. Eddison	*The Worm Ouroboros*
George R. R. Martin	A Song of Ice and Fire, starting with *A Game of Thrones*
J. R. R. Tolkien	The Lord of the Rings
Gene Wolfe	The Book of the New Sun, starting with *Shadow & Claw*

Keith Donohue

The Stolen Child

ABOUT THE AUTHOR

Keith Donohue lives in Maryland, near Washington, D.C. For many years, he was a speech-writer at the National Endowment for the Arts. Currently he is Director of Communications for the National Historical Publications and Records Commission, the grant-making arm of the U.S. National Archives in Washington, D.C. *The Stolen Child* was his first novel, followed by 2009's *Angels of Destruction*.

PLOT SUMMARY

Inspired by the Yeats poem of the same name and Flann O' Brien's *At Swim-Two-Birds*, *The Stolen Child* is the story of the abduction and replacement of seven-year-old Henry Day by a hobgoblin. The novel follows the new Henry and "Aniday," the boy who was Henry, through their lives as they narrate alternating chapters from the 1950s to the 1970s. Aniday becomes part of a wild troupe of changelings, all abducted from unhappy prior lives, who retain the guise of children through the years, while they live in the forest, waiting for their turn to abduct a child and rejoin the human world. A musical prodigy, the changeling Henry has difficulty adjusting to his human life and is nagged by distant memories of both his first life as a German-American boy and his time as a changeling in the wilds.

Publication Date: 2006

319p.

AUTHOR'S WEBSITE

http://www.keithdonohue.com

READER'S GUIDE

http://www.randomhouse.com/catalog/display.pperl?isbn=9781400096534&view=rg

APPEAL POINTS

The Stolen Child blends literary fiction and fantasy, an approach that has enjoyed a recent surge in popularity. It appeals in particular to those who appreciate lyrical language, psychological introspection, steady pacing, and a somewhat melancholy tone. This is highly rewarding reading for those who enjoy pondering symbols and thematic metaphors. In particular, the novel examines the inner lives of children and adolescents and their search for identity. Music, family, and reading are also important themes. The setting evokes the era after World War II, when America's small towns and country places gave way to growing cities and suburbs. Those who prefer lots of action, highly resolved plots, or detailed explanation of how magic works may find this book difficult, as may those who have difficulty following alternating narrators.

DISCUSSION QUESTIONS

- How are the two narrators alike? How do they differ? What are the possible explanations for their similarities?
- Who is this book's best audience? Adults or children? Fantasy or literary fiction readers?
- Do Henry's father and mother suspect or know that their child has been changed?
- Both narrators have difficulties maintaining relationships over the course of their lives. How is this rooted in their respective experiences?
- Experiences of music and literature have a prominent place in *The Stolen Child*. Why do both narrators find their artistic experiences so important?
- Are there parallels between Henry's feelings about childhood, adolescence, and belonging in the world and your own? Between Aniday's feelings and your own?
- Changes in the modern world encroach on the world of faerie in this novel. Have you encountered this theme before? What do you think authors intend to convey with this common theme?
- Donohue does little to explain the magic that allows goblin children to stay young. Does this vagueness work for you, or would you prefer a more detailed account?
- Do you notice anything interesting in how the author handles the concept of time? What do you think his intention is in handling the concept this way?
- Why do the faeries avoid discussing those who return to the human world?
- What kind of lives would you speculate that the narrators will live after the events in the novel?
- Compare this novel with other fantastic interpretations of eternal or long life. What examples come to mind? Which works best depict the consequences of living longer than others?

SUGGESTED READING IF YOU LIKE *THE STOLEN CHILD*

J. M. Barrie	*Peter Pan*
Kevin Brockmeier	*The Brief History of the Dead*
Andrew Sean Greer	*The Confessions of Max Tivoli*
Audrey Niffenegger	*The Time Traveler's Wife*
Jennifer Stevenson	*Trash Sex Magic*

David Anthony Durham

Acacia: The War with the Mein

ABOUT THE AUTHOR

Born in New York City in 1969 to parents of Caribbean ancestry, David Anthony Durham grew up in Maryland. He began to write seriously as an undergraduate, eventually completing an MFA at the University of Maryland, College Park. Since then, Durham has lived in Scotland, England, and France; taught at the University of Maryland, the University of Massachusetts, The Colorado College, and Cal State–Fresno; and received many awards and accolades for his three historical fiction novels. *Acacia*, his first work of fantasy fiction, made many best-of-the-year lists and has already been translated into six languages. He lives with his wife and two children in Fresno.

PLOT SUMMARY

The four Akaran children, heirs to the empire of Acacia, grow up without knowledge of the slave trade and drug addiction upon which their rule is based. Their father Leodan hopes they can find a gentler future, but his dreams come crashing down when the Mein, a long-banished Northern people, return with a wave of assassination, plague, and warfare. The four children are separated, each fleeing in different directions to very different fates, but years later Aliver, Corinn, Mena, and Dariel return, each using his or her own methods and allies to try to reclaim Acacia.

    Publication Date: 2007

    592 p.

AUTHOR'S WEBSITE

http://www.davidanthonydurham.com

APPEAL POINTS

Durham brings real-world sensibilities to this work of epic fantasy. Issues such as drug use and slavery are important to the plot. There is no simple right and wrong here, and leaders on all sides try to gloss over the corruption that underlies their power. Violence and other evils rear their ugly heads, and even likable lead characters are not safe from the results. Even the novel's sibling heroes suffer from discord, argument, and some truly nasty turns of fate. World building is a strength: the various societies depicted in the novel are diverse, yet believable and complex. Durham's style is more literary than that of most fantasy, so readers who prefer pulpy work might find his book a little slow, but there is no shortage of action, and pace builds as the novel races to a strong finish. With violence, sexuality, and its many real-world issues, this work may be too dark for sensitive readers. The finish to this book is satisfying, but two more series entries will follow.

DISCUSSION QUESTIONS

- With which of the Akaran children did you most identify?
- What do you think the cover image, which shows a tree with chains in place of roots, is intended to convey? How does this come through in the story?
- Do the Akarans deserve to rule? As you grow to understand them, how much do you sympathize with the Mein?
- Do you agree with the author's decision to jump forward in time several years, or would you like to see more of the intermediary events?
- Durham has been quoted as saying, "In epic fantasy, there is a lot of racism and sexism that I don't think the good people writing it are aware of." Do you agree? How are his convictions reflected in this work?
- If you had to choose between the different cultures portrayed in the book, which would you most want to visit? In which would you most like to make your home?
- How accurately does the book portray the relationship between siblings?
- Durham got his start as a historical fiction writer. Do you see similarities between his Known World and the real world? How much does the book draw on real-world geography, mythology, and political events?
- Contrast the family relationships of the Akarans and the Mein. How has each family reacted to rule? How do they react to the destruction of their empires?
- What do you expect from The League in the future of this series?
- Will you continue in the series? Why or why not?

SUGGESTED READING IF YOU LIKE *ACACIA: THE WAR WITH THE MEIN*

R. Scott Bakker	The Prince of Nothing, starting with *The Darkness That Comes Before*
David Anthony Durham	more from Acacia, starting with *The Other Lands*
Steven Erikson	Malazan Book of the Fallen, starting with *Gardens of the Moon*
Frank Herbert	*Dune*
George R. R. Martin	A Song of Ice and Fire, starting with *A Game of Thrones*

Gregory Frost

Shadowbridge

ABOUT THE AUTHOR

Gregory Frost, born in 1951, trained as an illustrator until an apartment fire claimed three years of work and sent his career in a new direction. He now directs the writing workshop at Swarthmore College. He's an instructor in the Clarion Workshop, a training ground for speculative fiction writers, and an active member of the Interstitial Arts Foundation, a group of writers and artists whose work falls between traditional genre lines. A fan of spaghetti westerns, Frost has found side work as an actor in low-budget horror films. He lives in Pennsylvania.

PLOT SUMMARY

In a world made from connected bridges, Leodora poses as Jax, a man, so that she can escape the life of a fishmonger and follow in the footsteps of her father Bardsham, the greatest of puppeteers and storytellers. Every span of the bridged world has a different culture and Leodora works to learn all of their stories as she travels between them. Her manager Soter, world-wise but often drunk, guides her development but knows more about the history of her parents than he tells. Along the way, she is joined by Diverus, a boy touched by the gods with a gift of musicianship. Frost alternates skillfully between revealing the pasts of the traveling trio, exploring the history and culture of the spans through tales from Jax's deep font of stories, and hinting ominously at the forces that claimed Leodora's parents and are now stalking her.

Publication Date: 2008

255 p.

AUTHOR'S WEBSITE

http://www.gregoryfrost.com

APPEAL POINTS

Frost explores the power of stories in a novel told as a series of stories, both those told by a puppeteer troupe and the histories of troupe members. It's a traveler's tale, full of marvelous settings: a world of bridges; a bustling market town; gardens inhabited by mischievous gods; and underground businesses that profit from the labor of impoverished children, dominated by Fagin-like overseers. Frost's suspense-building style hints of larger revelations to come about both the past and future of his characters. He manages the trick of building a large fantasy world with a fascinating mythos, exploring his characters in depth, and following many different tangents of his story while still keeping the book brief. This novel ends with little resolution. Readers must continue to *Lord Tophet* to complete the story (although the page count of both together is still lower than most of today's fantasy epics).

DISCUSSION QUESTIONS

- Is the author's notion of a world made of bridges believable? What factors in the story help or hinder your acceptance of this unusual geography?
- Leodora is estranged from her early life in many ways. Compare her treatment by the townspeople, her uncle, and her various childhood companions. Which treat her the most harshly? Which is her greatest friend?
- Is there a connection between the geography of the world that Frost creates and its mythology and sociology? Would the novel be the same if it were set in a more conventional world?
- What is the Coral Man?
- What is the relationship between a story and its teller? Where do stories originate?
- What do you think happened to Leodora's parents?
- Do you like the diversions that Frost takes in recounting Leodora's stories, or do you find them extraneous? Does the author use these tales to further his ends in any way?
- There are many instances of abuse, especially toward children, captured in *Shadowbridge*. Which of these do you find most deplorable? Is this a crueler world than most, or does it bear comparison to our world?
- Which of the three leads—Leodora, Diverus, or Soter—do you find most intriguing? Why?
- What does this novel say about the power and danger of stories? About how stories connect? What points does the author make about the skills required to tell stories well?
- What do you think will happen next? What is the nature of the ominous forces that Soter fears?
- Should *Shadowbridge* and *Lord Tophet* have been split or published as a single work?

SUGGESTED READING IF YOU LIKE *SHADOWBRIDGE*

Gregory Frost	*Lord Tophet*
Hussain Hadawwy, translator	*The Arabian Nights*
Scott Lynch	*The Lies of Locke Lamora*
Sarah Monette	Doctrine of Labyrinths, starting with *Mélusine*
Michael Swanwick	*The Iron Dragon's Daughter*; *The Dragons of Babel*
Catherynne M. Valente	The Orphan's Tales, starting with *In the Night Garden*

David Gemmell

Lord of the Silver Bow

ABOUT THE AUTHOR

Born in 1948 in West London, David Gemmell was expelled from school at the age of 16 for organizing a gambling ring. Several arrests followed. He was saved from life as a laborer and bouncer by an interview with a newspaper, in which his arrogance was mistaken for confidence and ability. He went on to become the editor-in-chief of five different papers. Diagnosed with cancer, Gemmell wrote *Legend* in an attempt to fulfill his dream of publishing a novel before he died. The illness was a misdiagnosis, but the novel, published in 1984, was a hit. In over 30 books that followed, Gemmell went on to become the leading contemporary practitioner of the kind of redemptive heroic fantasy that was one of the genre's early staples. Sadly, Gemmell succumbed to coronary artery disease after a quadruple bypass in 2006. His wife, Stella, completed the final volume in his Troy trilogy, based on Gemmell's extensive notes.

PLOT SUMMARY

Gemmell begins an alternative take on the history of Troy in this novel that focuses on Helikaon (Aeneas), a prince with a difficult past who has become a successful trader under the tutelage of Odysseus. When a seer foretells the Greek king Agamemnon's death by Helikaon's hand, the king responds by putting a bounty on the trader's head. Helikaon survives the first treacherous attempts on his life and thanks to the sacrifices of friends and the construction of his magnificent ship, wins a major sea battle. Aware of the plots against him now, he heads to Troy, where he courts an alliance against Agamemnon, pursues his love for the Trojan prince Hektor's betrothed Andromache, and moves toward a showdown with Greek foes led by Argurios, a bitter, but respectful foe.

Publication Date: 2005

449 p.

APPEAL POINTS

This book has many points of appeal, beginning with its fresh take on familiar literary and historical events. Gemmell is an old hand at fast-moving action and has a gift for sympathetic heroes who overcome tragic events. In this book, he outdoes himself with equally fine secondary characters and complex, well-motivated villains. There is little fantastic content here: gods and monsters have little impact on the story, and the only magic is a bit of minor precognition, so those who prefer realistic novels have no problems enjoying this. Fantasy fans are equally happy, with a hearty dose of exciting battle, high-class heroics, and even a dollop of romance. This is a violent novel (although not as gratuitously so as some modern heroic fantasy).

DISCUSSION QUESTIONS

- Is this fantasy or is it a historical novel? Is it possible for a book to be both?

- How does this story vary from other accounts of the Trojan War that you have encountered?

- Does this novel make you reexamine your view of ships and sailing? How was the act of going to sea different in ancient times?

- To what degree is Helikaon culpable for the tragic events that occur? What do you think of his decision to burn enemy ships?

- Gemmell's take on Odysseus is particularly unusual. What do you think of his portrayal?

- Which of the characters is your favorite?

- Are Gemmell's characters accurate for their historical period, or has he imbued them with more modern values?

- Is Argurios villainous or heroic? Is there some way in which he could have altered his conduct to achieve a better life?

- Will you continue reading this series? Does knowing that Gemmell's wife had to finish the trilogy detract from your desire to do so? What do you think will happen next?

SUGGESTED READING IF YOU LIKE *LORD OF THE SILVER BOW*

David Gemmell	Troy series: *Shield of Thunder*; *Fall of Kings*
David Gemmell	*The Lion of Macedon*; *Dark Prince*
Homer	*The Iliad* (Robert Fagles translation)
Michael Moorcock	Elric series
Mary Renault	*The King Must Die*
Eric Shanower	*Age of Bronze* graphic novels
Virgil	*The Aeneid* (Fagles translation)

William Goldman

The Princess Bride

ABOUT THE AUTHOR

Born in 1931, William Goldman was raised in the Chicago suburbs but now lives in New York City. He received a B.A. from Oberlin College in 1952, served two years in the U.S. Army, and then completed a master's degree in English at Columbia. He is a well-loved writer of novels (16), memoirs (5), plays (2), and screenplays (26 that have been produced). He won Academy Awards for his screenplays for *Butch Cassidy and the Sundance Kid* and *All the President's Men*. Other well-known screenplays include the original film of *The Stepford Wives*, *Misery*, *Maverick*, *Chaplin*, and the adaptations of his own novels, *Marathon Man* and *The Princess Bride*.

PLOT SUMMARY

Goldman presents this story as S. Morgenstern's classic history of the country Florin, as told to him as a boy (and greatly abridged) by his father. It's the love story of Buttercup, a princess who falls for farm boy Westley. When Westley is apparently lost at sea, Buttercup agrees to a loveless marriage with Prince Humperdinck. Before the wedding, Buttercup is kidnapped by three men: Vizzini, a self-proclaimed genius, Inigo Montoya, a swordfighter, and Fezzik, a strong giant. A mysterious man in black pursues the three kidnappers, defeating each at his specialty in turn. It is Westley, who was not killed by Dread Pirate Roberts but has instead taken his name. Buttercup and Westley escape, but when Humperdinck recaptures them, Buttercup agrees to marry him in exchange for Westley's freedom. She doesn't know that Humperdinck staged her kidnapping and intends to kill her and pin the murder on neighboring Guilder as an excuse to incite war. In the novel's climax, Westley must escape the Zoo of Death and, with help from Inigo and Fezzik—who now realize that they were Humperdinck's dupes—rescue Buttercup from marriage and murder.

Publication Date: 1973

464 p.

READER'S GUIDE

http://www.readinggroupguides.com/guides3/princess_bride1.asp

APPEAL POINTS

This amazing book works equally well as romance, fantasy adventure, satirical comedy, and metafiction about the power of reading and story. It does all this while maintaining a lightning-fast pace and a low page count. It can be enjoyed as light genre reading or as a satire of this kind of writing, so it's hard to imagine a reader who won't find it appealing on some level. It is also a good choice for film lovers, who are drawn to it by the loyal-in-spirit 1987 adaptation.

DISCUSSION QUESTIONS

- Does Goldman appreciate the fantasy and romance genres, or is he mocking them? Does he believe that the influence of stories like *The Princess Bride* improves children or warps them?

- Why does Goldman frame *The Princess Bride* within his tale of S. Morgenstern's version and how he first encountered the story through his father?

- Which of Wesley's many tests and perils is the greatest challenge?

- A recurring theme in the novel is the relationship between fathers and sons. What is Goldman trying to say on this subject?

- Do you like everything about Buttercup and Westley, or are there sides of their characters that are unattractive?

- What is your favorite line or joke from the book?

- How does the author portray himself, his family, and acquaintances within the framing story and his many interruptions of the narrative? Do you trust the honesty of this self-portrayal?

- Compare the portrayals of men and women in *The Princess Bride*. Is this an honest portrayal of the world, a case of sexism, or a satire of sexism?

- Did you encounter the movie or the book of *The Princess Bride* first? Does the order in which you experienced them change appreciation of the characters? Do any of the changes between film and book bother you? Why does Goldman makes these changes?

- Are you curious about S. Morgenstern's version of the story? Would you like to read it?

SUGGESTED READING IF YOU LIKE *THE PRINCESS BRIDE*

Peter S. Beagle	*The Last Unicorn*
Michael Ende	*Neverending Story*
Cornelia Funke	*Inkheart*; *Inkspell*
Neil Gaiman	*Stardust*
Diana Wynne Jones	*Dark Lord of Derkholm*
Walter Moers	*The 13 1/2 Lives of Captain Bluebear*
Lemony Snicket	A Series of Unfortunate Events, starting with *The Bad Beginning*

Lian Hearn

Across the Nightingale Floor

ABOUT THE AUTHOR

Lian Hearn is a pseudonym for Gillian Rubinstein. Born in England in 1942, she split her childhood between England and Nigeria. She studied languages at Oxford and worked as a film critic and arts editor before moving to Australia in 1973. Under her real name, she has a successful career as a playwright and author of over 30 children's books. A fascination with Japanese culture led her to immerse herself in the country's history, literature, film, and language. During a stay at the Akiyoshidai International Arts Village, she began writing *Across the Nightingale Floor*. Four other books in the <u>Otori</u> series have followed.

PLOT SUMMARY

Young Tomasu grows up in a mountain village populated by The Hidden, a persecuted religious caste. When the village is destroyed one night, Lord Otori Shigeru rescues the boy, takes him as his ward, and renames him Takeo. The Otori clan is embroiled in a series of long-standing feuds and political schemes, in which Takeo quickly becomes embroiled. He also learns that he is of the Tribe, a secret assassin group that has powers of hearing, stealth, invisibility, and mind control. Add Takeo's forbidden love for Kaede, and the protagonists have much to conquer as they battle with the evil Lord Iida.

   Publication Date: 2002
   287 p.

AUTHOR'S WEBSITE

http://www.lianhearn.com

READING GUIDE

http://us.penguingroup.com/static/rguides/us/across_the_nightingale.html

APPEAL POINTS

Hearn reimagines feudal Japan in a way that immediately enchants and makes it easy to suspend disbelief. Because of the exotic feeling that most Westerners attach to the Far East, this novel works both as fantasy and as alternate history. Its balanced characters appeal to men and women, old and young, equally. Strong characters, meaningful dilemmas, suspense, alliances and betrayals, and romance combine to give the work real emotional power as well. The prose style is elegant and austere, imparting an Asian feel to the writing. Unless a reader is a stickler for historical accuracy, easily confused by multiple characters and plots, or against some vivid violence or the death of likable characters, this book should make for fast, exciting, and resonant reading.

DISCUSSION QUESTIONS

- Does the author succeed in making you believe in this fantasy version of Japan?
- Would you guess on first reading that the author is a man or a woman? A native of Japan, or of some other nationality?
- How should Takeo ultimately resolve the conflicts between his loyalties to the Hidden, the Tribe, the Otori clan, and his romantic interests?
- Hearn works hard to appeal to the senses in the novel. What are some examples? How do they affect you as a reader?
- Are the sacrifices that the various characters make to exact revenge worth the price that they pay?
- How much does Hearn depend on historical (and fictional) character concepts, such as samurai, shogun, and ninja, in her plot? Do her characters follow these standards exactly, or are they somewhat different?
- The writer admits to being fascinated by the use of "silence and asymmetry" and works for a style that is "spare, elliptical, and suggestive." Does she succeed in imbuing her prose with these qualities? Does the style work for you as a reader?
- Why are Asian settings less common in fantasy than European settings? Why do films feature this setting more often? If it were available, would you seek out more Asian fantasy?
- Will you continue on in the series? Why?

SUGGESTED READING IF YOU LIKE *ACROSS THE NIGHTINGALE FLOOR*

Lian Hearn	More <u>Tales of the Otori</u>, beginning with *Grass for His Pillow*
Barry Hughart	*Bridge of Birds*
Kij Johnson	*The Fox Woman*
Takashi Matsuoka	*Cloud of Sparrows*; *Autumn Bridge*
Naomi Novik	*Throne of Jade*

Mark Helprin

A Winter's Tale

ABOUT THE AUTHOR

Raised in the Hudson River Valley and the British West Indies, Mark Helprin received an undergraduate degree from Harvard and did postgraduate work at Oxford, Princeton, and Columbia. He served briefly in the British merchant marines and the Israeli Air Force. Helprin has, in many ways, lived a double life: one as a distinguished writer of literary fiction that touches many genres and styles, and the second as a conservative essayist, speechwriter, pundit, and political advisor.

PLOT SUMMARY

Found and raised by the Baymen of the New Jersey marshes, Peter Lake becomes a member of the Short Tails, a burglary gang, until he makes an enemy of the gang's leader Pearly Soames. Thus begin Peter's years on the run from Pearly and his henchman, years when he falls in love with luminous but consumptive Beverly Penn and survives because of his wits, agility, and air-borne escapes on Athansor, his flying white horse. But these are just the events of the opening section of what may be the prime example of North American magical realism. Trying to describe its plot would take several pages and miss the point entirely . . .

Publication Date: 1983

688 p.

AUTHOR'S WEBSITE

http://www.markhelprin.com

APPEAL POINTS

Despite its length, *A Winter's Tale* is a novel to savor slowly for beautiful language and lush romanticism, not to rush through for plot. It bursts with metaphors, colors, and images that stay with the reader long after the book is done. Ultimately, these vignettes may be more enjoyable, certainly more accessible, than the whole, and readers who want explanations may be frustrated. It's a paean to New York City and the Hudson Valley and a celebration of larger-than-life characters. Some of the most beautiful winter scenes in literature are contained in the book. Helprin's political background may offend some, but readers who identify a political agenda in this novel stretch the point: It would be too reductive to say that this is political allegory. There are themes of justice, transcendence, beauty, and redemption. The first hundred pages, which are both more beautiful and more plot-driven than the ending, are a good test. If the reader doesn't enjoy the first part of this book, there's no reason to push on to the finish.

DISCUSSION QUESTIONS

- What images will stay with you from this book?
- Besides Peter Lake, which of the other characters stands out to you?
- What is the relationship between this book and the fantasy genre? What do they share? How are they different?
- *A Winter's Tale* is an ode to New York City, but it's a magical version of the city, particularly compared to the city in 1983, when Helprin wrote the book. Does he succeed in capturing the city's qualities? If so, how? Is the city symbolic of a broader concept?
- Is winter a symbol of something in this book? Why does Helprin choose to set so much of the book in that season?
- Some describe Peter Lake as a redeemer figure. Do you agree? If so, what does he redeem?
- Do you find the ending of this book satisfying?
- Helprin is also known for his extremely conservative political views. Do you see any clear political platform in this novel, or would that be a misreading?
- *A Winter's Tale* is a book that strongly divides readers. Who would you recommend it to? Who would not enjoy it?

SUGGESTED READING IF YOU LIKE *A WINTER'S TALE*

John Crowley	*Little, Big*
Gabriel Garcia-Márquez	*One Hundred Years of Solitude*
China Miéville	*Perdido Street Station*
Haruki Murakami	*The Wind-Up Bird Chronicle*
Tim Powers	*Last Call; Expiration Date; Earthquake Weather*

Robin Hobb

Ship of Magic

ABOUT THE AUTHOR

Robin Hobb has established herself as the queen of the epic fantasy trilogy, with four trilogies completed to date, most of them set in a shared world. She also publishes a different kind of fantasy under the name Megan Lindholm. Born in California, Hobb credits teen years spent living close to the land in Alaska as a major source of inspiration for her writing. She currently lives in Tacoma, Washington, where her non-writing time is taken up with her husband, children, grandchildren, gardening, and the renovation of a 35-foot boat.

PLOT SUMMARY

Set in Bingtown, the Pirate Isles, and Jamaillia, *Ship of Magic* opens the epic <u>Liveship Traders</u> trilogy. The novel follows a large cast of characters through a period in which disrupted trade and growing use of slaves change a regional economy. Things are particularly hard on Liveship traders, families whose sentient ships allow them to trade in magical goods with the mysterious Rain Wild traders. One Liveship trader, Ephron Vestrit, nears the end of his life and must decide whether to pass the family Liveship, Vivacia, to his brash daughter Althea or to his scheming son-in-law Kyle. Kyle's son Wintrow wants only to be a scholarly priest, but is forced to become a sailor to calm the agitated family ship. Brashen Trell, disinherited son of another trader family, is demoted from first mate on Vivacia and teeters on the edge of addiction. Kennit, a pirate captain, obsesses over the idea of obtaining a Liveship of his own and becoming King of the Pirates. These characters, along with a mad ship, some strange sea serpents, and a mysterious woodcarver, find themselves on an intersecting course full of magic, suffering, and adventure.
     Publication Date: 1999
     685 p.

AUTHOR'S WEBSITE

http://www.robinhobb.com

APPEAL POINTS

Hobb has a gift for multifaceted, often tormented characters, who must surmount many challenges, especially their own weaknesses, in order to win through. Readers who enjoy large casts and complex moral dilemmas should love this book. Setting is another strong point: this series may be the pinnacle of nautical fantasy and might appeal to fans of nautical historical fiction, if they can get over its magical trappings. Hobb's system of magic appeals to hardcore fantasy fans who enjoy complex magic with a tangible cost. Readers who like simple stories with clearly delineated heroes and villains may find this big book to be too challenging.

DISCUSSION QUESTIONS

- To which of Hobb's many characters do you most relate? Which frustrate you the most?

- How many different kinds of slavery and servitude can you identify in *Ship of Magic*?

- What are the core mistakes made by the Vestrit family? Can blame for their problems be leveled at one person?

- Many of the dilemmas in *Ship of Magic* stem from the struggles of women to function in a world designed for men. Can you cite examples? Do you see parallels in the real world?

- Three kinds of characters—Rain Wild traders, sea serpents, and the Liveships themselves—remain somewhat mysterious at the end of the volume. How will the author develop and use these characters later in the trilogy?

- Do you find Hobb's nautical setting believable?

- Hobb is known for putting her characters through incredible torments and challenges. Do you find the level of difficulty facing the lead characters here to be interesting or depressing?

- Will Kennit ultimately be hero or a villain? What are his strong points? His mistakes?

- Can the traders' control of Liveships be a positive thing, or is there something fundamentally wrong about this kind of magic?

- There are flashes of romance, or at least hints of impending coupling, between several of the novel's characters. Should Althea and Brashen get together? Does Kennit deserve Etta? What about Malta and the mysterious Reyn Khuprus?

- Will you continue in the series? Why or why not?

SUGGESTED READING IF YOU LIKE *SHIP OF MAGIC*

Robin Hobb	*Mad Ship; Ship of Destiny*
Robin Hobb	The Farseer Trilogy, beginning with *Assassin's Apprentice*
Paul Kearney	Sea Beggars series, beginning with *The Mark of Ran*
George R. R. Martin	A Song of Ice and Fire, beginning with *Game of Thrones*
Naomi Novik	Temeraire series, beginning with *His Majesty's Dragon*

Guy Gavriel Kay

Tigana

ABOUT THE AUTHOR

Born in Saskatchewan, Canada, in 1954, Guy Gavriel Kay read broadly in his youth, enjoying fantasy in particular. During his college years, he met Christopher Tolkien, who invited Kay to help work on his father's notes for *The Silmarillion*. That experience left Kay more interested than ever in writing fantasy, but nervous about the economic rewards of writing, so he finished a law degree instead. Although he passed the bar, his fascination with writing won out, and he never practiced law. He has now published 11 well-loved novels and also writes for television and film. He lives in Toronto.

PLOT SUMMARY

On the peninsula of the Palm, two sorcerers have invaded, conquering and dividing the Palm's nine provinces between them. Brandin, one of the conquerors, sends his son Stevan to subjugate the province of Tigana, but he is killed in battle. In retribution, Brandin crushes remaining resistance and curses Tigana with a spell that prevents those born outside the province from remembering it or even hearing its name. Twenty years after the conquest, a band of resistance grows around the charismatic Alessan, heir to Tigana. Disguised as a troupe of musicians with Catriana and Devin, two young people of Tiganan descent, Alessan travels the Palm, preparing a revolution. Meanwhile, Dianora, another survivor of Tigana, plots a more personal revenge, posing as a member of Brandin's harem to gain access and assassinate him.

    Publication Date: 1990

    640 p.

AUTHOR'S WEBSITE

http://www.brightweavings.com

APPEAL POINTS

Kay uses historical inspiration for his books. The setting of *Tigana* is inspired by 15th-century Italy, and its sensitive rendering makes this a natural choice for fans of history or historical fiction. Themes of cultural identity and oppression also echo 20th-century politics. Beyond historical realism, *Tigana* is a masterwork because of strong, complex characters, and fans of character-driven writing like this work. The book's tragic air appeals to readers with a sense of romanticism but may depress others. Other impressive motifs are the novel's musical sequences and tricky twists and turns of espionage. Kay's elegant language pleases fans of the Tolkien tradition. Finally, this is the rare epic fantasy that is complete in one volume. Series fans don't like this, but many readers appreciate that they are not committed to multiple books.

DISCUSSION QUESTIONS

- What parallels to Italy and Italian history can you see in *Tigana*? Does it remind you of other historical events as well?

- Kay is often cited as having a poetic style with language. Do you agree?

- Which of *Tigana*'s characters is your favorite? Your least favorite?

- What does this novel have to say about the idea of revenge?

- Does *Tigana* make you sad? More broadly, is there anything intrinsically sad about fantasy stories?

- The battle with the Night Walkers is controversial among readers of this book. Some find it out of step with the rest of the book, but others find it powerful and cite it as one of the best sequences in fantasy literature. What do you think?

- Loss of cultural identity has personal implications for many characters in the novel. Can you think of historical parallels? How important is cultural identity to individual personalities?

- Dianora falls for Brandin even as she plots her revenge on him. His love for her shows his character to have more facets than simply that of oppressor of Tigana. Is her continued plan for revenge appropriate, or should she change her position?

- One volume epic fantasy is unusual. Does Kay succeed in telling a vast story in only a few hundred pages? Do you want more? As a fantasy reader, do you prefer stand-alone books or series?

SUGGESTED READING IF YOU LIKE *TIGANA*

Peter S. Beagle	*The Last Unicorn*
Guy Gavriel Kay	*A Song for Arbonne*
Ellen Kushner	*Swordspoint*
George R. R. Martin	<u>A Song of Ice and Fire</u>, beginning with *A Game of Thrones*
Brandon Sanderson	*Elantris*
J. R. R. Tolkien	*The Lord of the Rings*

Greg Keyes

The Briar King

ABOUT THE AUTHOR

Born into a large Mississippi family in 1963, Greg Keyes also lived in Arizona as a child, where contact with the reservation and his own Choctaw relatives instilled him with a lifelong love of languages and storytelling. He received degrees in anthropology from Mississippi State and the University of Georgia before becoming a full-time writer. His novels include successful attempts at mythic fantasy, historical fantasy, epic fantasy, and the *Star Wars* and *Babylon 5* universes. He now lives in Savannah, Georgia, where he enjoys cooking and coaches a fencing club in his spare time.

PLOT SUMMARY

The world of Everon, especially the kingdom of Crotheny, is in upheaval. Plots against King William abound, the church is brewing trouble, and war with Hansa is imminent. Worse, there are rumors of destruction caused by ancient beasts once thought to be only myths. In this dangerous environment, action focuses on several characters. Princess Anne must grow up quickly when she unlocks something from an ancient crypt and then is forced to go on the run. Aspar White must protect the King's wood from strange creatures, battle a lifelong enemy, and keep the bookish monk Stephen Darige alive. Young Neil MeqVren finds new challenges to his dream of knighthood when he becomes the protector of a royal family in hiding.

Publication Date: 2003

560 p.

AUTHOR'S WEBSITE

http://www.gregkeyes.com

APPEAL POINTS

The Briar King is a fine example of epic high fantasy. It's told from multiple viewpoints by characters who are familiar to fantasy fans, but who are drawn so well that they escape the traps of cliché. By using short chapters and lots of action, Keyes creates a fast pace that makes this book read more quickly than other fat fantasies. The violence is explicit at times and may be a bit much for squeamish readers. The first in a series of four, this book leaves readers ready for the next installments.

DISCUSSION QUESTIONS

- Did you follow the events of the prologue and other references to Everon's ancient past? How will these manifest themselves in future volumes? How is history and its remembrance used as a theme? Is there a connection to our world's past?

- Which of Keyes's characters is your favorite? Are there any about whom you don't enjoy reading?
- Can you identify myths and legends that *The Briar King* develops? What other tellings of these legends have you encountered?
- Do you enjoy the author's method of ending chapters with cliffhangers, or do you find it frustrating?
- Many of the characters are familiar to epic fantasy fans: the feisty princess, the gruff man of action, the idealistic young knight, the bookish young man forced into a life of adventure, the cocky swordsman, the embattled king and queen, and the renegade brother. Does the author succeed in breathing new life into these familiar folk?
- Which of the romances initiated in the novel should continue? Which should end?
- Which of the monsters and villains is the most dangerous? Will one become the ultimate foe?
- What do you think of the novel's religion and its saints? Will the church people ultimately be heroes or villains?
- What will happen next in the series? Will you continue reading it?

SUGGESTED READING IF YOU LIKE *THE BRIAR KING*

David Anthony Durham	Acacia, starting with *The War with the Mein*
Raymond Feist	Riftwar, starting with *Magician: Apprentice*
Greg Keyes	More from Kingdoms of Thorn and Bone, starting with *The Charnel Prince*
George R. R. Martin	A Song of Ice and Fire, starting with *A Game of Thrones*
J. R. R. Tolkien	*The Lord of the Rings*
Tad Williams	Memory, Sorrow and Thorn, starting with *The Dragonbone Chair*

Laurie J. Marks

Fire Logic

ABOUT THE AUTHOR

Born in California, Laurie Marks discovered <u>The Chronicles of Narnia</u> in the 1950s and decided that she wanted to be a fantasist. She moved nine times through three countries during her college career before graduating from Brown University. At age 29, she realized that she was a lesbian, and that personal breakthrough soon led to publication of her first novel and discovery of her life partner. They live in Boston, where Marks teaches writing at the University of Massachusetts. The first two novels in her <u>Elemental Logic</u> series each won the Spectrum Award.

PLOT SUMMARY

Their land conquered by the Sainnites and their leader killed, the people of Shaftal are fighting a guerilla war. Zanja na'Tarwein joins the resistance when the Sainnites commit genocide on her people in an act of treachery. Emil is a Paladin scholar who must use his fire magic as a soldier when the war begins. Norina is an air elemental who watches over Zaris, a powerful earth healer addicted to smoke and barely able to function. The fates of these characters are bound together with the fate of Shaftal and through the four elemental magics.

Publication Date: 2002

336 p.

AUTHOR'S WEBSITE

http://lauriejmarks.com

APPEAL POINTS

Marks's saga opener is notable on many levels. Characters are vivid, especially women. The world the author creates—with equality of genders, same-sex relationships as norm instead of exception, and intricate elemental magic—is unusual and fascinating. Some of this may offend some readers, which is too bad for them: they'll miss a great work of fantasy! Marks has a show-don't-tell style that does not spoon-feed readers with explanations or too much exposition: they have to read carefully to catch the rich intricacies. The author also has a gift for showing the impact of politics and war on the emotional life of individuals, creating an empathy that appeals to sensitive readers, although the violence and other degradations that characters endure may be too much for some. Although the novel has a satisfying finish, readers need to continue the series to get more complete resolution.

DISCUSSION QUESTIONS

- Which of the focus characters do you find most compelling? With which do you identify the most?

- Does Marks succeed in creating equity between genders? In making same-sex relationships the norm?
- How realistic is the portrayal of Karis's addiction? How does that make you feel about her?
- Compare life in Shaftal with real-world examples of life under occupation. Does Marks get the details of this difficult existence right?
- Is this book primarily appealing to the GLBT population, or to women? Or should it appeal to all fantasy fans?
- What do you think of the conflicts between the "heroes" of the story? Do you find it off-putting, realistic, or some of each?
- Can you distinguish between the powers of the four kinds of elemental magic? Are the personality traits that go with them distinct?
- Does the author go too far in her depictions of torture, cruelty, and betrayal? Is it possible in an action genre such as fantasy to be too explicit in such matters?
- Which characters find justice by the end of the novel? Which achieve peace with their pasts?
- Will you continue in the series? What further events pique your curiosity the most?

SUGGESTED READING IF YOU LIKE *FIRE LOGIC*

Steven Erikson	*Gardens of the Moon*
Lynn Flewelling	<u>Nightrunner</u> series, starting with *Luck in the Shadows*
Ellen Kushner	*Swordspoint*; *The Privilege of the Sword*
Laurie J. Marks	more from the <u>Elemental Logic</u> series, starting with *Earth Logic*
Elizabeth Moon	*The Deed of Paksenarrion*
Catherynne M. Valente	<u>The Orphan's Tales</u>, starting with *In the Night Garden*

George R. R. Martin

A Game of Thrones

ABOUT THE AUTHOR

Born in 1948 in Bayonne, New Jersey, Martin holds an M.S. in journalism from Northwestern University. He sold his first science fiction story in 1970 and became a full-time writer in 1979. He was a writer for the 1980s revival of *The Twilight Zone* and a producer and writer for the series *Beauty and the Beast*. Once known for science fiction and horror, he became more widely known when he began his epic fantasy series, A Song of Ice and Fire, in 1996, a series that—although unfinished—has become recognized as one of the genre's masterworks. Martin lives in Santa Fe, New Mexico.

PLOT SUMMARY

In the Seven Kingdoms of Westeros, the ruling Targaryen house was deposed through a civil war led by the Barathaeons, Lannisters, and Starks. As the book opens, King Robert Barathaeon asks Lord Eddard Stark to come south from his northern stronghold to serve as King's Hand. Robert is unhappy as king and the Lannisters—incestuous siblings Jaime and Cersei, dwarf brother Tyrion, and arrogant nephew Joffrey—are scheming to take power. Eddard travels to King's Landing with daughters Arya and Sansa, although he knows the capital is a hornet's nest. Lord Stark's wife Catelyn and sons Robb and Bran are left to deal with intrigues at home, while his bastard son Jon Snow goes to join the Night Watch, a group that defends Westeros's northern borders, where new troubles seem to be brewing. Meanwhile, the last Targaryen, Daenerys, works to raise a force in the eastern isles so that she can return to reclaim the Iron Throne. These are the opening moves in the complex *Game of Thrones . . .*

    Publication Date: 1996

    694 p.

AUTHOR'S WEBSITE

http://www.georgerrmartin.com

OTHER WEB RESOURCES: WESTEROS

http://www.westeros.org/About/

APPEAL POINTS

Martin's series sets a standard for epic fantasy in complexity, realism, violence, and depth of characterization. The character point of view from which the story is told alternates with each chapter. This makes the book difficult for some, but others like its depth of plotting. The cast is enormous, and almost all of the characters are morally complex, not simply good or evil. There is a great deal of violence, swearing, and sexuality. Martin is not afraid to kill characters, even likable leads. For some, this makes his books believable and gripping, while others find the realism depressing or off-putting. The medieval world is rendered in astonishing detail: the reader can see how variations in climate affect the character of people inhabiting different regions. Those who enjoy plot twists love this book and its followers: they are full of exciting surprises, and although the books are long they read quickly, particularly after one meets the major players.

DISCUSSION QUESTIONS

- The violence, sexuality, and darkness of the world that Martin creates upsets some readers. Can a novel be too dark? Why or why not?
- The events of this series are somewhat based on The War of the Roses. Can you see any parallels? Parallels with other real-world historical events?
- Do you find the behavior of this novel's many child characters believable?
- What is the biggest threat to the world of Westeros? Infighting among its houses? Invaders from the North? The return of the Targaryens?
- Do you have a favorite among the many narrators of *Game of Thrones*? Is there any narrator whose chapters you do not find interesting?
- Does Eddard Stark do the right thing in leaving Winterfell?
- *Thrones* is unusual for a fantasy in that little magic is used. Do you enjoy this approach?
- How do geography and climate affect the behavior of people in this novel?
- Martin is unusually willing to kill off his lead characters. Does this bother you as a reader?
- Which character would make the best leader of Westeros?

SUGGESTED READING IF YOU LIKE *A GAME OF THRONES*

R. Scott Bakker	Prince of Nothing, starting with *The Darkness That Comes Before*
David Anthony Durham	*Acacia: The War with the Mein; The Other Lands*
Frank Herbert	*Dune*
J. V. Jones	Sword of Shadows, starting with *A Cavern of Black Ice*
Guy Gavriel Kay	*Tigana; The Lions of Al-Rassan*
Greg Keyes	Kingdoms of Thorn and Bone, starting with *The Briar King*
George R. R. Martin	More from Song of Ice and Fire, starting with *A Clash of Kings*

Sarah Micklem

Firethorn

ABOUT THE AUTHOR

Born in Virginia and raised in New York by her social activist parents, Sarah Micklem was a high school dropout but eventually made it into Princeton. She has held a variety of jobs: working in a printing plant, resettling refugees in New York City, and designing children's magazines. *Firethorn* is her first novel. Married to the poet and playwright Cornelius Eady, she now teaches at Notre Dame. Micklem's second novel in the Firethorn trilogy, *Wildfire*, was published in 2009.

PLOT SUMMARY

Brave, independent, but with limited power or prospects, Firethorn thinks that she has found a way out of a life in the brutish, backward countryside when she attracts the attentions of Sire Galan. She travels off to war with him, only to discover that she is in grave danger of becoming a "sheath," a common camp follower shared among the men, if Galan's attentions wander. Trapped in a dangerous camp while troops muster and prepare for war, Firethorn has to use all of her wits to survive.

> Publication Date: 2004
> 400 p.

AUTHOR'S WEBSITE

http://www.firethorn.info

APPEAL POINTS

Micklem calls *Firethorn* a "low fantasy." The central character does not have great power and the novel takes a dark, realistic view at medieval life, not the glorified version usual to high fantasy. At the novel's core is a great romance, but it is surrounded by dire, gritty circumstances that are not typical for that genre. The novel's realism includes fair doses of violence and sexuality that may deter some readers. Firethorn has mystical and herbal gifts, but it's not clear that any of this is real magic. Ultimately, this is a tale of bravery and heroism in the face of tragedy.

DISCUSSION QUESTIONS

- *Firethorn* portrays the dark side of medieval society. Do you like this, or do you prefer a more typical heroic fantasy portrayal of the times?
- How much magic is practiced in the book? Can the mystical elements be given more realistic explanations?

- Is Galan devoted to Firethorn from the beginning, or is she correct in doubting his constancy in the early stages of their relationship?
- Is the cover illustration for this novel appropriate?
- How do the religious beliefs of the clans contribute to their society and to the events of the novel?
- Would this novel work from a different character's point of view? From an omniscient point of view? How would it change?
- For what audience is this novel appropriate? How old should someone be before reading it? Will this novel work for men?
- How do the inequities of the "mud" and "Blood" castes contribute to the events of the novel?
- What does this story share in common with the typical romance? How does it differ?
- Should Firethorn and Sire Galan end up together? Will they?
- What would you predict will happen to Firethorn in future installments?

SUGGESTED READING IF YOU LIKE *FIRETHORN*

Jacqueline Carey	Kushiel series, starting with *Kushiel's Dart*
Mary Gentle	The Book of Ash, starting with *A Secret History*
Laurie Marks	Elemental Logic series, starting with *Fire Logic*
George R. R. Martin	A Song of Ice and Fire, starting with *A Game of Thrones*
Sarah Monette	*Mélusine*
Elizabeth Moon	*The Deed of Paksenarrion*

China Miéville
Perdido Street Station

ABOUT THE AUTHOR

Born in 1972, China Miéville is a lifelong resident of London (except for a year spent teaching English in Egypt). He holds a PhD in International Relations from the London School of Economics. He continues to write and advocate for socialist causes. He makes a distinction, however, between his politics and his fiction, which he writes, as he has stated, because he loves science fiction and fantasy, not because he is trying to make political points. He has consciously tried to move fantasy away from the Tolkien tradition and toward more original, less imitative styles. He is a frequent award nominee, including two wins of the British Fantasy Award and one of the Arthur C. Clarke Award.

PLOT SUMMARY

In the city of New Crobuzon, inhabited by a great mélange of humans and bizarre magical species, life teems and death runs rampant. Yagharek, a garuda (winged man) whose wings have been cruelly removed by his own kind, asks Dr. Isaac Grimnebulin to return him to the skies. Isaac's experiments with flight lead him to slake-moths, dangerous creatures that feed on dreams. The moths escape his laboratory and begin to terrorize the city. Meanwhile, Isaac's love Lin (a khepri: half human with a fly's head) takes a commission to sculpt Mr. Motley, a powerful underworld boss. The ripple of results expands, mixing with forces of oppression and revolution that battle for control of the city, particularly the process of "remaking": genetically combining people with machines or other species as punishment for crimes against the state.
   Publication Date: 2000
   710 p.

APPEAL POINTS

Miéville is a writer of atmosphere and creativity, devising a world that is something like Dickens's darkest cityscapes turned feverish and strange. This is not a fast-paced book, but sheer imagination, fascinating and complex characters, and suspense keep most readers moving forward. Any reader who loves great fantasy cities is pleased. Worldbuilding is a real strength here, and those who appreciate steampunk settings, newly imagined character species, or mixtures of magic and technology become instant fans. This book is not for those who cannot enjoy long novels, scary material, or rough language.

DISCUSSION QUESTIONS

- Which of the invented species in the book catches your imagination the most?

- Would you like to visit New Crobuzon, or would you rather stay far away? Does it remind you of any other cities in fiction?
- Is the world that the author creates modern or primitive in comparison with our own? Is racism more or less prevalent there?
- Should Isaac and Lin have accepted the commissions from Yagharek and Motley? Did they ignore signs of impending danger?
- Does Yagharek deserve redemption?
- Do you prefer the medieval traditions of fantasy, or would you like to see more unusual settings, such as that in *Perdido Street Station*?
- Can an argument be made that this is more science fiction than it is fantasy?
- What is the Weaver? An alien? A god? Something entirely new?
- Miéville is an avowed socialist. Can you see the influence of his politics on his writing?

SUGGESTED READING IF YOU LIKE *PERDIDO STREET STATION*

Clive Barker	*Imajica*
Neil Gaiman	*Neverwhere*
M. John Harrison	*Viriconium*
Mark Helprin	*A Winter's Tale*
China Miéville	Other Bas-Lag novels: *The Scar*; *Iron Council*
Mervyn Peake	*Gormenghast*
Tim Powers	*The Anubis Gates*

Naomi Novik

His Majesty's Dragon

ABOUT THE AUTHOR

Naomi Novik was born in New York in 1973. After studying English at Brown University and completing graduate work in computer science at Columbia, she worked on the development of a fantasy computer game. The first three novels in her Temeraire series were all published in 2006, resulting in her win of the Campbell Award for Best New Writer. She lives in New York City with her husband. Novik is a prominent user and advocate of Web 2.0 tools, in particular the rights of fans to transform works of their favorite writers through fan fiction. As of this writing, her Temeraire series has grown to five books.

PLOT SUMMARY

As the 18th century opens, young Captain Will Laurence captures a valuable dragon's egg from a French ship just as the egg begins to hatch. Dragons, in this alternate history, are highly intelligent and valued as a means of aerial support for military ships. They imprint on a rider at birth, and when none of Laurence's officers take the role, he feels bound to accept the task himself. This means that he must leave the Navy and join the Aerial Corps, a lonely life with little hope for social place or even marriage. Soon, however, Laurence's growing friendship with the brilliant Temeraire draws the sting from his strange new life, although Laurence has a hard time finding acceptance among lifelong Aerial Corps officers, jealous of the shortcut that brought him his dragon. Laurence, Temeraire, and his young crew must overcome prejudice and master new skills quickly as they head toward a crucial role in a climactic battle with the Napoleon's navy.

Publication Date: 2006

384 p.

AUTHOR'S WEBSITE

http://www.temeraire.org

APPEAL POINTS

There are many levels on which readers can enjoy this story: as a fantasy take on naval historical fiction, as a charming buddy story, or as a shining example of the dragon adventure. The two leads, Laurence and Temeraire, are both extremely likeable—it's easy to root for them. This is a light book, not a complex read. The plotting is quite simple and many readers finish in only a few sittings. Although the book is satisfying in its own right, most readers will want to continue deeper into the series.

DISCUSSION QUESTIONS

- How does Novik's version of the dragon compare with others that you have encountered? In what ways does she play with traditional tropes of the dragon legend?
- How completely does this book fit within the tradition of Napoleonic War fiction? Would you recommend it to a reader of that body of work who has not previously read fantasy?
- Which of these labels best describes the relationship between Laurence and Temeraire: father and son, best friends, captain and ship, commander and soldier, or comrades in arms?
- Do you find the tactics of the action scenes easy to follow? Believable?
- Do Laurence and Temeraire fit well within their historical social milieu? Is Laurence believable as a product of his background and time? Is it more accurate to say that Novik is depicting or commenting on the historical period?
- Clarke's work has been compared to such disparate works as Susanna Clarke's *Jonathan Strange & Mr. Norrell*, Patrick O'Brian's Aubrey and Maturin series, Jane Austen's novels, and Anne McCaffrey's Pern. Are these comparisons apt?
- How will the relationship of Laurence and Temeraire change over time?
- Can Laurence ultimately derive satisfaction from his life with Temeraire, or will his restriction from other relationships ultimately make him feel constrained?
- Should Temeraire ultimately be satisfied with his military role? Should he feel duty-bound to England?
- Will you further into the series?

SUGGESTED READING IF YOU LIKE *HIS MAJESTY'S DRAGON*

Anne McCaffrey	Dragonriders of Pern series, starting with *Dragonflight*
Naomi Novik	More of the Temeraire series, beginning with *Throne of Jade*
Patrick O'Brian	Aubrey and Maturin series, starting with *Master and Commander*
Mike Resnick	*Dragon America*
Harry Turtledove	Darkness series, starting with *Into the Darkness*
David Weber	Honor Harrington series, starting with *On Basilisk Station*

K. J. Parker

The Company

ABOUT THE AUTHOR

Little is known about Parker, except that the name is a pseudonym for an author who wanted to try a different style of writing. Some speculation has pointed toward the comic fantasist Tom Holt, while other evidence suggests that Parker is an Englishwoman (but one who spent her early years in rural Vermont). Previous biographical notes have mentioned that Parker has worked in law and journalism and enjoys coin collecting, woodworking, and metal working. Whoever Parker is, the pseudonym seems to be working: the author has written three successful trilogies and *The Company*, a stand-alone novel.

PLOT SUMMARY

Retired General Teuche Kunessin returns to his homeland Faralia and begins rounding up his old comrades from A Company, a group whose job in the war was to lower the enemy pike wall. Most line-breakers last only one battle, but somehow A Company, a small group of men who had known each other since boyhood, survived the war. The plot alternates between the events of the war and their actions in the present tense. Arranging marriages at the last minute, the five men sail for Sphoe, an island that Kunessin has requisitioned through back channels. They intend to settle there as gentlemen farmers. But for men who have seen horrible violence, who trust only each other, and who never expected to survive, settling down is difficult. To complicate matters, they discover gold on Sphoe, raising dissent with the indentured men whom they brought with them to work the island. Ugly secrets from the past and disagreements about Kunessin's leadership begin to emerge. The wives dislike each other and their husbands' fierce fraternity. Troubles mount as A Company faces its most difficult challenge yet: the struggle to come home.

Publication Date: 2008
448 p.

AUTHOR'S WEBSITE

http://www.kjparker.com

APPEAL POINTS

Magic-free and complete in one volume, this novel makes an ideal bridge to the fantasy genre for those who normally read action/adventure or historical fiction. Although the tone is dark and the action sometimes brutal, the characters are sympathetic. Parker depicts the details of building simple objects, mining, and settling barren land without becoming dull. The pace is steady and the story is full of suspense. The psychology of the Company, a group bonded through their survival in the face of insurmountable odds, is vividly portrayed. Parker creates sophisticated group dynamics and witty dialogue. Some readers may not care for the moral ambiguity of the characters, the lack of fantastic events in a fantasy, or the grimness of the ending, but many greatly appreciate the realism of this novel.

DISCUSSION QUESTIONS

- Who is K. J. Parker?
- The members of the Company and their wives are certainly morally ambiguous. Are any of them out-and-out evil?
- Do you have any favorites among the characters? Are there any whom you despise?
- What is the Company's biggest mistake, whether in the past or the present?
- Does this belong in the fantasy genre? If not, in which genre would you place it?
- Is there any good excuse for Kunessin's handling of the Company's money?
- What do you think of the author's handling of group dynamics? Do you find the interactions of the Company believable?
- What do you make of Menin? Do you like or dislike the effect of her actions on the novel's plot and climax?
- Is it possible for soldiers who have seen as much in war as the Company did to come home and settle down again?
- Are the loyalties of the Company only to one another? Do any of them show an affinity toward their wives that might, in some cases, transcend their feeling of duty toward each other?
- Is there any chance that the Company survived?

SUGGESTED READING IF YOU LIKE *THE COMPANY*

Joe Abercrombie	*Best Served Cold*
Glen Cook	*Chronicles of the Black Company*
Steven Erikson	Malazan Book of the Fallen, starting with *Gardens of the Moon*
David Gemmell	*Legend*
Elizabeth Moon	*The Deed of Paksenarrion*
K. J. Parker	The Engineer trilogy, starting with *Devices & Desires*

Tim Powers

Last Call

ABOUT THE AUTHOR

Tim Powers was born in 1952 in Buffalo, New York, the oldest of eight children in a large Irish Catholic family. They moved to California at a young age, where Powers still lives. He started writing early, receiving his first rejection slip at age 13. He specializes in blending historical fact and dark fantasy, and the results have garnered many awards, including two World Fantasy Awards for best novel. Powers is often associated with an early influence, Philip K. Dick, and two college friends who are also successful writers, James P. Blaylock and K. W. Jeter.

PLOT SUMMARY

If you find yourself playing poker with Tarot cards, fold your hand and leave the table! That's the lesson that young poker professional Scott Crane learns when he finds that a game he played 20 years ago will make him pay the ultimate price. His only hope is to follow a strange trail with his foster sister Diana and a few other ragged supporters through a Southwestern landscape of terrible villains, mad seers, and all of the other forces of fortune. Ultimately, Crane's path leads him to Las Vegas, the ghost of Bugsy Siegel, and a confrontation with his birth father, an American Fisher King.

  Publication Date: 1992

  535 p.

AUTHOR'S WEBSITE

http://www.theworksoftimpowers.com

APPEAL POINTS

Last Call is notable for bringing fantasy to a contemporary American setting, something rarely done in a genre dominated by medieval settings. The author's creation of a detailed and original system of the occult is notable, as is his use of the milieus of poker and gambling. Bugsy Siegel and the founding of Las Vegas figure prominently. Those who read for character enjoy many fine creations: a believably flawed protagonist and a fascinating crew of secondary characters. *Last Call* is at times frightening, at times brutally violent, which may make it too much for some readers. Powers's style is more literary than that of some fantasists, which makes him appealing to some, but difficult for others. In this book, readers must be patient as Powers slowly builds a history, develops the magical system, and assembles his cast of characters.

DISCUSSION QUESTIONS

- Have you encountered anything like the magical system that Powers puts together in this novel? Does it draw you in, or do you find it too incredible to believe?

- After reading this novel, how do you feel about the Tarot? Would you enjoy receiving a reading, find the idea disturbing, or do you find the practice of fortune-telling dubious?

- What about poker? Does *Last Call* make you more or less interested in gambling? Is the depiction of the gambling life in the novel believable?

- Who is Crane's most important ally? Which of his enemies is the most frightening?

- The violence and sudden deaths in *Last Call* are often surprising and quite unsettling. Do you find any of these scenes particularly powerful?

- How is Powers's novel influenced by the hard-boiled detective genre?

- Responsibility and parenting are ongoing themes in *Last Call*. What are the responsibilities of the major characters? Do they live up to these responsibilities? Which of the characters in the novel is the best parent? The worst?

- What are your impressions of Las Vegas? How does this novel contribute to those impressions? Compare the Las Vegas of the prologue, the Las Vegas of the last half of *Last Call*, and the real-world contemporary Las Vegas. Which would you most like to visit?

- What does this novel have to say about loss, grieving, and facing death?

- Are you satisfied by the ending of *Last Call*? Do you want to find out what happens next for the surviving characters?

SUGGESTED READING IF YOU LIKE *LAST CALL*

James Blaylock	*The Last Coin*
T. S. Eliot	*The Wasteland*
Neil Gaiman	*American Gods*
Stephen King	<u>The Dark Tower</u> series, starting with *The Gunslinger*
Tim Powers	*Expiration Date*; *Earthquake Weather*
Tim Powers	*The Drawing of the Dark*
Books about the Tarot, such as Rachel Pollack	*Seventy-Eight Degrees of Wisdom: A Book of Tarot*

Terry Pratchett

Small Gods

ABOUT THE AUTHOR

Born in 1948 in Beaconsfield, England, Pratchett sold his first story at age 13. He worked as a journalist and press officer for nuclear power stations before turning to full-time fiction writing. After three little-read science fiction novels, he began his Discworld series primarily as a parody of the fantasy genre, but has since expanded scope, satirizing almost every subject in a fantasy context. Pratchett has become the genre's best-loved humorist, arguably the best contemporary humor writer working in any form. In late 2007, Pratchett made the tragic announcement that he was afflicted with early-onset Alzheimer's, proving sadly that the universe also has a satirical sense of humor. Nearly 50 million copies of his books have been published in 35 languages. In 1998, Pratchett was awarded the OBE. In his spare time, he works for the Orang-Utan foundation.

PLOT SUMMARY

Brutha, a simple novice (who is not very bright, but possesses a photographic memory) has unshakable faith in the Omnian religion. The great god Om presents himself to Brutha as a tiny turtle. Om's powers have diminished because Brutha is his last true believer. The other Omnian leaders, particularly Vorbis, head of the nasty Quisition, have become obsessed with politics and power and have lost their faith. Unwittingly, Brutha uses his memory to aid Vorbis in his plot to hatch war between Omnia and neighboring Ephebe. As understanding finally begins to dawn through his denseness, Brutha (with Om grousing at him and guiding him from his pocket) must take an odyssey of travel, belief, and philosophy as he tries to stop a war and save his religion.

> Publication Date: 1994
> 272 p.

AUTHOR'S WEBSITE

http://www.terrypratchettbooks.com

OTHER INTERNET RESOURCES: L-SPACE AND DISCWORLD MONTHLY

http://www.lspace.org
http://www.discworldmonthly.co.uk

APPEAL POINTS

There are many theories about which Discworld novel to read first, but *Small Gods* is a good choice. It stands alone from the rest of the series, but is typical of Pratchett's humor. It's also one of his funniest. This novel appeals in particular to those interested in big questions: religion, philosophy, and science. Characters in this novel are humorous types: they won't appeal to readers who want characters with depth and development, but they are funny. Readers more interested in plot or character-based humor than satire or big issues might be better served with Discworld books about the Watch, the Witches, or William de Worde.

DISCUSSION QUESTIONS

- After reading this book, how do you interpret Pratchett's stance on religion?
- What is the funniest sequence in *Small Gods*?
- What do you think of Brutha? Is he likable or frustrating? Very smart or very dumb?
- Which of the many secondary characters encountered in the book is your favorite?
- Should Pratchett be shelved with fantasy in bookstores and libraries, or should his books go somewhere else?
- Which character demonstrates the most intelligence?
- What allusions to real-world religions can you catch in the novel?
- What references to famous philosophers and scientists are found in *Small Gods*?
- Those who have read a great deal of Pratchett's work have very different opinions about *Small Gods*. Is this one of his best books, or is it a weaker effort?
- Why did Pratchett choose to put Om in the form of a turtle?

SUGGESTED READING IF YOU LIKE *SMALL GODS*

Douglas Adams	*The Hitchhiker's Guide to the Galaxy*
Jasper Fforde	Thursday Next series, starting with *The Eyre Affair*
Tom Holt	any novel
Terry Pratchett	Discworld Death, starting with *Mort*
Terry Pratchett	Discworld Witches, starting with *Wyrd Sisters*
Terry Pratchett	Discworld Watch, starting with *Guards! Guards!*
Terry Pratchett	Discworld Tiffany Aching, starting with *Wee Free Men*
Robert Rankin	*Hollow Chocolate Bunnies of the Apocalypse*

Patrick Rothfuss

The Name of the Wind

ABOUT THE AUTHOR

Patrick Rothfuss was born in Wisconsin in 1973. He is a lecturer at the University of Wisconsin, Stevens Point. His first novel, *The Name of the Wind*, won the 2007 Quill Award for best science fiction/fantasy and the RUSA Reading List Award for best fantasy. A self-described late bloomer and itinerant student, he credits the "first real book" he read, *The Lion, The Witch, and the Wardrobe*, for shaping his mind and his life. He lists Terry Pratchett, Neil Gaiman, Peter S. Beagle, and Tim Powers as influences. Fans await the next book in the Kingkiller Chronicles.

PLOT SUMMARY

Kote appears to be nothing more than an innkeeper in a country town. But when an itinerant biographer called The Chronicler tracks him down, he reveals himself as Kvothe, a legendary hero and villain, magician and warrior. In this opener to the Kingkiller Chronicles trilogy, Kvothe tells the story of his childhood in a traveling troupe, the destruction of his family by the powerful Chandrian, his education at the magical University, and his time as a performing musician.

    Publication Date: 2007

    662 p.

AUTHOR'S WEBSITE

http://www.patrickrothfuss.com

APPEAL POINTS

The Name of the Wind is a fantasy lover's fantasy. Although it uses many of the genre's familiar tropes, it succeeds in making an old story feel brand new. Told in the form of a story, the book celebrates sheer storytelling ability. The characters are appealing, particularly the lead Kvothe. Rothfuss is also successful at creating a sense of mystery, revealing much, but still leaving the reader to wonder in suspense at half-revealed characters and plot points. The setting of the University is extremely well done, and worldbuilding in general is strong. Those with a musical bent love the in-depth descriptions of the act of performing on a stage.

DISCUSSION QUESTIONS

- The story of an orphan boy who becomes the legendary chosen one has been done many times in fantasy. Does Rothfuss succeed in making his story new?

- A book written in the first person depends greatly on the success of its main character. What did you think of Kvothe?

- How does the story-within-a-story structure of this novel enhance its storytelling power?

- What do you make of the tension between Bast and The Chronicler?

- Rothfuss has been lauded by many for his worldbuilding abilities. What are some of the elements that contribute to this success?

- Although this is heroic fantasy, Kvothe's challenges are sometimes very average: paying his tuition, problems with girls and school rivals, and so on. Does this make him more or less exciting for you as a reader?

- Magical universities have been used many times in fantasy, such as in *The Wizard of Earthsea* or the Harry Potter series. How does this author's version compare?

- Denna is an unusual love interest: independent and mysterious, she moves in and out of the story line at her own pace. Do you find her attractive or off-putting?

- What do you think of sympathy and naming, the two main elements of the book's magical system?

- How important to the story is Kvothe's lute playing? In what ways is it key to his development?

- Which of the many secondary characters in this novel catches your attention?

- Because of certain similarities (orphaned boy, magical school, etc.), *The Name of the Wind* has been compared by many to the Harry Potter series. Do you think this comparison is apt?

SUGGESTED READING IF YOU LIKE *THE NAME OF THE WIND*

David Eddings	The Belgariad, beginning with *Pawn of Prophecy*
Robin Hobb	The Farseer Trilogy, beginning with *Assassin's Apprentice*
Robert Jordan	*The Eye of the World*
Ursula K. Le Guin	*The Wizard of Earthsea*
Tad Williams	Memory, Sorrow, and Thorn, starting with *The Dragonbone Chair*

100 MORE RECOMMENDED FANTASY AUTHORS AND BOOKS FOR DISCUSSION

Here are 100 more authors whose work provides a worthwhile fantasy reading experience. For each author, a book is suggested that is in print (as of this writing), makes a good entry to the author's work, and supports discussion. If the book is part of a series, the series name is provided, but, for time considerations, only one book at a time should be assigned. This list does not exhaust the pool of interesting fantasy authors. In particular, it leaves out many authors and books from three categories that can be especially fruitful for fantasy fiction groups that are inclined to read them: genre classics, literary fantasies, and works for children and young adults. If these areas are of interest to your group, consult the appropriate lists in Chapter 5.

Author	Book or Series to Try First
Joe Abercrombie	The First Law, starting with *The Blade Itself*
Lloyd Alexander	The Chronicle of Prydain, starting with *The Book of Three*
Piers Anthony	Xanth series, starting with *A Spell for Chameleon*
R. Scott Bakker	The Prince of Nothing, starting with *The Darkness that Comes Before*
Clive Barker	*Weaveworld*
Christopher Barzak	*The Love We Share without Knowing*
Peter S. Beagle	*The Last Unicorn*
Carol Berg	Books of the Rai-Kirah, starting with *Transformation*
Anne Bishop	Black Jewels, starting with *Daughter of the Blood*
Ray Bradbury	*Dandelion Wine*
Marion Zimmer Bradley	Avalon series, starting with *The Mists of Avalon*
Peter Brett	*The Painted Man* (published in the U.K. as *The Warded Man*)
Patricia Briggs	Mercy Thompson series, starting with *Moon Called*
Kristen Britain	Green Rider series, starting with *Green Rider*
Steven Brust	Vlad Taltos series, starting with *The Book of Jhereg*
Lois McMaster Bujold	*Paladin of Souls*
Emma Bull	*War for the Oaks*
Jim Butcher	The Dresden Files, starting with *Storm Front*
Jacqueline Carey	Kushiel series, starting with *Kushiel's Dart*
Jonathan Carroll	*The Land of Laughs*
Lewis Carroll	*Alice's Adventures in Wonderland*
Angela Carter	*Burning Your Boats: Collected Stories*
Susanna Clarke	*Jonathan Strange & Mr. Norrell*
Storm Constantine	*Wraeththu*
Glen Cook	*Chronicles of the Black Company*
John Crowley	*Little, Big*
Pamela Dean	*Tam Lin*
Charles De Lint	Newford, starting with *Dreams Underfoot*
Gordon R. Dickson	Dragon Knight series, starting with *The Dragon and the George*
Sara Douglass	Wayfarer Redemption, starting with *The Wayfarer Redemption*

Dave Duncan	The King's Blades, starting with *The Gilded Chain*
Hal Duncan	The Book of All Hours, starting with *Ink*
David Eddings	The Belgariad, starting with *Pawn of Prophecy*
Steven Erikson	Malazan Book of the Fallen, starting with *Gardens of the Moon*
Jennifer Fallon	Hythrun Chronicles, starting with *Medalon*
David Farland	The Runelords, starting with *The Sum of All Men*
Raymond E. Feist	Riftwar, starting with *Magician: Apprentice*
Jasper Fforde	Thursday Next, starting with *The Eyre Affair*
Jack Finney	*Time and Again*
Lynn Flewelling	Tamir trilogy, starting with *The Bone Doll's Twin*
Neil Gaiman	*American Gods*
David Gemmell	Drenai Tales, starting with *Legend*
Felix Gilman	*Thunderer; Gears of the City*
Jo Graham	*Black Ships*
H. Rider Haggard	*She*
Charlaine Harris	Southern Vampire series, starting with *Dead until Dark*
Kim Harrison	The Hollows, starting with *Dead Witch Walking*
Elizabeth Haydon	Symphony of Ages, starting with *Rhapsody*
Robin Hobb	Farseer trilogy, starting with *Assassin's Apprentice*
Robert Holdstock	Ryhope Woods, starting with *Mythago Wood*
Robert E. Howard	Conan, starting with *The Coming of Conan the Cimmerian*
Barry Hughart	Master Li and Number Ten Ox, starting with *Bridge of Birds*
Kij Johnson	*Fudoki*
Diana Wynne Jones	Derkholm series, starting with *Dark Lord of Derkholm*
J. V. Jones	Sword of Shadows, starting with *A Cavern of Black Ice*
Robert Jordan	The Wheel of Time, starting with *The Eye of the World*
Guy Gavriel Kay	*The Lions of Al-Rassan*
Greg Keyes	The Age of Unreason, starting with *Newton's Cannon*
Katherine Kurtz	Deryni series, starting with *Deryni Rising*
Ellen Kushner	Swords of Riverside, starting with *Swordspoint*
Mercedes Lackey	The Last Herald Mage, starting with *Magic's Pawn*
Ursula K. Le Guin	Earthsea Cycle, starting with *A Wizard of Earthsea*
C. S. Lewis	Chronicles of Narnia, starting with *The Lion, the Witch, and the Wardrobe*
Kelly Link	*Stranger Things Happen*
Scott Lynch	Gentleman Bastards, starting with *The Lies of Locke Lamora*
John Marco	Tyrants and Kings, starting with *The Jackal of Nar*
Juliet Marillier	Sevenwaters, starting with *Daughter of the Forest*
Richard Matheson	*What Dreams May Come*
Anne McCaffrey	Dragonriders of Pern, starting with *Dragonflight*
Patricia McKillip	Riddle-Master omnibus
China Miéville	*The Scar*
L. E. Modesitt	The Saga of Recluce, starting with *The Magic of Recluce*

Sarah Monette	<u>Doctrine of Labyrinths</u>, starting with *Mélusine*
Elizabeth Moon	*<u>The Deed of Paksenarrion</u>*
Richard Morgan	<u>Land Fit for Heroes</u>, starting with *The Steel Remains*
Garth Nix	<u>Abhorsen</u> trilogy, starting with *Sabriel*
Andre Norton	<u>Witch World</u> series, starting with *Witch World*
Joshua Palmatier	<u>Throne of Amenkor</u>, starting with *The Skewed Throne*
K. J. Parker	<u>Engineer</u> trilogy, starting with *Devices and Desires*
Mervyn Peake	<u>Gormenghast</u> trilogy, starting with *Titus Groan*
Tim Powers	*The Anubis Gates*
Terry Pratchett	*Good Omens* (with Neil Gaiman)
Philip Pullman	<u>His Dark Materials</u>, starting with *The Golden Compass*
J. K. Rowling	<u>Harry Potter</u>, starting with *Harry Potter and the Sorcerer's Stone*
Brandon Sanderson	<u>Mistborn</u>, starting with *The Final Empire*
Ken Scholes	<u>The Psalms of Isaak</u>, starting with *Lamentation*
Ekaterina Sedia	*The Alchemy of Stone*
Sharon Shinn	<u>Twelve Houses</u>, starting with *Mystic and Rider*
Maria V. Snyder	<u>Study</u> series, starting with *Poison Study*
Matthew Woodring Stover	<u>Overworld</u>, starting with *Heroes Die*
Charles Stross	<u>Merchant Princes</u>, starting with *The Family Trade*
Jonathan Stroud	<u>Bartimaeus Trilogy</u>, starting with *The Amulet of Samarkand*
Michael Swanwick	*The Iron Dragon's Daughter*; *Dragons of Babel*
J. R. R. Tolkien	*<u>The Lord of the Rings</u>*
Catherynne M. Valente	<u>The Orphan's Tales</u>, starting with *In the Night Garden*
Jo Walton	*Tooth and Claw*
Brent Weeks	<u>Night Angel</u>, starting with *The Way of Shadows*
T. H. White	*<u>The Once and Future King</u>*
Tad Williams	<u>Memory, Sorrow, and Thorn</u>, starting with *The Dragonbone Chair*
Gene Wolfe	<u>Soldier in the Mist</u>, starting with *<u>Latro in the Mist</u>*
John C. Wright	<u>Chaos</u>, starting with *Orphans of Chaos*

Chapter 4
25 Great Science Fiction Novels for Book Groups

M. T. Anderson

Feed

ABOUT THE AUTHOR

Matthew Tobin Anderson lives in Cambridge, Massachusetts. Growing up in nearby Stow, he always knew he wanted to be a writer. After dropping out of Harvard, he earned degrees from Cambridge and the University of Syracuse. He worked as an editorial assistant for Candlewick Press, as an instructor at Vermont College, and as a classical music critic for The Improper Bostonian before turning to writing full-time. His young adult novels and children's books cover a wide swath of subject areas, but all of them show his intelligence, wit, and sense of satire.

PLOT SUMMARY

In a dystopian future (that seems uncomfortably believable), people are fitted at birth with implants through which they receive the "feed," an Internet-like mix of factoids, catch phrases, and advertising that is supposedly driven by individual preferences and interests. Titus, the book's narrator, is jarred from the chronically bored, trend-driven world of his circle of teen friends when he falls for Violet, an iconoclast who received her feed late and has fed it inaccurate information about her personal preferences. When a hacking attack causes her implant to malfunction, FeedTech, the company that controls the feeds, will not replace it. Titus is jolted out of his artificial world as he watches her brain begin to decline.

Publication Date: 2001

235 p.

APPEAL POINTS

Anderson's novel appeals to young adults and adults. Comfortably within the bounds of science fiction, the novel is also a satire of contemporary society and business currents. Anyone who enjoys language is fascinated by the author's clever-but-crude, funny-yet-scary mix of slang, coined words, and unusual usages. Short chapters keep the pace flying. Some readers find the language crude and *Feed*'s depictions of teen sexuality discomfiting (although this is exactly what the author is trying to do). The heart of the story is a simple tale of tragic romance, and some readers may appreciate that, even if the rest of the book's arguments don't appeal to them.

DISCUSSION QUESTIONS

- Do you find Titus sympathetic or annoying as a protagonist?
- Is the information coming through the feeds of individuals really driven by their interests, or are their personalities created by the feeds?

- Computer implants that interface with the human body and brain are a fast-developing field that might become common in the near future. After reading *Feed*, do you think such devices could be beneficial, or should they be avoided absolutely?

- Compare School with Violet's home education. Which is superior? Which is closer to education in our school systems today?

- What did you think of the trend to sport lesions as a personal style? Do people truly want the lesions, or are they making a fad of the debilitations that their society creates?

- Why does the ability to communicate in the book seem to decline as communication technology grows more advanced?

- How much of a comparison can be drawn between the ways in which we currently use the Internet and the resulting effects and the world that results from implanted feeds?

- If M-Chat were available would you sign up? Do you think it would become popular in society at large?

- Does Titus's experience with Violet change him in any permanent way?

- Is our society heading in the direction depicted in *Feed*? If so, what needs to be done to stop such a future from occurring?

SUGGESTED READING IF YOU LIKE *FEED*

Max Barry	*Jennifer Government*
Ray Bradbury	*Fahrenheit 451*
Anthony Burgess	*A Clockwork Orange*
Cory Doctorow	*Down and Out in the Magic Kingdom*
Pete Hautman	*Rash*
Lois Lowry	*The Giver*

Neal Asher

The Skinner

ABOUT THE AUTHOR

Born in England in 1961, Asher knocked about in a variety of jobs during his early years: engineer, barman, truck driver, coalman, boat window manufacturer, grass cutter, and builder. He began writing science fiction and fantasy at age 16, but his work didn't find much of an audience until after 2000, when Pan McMillan picked him up for a three-book contract (and Tor followed suit in the United States). Married to wife Caroline, he is now a full-time writer who will publish his twelfth novel in 2009.

PLOT SUMMARY

The ocean world of Spatterjay brims with nasty life forms that compete fiercely for survival. Its human inhabitants are also tough customers, pirates infected with a virus that make them almost impossible to kill. Three off-worlders come to Spatterjay, each with an agenda. Keech is a reification—a scientifically animated corpse—returned to take vengeance against one of the pirate captains and his crew. Erlin is a woman infected with the virus, searching for help from Captain Ambel. Janer is the servant of a hornet hive mind, sent to the planet on a mysterious scouting mission. All three are on a collision course with captains bearing old grudges, drone planetary monitors guided by artificial intelligence, and the alien Prador, who are determined to hide evidence of their past misdeeds on Spatterjay.

　　Publication Date: 2004
　　480 p.

AUTHOR'S WEBSITE

http://freespace.virgin.net/n.asher

AUTHOR'S BLOG

http://theskinner.blogspot.com

APPEAL POINTS

The Skinner balances exciting action with creative world building and vivid characters. Asher knows how to breathe new life into science fiction staples, such as cyborgs, mutations, and hive minds. His writing is just plain fun, teeming with incidental humor, cinematic action, and surprising twists. Fans of pirates or marine life are enthralled by his inventive setting and battling sea creatures. This is a violent book, set on a world where survival of the fittest requires everyday battle. As such, it is too violent for some readers but is just the ticket for others. *The*

Skinner is self-contained, but all of Asher's books are set in the universe of the Polity, and series readers find many avenues to explore in his other works.

DISCUSSION QUESTIONS

- Are the mysterious agendas of the visitors to Spatterjay intriguing or frustrating? Were you surprised as their goals were revealed, or did you see the plot twists coming?
- Which of Asher's creatures and characters do you find the most inventive? The most terrifying? The funniest?
- Did you look forward to the substories about Spatterjay's ecology at the beginning of each chapter?
- After reading this book, what would you guess about the author's background and education?
- Is the virus that infects the residents of Spatterjay a blessing or a curse to those who contract it?
- Justice is a theme at the center of this book. At its end, do you believe that justice has been served? Did all of the characters get what they deserved?
- Is the violence in this novel too strong, or do you find it exciting? Do any of the scenes cross the line into being offensive?
- If you were making a movie of *The Skinner*, who would you cast in the major parts?
- Would you classify this novel as pulp action, or is it deeper than that?
- After reading this book, would you rather continue to another book about Spatterjay or a book about the larger universe in which it is set?

SUGGESTED READING IF YOU LIKE *THE SKINNER*

Neal Asher	*The Voyage of the Sable Keech* (or other <u>Polity</u> novels)
Iain M. Banks	*Consider Phlebas*
Richard Morgan	*Thirteen*
Dan Simmons	*Hyperion*
Neal Stephenson	*Snow Crash*

Isaac Asimov

The Naked Sun

ABOUT THE AUTHOR

Born in the Smolensk region of Russia in 1920, Isaac Asimov immigrated with his family to Brooklyn when he was three. After civilian service during World War II and a short post-War stint in the U.S. Army, he became a professor of biochemistry at Boston University. Extremely prolific, he wrote or edited over 500 books, mostly science fiction, popular science, history, or mystery. Asimov enjoyed enclosed spaces but feared flying, traits that show up in some of his works, such as the Robot novels. He loved Gilbert and Sullivan, Nero Wolfe, and Sherlock Holmes stories and served as vice president of Mensa International. Often ranked with Arthur C. Clarke and Robert Heinlein as one of science fiction's "big three," Asimov is probably best known for two series: his Robot stories and novels and his series about galactic empire and trade, Foundation. His awards include five major Hugos, three Nebulas, and honorary doctorates from 14 universities. Asimov died from complications of AIDS, contracted from a blood transfusion in 1992.

PLOT SUMMARY

Earthman detective Elijah Baley is reunited with the Auroran robot R. Daneel Olivaw when they are called to Solaria, a planet with no police and very little contact between citizens. A bludgeoning murder has occurred, for which there is only one suspect, but no one can see how she could have committed the crime. Used to Earth's enclosed and crowded spaces, Baley must fight extreme agoraphobia while acclimatizing himself to Solaria's robot-intensive, contact-minimizing culture, as well as Solarian disdain for the people of Earth. When a second murder strikes down another prominent citizen, the race is on to discover the killer.

    Publication Date: 1956

    288 p.

AUTHOR'S WEBSITE

http://www.asimovonline.com

APPEAL POINTS

Asimov's style is heavy on plot, laced with droll humor, and moves along quickly because he keeps description to a minimum. *The Naked Sun* combines science fiction and mystery effectively and should appeal to fans of both genres. Although the social structures of the societies that he describes and some of the technology that he predicted have not aged particularly well, Asimov is very logical, and his basic story still holds up. Even though his characters aren't deep, their interactions are both entertaining and quirky. Although this is the second of his Robot novels featuring Baley and Olivaw, there is no need to read the series in order.

DISCUSSION QUESTIONS

- Which aspects of Asimov's story have become dated in the 50 years since its publication? Which still hold up?

- Which detective would you rather hire to work on a case for you, Baley or Olivaw?

- How concerned with the dangers of robots should we be? Is there anything in our technology and science that will prevent robots from acting inappropriately?

- Which interests you most, the mystery story or the social science fiction of *The Naked Sun*?

- Asimov has been credited by many with writing the first combination of science fiction and mystery. What elements of the classic mystery tale does he use in *The Naked Sun*?

- Could a society like Solaria's, with a phobia for contact between people, ever come to be?

- Is the behavior of Asimov's characters when using communication technology echoed anywhere today in real-world practice?

- Asimov has been accused of writing badly about women. Do you find his female characters believable?

- Are the people of Solaria and Earth fundamentally different or the same in what phobias created by technology have done to them? Does contemporary society resemble either of Asimov's projected worlds?

- Are there any holes in the solution to the mystery?

SUGGESTED READING IF YOU LIKE *THE NAKED SUN*

Isaac Asimov	*The Caves of Steel*
Isaac Asimov	Foundation series, starting with *Foundation* (written first) or *Prelude to Foundation* (chronologically first)
Alfred Bester	*The Demolished Man*
David Brin	*Sundiver*
Philip K. Dick	*Do Androids Dream of Electric Sheep?*

Kage Baker

In the Garden of Iden

ABOUT THE AUTHOR

A long-time resident of Pismo Beach, California, Kage Baker is the author of 10 science fiction and fantasy books. She is best known for her series of time travel novels about <u>The Company</u>, which begins with *In the Garden of Iden*. Baker has worked as a graphic artist, mural painter, and as a playwright and director for the Living History Centre. In particular, she is an expert in the Elizabethan period. Baker is a big fan of Frederick Marryat, Patrick O'Brien, C. S. Forester, Herman Melville, Robert Louis Stevenson, and Raymond Chandler. Baker describes herself as an "avid gardener, birdwatcher, spinster aunt, and Jethro Tull fan."

PLOT SUMMARY

Saved from the Spanish Inquisition as a girl, Mendoza becomes one of the immortal cyborg operatives of Dr. Zeus, Incorporated (also known as The Company), a mysterious cabal that uses time travel to attempt to mend the errors of history and create a better world. After her initial training, Mendoza is sent as a botanist to the countryside of 16th-century Kent to collect samples from the garden of the eccentric Sir Walter Iden. While there, she falls hard for Nicholas Harpole, a love that may undermine her mission and create ripples down through the centuries.

 Publication Date: 1997

 329 p.

AUTHOR'S WEBSITE

http://www.kagebaker.com

APPEAL POINTS

In the Garden of Iden appeals to a different readership than that of the average science fiction novel. There is no hard science, and the plot develops slowly, with few action sequences. Instead, this is a novel of delightful characters and clever, subtle dialogue. Period details in Spain and England are convincingly rendered. There's romance at the plot's center, handled with gentle, mannered comedy that can be read as either straight romance or as spoof. With a botanist as the lead character, this book also appeals to the gardening set. Behind everything lurks Dr. Zeus, adding a touch of mystery and impetus to send the series reader after the next volume.

DISCUSSION QUESTIONS

- Is this science fiction or not? To what other readers would it appeal?

- Mendoza and most of her colleagues are disappointed by their assignment to damp and dreary England. If you could travel in place and time as they do, would you be disappointed? Where would you like to go?
- As cyborgs whose future is determined, do the operatives of The Company truly have free will? Will they be able to act against their controllers wishes if they desire?
- Baker grew up in Hollywood and has a background in the theater. Can you see these influences in her writing?
- A question from the author's page: Could any group, no matter how benign its intentions, intervene in history without becoming responsible for the same evils that it sets out to prevent?
- In the novel, immortals seem to regard themselves as a separate species from humans. Is this the case? If immortality was possible, would such a conclusion be inevitable?
- Baker's characters are an eccentric batch. Which is your favorite? Do you find them believable?
- In Baker's version of time travel, one can only travel back in time, not to the future. Changes can only be made in history that has not been recorded. How does this compare to other accounts of time travel that you have read?
- What do you think of the romance between Mendoza and Nicholas Harpole? Of its conclusion? Is the pair well matched?
- Do you buy Baker's account of England during the reign of Queen Mary? Does she portray its people fairly and accurately?
- Does this novel make you want to continue the series? What is likely to happen to Mendoza and her colleagues? Will the Company do good, or is something sinister likely to develop?

SUGGESTED READING IF YOU LIKE *IN THE GARDEN OF IDEN*

Kage Baker	the rest of <u>The Company</u> series, starting with *Sky Coyote*
Jack Finney	*Time and Again*
Tim Powers	*The Anubis Gates*
Charles Stross	<u>The Merchant Princes</u> series, beginning with *The Family Trade*
Connie Willis	*The Doomsday Book*
Connie Willis	*To Say Nothing of the Dog*

Iain M. Banks

Consider Phlebas

ABOUT THE AUTHOR

Iain Banks, a Scot, was born in 1954, the son of an officer in the British Admiralty and a professional ice skater. He publishes literary fiction (12 novels to date) without his middle initial and science fiction (10 novels so far) with it included in his name. Considered a major writer in his homeland, he is just beginning to catch on in the United States. Most of his science fiction focuses on the Culture, an enormous intergalactic civilization. Once a car collector, he sold his collection in 2007, purchased an economy car, and vowed to fly as little as possible, declaring his opposition to global warming. He has espoused other political causes as well, in particular leading opposition to the Iraq War.

PLOT SUMMARY

Bora Horza Gobuchul is a Changer, who can alter physical appearance at will. Narrowly escaping death on a mission for his Idiran handlers in their war against the Culture, he is assigned to retrieve a Culture "Mind," an artificial intelligence that carries much of that society's knowledge. The Mind has hidden itself on Schar's World, a planet that only Changers can access. En route, Horza joins a band of mercenaries on the spaceship *Clear Air Turbulence*, becoming an enemy of their leader Kraiklyn and the lover of Yalson. Pursued by the Culture agent Balveda, and surviving a series of disastrous raids, crashes, and chases, Horza makes his way to Schar's World, where his small team of survivors descend into a network of deserted tunnels and battle a team of Idirans who don't know Horza is on their side while both groups search for The Mind.

Publication Date: 1988

471 p.

AUTHOR'S WEBSITE

http://www.iain-banks.net

APPEAL POINTS

Despite its significant length, *Consider Phlebas* is a fast-paced space opera loaded with over-the-top action. It's populated with morally ambiguous characters who become sympathetic as they survive disaster after disaster. Although this book moves quickly, Banks's style is descriptive and sometimes dense. His settings are massive and dramatic: enormous spaceships, strange islands, and spooky tunnels. The book has a grim tone and high violence that pleases fans of noir science fiction but may depress some readers, particularly those who like happy endings. The conflict between the Culture and rival civilizations is only sketched lightly here; it develops further in later novels as Banks delves into the shared worlds of his loosely connected <u>Culture</u> series.

DISCUSSION QUESTIONS

- How would you summarize the differences between the Idiran civilization and the Culture? Why do the two civilizations go to war? Which civilization do you prefer?
- Do you classify Horza as a self-centered character or as a heroic character?
- *Consider Phlebas* is full of action set pieces and narrow escapes. Which is your favorite?
- Why does Horza prefer the Idirans to the Culture? Is his decision a good one?
- This is Banks's first book of science fiction. Do you see the influence of other writers or works in *Consider Phlebas*?
- The grim and violent tone of the novel is too much for some readers. Does it go too far?
- The title of the novel comes from a line in T. S. Eliot's poem *The Wasteland* and refers to a man who has died, apparently from drowning, and forgotten his worldly cares as the sea breaks his body apart. The reader is asked to consider Phlebas and recall his or her own mortality. How does this title relate to the events of the book?
- How do you feel about the book's ending? Were you hoping for something different?
- *Consider Phlebas* is a very cinematic book. Who would you cast in the lead roles?
- Will you continue with the <u>Culture</u> series? What more would you like to know about their society after reading this book?

SUGGESTED READING IF YOU LIKE *CONSIDER PHLEBAS*

Neal Asher	<u>Polity</u> series, starting with *Gridlinked*
Iain M. Banks	More <u>Culture</u> novels, starting with *The Player of Games*
Peter F. Hamilton	<u>Commonwealth Saga</u>, starting with *Pandora's Star*
Larry Niven	*Ringworld*
Alistair Reynolds	<u>Revelation Space</u> series, starting with *Revelation Space*
Dan Simmons	<u>Hyperion Cantos</u>, starting with *Hyperion*

Max Brooks

World War Z: An Oral History of the Zombie War

ABOUT THE AUTHOR

Born in 1972 to director Mel Brooks and actress Anne Bancroft, Max Brooks worked as an actor, a voiceover artist, and a writer on *Saturday Night Live* before turning his attention to books. His first book was *The Zombie Survival Guide*, a nonfiction guide to surviving a zombie apocalypse. The reception for that book led Brooks to try a fictional alternate history on the same topic. *World War Z* has been met with rave reviews and a movie deal with Brad Pitt's Plan B films. Brooks splits his time between Los Angeles and New York City.

PLOT SUMMARY

Inspired by George Romero's <u>Living Dead</u> films and Studs Terkel's *The Good War*, Brooks has written an alternate history account of "The Zombie War," an apocalyptic struggle of people around the globe to survive and beat back a plague of zombies. Beginning with an account from China about what may have been the alpha patient, an unnamed historian interviews a series of diverse characters about the origins of the plague, the mistakes that allow it to become endemic, political and martial methods that succeed and fail in combating the undead, and the final campaign to eradicate them from the world.

 Publication Date: 2006

 342 p.

WEBSITE

http://www.randomhouse.com/crown/worldwarz/

APPEAL POINTS

World War Z's unusual format, a series of interview transcriptions, divides the book into short, fast-paced sections. The large cast pleases readers who like diversity, whereas those who like deep character development may find the book frustrating. The book's many settings should fascinate those who want to explore the world. Differences between zombies and humans and the mass disruption of the plague create dilemmas and thought problems for characters—political, philosophical, technical, and military—that many readers enjoy exploring. Although not as violent as a zombie novel could be, this is a graphic subject. Some readers may not wish to confront this violence, whereas others find it exciting. It is easy to picture the events of this book, which should appeal greatly to visual readers.

DISCUSSION QUESTIONS

- Do you like the oral history format used in this book? What are the challenges of the format?

- What factors allow a few zombies to become an epidemic? Could similar failures contribute to the spread of real diseases?
- Diverse methods are used to combat the zombies, with results ranging from disastrous to brilliant. Do you find them believable? Would you suggest other means of zombie fighting?
- In a real-world disaster, would and should governments come up with plans, such as the novel's Redeker plan, to sacrifice the majority of people for species survival?
- The book's many short interviews can be both a strength and a weakness. Which sections most catch your attention? Which would you like to see expanded to full-length? When the book is made into a film, which vignettes would you cut?
- *World War Z* explores how ethnicities and political systems respond to a cataclysm. Are these responses believable? Are any of them ethnically insensitive or otherwise offensive?
- If caught in a similar disaster, where would you go? What would you do? Which survival methods in the book would you emulate? Which would you avoid?
- Do you think that any of the characters, events, or political criticisms in the book are comparable to real-world analogs? Is Brooks going after any actual people or policies?
- When the majority of humans turn into zombies, some survivors go feral, in some cases even pretending to be zombies. Why do they choose this path? Could such a thing really happen?
- Survivor guilt, depression, and mental illness are poignant themes running through the book. Does Brooks portray these accurately? Could you cope with this kind of wide-scale disaster?
- Zombies have been explored more in film than they have in literature. Why do you suppose this is the case? What are the best zombie movies?

SUGGESTED READING IF YOU LIKE *WORLD WAR Z*

Jane Austen and Seth Grahame-Smith	*Pride and Prejudice and Zombies*
J. L. Bourne	*Day by Day Armageddon*
Max Brooks	*The Zombie Survival Guide* (nonfiction)
Stephen King	*Cell*
Robert Kirkman	The Walking Dead series (graphic novels)
Studs Terkel	*The Good War* (nonfiction oral history)

Arthur C. Clarke

Rendezvous with Rama

ABOUT THE AUTHOR

Born in England in 1917, Clarke spent his boyhood gazing at the stars and reading U.S. pulp science fiction magazines. After serving in World War II as a radar specialist, Clarke chaired the British Interplanetary Society, and his writing career began to take off. Clarke's ideas on geostationary satellites, meteorological research, and space elevators have proven revolutionary and will continue to influence space science long after his death. He was a dual citizen of the U. K. where he was made a Knight in 2000, and Sri Lanka, where he moved in 1956 because of his affinity for underwater exploration. He published over 50 novels and story collections, including classics such as *Childhood's End, 2001: A Space Odyssey*, and *The City and the Stars*. Awards for both the best British science fiction novel of the year and British achievement in space science bear his name, as do an asteroid and a species of dinosaur. Clarke died in 2008.

PLOT SUMMARY

In the 22nd century, an enormous cylindrical spaceship of unknown origins passes through Earth's solar system. After debate and controversy on Earth, a group of explorers intercept the ship and enter it in an attempt to discover its secrets. They find a microcosmic world tucked inside, an alien world without living aliens that, although elegant and simple, goes beyond the scope of their technology or the limits of their understanding.

Publication Date: 1972
214 p.

CLARKE AND ARTHUR C. CLARKE FOUNDATION WEBSITES

http://www.arthurcclarke.net
http://www.clarkefoundation.org

APPEAL POINTS

Rama is one of science fiction's most decorated novels, winning the Hugo, Nebula, Campbell, and Jupiter Awards, yet over 35 years after its publication, it maintains its sense of mystery. The novel appeals to fans of hard science fiction. Character development is rather thin, and, even though the novel has plenty of suspense, there is little action, because this is primarily a novel of ideas. *Rama* does not satisfy readers who require resolved endings, but it sticks with deep thinkers for a long time.

DISCUSSION QUESTIONS

- Do you find the novel suspenseful? Frightening? If so, why?
- One of Clarke's most celebrated quotes is that "any sufficiently advanced technology is indistinguishable from magic." How does this idea influence *Rendezvous with Rama*?
- If humans encounter alien civilizations, is the encounter likely to be as it is in *Rama*, or somehow different?
- How does the design of Rama (its size, its symmetry, its minimalism, etc.) affect your appreciation of it? Does it affect the mood of the novel?
- What would you hypothesize as the origins of Rama? What is its purpose? Where have the Ramans gone? Why does the ship come to our solar system?
- Do you find the science in *Rama* difficult to understand, or are Clarke's explanations easy to follow?
- What effect would the arrival of a ship like Rama have on Earth today? Would it affect various interests (political, religious, scientific) as it does in the novel?
- Do you find the explorers' failure to understand Rama frustrating, disappointing, or realistic? Would you prefer that Clarke allow them to discover more of the ship's secrets?
- As an explorer of Rama, would you do anything differently?
- Can you see the influence of *Rendezvous with Rama* on any science fiction films?

SUGGESTED READING IF YOU LIKE *RENDEZVOUS WITH RAMA*

Greg Bear	*Eon*
David Brin	*Sundiver*
Arthur C. Clarke	*2001: A Space Odyssey*
Arthur C. Clarke and Gentry Lee	*Rama II* and other sequels (warning: many readers find these disappointing)
Michael Crichton	*Sphere*
L. E. Modesitt	*The Eternity Artifact*

Cory Doctorow

Down and Out in the Magic Kingdom

ABOUT THE AUTHOR

Cory Doctorow is a Canadian, born in Toronto in 1971 to schoolteacher parents. He came to activism early, working for Greenpeace and nuclear disarmament as a child. He is equally well-known for science fiction and for activist writing on technology, particularly the causes of free, open access to all digital media and open source technology. As well as novels and stories, he writes for publications such as *Wired*, *The New York Times*, and *Popular Science*. *Boing Boing*, the technology and culture blog that he co-edits, is perhaps the most popular on the Internet. Although he holds no academic degree, he completed a visiting professorship at the University of Southern California in 2006–2007. He now lives in Los Angeles, where a daughter was born to him and Alice Taylor in 2008.

PLOT SUMMARY

On near-future Earth, Bitchun society has overcome death and scarcity. The economy is based on "whuffie," a digital measure of reputation based on how one is viewed by others. At death, one's consciousness is downloaded into a replica body and life begins anew, unless one becomes bored and opts to take a cryogenic nap until things get interesting again. "Ad-hocracies"—small communities of like-minded individuals—compete against each other to control the fields of endeavor that interest them. Narrator Julius, a specialist in crowd control, his girlfriend Lil, and his best friend Dan are leaders in a powerful ad-hoc at Disney's Magic Kingdom until Julius is assassinated. Although he quickly begins a new life, the distraction that his murder creates opens the door for another ad-hoc, freshly arrived from Disney Beijing, to hone in on their territory and take over the Haunted Mansion. Suddenly Julius is struggling to solve his own murder, connect it to his gifted competitors, and revive his relationships before his whuffie bottoms out.

    Publication Date: 2003

    208 p.

AUTHOR'S WEBSITE

Craphound: His Personal Website
http://craphound.com/
Boing Boing: His Technology, Culture, and Politics Blog
http://boingboing.net/

APPEAL POINTS

Doctorow's first novel is a jaunty book that explores a plethora of interesting ideas in the context of a fast-moving suspense plot that takes just over 200 pages. Even though the characters are likable, they are slight; highlights here are settings and the issues that Doctorow raises.

This novel fascinates readers interested in how the digital world is melding with the physical world to create new realities. Also of interest are the effects of eternal life on the workings of the world. This is a must-read for any fan—or critic—of Disney theme parks. The mystery at the core of the book provides crossover appeal to fans of that genre.

DISCUSSION QUESTIONS

- How many years would it take you to lose interest in the world if you had the kind of eternal life hypothesized in the book? Would it change your approach to living?
- Can a pure meritocracy function, or would other rules be necessary? What position does Doctorow seem to take on this question?
- Which version of The Hall of Presidents in the book do you prefer? Which version of the Haunted Mansion?
- Did you predict the changes that took place in the relationship of Julius, Dan, and Lil?
- Is Bitchun society a utopia or a dystopia?
- In what ways would the availability of eternal life change the world? Is Doctorow's imagined version of such a world accurate?
- Are the beings that replace someone after a physical death in *Down and Out* completely the same person?
- Are any of the predictions in Doctorow's novel already beginning to take form?
- What do you think of Disney theme parks? What do you think Doctorow thinks of them? Why did he choose to set his novel in this environment?
- Is basing an economy on respect, as in the whuffie system, a good idea? A feasible idea?
- What do you make of the tale of Julius's interlude with Zoya?

SUGGESTED READING IF YOU LIKE *DOWN AND OUT IN THE MAGIC KINGDOM*

Cory Doctorow	*Little Brother*
Cory Doctorow	*Overclocked*
Jasper Fforde	Thursday Next series, starting with *The Eyre Affair*
Clay Shirky	*Here Comes Everybody: The Power of Organizing without Organizations* (nonfiction)
Neal Stephenson	*Snow Crash*
Charles Stross	*Halting State*

Kathleen Ann Goonan

In War Times

ABOUT THE AUTHOR

Born in Cincinnati, Ohio, a graduate of Virginia Tech, Kathleen Ann Goonan started a Montessori school in Tennessee after college. When her husband was offered a job in Hawaii, she became a full-time writer. She broke through with her <u>Nanotechnology Quartet</u>, beginning with *Queen City Jazz*. In addition to her success as a novelist, Goonan is a travel writer and jazz aficionado. She currently divides her time between Knoxville, Tennessee, and Lakeland, Florida.

PLOT SUMMARY

In early December, 1941, young Sam Dance is recruited by the mysterious Dr. Eliani Hadntz for an elusive mission: development and experimentation with the Hadntz device, a kind of organic computer that allows humans some access to alternate strands of reality in the quantum world. When his brother is killed at Pearl Harbor the next day, Sam finds motivation for his lifelong pursuit of peace through technological means. The story follows Sam, his war friends, and his family through World War II and its Cold War aftermath as they try to solve the riddles of the time and space-warping device.

Publication Date: 2007

248 p.

AUTHOR'S WEBSITE

http://goonan.com

APPEAL POINTS

This unusual blend of historical and science fiction takes the reader on a whirlwind tour of the major events of the 20th century: you get the strong sense that you are there. Goonan integrates her father's actual diary entries of those years into the narrative as the journal of her lead character. It's by no means a thriller, but Goonan includes just enough suspense to keep the pages turning. Readers who enjoy subtle characterization appreciate this work, which has a nice balance of introspection and interaction. Music lovers appreciate Sam and his friend Wink's ongoing love affair with jazz. The moral dilemmas surrounding use of the mysterious and powerful Hadntz device also catch some readers. This relatively slim stand-alone novel doesn't tax readers who don't want too much science, too many pages, or cliffhanger endings.

DISCUSSION QUESTIONS

- One theme in this novel is a central question of our time: do advances in technology ultimately result in more good or harm?
- If you had been in Sam Dance's place, would you have attempted to use the Hadntz device? If so, in what way?
- What do you think of the author's use of her father's journal entries? Was their integration into the narrative successful?
- Family is central to this novel. What do you think of Sam and Bette's marriage? Of their parenting?
- Goonan draws interesting parallels between the kind of thought and skill required to play jazz music and that needed to make scientific breakthroughs. Is this convincing? Can you think of other examples of this kind of bond between art and science?
- The characters in this novel encounter the possibility that we all long for: a second chance. Does this make their lives better, or is it a burden?
- Many people find times of war, for all of their horrors, to be the most vivid years of their lives. Is that true in this novel?
- A shroud of mystery and foreboding surrounds several of the characters in this novel. Did you expect anyone to be a friend or foe of Sam Dance who ends up being something else?
- Do you find Goonan's scientific combination of biology and physics convincing? Is the idea of such technologies promising or threatening?
- Which of the historical events in the novel would you most like to experience firsthand?
- Goonan eschews flashy action sequences, taking a minor key approach to plot in the novel. Does this approach work for you?

SUGGESTED READING IF YOU LIKE *IN WAR TIMES*

Philip K. Dick	*The Man in the High Castle*
Kathleen Ann Goonan	Nanotech Quartet, starting with *Queen City Jazz*
Philip Roth	*The Plot against America*
Neal Stephenson	*Cryptonomicon*
Jo Walton	*Farthing; Ha'Penny*; and *Half a Crown*

Austin Grossman

Soon I Will Be Invincible

ABOUT THE AUTHOR

The son of Allen Grossman, an award-winning poet, Austin Grossman did his undergraduate work at Harvard and is now a doctoral candidate in English Literature at Berkeley, specializing in Romantic and Victorian literature. *Soon I Will Be Invincible* is his first novel. He has also worked as a computer game designer on games such as *Deus Ex* and *Tomb Raider*. Grossman splits his time between Brooklyn and San Francisco.

PLOT SUMMARY

Populating an alternate history with his own selection of superheroes and archvillains, Grossman tells the tale of Doctor Impossible, a supervillain doomed to a lonely and frustrating life of one near-complete—but eventually failed—world conquest after another. The story alternates between his narration and that of Fatale, a female cyborg superhero who is the newest member of the Champions superteam that always thwarts Impossible in the end.

Publication Date: 2007

287 p.

AUTHOR'S WEBSITE

http://austingrossman.blogspot.com

APPEAL POINTS

Any fan of superhero comics enjoys the way that *Invincible* embraces and plays with all of the genre's clichés and makes them into something new. The book's strengths are its fast pace, exciting action sequences, and sly humor (as when it satirizes smug heroes or the villain's self-knowledge of his tendency to make self-congratulating speeches before completing his plans). There's a good deal of mystery and suspense, as readers wonder what has happened to missing heroes, whether reformed villains will stay reformed, and if or how the villain will finally be defeated. Character-focused readers enjoy the book's exploration of the difficulties of the superpowerful and the psychology of their choice of good and evil. The cleverness of this book may be lost on readers who have no familiarity with superhero stories.

DISCUSSION QUESTIONS

- How does the superhero story change when told from the point of view of the villain?

- Why does the author choose Fatale, a new member and outsider, as his narrator for the perspective of the Champions? How would the story change if narrated by another member of the team?
- Does reading about superheroes work for you, or would you prefer to see this work in a graphic format?
- If Grossman continues to write books set in this universe, which hero or villain should he explore next?
- There are lots of inside jokes in the book about the clichés of superhero storytelling. Which of these bits of satire did you catch?
- Do you like the author's choice for the character that ultimately defeats Dr. Impossible? Would you rather see him succeed? Or be defeated by a different character?
- What traits do superheroes and villains share? How do they differ? Do they choose to follow one path or another, or is it genetic or in some way predestined?
- Grossman posits a world of heroes with corporate sponsorship and uneasy connections with the military and political institutions. If there were superheroes, how would they interact with other authorities?
- The Champions have a hard time coalescing as a team. What are the reasons for their difficulties in interacting with each other? Are all superteams doomed to discord? Do you see parallels to the real world?
- Are supervillains always doomed to failure?
- Which characters are your favorites? Whose powers would you most like to have?

SUGGESTED READING IF YOU LIKE *SOON I WILL BE INVINCIBLE*

Tom DeHaven	*It's Superman*
Minister Faust	*From the Notebooks of Dr. Brain*
Catherine Jinks	*Evil Genius*
George R. R. Martin, ed.	<u>Wild Cards</u> series (starting with *Wild Cards, Vol. 1*)
Alan Moore and Dave Gibbons	*Watchmen*
Perry Moore	*Hero*

Or revisit any of your favorite superhero comics, especially those with superteams.

Joe Haldeman

The Forever War

ABOUT THE AUTHOR

Joe Haldeman moved frequently in his youth, staying longest in Alaska and Bethesda, Maryland. His dream was to become a "spaceman," and he studied for a degree in astronomy. Before he could pursue his goals, he was drafted into the Vietnam War. His experience in the war factors into his writing, particularly *War Year*, his first short novel, and *The Forever* War, which won both the Hugo and the Nebula Awards for 1975. Upon return from Vietnam, Haldeman took the classes that he needed to graduate, including a creative writing course. He intended to write as a sideline, beginning graduate school in computer science, but contacts from a writing workshop convinced him to pursue the career full-time. He completed his M.F.A. at the University of Iowa in 1975 and has now published over 30 books. He also teaches writing, most recently at M.I.T. Haldeman enjoys traveling with his wife of over 40 years, bicycling, guitar, and amateur astronomy.

PLOT SUMMARY

William Mandella is conscripted into an elite unit of soldiers who are in fantastic health and have IQs over 150. After brutal training, they are sent to fight the alien Taurans. Traveling through wormhole-like collapsars, they cross the galaxy for horrible battles. Their near-light-speed travel means that many years pass on Earth during their tour of duty, and because of dilation of time, they become embroiled in a never-ending arms race with the Taurans, often encountering enemies who have made tremendous technical advances since they have had time to return to Earth and re-arm with the latest weapons. Mandella tries to return to civilian life with his love (and companion in arms) Marygay, but they encounter future shock in the drastically changed world. He returns to service, where, split from Marygay, he survives combat through some skill and even more sheer luck. When war with the Taurans (which turns out to have been a misunderstanding) finally ends, Mandella migrates to a colony of old-style humans, where he is reunited with Marygay.

> Publication Date: 1975
> 288 p.

AUTHOR'S WEBSITE

http://home.earthlink.net/~haldeman

APPEAL POINTS

The Forever War makes a fine primer for many of the most visited concepts of science fiction: alien warfare, relativistic travel, overpopulation, cloning, futuristic governments, and more. Unlike most works of military science fiction, this is clearly an anti-war novel. It's grim, but the ending is more positive. Characterization is on the sparse side, but it's easy to sympathize with the novel's narrator. The writer's sparse style results in a novel that has aged much better than most science fiction. Two books, *Forever Peace* and *Forever Free*, follow in a loosely connected series, but readers don't need to go beyond this volume, which has a clear resolution.

DISCUSSION QUESTIONS

- *The Forever War* is very much based on the author's experience in Vietnam. What similarities can you find between the two conflicts?
- Are there similarities between the author's version of the near future and our own?
- What would you do in Mandella's place if returned to an unfamiliar world?
- Does Haldeman portray the psychological experience of warfare accurately?
- Is Mandella a hero? What do you like best about him? Least?
- What do you think of the author's portrayal of sexuality? Do his heterosexual relationships exhibit equality? What do you think of his handling of homosexuality and heterosexuality in the future?
- Why does the war with the Taurans begin? Why does it last so long? Were you surprised by its finish?
- What factors contribute most to Mandella's alienation? Loss of family? Becoming a killer? The death of his comrades? Extreme jumps in technology? Something else?
- Which concepts in this novel have aged well? Which have not?
- Does the novel have a happy ending? Would you prefer something different?

SUGGESTED READING IF YOU LIKE *THE FOREVER WAR*

Robert Buettner	Jason Wander series, starting with *Orphanage*
Jack Campbell	The Lost Fleet series, starting with *Dauntless*
Joe Haldeman	*Forever Free*
Robert Heinlein	*Starship Troopers*
John Scalzi	*Old Man's War*; *The Ghost Brigades*; *The Last Colony*
John Steakley	*Armor*

Frank Herbert

Dune

ABOUT THE AUTHOR

Born in Washington in 1920, Frank Herbert was a bright child and knew from an early age that he wanted to be a writer. His independence made him an indifferent student and worker. His second wife Beverly supported him through many years of failure before *Dune* became a success. Published in 1968, it is now perhaps science fiction's most beloved novel. Beverly succumbed to cancer in 1984. Herbert's death followed in 1986. The father of three children, Herbert's oldest son Brian is also a well-known science fiction novelist, who continues to write books set in the <u>Dune</u> universe.

PLOT SUMMARY

The ongoing battle between the Houses of Atreides and Harkonnen leads to the near destruction of the Atreides on the desert planet of Arrakis. Hidden by the desert Fremen, and with help from his mother Jessica, a Bene Gesserit witch, young Paul Atreides plots revenge against the Harkonnens and the Padishah Emperor who allowed their treachery. He rises to the roles of the Lisan Al-Gaib, leader of the Fremen jihad, and the foretold Kwisatz Haderach, the first male Bene Gesserit whose powers will change the world forever. *Dune* mixes adventure, religion, politics, and ecology in an exciting blend.

    Publication Date: 1965

    516 p.

ONLINE DISCUSSION

http://www.lambdasf.org/lsf/books/bookdisc/dune.html

AUTHOR'S WEBSITE

http://www.dunenovels.com

OTHER INTERNET RESOURCES

Usul's Homepage
http://www.usul.net
Dune FAQ
http://www.faqs.org/faqs/sf/dune-faq

APPEAL POINTS

Dune has been described as the pinnacle of "soft" science fiction, meaning that it focuses less on technology and more on sociology, theology, politics, and human relations. The novel's complex politics, large cast of characters, philosophical tone, and tricky vocabulary may daunt some readers but richly reward others. Strong themes of coming of age, ecology, and mysticism appeal to certain readers. Herbert's language is more literary than is typical for science fiction, often achieving a loftiness of tone that draws comparisons to _The Lord of the Rings_.

DISCUSSION QUESTIONS

- _Dune_ is now over 40 years old. Does it hold up, or is it becoming dated?
- How does the climate of Arrakis shape the people who live there?
- Many forces and role models shape Paul Atreides. Can you identify how specific parts of his genetics, training, and experience create the man he finally becomes?
- Many pairs invite comparison in _Dune_. Contrast the methods and philosophies of the following: the Harkonnens and the Atreides, Paul and Feyd-Rautha, the Sardaukar and the Fremen, and the Bene Gesserit and the mentats.
- What do you think of Herbert's portrayal of gender relations? Of families?
- In reality, would the plotting and assassination attempts of the novel be more likely to produce people like the Harkonnens or like the Atreides? Can you see historical parallels?
- How important is the spice to _Dune_? What does it do to those who take it? How has it affected the novel's universe?
- Is charismatic leadership ultimately good or evil in this novel?
- Has _Dune_ shaped the course of science fiction, or is it a wonderful anomaly?
- Do modern political events change the way in which you interpret the Fremen and their progress toward jihad?
- Are either the film or miniseries adaptations of _Dune_ successful? Why or why not?

SUGGESTED READING IF YOU LIKE _DUNE_

Brian Aldiss	Helliconia trilogy, starting with _Helliconia Spring_
Isaac Asimov	Foundation series
Frank Herbert	_Dune Messiah_ and other sequels
George Lucas et al.	Star Wars series
Kim Stanley Robinson	Mars series, starting with _Red Mars_

Kay Kenyon

Bright of the Sky

ABOUT THE AUTHOR

Kay Kenyon has been a professional writer since the age of 18, when she got her first television copywriting job. She also acted in television commercials, but she quit acting upon the successful publication of her first novel. She and her husband split time between two small communities in Washington state and southern California. When she isn't writing, she's fond of riding her motorbike and spoiling her cat.

PLOT SUMMARY

Titus Quinn is a former pilot, who claims to have been thrown into another world where he lost his wife and daughter. Quinn's claim isn't helped by the fact that he cannot remember the details of his visit. He's considered delusional until an artificial intelligence uncovers the likelihood of just such a universe in a dimension next door to ours. The Minerva Corporation sends Quinn back to the other dimension to map new pathways for their commercial routes through the universe, but he's really in search of his lost loved ones (and protecting his remaining family from Minerva's dark influence). The universe that he discovers, The Entire, is a strange land, where the sky is always bright and the godlike Tarig (who look like giant mantises) rule over a Mandarin-like culture. Overmatched in every aspect except for his wits, and assuming a false identity, Quinn must stay alive while discerning allies from enemies as memories of his first visit to the Entire slowly return.

Publication Date: 2007

453 p.

AUTHOR'S WEBSITE

http://www.kaykenyon.com

APPEAL POINTS

Kenyon blends science fiction trappings with a story that reads like a heroic, alternate-world fantasy quest. In style, the book hearkens back to the planetary romances of early science fiction. Quinn is an appealing hero (although a few readers may find him, beyond his eccentric personality, to be too infallible). The worldbuilding is marvelous: Kenyon populates her Entire with an interesting culture and a plethora of unusual creatures. There is plenty of romance and family drama thrown into the mix, which should appeal to readers who need emotional weight. The scientific trappings of the story are used primarily as window dressing: this is probably not the series for readers who only like hard science fiction. Although the novel reaches a satisfying conclusion, many loose ends require readers to continue further in the series for full resolution.

DISCUSSION QUESTIONS

- Should Quinn's loyalties lie primarily with his wife and daughter, his remaining brother's family, or his new loved ones, such as Anzi? Is he honor-bound to protect his home universe, or should the needs of The Entire factor into his decisions?
- Which of Kenyon's invented beings and creatures catch your attention most?
- Who would you cast in the major roles in a film of *Bright of the Sky*?
- Many enemies stand in Quinn's way. Which do you think is ultimately the most dangerous to his mission?
- Why do you suppose Cixi supports Sydney, but not her father? What will become of Sydney and Mo Ti? Will Quinn and his daughter be reunited?
- What scenes or sequences from the book will stay with you?
- Is the culture of The Entire evil and corrupt, or simply different than that of our own?
- Are you able to suspend disbelief about the scientific underpinnings of the world that Kenyon creates? Do you care? Is this more fantasy or science fiction?
- Can Quinn be forgiven for his murder of Small Girl? What price will he have to pay for this crime? Is Quinn a hero?
- What will happen next in the series? Will you continue reading?

SUGGESTED READING IF YOU LIKE *BRIGHT OF THE SKY*

Edgar Rice Burroughs	Barsoom series, starting with *A Princess of Mars*
C. J. Cherryh	Foreigner Universe, starting with *Foreigner*
Stephen R. Donaldson	Chronicles of Thomas Covenant, starting with *Lord Foul's Bane*
Kay Kenyon	More of The Entire and the Rose, starting with *A World Too Near*
Rosemary Kirstein	*The Steerswoman's Road*
Julian May	*The Many-Colored Land*
Andre Norton	Witchworld series, starting with *The Gates to Witchworld*

Ursula K. Le Guin

The Dispossessed

ABOUT THE AUTHOR

Ursula Le Guin was born to a psychologist/writer mother and anthropologist father in 1929. Educated at Radcliffe and Columbia, she writes novels, short stories, essays, and poetry. Her work spans genres—including SF, fantasy, historical fiction, and literary works—and age groups—with books for adults, young adults, and children. She is one of our most decorated writers, with five Hugos and six Nebulas among her awards. Although very private, Le Guin has been an effective activist for causes from social justice to anti-war movements, from women's rights to respect for genre writing and ethnic diversity in fiction. She is a dedicated Taoist. Married to the historian Charles Le Guin, she lives in Portland, Oregon, and has three children and four grandchildren.

PLOT SUMMARY

Shevek, a gifted physicist, becomes the first person to return from the anarchist world of Anarres to the home world Urras in over a hundred years. The book alternates between two timelines. A historical timeline following Shevek's life on Anarres shows his development as a scientist, as a father and partner, and the convictions that lead him to visit Urras. A second timeline follows his visit to Urras, where capitalist and communist nations battle for control, his presence creates a stir in society, and the benefits of his science are in high demand. Ultimately, Shevek returns to Anarres with the help of Terrans (future Earth) and Hainish. The book ends ambiguously, with Shevek about to disembark on a home world that may not allow his return.

    Publication Date: 1974

    387 p.

READER'S GUIDE

http://www.wsu.edu/~brians/science_fiction/dispossessed.html

AUTHOR'S WEBSITE

http://www.ursulakleguin.com/

APPEAL POINTS

The Dispossessed places a comparison of anarchist, republican, and communist political systems in the personal context of one man's life. Thus, it appeals to those who are interested in politics or great characters, but less to those who read science fiction for science, technology, and action. It's easy for the reader to identify with the protagonist and wonder how he or she would respond if faced with the many choices that Shevek encounters. Le Guin uses a complex timeline, following Shevek in both past and present, a format that makes the novel difficult at first, but highly suspenseful as it progresses. The ending is highly ambiguous, which pleases readers who like to speculate but frustrates those who prefer a firm conclusion.

DISCUSSION QUESTIONS

- Do you find the alternating chapters effective in building suspense? What do you most want to discover about Shevek's past? About what would happen to him in the present?
- How do the events of Shevek's youth affect his later decisions?
- For a novel set far in the future, have science and technology advanced significantly? Does this have any impact on your enjoyment of the novel?
- Why does Shevek decide to visit Urras? Why does he return to Anarres?
- What does this book have to say about the importance of family? Of community?
- Le Guin's subtitle calls Anarres an "ambiguous utopia." In what ways is it utopian? In what ways is it not?
- Compare the histories of Terra (Earth) and Urras. Are there any major differences?
- Should Le Guin have used a female protagonist? How would this change the book?
- What does the evolution of society on Annares say about the ability of people to act with complete freedom?
- In which of the book's societies would you most like to live?
- What will happen to Shevek? To the societies that he encounters?

SUGGESTED READING IF YOU LIKE *THE DISPOSSESSED*

Ursula K. Le Guin	*The Lathe of Heaven*
Ursula K. Le Guin	*The Left Hand of Darkness*
Marge Piercy	*Woman on the Edge of Time*
Kim Stanley Robinson	Mars trilogy, starting with *Red Mars*
Kim Stanley Robinson	*Pacific Edge*
B. F. Skinner	*Walden Two*
Yevgeny Zamyatin	*We*

Richard K. Morgan

Thirteen

ABOUT THE AUTHOR

Born in 1965, Richard Morgan studied political history at Queens' College, Cambridge. After graduating, he taught English as a way to travel, making long stops in Istanbul, Glasgow, and Madrid. While teaching, he worked on his writing until *Altered Carbon*, his first science fiction novel featuring detective Takeshi Kovacs, was published in 2002. The success of that book allowed him to become a full-time writer. He has published five science fiction novels, two graphic novels, and will publish the first book in a fantasy trilogy in 2008.

PLOT SUMMARY

Thirteen (published as *Black Man* in Britain) is the dystopian near-future story of Carl Marsalis, an antiheroic bounty hunter. Marsalis is a genetic variant known as a "thirteen," a return to the hunter-gatherer, bred for aggression and military capacity, but then abandoned as too dangerous in a world that wants to pretend it has found peace. He's employed by the United Nations (UN) on contracts to hunt down and kill other thirteens. When he lands in a Florida prison after a mission (civil war has divided the United States into fundamentalist Jesusland, the UN-aligned North Atlantic Union, and the technology-focused Pacific Rim), Marsalis is bailed out by COLIN officials to help them hunt a thirteen who escaped Mars by brutally murdering everyone on a spaceship and crash-landing it in the ocean. The investigation leads Marsalis and two COLIN security officers, Sevgi Ertekin and Tom Norton, on a harrowing, violent, and twisty trip around the world.

Publication Date: 2007

560 p.

AUTHOR'S WEBSITE

http://www.richardkmorgan.com

APPEAL POINTS

Thirteen blends dystopian science fiction and the hard-boiled detective novel. Morgan writes in a highly descriptive, slowly building style that pleases patient readers. His near future is dark and unhappy, but highly plausible and brimming with interesting ideas. Morgan examines complex issues such as the nature/nurture debate and racism in the context of an action thriller. This book definitely gets an "R" rating for graphic violence, gritty, profane language, and even a few sex scenes. Along the way, the reader should expect plenty of twists and turns, a touch of moving, bittersweet romance, and stoic but thoughtful tough-guy heroics.

DISCUSSION QUESTIONS

- The British title for *Thirteen* is *Black Man*. In what senses is he black? Which status, being black or being a thirteen, is more important to Marsalis's isolation in the world? Which title is better?

- What characteristics does *Thirteen* share with hard-boiled detective fiction? How is it different?

- Do you find Morgan's vision of the future Earth believable? Would you make a different prediction for our future? Is this book entirely about the future, or has much of its vision already occurred?

- What do you think of Morgan's philosophical take on male and female natures? Is this a sexist novel?

- What is the irony of Morgan's version of space colonization? Why is the Mars of his future so undesirable?

- In the end, what separates Marsalis from Merrin or Onbekend? From Ren? Are thirteens controlled by their genetic nature, their nurturing, or something else?

- Who, in the end, is Marsalis's biggest enemy?

- Who is more damaged in the novel, the "normal" humans or the "variant" thirteens?

- What accounts for the closeness of the bond between Marsalis and Sevgi Ertekin? In alternate circumstances, could their relationship survive?

- Do you like the ending of the book? Do you have any questions about what will happen next, or are you certain of the result?

SUGGESTED READING IF YOU LIKE *THIRTEEN*

Neal Asher	*Gridlinked*
Philip K. Dick	*Do Androids Dream of Electric Sheep?* (*Blade Runner*)
William Gibson	*Neuromancer*; *Count Zero*
Jonathan Lethem	*Gun, with Occasional Music*
Richard K. Morgan	Takeshi Kovacs series, starting with *Altered Carbon*
Haruki Murakami	*Hard-Boiled Wonderland and the End of the World*

Audrey Niffenegger

The Time Traveler's Wife

ABOUT THE AUTHOR

Born in Michigan in 1963, Audrey Niffenegger is a writer and artist. She also works as a professor of Interdisciplinary Book Arts, teaching writing to visual artists, handset printing, lithography, and book making. After her bestselling first novel, she published two graphic novels. Among her visual influences, she lists Aubrey Beardsley, Joseph Cornell, Goya, and Kathe Kollwitz. A new novel, *Her Fearful Symmetry*, arrives in 2009. Writing influences include Richard Powers, Rainer Maria Rilke, Henry James, and Edgar Allan Poe. She lives in Chicago.

PLOT SUMMARY

Henry DeTamble, a Chicago librarian, has a problem: a genetic disorder causes him to come "unstuck" in time. At random times, but especially under stress, Henry travels to times in his past or future, arriving awkwardly without any clothing. The novel is the story of Henry's life with Clare Abshire, an artist, whom he meets first in 1991, when she has known him since age six, but he has never seen her before (a paradox explained in the course of the novel). Following them through their unusual courtship, marriage, and the foreshadowing of future events, the novel is, at core, a tragic romance, as Henry is unable to make any changes to history, including his own.

    Publication Date: 2003

    525 p.

READER'S GUIDE

http://www.readinggroupguides.com/guides3/time_travelers_wife1.asp

AUTHOR'S WEBSITE

http://www.audreyniffenegger.com

OTHER INTERNET RESOURCES

The Time Traveler's Wife Forum
http://tttw.conforums.com/index.cgi
The Novel's Timelines
http://youknowjack.fivewells.com/archives/2006/01/time_travelers.html

APPEAL POINTS

The Time Traveler's Wife is a book for classic romantics. It takes the science fiction staple of time travel and uses it to explore tragic but beautiful love in the face of the impending ravages of time and death. That said, this is not a traditional romance, and most men enjoy it as much as women. Other appeals include the strong use of Chicago settings, the dangerous-yet-comic aspect of Henry's time trips, and interesting relationship dilemmas that are exacerbated by Henry's time travel but very much like those faced by other couples.

DISCUSSION QUESTIONS

- How are the concepts of waiting, anticipating, and longing developed in the novel? Do regular relationships face similar challenges?
- Is Clare and Henry's relationship healthy or unhealthy?
- Is the explanation for Henry's time travel satisfying? In general, is it necessary for writers to provide a plausible scenario for speculative events? Should science fiction readers, in particular, ever be satisfied by explanations that don't fit the laws of science?
- How is Henry's character shaped by chrono-displacement? Do you find his reaction to his dilemma convincing? What about Clare's reaction?
- What do you think of Henry's encounters with himself? If you could visit yourself at a younger time, would you do so? What would you say to your past self?
- Is Henry's time travel a gift or a curse?
- How does Henry and Clare's longing for a child affect their relationship? How does a child change their relationship?
- How are Henry and Clare's careers affected by their life experience?
- Compare this to other time-travel stories. How do the means of travel differ? The traveler's ability to affect history? The direction of travel? The ability to take along objects? The possibility of meeting oneself?
- A movie of *The Time Traveler's Wife* stars Eric Bana and Rachel McAdams. Who would you cast in the lead roles? Is Hollywood likely to get the tone of such a story right?

SUGGESTED READING IF YOU LIKE *THE TIME TRAVELER'S WIFE*

Charles Dickinson	*A Shortcut in Time*
Jack Finney	*Time and Again*
Ken Grimwood	*Replay*
Alice Sebold	*The Lovely Bones*
Donna Tartt	*The Secret History*
Connie Willis	*To Say Nothing of the Dog*

Larry Niven and Jerry Pournelle

Lucifer's Hammer

ABOUT THE AUTHORS

Born in Los Angeles in 1938, Larry Niven graduated from Washburn University in 1962 with a degree in mathematics, but he quickly gave up work in that field for full-time writing. On his own, he is best known for books set in his Known Space universe, especially the series starting with *Ringworld*, which won the Hugo and Nebula awards. His ideas about the Ringworld have been influential to real scientists.

Jerry Pournelle was born in Shreveport, Louisiana, in 1933 and served as an artillery officer in the Korean War. He has had careers in politics (executive assistant to the mayor of Los Angeles; campaign manager for Barry Goldwater and others), military and aerospace strategy (co-writer of military textbooks; operations research at Boeing and Rockwell; founding president of the Pepperdine Research Institute), and science fiction writing (mostly in collaboration with Niven). He served a term as president of the Science Fiction and Fantasy Writers of America.

PLOT SUMMARY

When Tim Hamner first sights the Hamner-Brown comet, the odds are millions-to-one against it hitting Earth; scientists and astronauts can't wait to study the close-passing comet. But those odds keep shrinking, and ultimately the comet, renamed the Hammer, "calves" off large pieces that slam into locations around the globe, setting off enormous earthquakes, tidal waves, and a new ice age. This novel follows various Californians with connections to the comet before its fall through the travails of life afterward. Most of them head for the mountain ranch of a U.S. senator. These inhabitants of the "Stronghold" must make difficult choices to survive the upcoming winter in a world full of refugees, with little food, rapidly dwindling technology, and a growing cannibal army run by street gangs, renegade soldiers, and religious fanatics.

Publication Date: 1977
494 p.

AUTHOR WEBSITES

Known Space: The Future Worlds of Larry Niven (Fan Site)
http://www.larryniven.org
Jerry Pournelle's Chaos Manor
http://www.jerrypournelle.com

APPEAL POINTS

This disaster tale balances action, science, and characterization. The first third builds pressure slowly, but once the Hammer hits, pages fly by quickly. With a broad cast of characters and many competing plots, this novel pleases most readers, but may confuse a few who like simpler plots. Niven and Pournelle's characters are good for science fiction, but they do write men better than women. Some may find their views of race and gender relations dated. Despite the rebuilding that faces Earth's survivors at the end of the novel, the book reaches a rousing conclusion that pleases those who prefer strong resolutions.

DISCUSSION QUESTIONS

- Some 30 years after publication, how well does this novel hold up?
- Which story lines do you find most fascinating? Which seem superfluous?
- Do you find the authors' portrayal of the disaster's aftermath convincing on an emotional level? In its science? In sociopolitical terms?
- What personality traits, skills, or occupations would be most useful in the event of such a disaster? How would your own skill set fare?
- Which of Maureen Jellison's suitors should she pursue?
- Is Alim Nassor entirely a villain? If so, what makes him a villain?
- Is the authors' portrayal of race relations believable, inaccurate, or offensive? Why? What about their portrayal of women?
- How would you prepare for an asteroid strike? Would any preparations matter?
- What do you think of Dan Forrester's stockpile? Would knowledge become as valuable, or as scarce, in the event of such an emergency as it did in *Lucifer's Hammer*?
- Do extreme circumstances justify changes in what we view as right or wrong? Which of the novel's "unethical" actions can be justified by the circumstances? Dynamiting roads and dams? Refusal to help refugees? The decisions of the scout troops? Cannibalism?

SUGGESTED READING IF YOU LIKE *LUCIFER'S HAMMER*

Octavia Butler	*Parable of the Sower*; *Parable of the Talents*
Pat Frank	*Alas, Babylon*
Larry Niven and Jerry Pournelle	*Footfall*
S. M. Stirling	Dies the Fire series, starting with *Dies the Fire*
Walter Jon Williams	*The Rift*

Alastair Reynolds

Revelation Space

ABOUT THE AUTHOR

Born in Wales in 1966, Alistair Reynolds grew up in the ruins of Britain's coal country. After earning a PhD in astronomy from St. Andrews in Scotland, he spent 16 years working in the Netherlands for the European Space Agency. He published his first novel, *Revelation Space*, in 2000 and as of 2008 had published a total of eight books, most set in the same well-imagined universe. A full-time writer since 2004, he returned to Wales in 2008. Reynolds is married, enjoys old films, classic rock, birding, and horseback riding.

PLOT SUMMARY

Archaeologist Dan Sylveste, a man with a complicated past dominated by his visit to the Revelation Space of the mysterious and powerful Pattern Jugglers, must cope with a barrage of political flak to continue his research into the extinction of the Amarantin species on the remote planet Resurgam. Meanwhile, on a vast but mostly empty spaceship, *Nostalgia for Infinity*, weapons officer Ilia Volyova must cope with a gunnery officer gone insane, the machinations of fellow crew members, a captain whose implants are infected (as is much of the ship) with a nanotech plague, and a set of mysterious weapons with planet-destroying capabilities. The ship picks up ex-soldier Ana Khouri to replace the gunnery officer and heads off in search of Sylveste and his father Calvin, who the crew members believe can repair the captain. Khouri, however, is an infiltrator, sent under duress by the mysterious Mademoiselle to assassinate Sylveste. On a final trip to the neutron star Hades and its orbiting planet Cerberus, Sylveste's past, the ancient Amarantin extinction, Volyova's weapons, Khouri's mission, and a mysterious stowaway, Sun Stealer, all come together in a fateful collision.

    Publication Date: 2000

    480 p.

AUTHOR'S WEBSITE

http://members.tripod.com/~voxish/

APPEAL POINTS

Reynolds mixes hard science fiction, space opera, and the gothic tradition in a challenging, atmospheric blend. His characters are more intriguing than most found in hard science fiction. Settings, particularly the mysterious expanse of the spaceship, are especially well done, evoking the haunted houses of Victorian gothic fiction. Action sequences come infrequently, but are well staged when they do. The author slowly reveals secret pasts, advanced technologies, hidden motives, and political factions, building suspense at a deliberate pace. The characters and their universe are complex: this is not for impatient or faint-hearted readers. Those familiar with science fiction tropes and who don't need quick gratification enjoy it most. It can serve as the introduction to Reynolds's <u>Revelation Space</u> universe, where themes and ideas recur, but lead characters change.

DISCUSSION QUESTIONS

- Are all of the novel's plotlines of equal interest, or are some more absorbing than others?
- Which of the future technologies in this book do you find the most intriguing?
- Who are the heroes and who are the villains in this story? For which characters do you find yourself rooting?
- A great deal of technology in this universe was created by earlier civilizations and is little understood by its current operators. Do you find this believable? Are there any analogs in current civilization?
- Are the implants that many characters employ ultimately a help or a hindrance to them?
- Do you find Reynolds's style absorbing and suspenseful, or difficult and slow?
- Could you handle the emotional isolation created by the slow-passing time of reefersleep and other conditions on the lighthugger ships?
- Are there elements of this universe that are still confusing at the end of the book? Do you think Reynolds's incomplete explanations are intentional?

  Will you continue the *Revelation Space* series?

SUGGESTED READING IF YOU LIKE *REVELATION SPACE*

Iain Banks	<u>Culture</u> series, beginning with *Consider Phlebas*
Stephen Baxter	<u>Manifold</u> trilogy, starting with *Manifold Time*
Peter F. Hamilton	<u>The Reality Dysfunction</u>, beginning with *Emergence*
Alistair Reynolds	Further works in the <u>Revelation Space</u> series, beginning with *Redemption Ark*, or the story collection *Galactic North*
Dan Simmons	<u>Hyperion</u> series, starting with *Hyperion*

Kim Stanley Robinson

Forty Signs of Rain

ABOUT THE AUTHOR

A native Californian, Kim Stanley Robinson is the author of 14 novels and 4 story collections to date. He is one of science fiction's most decorated writers, having won the Nebula, Hugo, Asimov, John W. Campbell, Locus, and World Fantasy Awards. His Mars Trilogy is considered his master work. Frequently addressing themes of environment, politics, justice, Buddhism, and what it is like to be a scientist, Robinson is considered a master of hard science fiction. Known for his utopian ideals, Robinson is a favorite with interviewers. An enthusiastic mountain climber in his spare time, Robinson lives in California with his chemist wife and two sons.

PLOT SUMMARY

A near-future thriller and first in a trilogy, *Forty Signs of Rain* follows a group of Washington, D.C., scientists and politicians through their work and social lives. Charlie Quibler works from home as a political advisor on environmental questions while he tends to his two boys. His wife Anna works for the National Science Foundation (NSF). Frank Vanderwal is working for a year with the NSF but longs to return home to San Diego. All three become acquainted with Buddhists from Khembalung, who are setting up an embassy in the United States to lobby for attention to the rising levels of global seas that threaten their tiny island nation of Tibetan refugees. As global warming worsens and climate change passes beyond a crucial tipping point, these characters find their lives on an intersecting course.

    Publication Date: 2004
    358 p.

APPEAL POINTS

Forty Signs of Rain is an unusual thriller—where action is secondary to character development and matters of scientific and political process. It carefully documents the daily work of scientists, particularly their attempts to survive within the U.S. political process. The novel's Washington D.C., political setting is well developed and believable. Robinson builds tension very slowly, but finishes the book with a flurry of exciting but disastrous events, leaving the reader primed to continue the series. Readers of a philosophical bent enjoy the interplay between characters and their different approaches to the practice of science.

DISCUSSION QUESTIONS

- Is this primarily science fiction? A thriller? A political novel?
- Does Robinson make a convincing case for the likelihood of climate change?

- What did you learn about the process of science from this novel? Does what you learned make you more optimistic or more pessimistic about the future?

- What do you think of Frank Vanderwal's attitude change? Do you find it believable? Do you like him better before or after his change of heart?

- In the book, it takes extreme events before climate change is taken seriously by politicians. Do you believe that humanity is doomed to learn only from tragedy, or can we make proactive solutions before crises occur?

- Do you agree with Rudra Cakrin's statement that "an excess of reason is itself a form of madness"?

- Are details of the characters' private lives (i.e., Charlie's challenges in caring for Joe, Frank's encounter with the woman in the elevator) distractions, or are they of a piece with the challenges that they face in work roles?

- A central theme of this book is balance. What examples of this theme do you find in the narrative?

- Some critics complain that this book does not stand on its own. Do you find its ending satisfying? Do you feel compelled to continue to the next book?

- What do you think will happen next in the series?

SUGGESTED READING IF YOU LIKE *FORTY SIGNS OF RAIN*

John Barnes	*Mother of Storms*
Michael Crichton	*State of Fear* (but only for a contrasting view)
Kim Stanley Robinson	*Fifty Degrees Below; Sixty Days and Counting*
Kim Stanley Robinson	Mars trilogy, starting with *Red Mars*
Bruce Sterling	*Heavy Weather*

Mary Doria Russell

The Sparrow

ABOUT THE AUTHOR

Mary Doria Russell was born to a drill sergeant father and navy nurse mother in Chicago in 1950. She earned a doctorate in biological anthropology and taught gross anatomy at Case Western Reserve University before she quit to take up full-time writing. Her five novels to date explore many traditional genres, such as science fiction, historical fiction, and the mystery, but with a very literary slant. *The Sparrow* has been used as the basis for an opera and is under option to become a motion picture. Russell lives in Cleveland with her husband, a son, a golden retriever, and a dachshund.

PLOT SUMMARY

In 2019, a musical signal is heard in space, and the Jesuit order quickly organizes a mission to investigate. The story is told in two alternating time frames. One is from the perspective of the mission members, as they plan the covert trip, reach Rakhat, and make contact with a simple alien race. The second is through flashbacks from the perspective of Father Emilio Sandoz, a linguist who was the only survivor of the mission and is now under inquest from the Jesuits regarding his actions on Rakhat. Sandoz returned to earth on a UN ship, which has now gone missing itself. As Sandoz's story unfolds, the reader is left to wonder at the limits of good intentions, our right to judge other cultures, and the extent of personal guilt in unpredictable circumstances.

> Publication Date: 1996
> 408 p.

READER'S GUIDE

http://www.readinggroupguides.com/guides_S/sparrow1.asp

AUTHOR'S WEBSITE

http://www.marydoriarussell.info

APPEAL POINTS

The Sparrow is a first-contact story that works on many levels: as dark space opera, as literary fiction, and as a theological treatise. The novel is populated with interesting, complex characters. Some readers may find it difficult to cope with the deaths of significant likable characters. This story appeals to anyone interested in linguistics, anthropology, moral philosophy, or theology, all of which are central to the plot. Some may find *The Sparrow* too dark, too violent, or too slowly paced for their liking, but most readers find this to be a compelling read.

DISCUSSION QUESTIONS

- The title of the book comes from Matthew 10:29–31, which says that not even a sparrow falls to earth without God's knowing of it. How does the title relate?
- Do you like the structure of the novel? Do you prefer the forward-looking or backward-looking timeline?
- Why does Russell pick Jesuits as the protagonists for her tale? Is their mission primarily undertaken in pursuit of theology, anthropology, or science?
- What historical parallels or literary allusions do you see in *The Sparrow*?
- Does the novel succeed as both science fiction and literary fiction? Does it appeal to readers of one style more than the other?
- Are the mistakes made by the members of the mission believable?
- If humans make contact with other cultures, do we have the right to judge the morality of the civilizations that we encounter?
- Is there tension between the degree of scientific and sociological advancement in the Jana'ata society? In your opinion, can one kind of advancement occur without the other?
- Are Sandoz and his colleagues following the will of God? Is his belief ultimately supporting or harmful to Sandoz?
- If the film of *The Sparrow* is made (it has been optioned for some time now), who should play the lead parts?
- Will you read *The Sparrow*'s sequel, *Children of God*?

SUGGESTED READING IF YOU LIKE *THE SPARROW*

James Blish	*A Case of Conscience*
Orson Scott Card	*Speaker for the Dead*
Ursula K. Le Guin	*The Left Hand of Darkness*
Ian McDonald	*Brasyl*
Mary Doria Russell	*Children of God*

John Scalzi

Old Man's War

ABOUT THE AUTHOR

Scalzi was born in 1969 in southern California. His first job after graduating from the University of Chicago was as film critic for the *Fresno Bee*, and he has been a working writer ever since. His writing jobs have included everything from corporate brochures to video game reviews to blogs. He contributed to many volumes of Uncle John's Bathroom Reader and the Rough Guide series. The success of *Old Man's War*, which was nominated for the Hugo Award and led to his win of the Campbell Award, has allowed him to focus on fiction. He has published five novels and one anthology to date. Scalzi lives in Bradford, Ohio, with his wife and daughter.

PLOT SUMMARY

On his seventy-fifth birthday, John Perry makes the decision that many citizens of Earth choose: he joins the Colonial Defense Forces (CDF). Nobody on Earth knows who the CDF is fighting or how it makes political decisions, but they know that it protects Earth and suspect that it can rejuvenate old bodies, a process otherwise unavailable. So Perry, like many others, leaves everything he knows behind (he can never return) and heads for the stars. He discovers that CDF soldiers indeed receive fantastic new bodies (although perhaps not in the way that they expect), but that his odds of surviving 10 years of enlistment are very slim. Fighting a wide array of aliens, Perry rises through the ranks, while watching friends die all around him. He's put to the ultimate test when battle with a foe possessing dangerously advanced technology leads him into contact with a female soldier who looks just like the dead wife he left behind on Earth.

    Publication Date: 2005

    316 p.

AUTHOR'S WEBSITE

http://www.scalzi.com

APPEAL POINTS

Old Man's War follows in the entertaining tradition of military science fiction, but with better character development, more humor, and more moral questioning than is typical of the subgenre. Some may find the characters, particularly the lead, to be too perfect, but Scalzi develops John Perry's personality quirks, relationships, and humor enough to make him a truly entertaining narrator. The variety of alien species depicted in the novel show good creativity, and the methods of the CDF in recruiting and building its soldiers introduce interesting dilemmas. This is a fast-paced, easy-to-read book that can still induce thought and stoke successful discussion.

DISCUSSION QUESTIONS

- Many compare Scalzi to Robert Heinlein as an author. Have you read Heinlein? If so, do you find the writers comparable?
- Which of the CDF improvements to the human body would you most like to have?
- A Mary Sue is a character who is a bit too perfect, used by authors and readers as a kind of wish fulfillment. Is John Perry a Mary Sue?
- What do old people bring to a war experience that young people wouldn't? Would someone with a life of experiences make a good soldier?
- Should the CDF soldiers be more concerned about the political systems for which they fight? Is the fact that they fight for humanity against aliens enough to justify any means to the end?
- What is the funniest scene in the novel?
- If you knew your odds of survival in advance, would you choose to undergo the procedure that CDF soldiers undergo at age 75?
- What exactly is the self? Does the process that CDF soldiers undergo transfer the same person to a new body, or is a new being created? What about ghost brigade soldiers?
- Which alien species do you find most interesting? Which would you most fear?
- Is the creation of the ghost brigades a moral choice? Why do you suppose the CDF chooses to implant specific personalities into the ghost brigades instead of using one personality for all of their soldiers?
- Will you continue forward in the series? Which question left open at the end of *Old Man's War* do you most want answered?

SUGGESTED READING IF YOU LIKE *OLD MAN'S WAR*

Jack Campbell	The Lost Fleet series, starting with *Dauntless*
Joe Haldeman	*The Forever War*
Robert Heinlein	*Starship Troopers*
Robert J. Sawyer	*Rollback*
John Scalzi	*The Ghost Brigades*; *The Last Colony*
David Weber	Honor Harrington series, starting with *On Basilisk Station*

Dan Simmons

Hyperion

ABOUT THE AUTHOR

Born in 1948 in Peoria, Illinois, Dan Simmons grew up in various Midwestern towns and took degrees from Wabash College in Indiana and Washington University in St. Louis. He taught elementary school and coordinated gifted and talented programs for 18 years. He published his first story in 1982 and became a full-time writer in 1987. Simmons is known for his diversity, having written successful science fiction, horror, literary fiction, historical fiction, and hard-boiled detective fiction. Simmons lives with his wife and family at the base of the Rockies in Colorado, where he does much of his writing in an isolated mountain cabin near Rocky Mountain National Park.

PLOT SUMMARY

Winner of the Hugo and Locus awards, *Hyperion* takes its structure from *The Canterbury Tales*: seven varied individuals are making a pilgrimage, each with a different purpose, to the planet Hyperion. As they travel, each tells the tale of why he or she has come. The tales are varied, each exploring a different aspect of science fiction: military SF from a soldier, cyberpunk noir from a detective character, a writer's tale and aesthetic pondering from a poet, religious anthropological SF from a priest, a time-travel conundrum from a scholar and father, a political and ecological tale from a planetary consul. These six pilgrims and the captain of the tree ship that carries them to Hyperion each seek something different from the Shrike, a mysterious and dangerous demon-god. All of this is set against the background of the 29th century, a time when humanity is under threat from within by powerful artificial intelligences, and without by the Ousters.

    Publication Date: 1989

    481 p.

AUTHOR'S WEBSITE

http://www.dansimmons.com

APPEAL POINTS

Simmons writes highly creative science fiction that is full of literary allusions. He's a challenging writer with a metaphysical style, but it isn't necessary to understand all of his references to appreciate his books. *Hyperion* plays on the conceit of Chaucer's *Canterbury Tales*: it's a set of pilgrims' tales, each told from a different perspective. This book serves as kind a primer to science fiction styles. Readers should see which tales they enjoy most and then pursue other books in the same style. Because the book is told from many perspectives, pacing is slow. It takes time to meet the characters, but once this introduction is accomplished, the tales are rewarding and the characters are deep and highly varied. Readers who seek a strong resolution should be forewarned that they need to continue to *The Fall of Hyperion*.

DISCUSSION QUESTIONS

- What literary allusions can you identify in *Hyperion*?
- Which of the pilgrims do you wish the most success in their encounter with the Shrike? Which do you find the least sympathetic?
- Do any of the stories within the story stand out to you? Is this because of style or because of content? Do you find any of the narrators unlikable? Are any of their stories tiresome?
- Do you ultimately care more about the big picture—the battles between Ousters and humanity, the development of the UI, and the mystery of the Shrike—or the tales of the individual pilgrims?
- The Shrike seems to twist fundamental human concepts—death, family, romance, and art—into horrors. How do you account for it? Is the Shrike a god or a devil? Evil or something more complex?
- What do you think of the datasphere that Simmons describes? Is this the likely future of computer networks and the Internet?
- How does Father Hoyt's tale relate to the idea of original sin? To the story of Christ? Or is it some kind of anthropological fable? What should Father Duré have done?
- Is Sol and Sarai Weintraub's experience with daughter Rachel more or less difficult than the death of a child?
- Who would you cast as the characters in a miniseries adaptation of *Hyperion*?
- Will you continue to *The Fall of Hyperion*? Why?

SUGGESTED READING IF YOU LIKE *HYPERION*

China Miéville	*Perdido Street Station*
Walter M. Miller, Jr.	*A Canticle for Leibowitz*
Kim Stanley Robinson	Mars trilogy, starting with *Red Mars*
Dan Simmons	*The Fall of Hyperion*
Dan Simmons	*Ilium*; *Olympos*

Neal Stephenson

Snow Crash

ABOUT THE AUTHOR

Stephenson was born in 1959 to a scientific family: both his parents and grandparents are scientists. He was raised in Illinois and Iowa, graduated from Boston University, and now lives in Seattle. He pursued a degree in geography, mostly because it gave him time on his university's mainframe computer, but after graduation he turned to other pursuits. He has written novels in many styles: cyberpunk, neo-Victorian, eco-thriller, historical novels, and even an academic comedy. His work is concerned with subjects such as computers, the history of science, and economic systems. Stephenson contributes articles on the impact of technology to journals and magazines such as *Wired*. He's an advisor to Blue Origin, a private-sector space company.

PLOT SUMMARY

Full of dark comedy and satire, *Snow Crash* is set in an early 21st century dominated by a mix of anarchy and monolithic big business enclaves. Having lost his job delivering pizza for the Mafia, Hiro Protagonist decides to focus on other work: selling information to the Central Intelligence Corporation. On the prowl in the Metaverse (a more advanced version of the Internet), he witnesses the use of Snow Crash, a virus that wipes out data in the Metaverse and the minds of those connected to it in reality. This leads him (and Y. T., a smart-ass teenage girl skateboard courier) into a plot involving a huge raft of refugees who speak in tongues; a nuke-wielding, motorcycle-riding Aleut harpoon master named Raven; and the revival of an ancient Sumerian religious order that wants to use Snow Crash to fragment computer use in the same way that the Tower of Babel fragmented language.

    Publication Date: 1992
    470 p.

AUTHOR'S WEBSITE

http://www.nealstephenson.com

READER'S GUIDE

http://www.english.ucsb.edu/teaching/resources/unlocked/coursematerials/english_192/snow_crash_topics.asp

APPEAL POINTS

With smart-aleck humor, trend-setting use of techno-language, and youthful protagonists, *Snow Crash* is the perfect book for the Internet generation. With a samurai hero, Aleut villain, and hearty doses of Sumerian mythology, the book also incorporates a strong vein of mysticism. Exciting action sequences please those who think visually and those who like quick pacing. As is usual with Stephenson, political and sociological ideas underpin the action. Traditional readers may find *Snow Crash*'s humor, focus on technology, or use of jargon off-putting. One sexual encounter involving the young Y. T. offends some readers. *Snow Crash* is a good gateway to Stephenson's later work, which addresses similar themes but becomes increasingly complex.

DISCUSSION QUESTIONS

- Written in 1992, when the Internet was in its infancy, how prescient is *Snow Crash*?
- Compare Stephenson's Metaverse with current online sites such as Second Life. What separates our Internet from his future version?
- Hiro Protagonist and Y. T. are youthful in both age and attitude. Do you enjoy them as lead characters? Will young people play increasing roles in the future? Do they already?
- Stephenson paints a bleak history for the future of the United States, with the central government withered away and a few retail franchises battling for control. Are we headed in this direction? Is there anything positive in such a development?
- Which of *Snow Crash*'s humorous secondary characters and subplots are your favorites?
- Do you find the sexual encounter in *Snow Crash* inappropriate or off-putting?
- Is an interest in computers necessary to appreciate this novel? Can someone who doesn't use the Internet regularly grasp it fully?
- Some complain that *Snow Crash* bogs down in sections that focus on Sumerian mythology. Others find these sections fascinating. With which view do you side?
- What aspects of Stephenson's future world do you see mirrored in contemporary society?
- What did you think of Stephenson's connection of words and ideas with the concept of computer viruses? Is there anything to this thinking?

SUGGESTED READING IF YOU LIKE *SNOW CRASH*

Max Barry	*Jennifer Government*
Cory Doctorow	*Down and Out in the Magic Kingdom*
William Gibson	*Neuromancer*
Neal Stephenson	*Cryptonomicon*

S. M. Stirling

Dies the Fire

ABOUT THE AUTHOR

S. M. Stirling was born in France, has Canadian ancestry, and is now a naturalized U.S. citizen. He lives in New Mexico. He has written over 40 novels of science fiction and fantasy, including collaborations with such notables as Anne McCaffrey, David Drake, Raymond Feist, and Jerry Pournelle. His work often focuses on alternative history and military adventures. Stirling is interested in history, archaeology, anthropology, and the martial arts.

PLOT SUMMARY

On a day in March 1998, the world undergoes what comes to be called "the change," an event that stops electrical devices and turns explosions (such as those that propel bullets) into nothing more than fizzles. Without cars, computers, stores, and modern weapons (to name just a few), people are quickly thrown into a primitive state. Violence and disease rapidly become the norm. *Dies the Fire* follows the adventures of two groups: one led by pilot and former commando Mike Havel, and another led by Juniper Mackenzie, a Wiccan witch and folksinger. They need skill, luck, and masterful leadership to help their people survive the advances of The Protector, a former professor intent on turning Oregon into his own feudal state.

Publication Date: 2004

496 p.

AUTHOR'S WEBSITE

http://www.smstirling.com

APPEAL POINTS

Dies the Fire explores what would become of our world if we suddenly lost modern technologies and comforts. Readers enjoy puzzling out the challenges of this sudden change along with the characters. Many action scenes provide plenty of thrills and keep pages turning quickly. Some plot developments may strike some readers as too convenient. For the most part, characters in the book are simple: either clearly good or clearly evil, but they are given depth by the skills they practice and the beliefs they espouse. Archery, hand-to-hand combat, agriculture, horse riding, and construction are among the fields explored, as are different modes of leadership and government. The book also features some mild romance. The Wiccan religion is explained and promoted heavily in the book, a focus that interests some readers, bores others, and offends a few.

DISCUSSION QUESTIONS

- If such a catastrophe were to occur, do you think that the world would deteriorate as quickly as it does in this book?

- Does the author succeed in getting you to suspend disbelief and become involved in the story?
- Compare and contrast the approaches of the Bearkillers and Clan Mackenzie. Which is best organized for long-term survival?
- Readers have strong reactions to the Wiccan material in the novel. What do you think of it? Does the book dispel any myths that you might have had about witchcraft?
- Which of the book's characters is best adapted to the events of the change? Which would you want as your leader in such a situation?
- What modern conveniences would you miss most if you were caught in the novel's scenario?
- Should Mike get together with Signe or with Juniper?
- Do you find the author's attention to detail interesting or burdensome?
- What skills do you have that would be useful if you were thrown into a primitive state? Are there any skills that *Dies the Fire* either undervalues or overvalues?
- What would you speculate is the force behind the change? What will happen next in the series?

SUGGESTED READING IF YOU LIKE *DIES THE FIRE*

David Brin	*The Postman*
Octavia Butler	*Parable of the Sower*; *Parable of the Talents*
Eric Flint	*1632*
Pat Frank	*Alas, Babylon*
George R. Stewart	*Earth Abides*
S. M. Stirling	More from <u>The Change</u>, beginning with *The Protector's War*
S. M. Stirling	*Island in the Sea of Time*

Charles Stross

Halting State

ABOUT THE AUTHOR

Born in Leeds, England, in 1964, Charles Stross knew by the age of 6 that he wanted to write science fiction. Success, however, was intermittent, and he trained and worked as both a pharmacist and a computer scientist. A side job, writing a column about Linux, turned into full-time work as a freelance writer on technology and then reinvigorated Stross's career as a fiction writer. Since 2003, he has published 14 novels, with more on the way. Three of those novels—*Singularity Sky, Iron Sunrise,* and *Accelerando*—have been nominated for the Hugo Award.

PLOT SUMMARY

In Scotland, in the year 2018, a bank is robbed. What makes this theft unusual is that the bank resides in an online fantasy role-playing game, and the thieves invade and escape from another game. If Hayek Associates, a multimillion dollar company that contracts to maintain economic systems in several games, can't solve the problem, not only will it go out of business, but the stability of all such games will be compromised. Three narrators—a policewoman, an auditor, and a gaming expert—are brought in by various entities to solve the case. They soon discover that computer games and software companies are more than what they seem and that the survival of an entire networked world—communication, finance, transportation, law enforcement, and government—is at stake.

    Publication Date: 2007

    351 p.

AUTHOR'S WEBSITE

http://www.antipope.org/charlie

APPEAL POINTS

Halting State can be read as science fiction, as near-future thriller, or even as a crime novel. Stross's vision of 2018 brims with believable changes in the conduct of everyday life. Some are exciting, some scary, and many are a combination of both. Anyone with interest in gadgets, gaming, computer networking, or security is fascinated. There are elements of mystery and romance. The plot of the story is fun and fast-paced, but some find the ending abrupt. The book is self-contained: no prequels or sequels. Stross has an over-the-top, jargon-filled style, with unusual language that often soars but can occasionally confuse. Readers who like great characters should enjoy some aspects of the three narrators but may find their personalities too similar.

DISCUSSION QUESTIONS

- What is the most exciting technological development in the book? The most frightening? The most life-changing?
- Do you prefer any one of the three narrators to the others?
- Have you tried online gaming or social communities? What was your experience like? How did it compare to the experience in the novel?
- Do you find Stross's jargon-filled style in this novel interesting, irritating, or confusing?
- Many people in this novel have alternate or false identities. Will the advance of technology increase or decrease this practice?
- Under what conditions would you ride in the automated vehicles predicted in *Halting State*?
- If they were available, would you use the implants and augmenting devices described in *Halting State*?
- Is this novel part of the cyberpunk genre?
- Will advancing technologies make us closer to other people and enhance communication, or will they leave us more isolated?
- What do you think of the use of regular people as unwitting spies in the novel's *Spooks* game? How real can alternate worlds become?
- Why is the novel called *Halting State*?

SUGGESTED READING IF YOU LIKE *HALTING STATE*

Philip K. Dick	*Do Androids Dream of Electric Sheep?* (*Blade Runner*)
Cory Doctorow	*Down and Out in the Magic Kingdom*
James Patrick Kelly and JohnKessel, eds.	*Rewired: The Post-Cyberpunk Anthology*
Ken MacLeod	*The Execution Channel*
Paul McAuley	*Whole Wide World*
Neal Stephenson	*Snow Crash*

Karen Traviss

City of Pearl

ABOUT THE AUTHOR

Originally from Portsmouth, Karen Traviss now lives in Wiltshire, England. After serving in the U.K. Army and the Royal Navy Auxiliary, then working as an advertising copywriter, a media liaison officer for the police, and a journalist in television and newspapers, she's now settled into the life of a full-time novelist. Her writing is best known in the U.S. market, where she broke through to success with *City of Pearl*, which was nominated for both the Campbell and Philip K. Dick awards. Five more books in the Wess'Har series have followed. Traviss also writes tie-in novels in the Star Wars universe for LucasFilm.

PLOT SUMMARY

On the eve of retirement from the Environmental Hazard police, Shan Frankland agrees on a 150-year mission to Cavanagh's Star. She awakes from cryogenic travel to find herself in charge of a small team, but unclear about her mission because of a suppressed briefing—a biological block that only allows memory of the information she was given as need requires. Three sentient species inhabit the planet: a small human religious colony, descended from travelers who left Earth long ago; a native aquatic species called the Bezeri; and the Wess'Har, a matriarchal species whose technology far outpaces that of Earth. The Wess'Har are represented by Aras, a caretaker quarantined on the planet because he is infected by a parasite that makes him nearly invulnerable by selecting the best genetic traits from each species that he encounters. Respectful of the rights of even the simplest creatures, the Wess'Har destroyed the cities of an invasive species, the Isenj. Shan must balance the needs of her mysterious mission with the rebelliousness of the scientists under her command, her growing friendship with Aras, and a new Isenj invasion.

    Publication Date: 2004

    392 p.

AUTHOR'S WEBSITE

http://www.karentraviss.com

APPEAL POINTS

Traviss's style balances well-developed characters, suspenseful plotting, and a story that brings up many interesting ethical dilemmas. It is thought-provoking without becoming ponderous, exciting without an overabundance of action, and scientifically stimulating but not difficult. Environmentalists and vegetarians find much to embrace, and women appreciate the strong lead, Shan Franklin. Readers who prefer military solutions to interspecies diplomacy may find a clear challenge to their beliefs. Although the book leaves some issues unresolved, readers who don't want to continue with the series can stop here with satisfaction.

DISCUSSION QUESTIONS

- Do you find the author's depiction of the 23rd century to be convincing? Is her future Earth more or less developed than you predict?
- Does Shan Franklin make any mistakes in the leadership of her mission?
- Is the c'naatat ultimately a boon or a danger to those who encounter it?
- Do you find devices such as the suppressed briefing and Aras's secretiveness an enjoying source of suspense, or do you want the author to spill the beans a little faster?
- With full knowledge of the worlds and species they encounter, would humans prove to be more like the Wess'Har or more like the Isenj? If we do make contact with other species, do you think that we are likely to be more or less advanced than they are?
- Would you commit to space travel, knowing that most of the people you know would be gone by the time that you returned?
- Is Traviss fair in her depiction of the scientists? Are these typical scientists?
- Why are Shan and Aras so compatible?
- Does this book make you think differently about the utility of implant technology?
- Who would you cast in the major roles in a film of this novel? Would it work as a movie?

SUGGESTED READING IF YOU LIKE *CITY OF PEARL*

C. J. Cherryh	Foreigner series, starting with *Foreigner*
Ursula K. Le Guin	*The Dispossessed*
George R. R. Martin	*Tuf Voyaging*
Kristine Kathryn Rusch	The Retrieval Artist series, starting with *The Disappeared*
Karen Traviss	More titles in the Wess'Har series, starting with *Crossing the Line*

100 MORE RECOMMENDED SCIENCE FICTION AUTHORS AND BOOKS FOR DISCUSSION

Here are 100 more authors whose work provides a worthwhile reading group experience. For each, a book is suggested that is in print as of this writing (a factor that, sadly, takes many writers off the list) and that makes a good entry point to discussion of the author's work. When that book is part of a series, the series name is provided, but, for time considerations, most groups should assign only one book at a time. Even with a list this long, the great science fiction authors are nowhere near exhaustion. In particular, three kinds of books—older SF classics, young adult SF, and literary fiction crossovers—are little represented on this list. If your group enjoys these fruitful areas of the genre, please refer to related lists in Chapter 5.

Author	Book or Series to Try First
Douglas Adams	*The Ultimate Hitchhiker's Guide* omnibus
Catherine Asaro	Saga of the Skolian Empire, starting with *Catch the Lightning*
Isaac Asimov	Foundation series, starting with *Foundation*
Margaret Atwood	*The Handmaid's Tale*
J. G. Ballard	*The Complete Stories of J. G. Ballard*
Iain M. Banks	*The Player of Games*
Max Barry	*Jennifer Government*
Stephen Baxter	*The Time Ships*
Elizabeth Bear	Jenny Casey, starting with *Hammered*
Alfred Bester	*The Stars My Destination*
Ben Bova	*Jupiter*
Ray Bradbury	*The Martian Chronicles*
David Brin	Uplift Saga, starting with *Sundiver*
Tobias Buckell	Xenowealth Saga, starting with *Crystal Rain*
Lois McMaster Bujold	Vorkosigan Saga, starting with *Cordelia's Honor* omnibus
Anthony Burgess	*A Clockwork Orange*
Octavia Butler	*Lilith's Brood* omnibus
Ernst Callenbach	*Ecotopia*
Orson Scott Card	Ender Saga, starting with *Ender's Game*
C. J. Cherryh	Foreigner series, starting with *Foreigner*
Ted Chiang	*Stories of Your Life and Others*
Arthur C. Clarke	*Childhood's End*
Julie E. Czerneda	Web Shifters, starting with *Beholder's Eye*
Philip K. Dick	*The Three Stigmata of Palmer Eldritch* or other work from the *Four Novels of the 1960s* omnibus
Cory Doctorow	*Little Brother*
Harlan Ellison	*The Essential Ellison*
Philip Jose Farmer	Riverworld series, *To Your Scattered Bodies Go*
Eric Flint	Assiti Shards series, starting with *1632* (series has multiple writers)
Michael Flynn	*Eifelheim*
C. S. Friedman	Coldfire Trilogy, starting with *Black Sun Rising*
William Gibson	The Sprawl, starting with *Neuromancer*

Jon Courtenay Grimwood	<u>Arabesk</u> series, starting with *Pashazade*
Peter F. Hamilton	<u>Night's Dawn</u>, starting with *The Reality Dysfunction*
Harry Harrison	*A Stainless Steel Trio*
Robert Heinlein	*The Moon Is a Harsh Mistress*
Zenna Henderson	*Ingathering: The Complete People Stories of Zenna Henderson*
Aldous Huxley	*Brave New World*
Kazuo Ishiguro	*Never Let Me Go*
Matthew Jarpe	*Radio Freefall*
James Patrick Kelly	*Burn*
Daniel Keyes	*Flowers for Algernon*
Rosemary Kirstein	<u>Steerswoman</u>, starting with <u>*The Steerswoman's Road*</u> omnibus
Nancy Kress	<u>Sleepless</u> series, starting with *Beggars in Spain*
Ursula K. Le Guin	*The Lathe of Heaven*
Lois Lowry	*The Giver*
Ken MacLeod	<u>The Fall Revolution</u>, starting with *Fractions* omnibus
George R. R. Martin	*Hunter's Run* (with Daniel Abraham and Gardner Dozois)
David Marusek	*Counting Heads*
Jack McDevitt	<u>"Hutch" Hutchins</u> series, starting with *The Engines of God*
Ian McDonald	*River of Gods*
Paul Melko	*The Walls of the Universe*
Walter M. Miller, Jr.	*A Canticle for Leibowitz*
Elizabeth Moon	<u>Vatta's War</u>, starting with *Trading in Danger*
Alan Moore	*V for Vendetta*
Richard K. Morgan	<u>Takeshi Kovacs</u> series, starting with *Altered Carbon*
Linda Nagata	*Memory*
Larry Niven	<u>Ringworld</u> series, starting with *Ringworld*
George Orwell	*1984*
Marge Piercy	*Woman on the Edge of Time*
Frederik Pohl	<u>Heechee Saga</u>, starting with *Gateway*
Philip Reeve	<u>Hungry City Chronicles</u>, starting with *Mortal Engines*
Alastair Reynolds	*House of Suns*
John Ringo	<u>Posleen War</u> series, starting with *A Hymn before Battle*
Keith Roberts	*Pavane*
Kim Stanley Robinson	<u>Mars</u> series, starting with *Red Mars*
Justina Robson	*Natural History*
Rudy Rucker	<u>Postsingular</u> series, starting with *Postsingular*
Joanna Russ	*The Female Man*
Robert J. Sawyer	<u>The Neanderthal Parallax</u>, starting with *Hominids*
John Scalzi	*The Android's Dream*
Karl Schroeder	<u>Virga</u>, starting with *Sun of Suns*
Nevil Shute	*On the Beach*
Robert Silverberg	*Dying Inside*
Dan Simmons	*Ilium*; *Olympos*
Olaf Stapledon	*Star Maker*

John Steakley	*Armor*
Allen Steele	<u>Coyote</u> series, starting with *Coyote*
Neal Stephenson	*Cryptonomicon*
Bruce Sterling	*Schismatrix Plus*
Charles Stross	*Accelerando*
Theodore Sturgeon	*More than Human*
Sheri S. Tepper	*Grass*
Harry Turtledove	*Guns of the South*
John Varley	<u>Gaea</u> trilogy, starting with *Titan*
Jules Verne	*Twenty Thousand Leagues Under the Sea*
Vernor Vinge	<u>Queng Ho</u>, starting with *A Fire upon the Deep*
Kurt Vonnegut	*Slaughterhouse-Five*
Peter Watts	*Blindsight*
David Weber	<u>Honor Harrington</u> series, starting with *On Basilisk Station*
H. G. Wells	*The Time Machine*
Scott Westerfeld	<u>Succession</u> duology, starting with *The Risen Empire*
Kate Wilhelm	*Where Late the Sweet Birds Sang*
Walter Jon Williams	<u>Dread Empire's Fall</u>, starting with *The Praxis*
Connie Willis	*The Doomsday Book*
Robert Charles Wilson	*Spin*; *Axis*
Gene Wolfe	<u>Book of the New Sun</u>, starting with <u>*Shadow & Claw*</u> omnibus
John C. Wright	<u>Golden Age</u> series, starting with *The Golden Age*
John Wyndham	*The Day of the Triffids*
Yevgeny Zamyatin	*We*
Roger Zelazny	*Lord of Light*

Chapter 5
Themes for Speculative Fiction Discussion

A NOTE ON THEMATIC BOOK SELECTIONS

Whenever book groups use themes, some books fit the theme more closely than others. In practice, it works best to interpret the theme loosely. This gives readers more latitude in book selection and encourages discussion about the parameters of the theme. Thus, the selection of books for the themes that follow uses similar criteria. I've played as loosely with the theme as necessary to get a high-quality list of books that are indicative of the full scope of the theme. As I always tell my group, if you find other books that fit the theme, please feel free to use them.

Two further criteria have been applied to these selections. First, I have limited lists mainly to books that are in print at the time of this writing in order to emphasize contemporary writers and make it easy for readers to obtain books in a timely fashion. If your group has a strong preference for classic works or is especially good at obtaining out-of-print works in a timely fashion, you may want to amend the lists.

Second, the number of books that fit many of these themes is greater than the space that I can devote to the booklists. In such cases, I have selected a list of titles that represent the theme, provide a first-rate reading experience, and balance critical acclaim and reader popularity. If you think that I got the selection wrong, please debate it in your group!

In addition to thematic book groups, libraries are encouraged to use the lists that follow to create displays, booklists, and finding aids for readers.

ADAPTED INTO FILMS: SCREEN-WORTHY SPECULATIVE FICTION

We made a promise to ourselves at the beginning of the process that we weren't going to put any of our own politics, our own messages, or our own themes into these movies. What we were trying to do was analyze what was important to Tolkien and to try to honor that. In a way, we were trying to make these films for him, not for ourselves.

—Peter Jackson

When I tried to suggest the unwisdom of making radical changes to characters, events, and relationships which have been familiar to hundreds of thousands of readers all over the world for over thirty years, I was sent a copy of the script and informed that production was already under way.

—Ursula K. Le Guin on the adaptation of her Earthsea books

With a few delightful exceptions, films adapted from science fiction/fantasy novels generally emphasize special effects to the detriment of the story and characters, but the results can still be entertaining, eye-boggling fun. Adaptations make for delightful discussion, because many people have experienced the film, the book, or both and thus have shared moments to compare. Even if the adaptation is a mess, it's fun to discuss where the director went wrong. For added fun, serve popcorn and leave extra time to queue up the DVD player and show everyone's favorite scenes.

SUGGESTED WORKS

Douglas Adams	*The Hitchhiker's Guide to the Galaxy*
Richard Adams	*Watership Down*
Isaac Asimov	*I, Robot*
Margaret Atwood	*The Handmaid's Tale*
L. Frank Baum	*The Wonderful Wizard of Oz*
Peter S. Beagle	*The Last Unicorn*
Holly Black and Tony DiTerlizzi	Spiderwick Chronicles, starting with *The Field Guide*
Pierre Boulle	*Planet of the Apes*
Ray Bradbury	*Fahrenheit 451*
Marion Zimmer Bradley	*The Mists of Avalon*
David Brin	*The Postman*
Anthony Burgess	*A Clockwork Orange*
Arthur C. Clarke	*2001: A Space Odyssey* (film came first)
Arthur C. Clarke	*2010*
Susan Cooper	*The Dark Is Rising*
Michael Crichton	*The Andromeda Strain*
Michael Crichton	*Jurassic Park*; *The Lost World*
Michael Crichton	*Eaters of the Dead*
Philip K. Dick	*Do Androids Dream of Electric Sheep* (later sold as *Blade Runner*)
Philip K. Dick	*A Scanner Darkly*
Michael Ende	*The Neverending Story*

Cornelia Funke	*Inkheart*
Neil Gaiman	*Stardust*
Neil Gaiman	*Coraline*
William Goldman	*The Princess Bride*
Steven Gould	*Jumper*
Robert Heinlein	*Starship Troopers*
Frank Herbert	*Dune*
Alice Hoffman	*Practical Magic*
Diana Wynne Jones	*Howl's Moving Castle*
Daniel Keyes	*Flowers for Algernon*
Stephen King	*The Stand*
Stanislaw Lem	*Solaris*
Ira Levin	*The Stepford Wives*
C. S. Lewis	*The Lion, the Witch, and the Wardrobe*; *Prince Caspian*
Sergei Lukyanenko	*Night Watch*; *Day Watch*
Richard Matheson	*I Am Legend*
Frank Miller	*300*
Alan Moore and David Lloyd	*V for Vendetta*
Alan Moore and Dave Gibbons	*Watchmen*
Cormac McCarthy	*The Road*
Audrey Niffenegger	*The Time Traveler's Wife*
George Orwell	*Animal Farm*
George Orwell	*1984*
Christopher Paolini	*Eragon*
Christopher Priest	*The Prestige*
Philip Pullman	*The Golden Compass*
J. K. Rowling	<u>Harry Potter</u>, starting with *Harry Potter and the Sorcerer's Stone*
Carl Sagan	*Contact*
Nevil Shute	*On the Beach*
Lemony Snicket	<u>A Series of Unfortunate Events</u>, starting with *The Bad Beginning*
Walter Tevis	*The Man Who Fell to Earth*
J. R. R. Tolkien	<u>*The Lord of the Rings*</u>
John Updike	*The Witches of Eastwick*
Jules Verne	*Journey to the Center of the Earth*
Jules Verne	*20,000 Leagues under the Sea*
Kurt Vonnegut	*Slaughterhouse-Five*
H. G. Wells	*The War of the Worlds*
H. G. Wells	*The Island of Dr. Moreau*
H. G. Wells	*The Time Machine*
Philip Wylie and Edwin Balmer	*When Worlds Collide*
John Wyndham	*The Day of the Triffids*

THEMATIC QUESTIONS

- On the whole, have science fiction/fantasy films done justice to the literature?
- Would science fiction and fantasy films be better if more were derived from and loyal to novels, or are the two media just too different for loyal adaptation to work?
- How is the film you watched different from the novel you read? Were changes necessary for transfer from one medium to the other, for purposes of length, or were they simply the creative choices of the filmmakers?
- Do you recommend reading the book or watching the film first? Why?
- What moment from the book were you most excited to see brought to a visual medium?
- Are there significant differences between the way you picture characters and places from the book in your mind and the way that they appear on film?
- What moment from the film most disappoints you as a depiction of the events of the novel?
- What work of speculative fiction most needs to be made into a film? If you were producing the project, who would you get to direct it? Who would you cast in the major roles?

RESOURCES

Internet Movie Database

http://www.imdb.com

Mid-Continent Public Library Based on the Book

http://www.mcpl.lib.mo.us/readers/movies

———————————

ALTERNATE HISTORIES: STITCHES IN TIME

History is merely a list of surprises. It can only prepare us to be surprised again.

—Kurt Vonnegut

A new future requires a new past.

—Eric Foner

Alternative history follows time's road until the author takes a fork—a ship displaced to a different time, a war won by the other side, or the intrusion of wizards in court politics, for instance. World War II, the U.S. Civil War, and the reign of British royals are the most popular for timeline tinkering, but authors ask "What if . . . ?" about almost every historic period and geographic location. The best alternate histories balance a tightrope between historical verisimilitude and an active imagination—maintaining a detailed sense of the period, but using judiciously applied speculation to play with political possibilities. When using this theme, your group can specify a particular era, place, or event, or you can leave the halls of history wide open.

SUGGESTED WORKS

Lou Anders, ed.   *Sideways in Crime*

Poul Anderson	*Time Patrol*
Taylor Anderson	<u>Destroyermen</u>, starting with *Into the Storm*
Kage Baker	<u>The Company</u> series, starting with *In the Garden of Iden*
John Birmingham	<u>Axis of Time</u>, starting with *Weapons of Choice*
Gillian Bradshaw	*Cleopatra's Heir*
Ernst Callenbach	*Ecotopia*
Orson Scott Card	<u>The Tales of Alvin Maker</u>, starting with *Seventh Son*
Michael Chabon	*The Yiddish Policeman's Union*
Susannah Clarke	*Jonathan Strange & Mr Norrell*
Robert Conroy	*1945*
Julie Czerneda, ed.	*ReVisions*
L. Sprague de Camp	*Lest Darkness Fall*
Philip K. Dick	*The Man in the High Castle*
Paul Di Filippo	*The Steampunk Trilogy*
Gardner Dozois and Stanley Schmidt, eds.	*Roads Not Taken*
Jasper Fforde	<u>Thursday Next</u>, starting with *The Eyre Affair*
Eric Flint and others	<u>Assiti Shards</u>, starting with *1632*
Stephen Fry	*Making History*
Randall Garrett	<u>Lord Darcy</u> omnibus
Nick Gevers and Jay Lake, eds.	*Other Earths*
William Gibson and Bruce Sterling	*The Difference Engine*
Kathleen Ann Goonan	*In War Times*
Thomas Harlan	<u>Oath of Empire</u>, starting with *The Shadow of Ararat*
Thomas Harlan	<u>Sixth Sun</u>, starting with *Wasteland of Flint*
Robert Harris	*Fatherland*
Alexander Irvine	*The Narrows*
Ben Jeapes	*The New World Order*
J. Gregory Keyes	<u>The Age of Unreason</u>, starting with *Newton's Cannon*
Mercedes Lackey, et al.	<u>Heirs of Alexandria</u>, starting with *The Shadow of the Lion*
Ian MacLeod	*The Light Ages*; *The House of Storms*
Paul Melko	*The Walls of the Universe*
Alan Moore and Dave Gibbons	*Watchmen*
Naomi Novik	<u>Dragon Temeraire</u>, starting with *His Majesty's Dragon*
Tim Powers	*The Anubis Gates*
Christopher Priest	*The Separation*
Adam Roberts	*Swiftly*
Keith Roberts	*Pavane*
Kim Stanley Robinson	<u>Capital Science</u> series, starting with *Forty Signs of Rain*
Kim Stanley Robinson	*The Years of Rice and Salt*
Robert J. Sawyer	<u>The Neanderthal Parallax</u>, starting with *Hominids*
S. M. Stirling	*The Domination*
S. M. Stirling	<u>Nantucket</u> series, starting with *Island in the Sea of Time*

S. M. Stirling	*Conquistador*
J. N. Stroyar	*The Children's War*; *A Change of Regime*
Harry Turtledove, ed.	*The Best Alternate History Stories of the 20th Century*
Harry Turtledove	*The Guns of the South*
Harry Turtledove	<u>Crosstime Traffic</u>, starting with *Gunpowder Empire*
Harry Turtledove	<u>Worldwar</u> series, starting with *In the Balance*
Harry Turtledove	<u>Settling Accounts</u>, starting with *Return Engagement*
Harry Turtledove	<u>Great War</u> series, starting with *American Front*
Harry Turtledove	<u>American Empire</u> series, starting with *Blood & Iron*
Harry Turtledove	<u>Videssos Cycle</u>, starting with *The Misplaced Legion*
Ann and Jeff VanderMeer	*Steampunk*
Jo Walton	*Farthing*; *Ha'Penny*; *Half a Crown*
Robert Charles Wilson	*Darwinia*
Jack Womack	*Terraplane*
Jack Womack	*Random Acts of Senseless Violence*

THEMATIC QUESTIONS

- At what point does your book diverge from history as we know it? To what historical changes does this divergence lead?
- Are the speculative elements jarring, or does the author blend them into the history well?
- Are the characters, their actions, and their beliefs appropriate for the era in which the book is set, or do they read more like modern people?
- Did you catch any anachronisms, or is the historical period captured with accuracy?
- What historical alternatives would you like to see explored in fiction? Which historical events have been overworked?

RESOURCES

UChronia: The Alternate History List

http://uchronia.net

ANCIENT AND MEDIEVAL WORLDS: GIVE 'EM AN OLD TIMES REVISION

The past: our cradle, not our prison; there is danger as well as appeal in its glamour. The past is for inspiration, not imitation, for continuation, not repetition.

—Israel Zangwill

The past is a foreign country; they do things differently there.

—L. P. Hartley

Once upon a time, it was difficult to find a work of fantasy fiction that was not set in medieval times. Recent trends favor more contemporary settings, but medieval and ancient world fantasies are still plentiful, whether set in alternate versions of our own historical world or in imagined lands with historical levels of technology. For some readers, it's just not a fantasy if it isn't set in this era. To enhance your experience, bring food for group members to eat with their hands, preferably meat, and a mug of mead or cider.

SUGGESTED WORKS

Joe Abercrombie	The First Law, starting with *The Blade Itself*
Justin Allen	*Slaves of the Shinar*
Poul Anderson	*Mother of Kings*
R. Scott Bakker	The Prince of Nothing, starting with *The Darkness That Comes Before*
Marion Zimmer Bradley	Avalon series, starting with *The Mists of Avalon*
Lois McMaster Bujold	Chalion series, starting with *The Curse of Chalion*
Jim Butcher	Codex Alera, starting with *The Furies of Calderon*
Jacqueline Carey	Kushiel series, starting with *Kushiel's Dart*
Sara Douglass	*Threshold*
Sara Douglass	The Troy Game, starting with *Hades' Daughter*
Sara Douglass	The Crucible series, starting with *The Nameless Day*
Dave Duncan	The King's Blades, starting with *The Gilded Chain*
Dave Duncan	Alchemist series, starting with *The Alchemist's Apprentice*
Kate Elliott	Crown of Stars, starting with *King's Dragon*
Catherine Fisher	Oracle Prophecies, starting with *The Oracle*
John Gardner	*Grendel*
David Gemmell	*Lion of Macedon*
David Gemmell	Troy series, starting with *Lord of the Silver Bow*
Mary Gentle	The Book of Ash, starting with *A Secret History*
Mary Gentle	Ilario, starting with *The Lion's Eye*
William Goldman	*The Princess Bride*
Jo Graham	*Black Ships*
Jo Graham	*Hand of Isis*
Thomas Harlan	Oath of Empire, starting with *Shadow of Ararat*
Lian Hearn	Tales of the Otori, starting with *Across the Nightingale Floor*
Robin Hobb	Farseer trilogy, starting with *Assassin's Apprentice*
Robert Holdstock	Merlin Codex, starting with *Celtika*
Cecelia Holland	Soul Thief series, starting with *The Soul Thief*
Barry Hughart	*Bridge of Birds*
Robert Jordan	The Wheel of Time, starting with *The Eye of the World*
Guy Gavriel Kay	*The Lions of Al-Rassan*
Guy Gavriel Kay	*A Song for Arbonne*
Guy Gavriel Kay	*Tigana*
David Keck	*In the Eye of Heaven; In a Time of Treason*
Greg Keyes	Kingdoms of Thorn and Stone, starting with *The Briar King*
Katherine Kurtz	Deryni series, starting with *Deryni Rising*
Mercedes Lackey	Valdemar, starting with *Arrows of the Queen*
Stephen Lawhead	Pendragon series, starting with *Taliesin*

Stephen Lawhead	Albion trilogy, starting with *The Paradise War*
Ursula K. Le Guin	Earthsea Chronicles, starting with *The Wizard of Earthsea*
Juliet Marillier	Saga of the Light Isles, starting with *Wolfskin*
Juliet Marillier	Sevenwaters trilogy, starting with *Daughter of the Forest*
George R. R. Martin	A Song of Ice and Fire, starting with *A Game of Thrones*
Sarah Micklem	*Firethorn*; *Wildfire*
Elizabeth Moon	*The Deed of Paksenarrion*
Tim Powers	*The Drawing of the Dark*
Terry Pratchett	*Pyramids*; *Small Gods*
Patrick Rothfuss	Kingkiller Chronicles, starting with *The Name of the Wind*
Brian Ruckley	The Godless World, starting with *Winterbirth*
Mary Stewart	Merlin series, starting with *The Crystal Cave*
Judith Tarr	*The Hound and the Falcon*
Harry Turtledove	Videssos Cycle, starting with *The Misplaced Legion*
Brent Weeks	Night Angel trilogy, starting with *The Way of Shadows*
Jack Whyte	Camulod Chronicles, starting with *The Skystone*
Gene Wolfe	Soldier series, starting with *Soldier of the Mist*

THEMATIC QUESTIONS

- Is the book you read set in a mostly realistic or imagined historical setting? Does historical verisimilitude make a great difference to you as a reader?

- Does fantasy fiction work better when it is set in a world before steam engines, gunpowder, or electricity? Or is this simply the way that the genre developed?

- Did the setting in your book evoke a particular place or time? If so, where or when?

- How would you characterize daily life for the common person in the time and place in which your book is set? Does this match the depiction of daily life in the book?

- Are there aspects of medieval or ancient life that are typically left out of fantasy fiction?

- How did combat and battle differ in earlier eras compared to the modern era? Did these differences change the way in which war and violence were approached strategically? Psychologically?

ANIMALS: FEATURE CREATURES IN SPECULATIVE FICTION

Listen to them—the children of the night. What music they make!

—Bram Stoker

All animals are equal
But some animals are more equal than others.

—George Orwell

The creatures outside looked from pig to man, and from man to pig, and from pig to man again; but already it was impossible to say which was which.

—George Orwell

Personally, I'm glad that cats and dogs don't talk to me. I suspect that the former would be clever but verbally abusive and the latter would be like a sweet, well-intentioned friend who just won't shut up and becomes intolerable. But fears of abusive Abyssinians and chatty Chows aside, there is an undeniable, longstanding connection between animal appreciation and fantastic fiction. Readers can find fantasy animals of all descriptions, from the mythic to the mundane, including loyal companions, dangerous beasts, and dashing lead characters. Bring pictures of your pets and—for obvious reasons—vegetarian snacks on the night you tackle this theme!

SUGGESTED WORKS

Richard Adams	*Watership Down*
Richard Adams	*Shardik*
Richard Adams	*The Plague Dogs*
Stephen Baxter	Behemoth trilogy, starting with *Silverhair*
Peter S. Beagle	*The Last Unicorn*
Alice Borchardt	Legends of the Wolves, starting with *The Silver Wolf*
David Brin	Uplift Saga, starting with *Sundiver*
Jonathan Carroll	*The Ghost in Love*
David Clement-Davies	*The Sight*; *Fell*
David Clement-Davies	*Fire Bringer*
David B. Coe	Lon-Tobyn Chronicles, starting with *Children of Amarid*
Michael Crichton	*Jurassic Park*; *The Lost World*
Peter Dickinson	*Eva*
Diane Duane	*The Book of Night with Moon*; *To Visit the Queen*
Eric Flint and Dave Freer	*Rats, Bats & Vats*; *The Rats, the Bats & the Ugly*
Alan Dean Foster	The Taken trilogy, starting with *Lost and Found*
Lorna Freeman	Borderlands, starting with *Covenants*
Shannon Hale	*The Goose Girl*
Robin Hobb	Farseer trilogy, starting with *Assassin's Apprentice*
Tanya Huff	Keeper's Chronicles, starting with *Summon the Keeper*
Brian Jacques	Redwall series, starting with *Redwall*
Kij Johnson	*The Fox Woman*
Kij Johnson	*Fudoki*
William Kotzwinkle	*The Bear Went over the Mountain*
C. S. Lewis	The Chronicles of Narnia, starting with *The Lion, the Witch & the Wardrobe*
Jane Lindskold	Firekeeper series, starting with *Through Wolf's Eyes*
Patricia McKillip	*The Forgotten Beasts of Eld*
China Miéville	*King Rat*
Walter Moers	*The 13 1/2 Lives of Captain Bluebear*
Christopher Moore	*Fluke*
Andre Norton	*Beast Master's Planet*
George Orwell	*Animal Farm*
Edith Pattou	*East*
Tamora Pierce	The Immortals, starting with *Wild Magic*

Philip Pullman	His Dark Materials, starting with *The Golden Compass*
Jean Rabe	Finest trilogy, *The Finest Creation*
Mickey Zucker Reichert	Barakhai series, starting with *The Beasts of Barakhai*
J. K. Rowling	*Harry Potter & the Prisoner of Azkaban*
Jennifer Stevenson	*Trash Sex Magic*
Sheri S. Tepper	*The Companions*
Catherynne M. Valente	The Orphan's Tales, starting with *In the Night Garden*
H. G. Wells	*The Island of Dr. Moreau*
Tad Williams	*Tailchaser's Song*

THEMATIC QUESTIONS

- Do animal portrayals in your book give insight into animal life, or are they completely fantastic creations?

- How would a PETA (People for the Ethical Treatment of Animals) activist view the book that you read?

- Most of the books in this thematic list come from fantasy, not from science fiction. Is there a reason why animals are so well represented in fantasy? So rarely represented in science fiction?

- What are the advantages and disadvantages for an author of choosing an animal character, particularly a talking animal character, instead of a human?

- How is the relationship between animals and humans portrayed in the book that you chose?

- If there are multiple animal characters in your book, what is the relationship between them like? Is it analogous to relationships between people, or does it differ somehow?

- Some people, particularly those with environmental interests, have been critical of anthropomorphizing animals—depicting them as human. What are the potential problems of portraying animals as having human thoughts and values? Is there any value to this practice?

ANTIHEROES: BLACK HAT, HEART OF GOLD

The successful revolutionary is a statesman, the unsuccessful one a criminal.
—Erich Fromm

The real hero is always a hero by mistake; he dreams of being an honest coward like everyone else.
—Umberto Eco

In early works of science fiction and fantasy, the protagonists were almost always heroes—simply and straightforwardly battling for good. Today, the hero is as likely to be a small-time criminal as a shining white knight, a manipulative witch as often as an infallible princess. Works that feature antiheroes are sure to spur discussion. For some readers, antiheroes are morally complex and realistic; others resent the intrusion of darkness and cynicism into a genre that they enjoy because of its youthful simplicity.

SUGGESTED WORKS

Joe Abercrombie	*Best Served Cold*
Joe Abercrombie	The First Law, starting with *The Blade Itself*
R. Scott Bakker	The Prince of Nothing, starting with *The Darkness That Comes Before*
Alfred Bester	*The Stars My Destination*
Steven Brust	Vlad Taltos series, starting with *Jhereg*
Anthony Burgess	*A Clockwork Orange*
Eoin Colfer	Artemis Fowl series, starting with *Artemis Fowl*
Glen Cook	Black Company, starting with *Chronicles of the Black Company*
Peter David	Apropos of Nothing, starting with *Sir Apropos of Nothing*
Stephen R. Donaldson	Chronicles of Thomas Covenant, starting with *Lord Foul's Bane*
Sara Douglass	The Crucible, starting with *The Nameless Day*
Steven Erikson	Malazan Book of the Fallen, starting with *Gardens of the Moon*
C. S. Friedman	Coldfire trilogy, starting with *Black Sun Rising*
John Gardner	*Grendel*
David Gemmell	*Waylander*
William Gibson	*Neuromancer*
Jon Courtenay Grimwood	Arabesk series, starting with *Pashazade*
Austin Grossman	*Soon I Will Be Invincible*
David Gunn	Death's Head series, starting with *Death's Head*
Harry Harrison	Stainless Steel Rat series, starting with *The Stainless Steel Rat*
Charlie Huston	Joe Pitt series, starting with *Already Dead*
Paul S. Kemp	Erevis Cale series, starting with *Twilight Falling*
Stephen King	The Dark Tower, starting with *The Gunslinger*
Ellen Kushner	*Swordspoint*
Fritz Leiber	Fafhrd and the Gray Mouser, starting with *Swords and Deviltry*
Scott Lynch	Gentlemen Bastards, starting with *The Lies of Locke Lamora*
Gregory Maguire	*Wicked*
George R. R. Martin	A Song of Ice and Fire, starting with *A Game of Thrones*
George R. R. Martin, Gardner Dozois, and Daniel Abraham	*Hunter's Run*
Michael Moorcock	Elric series, starting with *Elric of Melniboné*
Alan Moore and Dave Gibbons	*Watchmen*
Alan Moore and David Lloyd	*V for Vendetta*
Richard K. Morgan	Takeshi Kovacs series, starting with *Altered Carbon*
Richard K. Morgan	*Thirteen* (published in the United Kingdom as *Black Man*)
Richard K. Morgan	*The Steel Remains*

K. J. Parker	Engineer trilogy, starting with *Devices and Desires*
Mervyn Peake	Gormenghast trilogy, starting with *Titus Groan*
Neal Stephenson	*Snow Crash*
Matthew Woodring Stover	Overworld series, starting with *Heroes Die*
Jack Vance	*Tales of the Dying Earth*
Brent Weeks	The Night Angel series, starting with *The Way of Shadows*
Gene Wolfe	The Book of the New Sun, starting with *Shadow & Claw* omnibus

THEMATIC QUESTIONS

- In what ways are the characters of your book more morally complex than simple heroes? Do you still like the characters? Would you want them as close friends? As party guests? As your defender in difficult times? As a romantic partner? As a partner for your child?

- Should the book you chose only be read by those of a particular age? Why or why not?

- Can works that depict the contest between good and evil as straightforward be realistic?

- Would you call the book that you read more violent or obscene than the average speculative fiction book? Are such results inextricably linked with works featuring antiheroes?

- Did the use of antiheroes in your book create situational irony or dark humor? Can you give examples?

- How are societal institutions—political leaders, law enforcement, family values—portrayed in your book? Is there a connection between this portrayal and the antiheroic point of view?

APOCALYPTIC FICTION: STOP THE WORLD; WE WANT TO GET ON

This is the way the world ends
Not with a bang but a whimper

—T. S. Eliot

"Look," whispered Chuck, and George lifted his eyes to heaven. (There is always a last time for everything.)
Overhead, without any fuss, the stars were going out.

—Arthur C. Clarke

Ever since Noah (and other flood myths found in many world cultures), humans have been nervously scanning the horizon, waiting for the big event, so it's not surprising that a staple of speculative fiction is the apocalyptic novel. The population of Earth has been decimated repeatedly over the years by authors wielding bombs, viruses, asteroids, invasions, and other varieties of nastiness. This subgenre of the literature is about confronting fears, heroism (or depravity) in the face of the unthinkable, and, at its core, the basics of human behavior when people are returned to a state of nature. Think you have what it takes to survive? Try yourself against the scenarios in these classic and contemporary novels. Bring some freeze-dried food or conduct your meeting without electric lights to add verisimilitude.

SUGGESTED WORKS

John Joseph Adams	*Wastelands: Stories of the Apocalypse*
Chris Adrian	*The Children's Hospital*
Kevin J. Anderson and Doug Beason	*Ill Wind*
Margaret Atwood	*Oryx & Crake*
J. G. Ballard	*The Crystal World*
Stephen Baxter	*Flood*
Greg Bear	*The Forge of God*
David Brin	*The Postman*
William Brinkley	*The Last Ship*
Kevin Brockmeier	*A Brief History of the Dead*
Max Brooks	*World War Z: An Oral History of the Zombie War*
John Brunner	*Stand on Zanzibar*; *The Sheep Look Up*
Octavia Butler	*Parable of the Sower*; *Parable of the Talents*
Adam Celaya	*Earth, the New Frontier*
John Christopher	*A Wrinkle in the Skin*
Jim Crace	*The Pesthouse*
Philip K. Dick	*The Penultimate Truth*
Thomas Disch	*The Genocides*
Pat Frank	*Alas, Babylon*
Jean Hegland	*Into the Forest*
Robert A. Heinlein	*Farnham's Freehold*
Russell Hoban	*Riddley Walker*
P. D. James	*Children of Men*
Stephen King	*The Stand*
Stephen King	*Cell*
Tim LaHaye and Jerry Jenkins	<u>Left Behind</u> series, starting with *Left Behind*
Jeff Long	*Year Zero*
Richard Matheson	*I Am Legend*
Robert McCammon	*Swan Song*
Sean McMullen	<u>Greatwinter</u> trilogy, starting with *Souls in the Great Machine*
Larry Niven and Jerry Pournelle	*Lucifer's Hammer*
Robert C. O'Brien	*Z for Zachariah*
Kim Stanley Robinson	<u>Science in the Capital</u>, starting with *Forty Signs of Rain*
Jose Saramago	*Blindness*
Nevil Shute	*On the Beach*
George R. Stewart	*Earth Abides*

S. M. Stirling	<u>The Change</u> series, starting with *Dies the Fire*
Sam Taylor	*The Island at the End of the World*
Brian K. Vaughan, et al.	<u>Y: The Last Man</u> graphic novels
Kurt Vonnegut	*Cat's Cradle*
Kurt Vonnegut	*Galapagos*
H. G. Wells	*The War of the Worlds*
Kate Wilhelm	*Where Late the Sweet Birds Sang*
Walter Jon Williams	*The Rift*
Philip Wylie and Edwin Balmer	*When Worlds Collide*
John Wyndham	*The Day of the Triffids*

THEMATIC QUESTIONS

- What does the reaction of characters to the catastrophe in your novel say about human nature? Do characters in your book react believably to the disasters that they encounter?
- Can anything hopeful come out of the aftermath of a disaster? Is this reflected in the book that you read?
- How do societal institutions (government, law enforcement, community, religion, etc.) fare in the face of disaster in the book that you read? Are these reactions convincing? Faced with such a disaster, do you think that real-world institutions would be a help or a hindrance to survival?
- If you survived a world-shattering event, what possessions or technologies would you most want to retain?
- What fundamental skills and technologies does the average person take for granted that would be difficult to maintain if an apocalyptic event occurred?

RESOURCES

Empty World

http://www.empty-world.com

COMPUTERS, INTERNET, AND VIRTUAL REALITIES: BOOKS WITH BYTE

I do not fear computers. I fear lack of them.

—Isaac Asimov

Dave: *Open the pod bay doors, HAL.*
HAL: *I'm sorry Dave, I'm afraid I can't do that.*

—2001: A Space Odyssey

Whether it's fair or accurate, science fiction and fantasy readers are stereotyped as being much more connected to computers than the average member of society. Is this true for your book group? As the difficulties of space travel have become clear, computer advances have risen to rival space as science fiction's most popular field. Is computer technology the great hope for a glorious human future or could it ultimately enslave us? Read some of these works and consider.

SUGGESTED WORKS

Douglas Adams	*The Hitchhiker's Guide to the Galaxy*
M. T. Anderson	*Feed*
Catherine Asaro	*The Veiled Web*
Dan Brown	*Digital Fortress*
Arthur C. Clarke	*2001: A Space Odyssey*
Josh Conviser	*Echelon*; *Empyre*
Charles de Lint	*Spirits in the Wires*
Cory Doctorow	*Down and Out in the Magic Kingdom*
Cory Doctorow	*Eastern Standard Tribe*
Cory Doctorow	*Little Brother*
William Gibson	Novels of <u>The Sprawl</u>, starting with *Neuromancer*
William Gibson	<u>Bridge</u> series, starting with *Virtual Light*
William Gibson	*Pattern Recognition*
William Gibson and Bruce Sterling	*The Difference Engine*
Marc D. Giller	*Hammerjack*; *Prodigal*
Kathleen Ann Goonan	*In War Times*
Margaret Peterson Haddix	*Escape from Memory*
Robert Heinlein	*The Moon Is a Harsh Mistress*
Howard V. Hendrix	*The Labyrinth Key*
Matthew Jarpe	*Radio Freefall*
Catherine Jinks	*Evil Genius*; *Genius Squad*
James Patrick Kelly and John Kessel, eds.	*Rewired: The Post-Cyberpunk Anthology*
Hari Kunzru	*Transmission*
Ken MacLeod	<u>The Fall Revolution</u>, starting with *Fractions*
Paul J. McAuley	*Whole Wide World*
Kelly McCullough	<u>Ravirn</u> series, starting with *WebMage*
Jeff Noon	*Vurt*
Susan Palwick	*Shelter*
Alastair Reynolds	<u>Revelation Space</u> series, starting with *Revelation Space*
Rudy Rucker	*The Hacker and the Ants*
Neal Stephenson	*Snow Crash*
Neal Stephenson	*Cryptonomicon*
Bruce Sterling	*The Zenith Angle*
Charles Stross	*The Atrocity Archives*
Charles Stross	*Halting State*
Charles Stross	*Singularity Sky*; *Iron Sunrise*
David J. Williams	*Mirrored Heavens*
Tad Williams	<u>Otherland</u> series, starting with *City of Golden Shadow*

| Walter Jon Williams | *Hardwired* |
| Walter Jon Williams | *This Is Not a Game* |

THEMATIC QUESTIONS

- How has the improvement of technology changed the way in which science fiction portrays computers?
- Are computers viewed mainly as an aid to humanity or a danger in the novel you read? Are the dangers or benefits of computers overclaimed or underrepresented in fiction?
- How do your own views toward computers affect your reaction to the book you read?
- In retrospect, did the cyberpunk movement deserve the importance that it gained in science fiction circles, or is it a limited subgenre?
- What lessons about the use of computers can society learn from science fiction?
- How has computer technology changed your life so far? How might it change our lives in the future? Which works of science fiction best capture these changes?

RESOURCES

The Computer History Museum

http://www.computerhistory.org

THE COST OF MAGIC: SPELL-BOUND AND OVER-CAST IN FANTASY FICTION

"Precious!" Gollum cried. And with that, even as his eyes were lifted up to gloat on his prize, he stepped too far, toppled, wavered for a moment on the brink, and then with a shriek he fell. Out of the depths came his last wail Precious, and he was gone.
—J. R. R. Tolkien

Power tends to corrupt, and absolute power corrupts absolutely.
—Lord Acton

Without clear limits or costs, the unrestricted use of magic can reduce a fantasy novel to an arbitrary series of events with no internal logic. The best writers recognize this danger and carefully develop systems of magic that can't be used to solve every problem easily and that present real challenges to practitioners. Taking a month to consider this most intrinsic element of fantasy fiction, yields rewards for any fantasy book group. Once readers understand the reasons why it is difficult to write believably about magic, their appreciation for the genre grows.

SUGGESTED WORKS

| Daniel Abraham | Long Price Quartet, starting with *A Shadow in Summer* |
| Sarah Ash | Tears of Artamon series, starting with *Lord of Snow and Shadows* |

Clive Barker	<u>The Art</u>, starting with *The Great and Secret Show*
Peter S. Beagle	*The Innkeeper's Song*
Anne Bishop	<u>*The Black Jewels Trilogy*</u>
Lois McMaster Bujold	*The Curse of Chalion*; *Paladin of Souls*
Orson Scott Card	*Hart's Hope*
Susanna Clarke	*Jonathan Strange & Mr. Norrell*
Dawn Cook	<u>Truth</u> series, starting with *First Truth*
Stephen R. Donaldson	<u>Chronicles of Thomas Covenant</u>, starting with *Lord Foul's Bane*
Keith Donohue	*The Stolen Child*
Sara Douglass	*Threshold*
Dave Duncan	<u>The King's Blades</u>, starting with *The Gilded Chain*
David Eddings	<u>The Belgariad</u> omnibus
David Farland	<u>Runelords</u> series, starting with *The Runelords: the Sum of All Men*
S. L. Farrell	<u>Cloudmages</u> series, starting with *Holder of Lightning*
C. S. Friedman	*Feast of Souls*
Gregory Frost	*Shadowbridge*; *Lord Tophet*
Cornelia Funke	<u>Inkheart</u> series, starting with *Inkheart*
Neil Gaiman	*Anansi Boys*
Neil Gaiman	*Stardust*
Ed Greenwood	*The Silent House*
Shannon Hale	<u>Bayern</u> series, starting with *The Goose Girl*
Robin Hobb	<u>The Farseer Trilogy</u>, starting with *Assassin's Apprentice*
Robin Hobb	<u>The Liveship Traders</u>, starting with *Ship of Magic*
Robin Hobb	<u>Soldier Son</u> trilogy, starting with *Shaman's Crossing*
J. V. Jones	<u>Sword of Shadows</u>, starting with *A Cavern of Black Ice*
Tamara Siler Jones	<u>Dubric Bryerly</u> series, starting with *Ghosts in the Snow*
Robert Jordan	<u>The Wheel of Time</u>, starting with *The Eye of the World*
Guy Gavriel Kay	*Tigana*
Mercedes Lackey and James Mallory	<u>Obsidian</u> trilogy, starting with *The Outstretched Shadow*
Justine Larbalestier	<u>Magic or Madness</u> series, starting with *Magic or Madness*
Ursula K. Le Guin	<u>Earthsea Cycle</u>, starting with *The Wizard of Earthsea*
Ursula K. Le Guin	<u>Annals of the Western Shore</u>, starting with *Gifts*
Laurie J. Marks	<u>Elemental Logic</u> series, starting with *Fire Logic*
Patricia A. McKillip	*The Book of Atrix Wolfe*
Patricia A. McKillip	*Ombria in Shadow*
L. E. Modesitt	<u>Recluce</u> series, starting with *The Magic of Recluce*
Garth Nix	<u>Abhorsen</u> trilogy, starting with *Sabriel*
Terry Pratchett	*The Colour of Magic*; *The Light Fantastic*
Patrick Rothfuss	*The Name of the Wind*
Brian Ruckley	<u>The Godless World</u>, starting with *Winterbirth*
Ellen Steiber	*A Rumor of Gems*
Jonathan Stroud	<u>Bartimaeus</u> trilogy, starting with *The Amulet of Samarkand*
J. R. R. Tolkien	<u>*The Fellowship of the Ring*</u>

| Lawrence Watt-Evans | <u>Annals of the Chosen</u>, starting with *The Wizard Lord* |
| Lawrence Watt-Evans | <u>Ethshar</u>: *Night of Madness*; *The Misenchanted Sword*; *With a Single Spell* |

THEMATIC QUESTIONS

- What kinds of costs for the performance of magic have you seen in works of fantasy?
- Can you think of a successful fantasy novel where magic is prevalent but does not have a clear cost? What is the potential problem of a magical system in which the dangers of practice are not defined?
- Does the book that you read make distinctions between how good characters and evil characters use magic? Is magic ultimately a force for good or evil?
- What is the difference between magic and science?
- Does magic serve as a metaphor for other kinds of power, talent, or obsession in the book you read? Can reading fantasy fiction lead to insights about our lives in the real world?
- Can a novel be part of the fantasy genre without any magic?

———————————

DIVERSITY: A FANTASTIC CHOIR OF MANY VOICES

We don't want the melting pot where everybody ends up with thin gruel. We want diversity, for strangeness breeds richness.

—Marge Piercy

Racism was not a problem on the Discworld, because—what with trolls and dwarfs and so on—speciesism was more interesting. Black and white lived in perfect harmony and ganged up on green.

—Terry Pratchett

By any objective measure, science fiction and fantasy have been among the slowest genres to integrate writers and characters whose skins are not pale and pink. Because of their inclusion of many different sentient species from this world, the alien, and the fantastic, SF & F often can't help but make points about diversity, but that doesn't mean that the color line has been thoroughly broken by the genres' writers, fans, or protagonists. Still, progress is being made: more minority writers find publication in each passing year, and more minority fans read the genres. Books listed in this theme are by minority writers or feature strong depictions of minority characters.

SUGGESTED WORKS

Justin Allen	*Slaves of the Shinar*
Ashok Banker	<u>Ramayana</u> series, starting with *Prince of Ayodhya*
L. A. Banks	<u>Vampire Huntress Legends</u>, starting with *Minion*
Elizabeth Bear	*Carnival*

Tobias Buckell	Xenowealth Saga, starting with *Crystal Rain*
Lois McMaster Bujold	Miles Vorkosigan novels, starting with *Young Miles*
Octavia Butler	*Kindred*
Octavia Butler	*Fledgling*
Octavia Butler	*Lilith's Brood*
Orson Scott Card	*Magic Street*
Samuel R. Delaney	Return to Neveryon, starting with *Tales of Neveryon*
Samuel R. Delaney	*Dhalgren*
Junot Diaz	*The Brief Wondrous Life of Oscar Wao*
Tananarive Due	*My Soul to Keep*
Tananarive Due	*The Living Blood*
David Anthony Durham	Acacia, starting with *The War with the Mein*
Minister Faust	*Coyote Kings of the Space-Age Bachelor Pad*; *From the Notebooks of Doctor Brain*
Lynn Flewelling	Nightrunner trilogy, starting with *Luck in the Shadows*
Neil Gaiman	*Anansi Boys*
Jon Courtenay Grimwood	*9Tail Fox*
Jesse Hajicek	*The God Eaters*
Ginn Hale	*Wicked Gentlemen*
Lian Hearn	Tales of the Otori, starting with *Across the Nightingale Floor*
Nalo Hopkinson	*The Salt Roads*
Nalo Hopkinson	*Brown Girl in the Ring*
Nalo Hopkinson and Uppinder Meehan, eds.	*So Long Been Dreaming: Postcolonial Science Fiction & Fantasy*
Kij Johnson	*Fudoki*
Kij Johnson	*Fox Woman*
Ellen Kushner	*Swordspoint*; *The Privilege of the Sword*
Mercedes Lackey	The Last Herald Mage, starting with *Magic's Pawn*
Laurie J. Marks	Elemental Logic series, starting with *Fire Logic*
Ian McDonald	*River of Gods*
Ian McDonald	*Brasyl*
Sarah Monette	Doctrine of Labyrinths, starting with *Mélusine*
Perry Moore	*Hero*
Richard K. Morgan	*Thirteen* (a.k.a. *Black Man*)
Walter Mosley	*Futureland*
Nnedi Okorafor-Mbachu	*The Shadow Speaker*
Gary Phillips and Christopher Chambers, eds.	*The Darker Mask*
Ricardo Pinto	Stone Dance of the Chameleon, starting with *The Chosen*
Terry Pratchett	Discworld—the Watch, starting with *Guards! Guards!*
Kim Stanley Robinson	*The Years of Rice and Salt*
Charles Saunders	*Imaro*
Sheree R. Thomas, ed.	*Dark Matter: A Century of Speculative Fiction from the African Diaspora*
Catherynne M. Valente	Orphan's Tales, starting with *In the Night Garden*

THEMATIC QUESTIONS

- How do questions of race, gender, sexuality, or ability impact characters in the novel that you read?
- Do the race, gender, or sexual preferences of the author influence your likelihood to pick up and enjoy a work? Do authors of color create better characters of color?
- Why have science fiction and fantasy been slow to find diversity? Are there obvious examples of racism in the genres? What can be done to improve diversity in these genres? Which would help most: more diversity among the writers, the readers, or the characters?
- Is it enough for science fiction and fantasy to depict relations between creatures of different species, or do characters of particular ethnicities need to be used?
- Have science fiction and fantasy been more successful in their representation of women than of people of color? In representation of different physical and mental abilities? In its consideration of homosexuality?

RESOURCES

Diversicon

http://www.diversicon.org

ENVIRONMENTAL ISSUES: READING THE GREEN

The Earth is beautiful, and bright, and kindly, but that is not all. The Earth's also terrible, and dark, and cruel.
—Ursula K. Le Guin

Nature was his real antagonist—the friendly enemy who never cheated, always played fair, but never failed to take advantage of the tiniest oversight or omission.
—Arthur C. Clarke

Both fantasy and science fiction provide good platforms for addressing environmental issues: fantasy because it often features outdoor settings and values the pretechnological, natural world; science fiction because it is often concerned with technological mistakes, population concerns, and sustenance of life on this planet and others.

SUGGESTED WORKS

Richard Adams	*Watership Down*
Isaac Asimov	*Caves of Steel*
Margaret Atwood	*Oryx and Crake*
J. G. Ballard	*The Drowned World*
T. A. Barron	Great Tree of Avalon, starting with *Child of the Dark Prophecy*

Gregory Benford	*Timescape*
Julie Bertagna	*Exodus*
David Brin	*Earth*
John Brunner	*The Sheep Look Up*
John Brunner	*Stand on Zanzibar*
Ernest Callenbach	*Ecotopia*
David B. Coe	<u>Lon-Tobyn Chronicles</u>, starting with *Children of the Amarid*
Michael Crichton	*State of Fear*
Ellen Datlow and Terri Windling, eds.	*The Green Man: Tales from the Mythic Forest*
Stephen R. Donaldson	<u>Chronicles of Thomas Covenant</u>, starting with *Lord Foul's Bane*
Diane Duane	*Deep Wizardry*
Harry Harrison	*Make Room! Make Room!*
Frank Herbert	*The Green Brain*
Frank Herbert	*Dune*
David Klass	<u>Caretaker Trilogy</u>, starting with *Firestorm*
George R. R. Martin	*Tuf Voyaging*
Dennis McKiernan	*The Eye of the Hunter*
Janet Elizabeth McNaughton	*The Secret under My Skin*
China Miéville	*Un Lun Dun*
Hayao Miyazaki	*Nausicaä of the Valley of the Wind*
Charles Pellegrino	*Dust*
Philip Reeve	<u>The Hungry Cities</u>, starting with *Mortal Engines*
Kim Stanley Robinson	<u>Mars</u> trilogy, starting with *Red Mars*
Kim Stanley Robinson	*Antarctica*
Kim Stanley Robinson	<u>Science in the Capital</u>, starting with *Forty Signs of Rain*
Neal Stephenson	*Zodiac*
Bruce Sterling	*Heavy Weather*
Jennifer Stevenson	*Trash Sex Magic*
Sheri S. Tepper	*Grass*
J. R. R. Tolkien	<u>*The Lord of the Rings*</u>
Karen Traviss	<u>Wess'har Wars</u>, starting with *City of Pearl*

THEMATIC QUESTIONS

- Which environmental issues are addressed by the book that you read? Is environment the major theme, or is it a minor one?

- Are environmental issues generally handled believably in fiction? Or are they exaggerated or distorted? Does the book that you read make a good case, or is it weakly argued or alarmist?

- On the whole, has science fiction explored environmental issues adequately? Are there particular environmental concerns that deserve more coverage?

- What challenges face a writer who attempts to craft environmental concerns into interesting fiction? Does the book that you read overcome them?
- After hearing about each book read by your group members, which scenarios do you find the most convincing or frightening? Which do not seem likely?
- Will technology solve environmental problems in the future, or will more advanced technologies create bigger environmental damage?

THE FAIRY WORLD: "SIDHE" MOVES IN MYSTERIOUS WAYS

Every time a child says "I don't believe in fairies," there is a fairy somewhere that falls down dead.

—J. M. Barrie

Any man can lose his hat in a fairy-wind.

—Irish saying

Excursions into the world of fairy are a prime source of the fantasy genre. Whether you spell it faerie or fairy, call them the wee folk, the fey, or something else entirely, this part of the genre is still alive, well, and not just for little kids. This list focuses on books about contacts between human and the fairy world, but for related work, including fairy tales, see the Myths, Fables, and Legends theme.

SUGGESTED WORKS

Steve Augarde	Touchstone Trilogy, starting with *The Various*
Elizabeth Bear	Promethean Age, starting with *Blood and Iron*
Anne Bishop	Tir-Alainn trilogy, starting with *The Pillars of the World*
Holly Black	*Tithe*; *Valiant*; *Ironside*
Herbie Brennan	Faerie Wars, starting with *Faerie Wars*
Marie Brennan	*Midnight Never Come*; *In Ashes Lie*
Emma Bull	*War for the Oaks*
Emma Bull	*Finder*
Jim Butcher	Dresden Files, especially *Summer Knight*
Michael Chabon	*Summerland*
Susannah Clarke	*Jonathan Strange & Mr. Norrell*
Susannah Clarke	*The Ladies of Grace Adieu and Other Stories*
Eoin Colfer	Artemis Fowl series, starting with *Artemis Fowl*
Ellen Datlow and Terri Windling, eds.	*Snow White, Blood Red*; *Black Thorn, White Rose*; *Ruby Slippers, Golden Tears*; *Black Swan, White Raven, Silver Birch, Blood Moon*; *Black Heart, Ivory Bones*; *The Faery Reel*
Peter David	*Tigerheart*
Pamela Dean	*Tam Lin*
Charles de Lint	*Jack of Kinrowan*
Charles de Lint	Newford stories, starting with *Dreams Underfoot*

Charles de Lint	*Greenmantle*
Paul di Filippo	*Harp, Pipe & Symphony*
Keith Donohue	*The Stolen Child*
Lord Dunsany	*The King of Elfland's Daughter*
Sally Gardner	*I, Coriander*
Laurell K. Hamilton	Meredith Gentry series, starting with *A Kiss of Shadows*
Kim Harrison	The Hollows, starting with *Dead Witch Walking*
Robert Holdstock	Ryhope Wood series, starting with *Mythago Wood*
Anne Kelleher	Shadowlands series, starting with *Silver's Edge*
Ellen Kushner	*Thomas the Rhymer*
Sharon Lee and Steve Miller	*Duainfey*; *Longeye*
George MacDonald	*Phantastes: A Fairy Romance*
Juliet Marillier	Bridei Chronicles, starting with *The Dark Mirror*
Juliet Marillier	*Wildwood Dancing*; *Cybele's Secret*
Patricia McKillip	*Solstice Wood*
Robin McKinley	*Spindle's End*
O. R. Melling	The Chronicles of Faerie, starting with *The Hunter's Moon*
Hope Mirrlees	*Lud-in-the-Mist*
Robin D. Owens	The Summoning, starting with *Guardian of Honor*
Christopher Pike	Alosha trilogy, starting with *Alosha*
Terry Pratchett	*Lords and Ladies*
Terry Pratchett	*The Wee Free Men*
Justina Robson	Quantum Gravity, especially *Going Under*
Will Shetterly	*Elsewhere*; *Nevernever*
Adam Stemple	*Singer of Souls*; *Steward of Song*
Michael Swanwick	*The Iron Dragon's Daughter*; *The Dragons of Babel*
Kate Thompson	*The New Policeman*
Lisa Tuttle	*The Mysteries*
Tad Williams	*The War of the Flowers*
Tad Williams	Shadowmarch series, starting with *Shadowmarch*

THEMATIC QUESTIONS

- What parts of the fairy world tradition does the book that you read incorporate?

- Do you find it easier to suspend disbelief when reading fantasies that posit a fairy world bordering the real world or when reading fantasies set in completely separate alternate worlds?

- What are some of the archetypal fairy tales? See if your group can collectively brainstorm a list. Were the novels that you read influenced by these tales? Is there a difference between fairy tales and books about contact with the fairy world?

- What's the difference between fairies and elves? Pixies? Dwarves? Goblins? Gnomes? Elementals? Trolls? What is the most interesting type of fairy creature in the book that you read?

- Some say that fairy tales were originally intended as cautionary stories, aimed at children and used to frighten away misbehavior. Is that tradition reflected in the book that you read?

FAMILIES: RELATIVE-LY GOOD SPECULATIVE FICTION

We lived like that "Happy Family" you sometimes see in traveling zoos: a lion caged with a lamb. It is a startling exhibit, but the lamb has to be replaced frequently.

—Robert A. Heinlein

A boy's best friend is his mother.

—from *Psycho*

One of the great pleasures of fantasy and science fiction is that they are genres parents and children can enjoy together. It's appropriate then, that family relationships are a common theme. Whether it's an evil stepparent, a secession crisis, sibling rivalry, a multigenerational saga, or just a classic family adventure, speculative fiction has got it. For a fun variation, consider inviting family members or asking about their genre reading when your group tackles this theme.

SUGGESTED WORKS

Lois McMaster Bujold	<u>Vorkosigan Saga</u>, starting with <u>*Cordelia's Honor*</u> omnibus
Octavia E. Butler	*Fledgling*
Orson Scott Card	*Ender's Game*
Suzanne Collins	*The Hunger Games*
Dawn Cook	<u>Truth</u> series, starting with *First Truth*
Jim Crace	*The Pesthouse*
John Crowley	*Little, Big*
Keith Donohue	*The Stolen Child*
David Anthony Durham	<u>Acacia</u>, starting with *The War with the Mein*
S. L. Farrell	<u>Cloudmages</u>, starting with *Holder of Lightning*
Cornelia Funke	<u>Inkheart</u> series, starting with *Inkheart*
Neil Gaiman	*Anansi Boys*
Neil Gaiman	*Coraline*
Gabriel Garcia Márquez	*One Hundred Years of Solitude*
Kathleen Ann Goonan	*In War Times*
Frank Herbert	*Dune*
Robin Hobb	<u>Farseer</u> trilogy, starting with *Assassin's Apprentice*
Robin Hobb	<u>Liveship Traders</u> trilogy, starting with *Ship of Magic*
Guy Gavriel Kay	*A Song for Arbonne*
Greg Keyes	<u>Kingdoms of Thorn and Bone</u>, starting with *The Briar King*
Ursula K. Le Guin	<u>Annals of the Western Shore</u>, starting with *Gifts*
Madeleine L'Engle	<u>Time Quintet</u>, starting with *A Wrinkle in Time*
C. S. Lewis	*The Lion, the Witch, and the Wardrobe; Prince Caspian*
Lois Lowry	*The Giver*
Gregory Maguire	<u>Wicked Years</u>, starting with *Wicked*
Juliet Marillier	<u>Sevenwaters</u> series, starting with *Daughter of the Forest*
George R. R. Martin	<u>A Song of Ice and Fire</u>, starting with *Game of Thrones*
Cormac McCarthy	*The Road*

Audrey Niffenegger	*The Time Traveler's Wife*
Susan Palwick	*The Necessary Beggar*
Susan Pfeffer	*Life as We Knew It*; *The Dead & the Gone*
J. K. Rowling	<u>Harry Potter</u>, starting with *Harry Potter and the Sorcerer's Stone*
Brian Ruckley	<u>Godless World</u>, starting with *Winterbirth*
Lemony Snicket	<u>A Series of Unfortunate Events</u>, starting with *The Bad Beginning*
Midori Snyder	*Hannah's Garden*
Michael Stackpole	<u>Age of Discovery</u> series, starting with *A Secret Atlas*
Jennifer Stevenson	*Trash, Sex, Magic*
Charles Stross	*Accelerando*
Charles Stross	<u>Merchant Princes</u>, starting with *The Family Trade*
Rob Thurman	<u>Cal Leandros</u> series, starting with *Nightlife*
Robert Charles Wilson	*Spin*

THEMATIC QUESTIONS

- Are there more examples of happy families or dysfunctional families in speculative fiction? Which are more fun to read about? How would you describe the families in the book that you read?

- Do you ever share science fiction or fantasy with your family members? Are your parents or siblings readers of these genres? Have younger readers picked up an interest in the genres?

- Is the number of orphans and other characters without families unusually high in science fiction and fantasy? If so, why?

- Are the family relationships depicted in the book that you read believable? Or do the characters behave differently than real people?

- Which is the happiest family in speculative fiction? Which is the most dysfunctional?

FANTASY BEFORE 1970: THE GENRE BEFORE TOLKIEN

All we who write put me in mind of sailors hastily making rafts upon doomed ships. When we break up under the heavy years and go down into eternity with all that is ours our thoughts like small lost rafts float on awhile upon Oblivion's sea. They will not carry much over those tides, our names and a phrase or two and little else.

—Lord Dunsany

But whatever my failure, I have this thing to remember—that I was a pioneer in my profession . . .

—Robert E. Howard

Tolkien's <u>The Lord of the Rings</u> was published in 1955. It's popularity built slowly, but by the mid 1960s, it had become a cultural force. By 1970, it had become the prime influence on the fantasy genre. Tolkien and his imitators dominated the fantasy landscape until the turn of the century. Tolkien's writing had such a strong effect on the genre that it's easy to forget that the genre was already well established before 1970, with many interesting and durable traditions already created.

SUGGESTED WORKS—FOLKLORE

Folklore differs from modern fantasy in at least two significant ways. Most of it derived from an oral tradition that was only transcribed after many storytellers made their contributions. Also, most folklore was not viewed as fiction, at least not in the sense that a modern writer thinks of fiction, by those who originally wrote it. Still, one can't deny the influence of folklore (and mythology) on modern fantasists, and folklore reads like fantasy to modern eyes. No authors are listed for the folklore, as most of these works are available in many different editions and translations.

Beowulf
The Epic of Gilgamesh
The Iliad
The Kalevala
The Mabinogion
The Nibelungenlied
The Odyssey
One Thousand and One Nights
The Poetic Edda
The Prose Edda
The Sagas of the Icelanders
The Song of Roland
The Tain

NOVELS AND STORIES

Joan Aiken	*The Wolves of Willoughby Chase*
Lloyd Alexander	The Chronicles of Prydain, starting with *The Book of Three*
Douglas A. Anderson, ed.	*Tales before Tolkien*
Douglas A. Anderson, ed.	*Tales before Narnia*
Poul Anderson	*The Broken Sword*
J. M. Barrie	*Peter Pan*
L. Frank Baum	The Land of Oz, starting with *The Wonderful Wizard of Oz*
Peter S. Beagle	*A Fine and Private Place*
Peter S. Beagle	*The Last Unicorn*
James Branch Cabell	*Jurgen*
L. Sprague de Camp	*Lest Darkness Fall*
L. Sprague de Camp and Fletcher Pratt	*The Mathematics of Magic*

Lewis Carroll	*Alice's Adventures in Wonderland*; *Through the Looking Glass*
Charles Dickens	*A Christmas Carol*
Lord Dunsany	*The King of Elfland's Daughter*
E. R. Eddison	*The Worm Ouroboros*
Randall Garrett	*Lord Darcy*
Geoffrey of Monmouth	*The History of the Kings of Britain*
H. Rider Haggard	*She*
Robert E. Howard	<u>Conan</u> stories, starting with *The Coming of Conan the Cimmerian*
Robert E. Howard	*Bran Mak Morn: The Last King*
Robert E. Howard	*Kull: Exile of Atlantis*
Robert E. Howard	*The Savage Tales of Solomon Kane*
Ursula K. Le Guin	*A Wizard of Earthsea*
Madeleine L'Engle	*A Wrinkle in Time*
C. S. Lewis	<u>Chronicles of Narnia</u>, starting with *The Lion, the Witch, and the Wardrobe*
Fritz Leiber	<u>Fafhrd and the Gray Mouser</u>, starting with <u>*Lankhmar: Sword and Deviltry*</u> omnibus
George MacDonald	*Phantastes*
George MacDonald	*The Princess and the Goblin*
Sir Thomas Malory	*L'Morte d'Arthur*
Anne McCaffrey	*Dragonflight*
A. Merritt	*The Moon Pool*
A. Merritt	*The Ship of Ishtar*
Hope Mirrlees	*Lud-in-the-Mist*
William Morris	*The Wood beyond the World*
John Myers Myers	*Silverlock*
Andre Norton	<u>Witch World Estcarp Cycle</u>, starting with *Witch World*
Mervyn Peake	<u>Gormenghast</u>, starting with *Titus Groan*
Howard Pyle	*The Merry Adventures of Robin Hood*
Clark Ashton Smith	*The Collected Fantasies of Clark Ashton Smith*
J. R. R. Tolkien	*The Hobbit*; <u>*The Lord of the Rings*</u>
Jack Vance	*Tales of the Dying Earth*
Manly Wade Wellman	*The Selected Stories of Manly Wade Wellman*
T. H. White	<u>The Once and Future King</u>, starting with *The Sword in the Stone*
Oscar Wilde	*The Picture of Dorian Grey*

THEMATIC QUESTIONS

- How has the fantasy genre changed since the time when your chosen book was written? Is the genre better or worse on the whole?

- Do you see the influence of the book or author that you read on any later writers or works?

- How well has the work that you selected aged? Will contemporary readers still enjoy it? How well does the fantasy genre age, on the whole, compared to other genres?

- Did you have difficulty finding a copy of the book that you read? Are there enough reprints of classic works of fantasy? Has technology improved your ability to find older books? What older work of fantasy would you most like to see back in print?

- Can you see the influence of original folklore clearly in the book that you chose to read?

RESOURCES

Wikipedia History of Fantasy

http://en.wikipedia.org/wiki/History_of_fantasy

GENDER ROLES: A WOMAN'S PLACE IS IN THE TOME

Being a man or a woman is, in a large measure, just an act, a certain culturally determined role that may have very little to do with how we really are inside.
—Philip K. Dick and Ray Nelson

The most important thing, the heaviest single factor in one's life, is whether one's born male or female. In most societies it determines one's expectations, activities, outlook, ethics, manners—almost everything. Vocabulary. Semiotic usages. Clothing. Even food.
—Ursula K. Le Guin

Reviews are mixed on the success of fantasy and science fiction at reaching gender equity. On one hand, some argue that the genres are marketed to young men and dominated by male characters, often leaving female characters the stereotypical roles of damsel in distress, love interest, perky princess, or, on the side of evil, the femme fatale or hideous hag. Science fiction, in particular, has often been guilty of imagining major technological changes centuries into the future while maintaining gender stereotypes from the distant past. On the other hand, female authors and strong female characters are readily available in F & SF. From new wave science fiction forward, speculative novels often directly address questions of gender. No matter what your views of gender, your group will find that this subject generates interesting discussion.

SUGGESTED WORKS

Catherine Asaro	*The Last Hawk*
Margaret Atwood	*The Handmaid's Tale*
Marion Zimmer Bradley	Avalon series, starting with *The Mists of Avalon*
Lois McMaster Bujold	*Cordelia's Honor*
Lois McMaster Bujold	*Paladin of Souls*
Octavia Butler	*Kindred*
Octavia Butler	*Parable of the Sower; Parable of the Talents*
Octavia Butler	Xenogenesis trilogy, starting with *Dawn*
Jacqueline Carey	Kushiel series, starting with *Kushiel's Dart*

Angela Carter	*Burning Your Boats: The Collected Stories*
Storm Constantine	*Wraeththu*
Karen Joy Fowler and Pat Murphy, eds.	*James Tiptree Award Anthologies, 1–3*
Mary Gentle	<u>The Secret History</u>, starting with *The Book of Ash*
Charlotte Perkins Gilman	*Herland*
Molly Gloss	*Wild Life*
Robin Hobb	<u>Liveship Traders</u>, starting with *Ship of Magic*
Nalo Hopkinson	*Brown Girl in the Ring*
P. D. James	*Children of Men*
Guy Gavriel Kay	*The Lions of al-Rassan*
Naomi Kritzer	<u>Dead Rivers</u> trilogy, starting with *Freedom's Gate*
Mercedes Lackey	<u>Vows and Honor</u> series, starting with *The Oathbound*
Ursula K. Le Guin	*The Left Hand of Darkness*
Ursula K. Le Guin	*The Dispossessed*
Ira Levin	*The Stepford Wives*
Gregory Maguire	*Wicked*
Juliet Marillier	<u>Sevenwaters</u> trilogy, starting with *Daughter of the Forest*
Laurie J. Marks	<u>Elemental Logic</u>, starting with *Fire Logic*
George R. R. Martin	<u>A Song of Ice and Fire</u>, starting with *Game of Thrones*
Robin McKinley	*Beauty*
Sarah Micklem	*Firethorn*
Elizabeth Moon	<u>*The Deed of Paksenarrion*</u>
James Morrow	*The Last Witchfinder*
Tamora Pierce	<u>Song of the Lioness</u>, starting with *Alanna: The First Adventure*
Marge Piercy	*He, She, and It*
Marge Piercy	*Woman on the Edge of Time*
Terry Pratchett	*Equal Rites*
Terry Pratchett	<u>Discworld-Tiffany Aching</u>, starting with *Wee Free Men*
Lane Robins	*Maledicte*
Joanna Russ	*The Female Man*
Pamela Sargent, ed.	*Women of Wonder: The Classic Years*; *Women of Wonder: The Contemporary Years*
Sheri S. Tepper	*The Gate to Women's Country*
Sheri S. Tepper	*Grass*
Sheri S. Tepper	*Beauty*
James Tiptree	*Her Smoke Rose Up Forever*
John Varley	<u>Gaean Trilogy</u>, starting with *Wizard*
Joan D. Vinge	*The Summer Queen*
Virginia Woolf	*Orlando*
Jane Yolen	<u>Great Alta Saga</u>, starting with *Sister Light, Sister Dark*

THEMATIC QUESTIONS

- What does your novel have to say about the role of women (or the role of gender)?

- Do you believe that science fiction and fantasy have done a good job of exploring the roles of women and improving the place of women? Do stereotypes persist in these genres that are harmful to women?
- Does the book that you chose have a strong female lead? A female villain? Strong older female characters? Stereotypical female characters? Friendships (or significant relationships of any kind) between women?
- Has the position of women writers improved over time, or has it held steady? Do women writers produce more complex, well-developed female characters?
- Which science fiction and fantasy books would you recommend to a young woman reader? To an elderly woman reader?
- Is coverage of gender issues better in the science fiction or fantasy genre
- Does appreciation of gender themes differ between men and women in your group?

RESOURCES

Feminist Science Fiction, Fantasy, and Utopian Literature

http://www.feministsf.org

GODS AND RELIGION: A DIVINE COLLECTION OF SPECULATIVE FICTION

I'm not good in groups . . . It's difficult to work in a group when you're omnipotent.
—Q, in "Deja Q," episode of *Star Trek, The Next Generation*

God is:
A) An invisible spirit with a long beard.
B) A small dog dead in a hole.
C) Everyman.
D) The Wizard of Oz.

—Harlan Ellison

Can religion and speculative fiction mix? Some argue that science is fundamentally atheistic, that fantasy fiction is, by its nature, heretical, or that religion is simply left out of the equation by most SF & F writers. If that's true, somebody forgot to relay the message to the authors in this list. Although I don't argue that science fiction and fantasy are always kind to religious belief systems, many works do address religion and spirituality. Many variations on the role of a god have been examined, and interesting examples of both believers and nonbelievers are available to speculative fiction readers.

SUGGESTED WORKS

Richard Adams	*Shardik*
Margaret Atwood	*The Handmaid's Tale*
Wayne Barlowe	*God's Demon*

James Blish	*A Case of Conscience*
Marion Zimmer Bradley	<u>Avalon</u> series, starting with *The Mists of Avalon*
Lois McMaster Bujold	*The Curse of Chalion; The Hallowed Hunt*
Octavia Butler	*Parable of the Sower; Parable of the Talents*
Trudi Canavan	<u>Age of the Five</u>, starting with *Priestess of the White*
Orson Scott Card	<u>The Tales of Alvin Maker</u>, starting with *Seventh Son*
Orson Scott Card	*Xenocide* (in the <u>Ender</u> series)
P. C. Cast	<u>Divine Fantasies</u>, starting with *Divine by Mistake*
G. K. Chesterton	*The Man Who Was Thursday*
Philip K. Dick	*Valis*
Sara Douglass	<u>The Crucible</u>, starting with *The Nameless Day*
Hal Duncan	<u>The Book of All Hours</u>, starting with *Vellum*
Philip Jose Farmer	<u>Riverworld</u>, starting with *To Your Scattered Bodies Go*
Michael Flynn	*Eifelheim*
Felix Gilman	*Thunderer; Gears of the City*
Lisa Goldstein	*The Red Magician*
Karen Hancock	<u>Legends of the Guardian King</u>, starting with *Light of Eidon*
Robert Heinlein	*Stranger in a Strange Land*
Robert Heinlein	*Job: A Comedy of Justice*
Frank Herbert	<u>Dune</u> series, starting with *Dune*
Nalo Hopkinson	*The Salt Road*
Greg Keyes	<u>Kingdoms of Thorn and Bone</u>, starting with *The Briar King*
Tim LaHaye and Jerry Jenkins	<u>Left Behind</u> series, starting with *Left Behind*
C. S. Lewis	<u>The Chronicles of Narnia</u>, starting with *The Lion, the Witch, and the Wardrobe*
C. S. Lewis	<u>Space</u> trilogy, starting with *Out of the Silent Planet*
Kathryn Mackel	<u>Birthright Project</u>, starting with *Outriders*
Ian McDonald	*River of Gods*
Walter M. Miller	*A Canticle for Leibowitz*
Christopher Moore	*Lamb: the Gospel According to Biff, Christ's Childhood Pal*
James Morrow	<u>Godhead</u> series, starting with *Towing Jehovah*
Donita K. Paul	<u>The Dragonkeeper Chronicles</u>, starting with *Dragonspell*
Terry Pratchett	*Small Gods*
Philip Pullman	<u>His Dark Materials</u>, starting with *The Golden Compass*
Mary Doria Russell	*The Sparrow; Children of God*
Carl Sagan	*Contact*
Robert J. Sawyer	*Calculating God*
Sharon Shinn	<u>Samaria</u> series, starting with *Archangel*
Dan Simmons	<u>Hyperion Cantos</u>, starting with *Hyperion*
Jeff Somers	*The Electric Church*
Olaf Stapledon	*The Star Maker*
Judith Tarr	*The Hound and the Falcon*
Walter Wangerin	*The Book of the Dun Cow*
Roger Zelazny	*Lord of Light*

THEMATIC QUESTIONS

- What role does religion play in the lives of major characters in the novel that you chose?

- Does the author create or explore any unusual variations on religion in the book that you read? What is the most interesting religion in speculative fiction?

- Is your novel basically respectful or disrespectful of religion? Which is true for science fiction as a whole? For fantasy as a whole?

- What is the most interesting portrayal of a god or goddess in speculative fiction?

- Compare religion and mythology. What are the significant similarities or differences in these two traditions?

- Fantasy fiction has been called fundamentally heretical by people of some religious persuasions. Is there anything to this argument? Is science fiction/fantasy likely to be satisfying for religious readers? Is religion as important in fantasy and science fiction fiction on the whole as it is in the real world?

GOLDEN AGE AND NEW WAVE: SCIENCE FICTION THROUGH 1980

Two of the most prominent schools of science fiction writing were the Golden Age and the New Wave. The Golden Age of science fiction, typically defined as occurring from 1930 to 1960, emphasizes a style of writing that focuses on hard science fiction and adventure plots, most typically written in the short story format. The editorial style of John W. Campbell, who wielded influence at *Astounding Science Fiction* and other magazines, is typical of the Golden Age.

In reaction to Golden Age style and in line with societal changes, the New Wave began to gain steam in the early 1960s and remained prominent into the late 1970s. Developing under the guidance of writers such as Michael Moorcock and Brian Aldiss in Britain and Harlan Ellison, Ursula K. Le Guin, and Samuel R. Delany in the United States, New Wave science fiction is more literary and experimental than Golden Age writing. It explores "soft" and social sciences, focusing on the individual and on questions of morals or politics. In this period, the pulp magazine market began to decline, and novels became the most common format for genre writing.

Both styles continue to influence contemporary writers. Either makes an interesting theme for a book group meeting, or both can be combined in a comparative exercise.

SUGGESTED GOLDEN AGE WORKS

Poul Anderson	*Time Patrol*
Poul Anderson	*To Outlive Eternity and Other Stories*
Poul Anderson	Flandry series, starting with *Ensign Flandry*
Poul Anderson	*The Collected Short Works of Poul Anderson, Vol. 1: Call Me Joe*
Isaac Asimov	Foundation series, starting with *Foundation*
Isaac Asimov	*The Caves of Steel*; *The Naked Sun*
Isaac Asimov	Robot series, starting with *I, Robot*
Isaac Asimov	*Pebble in the Sky*
Isaac Asimov	*The Complete Stories, Vols. 1 & 2*

Isaac Asimov, et al., eds.	*The Mammoth Book of Golden Age Science Fiction*
James Blish	*A Case of Conscience*
Leigh Brackett	*The Secret of Sinharat*
Leigh Brackett	*Lorelei of the Red Mists: Planetary Romances*
Fredric Brown	*From These Ashes: The Complete Short Science Fiction of Fredric Brown*
Arthur C. Clarke	*The Collected Stories of Arthur C. Clarke*
Hal Clement	*Heavy Planet: The Classic Mesklin Stories*
Hal Clement	*The Essential Hal Clement: Volumes 1–3*
L. Sprague de Camp	*Years in the Making: The Time Travel Stories of L. Sprague de Camp*
Robert A. Heinlein	*Starship Troopers*
Henry Kuttner	*The Lost Mimzy and Other Stories*
Henry Kuttner	*The Dark World*
Murray Leinster	*First Contacts: The Essential Murray Leinster*
C. L. Moore	*Northwest of Earth: The Complete Northwest Smith*
C. L. Moore	*The Black God's Kiss*
Chad Oliver	*Far from This Earth and Other Stories*
Chad Oliver	*From Other Shores: An Omnibus*
Frederik Pohl	*Platinum Pohl: The Collected Best Stories*
Frederik Pohl and C. M. Kornbluth	*The Space Merchants*
Frederik Pohl, ed.	*The SFWA Grand Masters, Volumes 1–3*
Eric Frank Russell	*Entities: The Selected Novels of Eric Frank Russell*
Eric Frank Russell	*Major Ingredients*
Robert Silverberg, ed.	*The Science Fiction Hall of Fame, Volume One*
Clifford D. Simak	*City*
E. E. "Doc" Smith	*Skylark of Space*
E. E. "Doc" Smith	*Triplanetary*
William Tenn	*Immodest Proposals: The Complete Science Fiction of William Tenn, Vol. 1*
William Tenn	*Here Comes Civilization: The Complete Science Fiction of William Tenn, Vol. 2*
A. E. Van Vogt	*Slan*
A. E. Van Vogt	*The World of Null-A*
A. E. Van Vogt	*Transfinite: The Essential A. E. Van Vogt*
Jack Vance	*The Demon Princes*, starting with *The Star King*
Jack Vance	*The Jack Vance Reader*
John Wyndham	*The Day of the Triffids*
John Wyndham	*The Chrysalids*

TRANSITIONAL WORKS

Brian Aldiss	*Non-Stop*
Alfred Bester	*The Stars My Destination*
Alfred Bester	*The Demolished Man*

Ray Bradbury	*Bradbury Stories*
Tom Shippey, ed.	*The Oxford Book of Science Fiction Stories*
Cordwainer Smith	*The Rediscovery of Man: The Complete Short Science Fiction of Cordwainer Smith*
Theodore Sturgeon	*More Than Human*

SUGGESTED NEW WAVE WORKS

Brian Aldiss	*Non-Stop*
J. G. Ballard	*The Best Short Stories of J. G. Ballard*
J. G. Ballard	*The Crystal World*
John M. Brunner	*The Sheep Look Up*
John M. Brunner	*Stand on Zanzibar*
Anthony Burgess	*A Clockwork Orange*
Samuel Delany	*Babel-17*
Samuel Delany	*Dhalgren*
Philip K. Dick	*Four Novels of the 1960s*
Philip K. Dick	*Five Novels of the 1960s & 70s*
Thomas Disch	*334*
Thomas Disch	*The Genocides*
Philip Jose Farmer	<u>Riverworld</u> series, starting with *To Your Scattered Bodies Go*
Philip Jose Farmer	*The Best of Philip Jose Farmer*
Harlan Ellison, ed.	*Dangerous Visions*; *Again, Dangerous Visions*
Harlan Ellison	*The Essential Ellison*
Robert A. Heinlein	*Stranger in a Strange Land*
Frank Herbert	*Dune*
Daniel Keyes	*Flowers for Algernon*
Ursula K. Le Guin	*The Left Hand of Darkness*
Ursula K. Le Guin	*The Lathe of Heaven*
Ursula K. Le Guin	*The Dispossessed*
Michael Moorcock	*The Cornelius Quartet*
Joanna Russ	*The Female Man*
Joanna Russ	*We Who Are About To . . .*
Robert Silverberg	*The Book of Skulls*
Robert Silverberg	*Dying Inside*
Robert Silverberg	*Son of Man*
Robert Silverberg	*Nightwings*
Robert Silverberg	*Phases of the Moon: Six Decades of Masterpieces*
John Sladek	*The Complete Roderick*
Norman Spinrad	*Bug Jack Barron*
James Tiptree, Jr.	*Her Smoke Rose Up Forever: The Great Years of James Tiptree, Jr.*
Sean Wright, ed.	*The New Wave of Speculative Fiction: The What If Factor*
Roger Zelazny	*Lord of Light*

THEMATIC QUESTIONS

- Is the book that you chose a good example of Golden Age or New Wave science fiction, or does it fall between the two camps?
- Do you see a clear delineation between these two different eras of science fiction writing? If so, how do you characterize the difference?
- Which of these two styles have you read more extensively? Which holds up better over time?
- Did Golden Age or New Wave science fiction have more influence on the contemporary genre? Do contemporary authors that you read fit into one style or the other?
- Which writers fit most comfortably in the style of each of these two eras? Can you think of writers who were out of place in the era in which they wrote? Writers whose style changed with the times?

GOOD AND EVIL: THE STORY OF THE MORAL IS . . .

Evil is relative. You can't hang a sign on it. You can't touch it or taste it or cut it with a sword. Evil depends on where you are standing, pointing your indicting finger.
—Glen Cook

Even the most evil of men and women, if you understand their hearts, had some generous act that redeems them, at least a little, from their sins.
—Orson Scott Card

Questions of morality are central to fantasy and science fiction, although the way that they are handled has changed over time. In early genre works, good typically battles evil and the heroes win the day. A bright line of demarcation separates right from wrong. Contemporary writing often takes a more ambivalent approach, featuring characters who exhibit both good and bad behaviors, or whose good intentions are twisted sometimes into bad results. In such works, it can be difficult to separate heroes from villains, and the results of their morally murky actions are often ironic, darkly humorous, relative, and tragic, yet highly believable.

SUGGESTED WORKS

Joe Abercrombie	*Best Served Cold*
Clive Barker	The Art, starting with *The Great and Secret Show*
Greg Bear	*The Forge of God; Anvil of Stars*
Anne Bishop	Black Jewels trilogy, starting with *Daughter of the Blood*
James Blish	*A Case of Conscience*
Peter V. Brett	*The Warded Man*
Terry Brooks	The Word & the Void, starting with *Running with the Demon*
Terry Brooks	Genesis of Shannara, starting with *Armageddon's Children*
Lois McMaster Bujold	The Sharing Knife, starting with *Beguilement*
Orson Scott Card	*Ender's Game*
James Clemens	The Banned and the Banished, starting with *Wit'ch Fire*

Sara Douglass	The Crucible series, starting with *The Nameless Day*
Hal Duncan	The Book of All Hours, starting with *Vellum*
David Anthony Durham	Acacia, starting with *The War of the Mein*
Chris Evans	Iron Elves series, starting with *A Darkness Forged in Fire*
Mark J. Ferrari	*The Book of Joby*
C. S. Friedman	Coldfire Trilogy, starting with *Black Sun Rising*
Neil Gaiman and Terry Pratchett	*Good Omens*
John Gardner	*Grendel*
Felix Gilman	*Thunderer*; *Gears of the City*
Terry Goodkind	The Sword of Truth, starting with *Wizard's First Rule*
Austin Grossman	*Soon I Will Be Invincible*
Elizabeth Haydon	Symphony of Ages, starting with *Rhapsody: Child of Blood*
Robert A. Heinlein	*Job: A Comedy of Justice*
Robert Jordan	The Wheel of Time, starting with *The Eye of the World*
Guy Gavriel Kay	*Tigana*
Stephen King	The Dark Tower, starting with *The Gunslinger*
Stephen King	*The Stand*
Madeleine L'Engle	Time Quintet, starting with *A Wrinkle in Time*
C. S. Lewis	The Chronicles of Narnia, starting with *The Lion, the Witch and the Wardrobe*
C. S. Lewis	Space trilogy, starting with *Out of the Silent Planet*
Sergei Lukyanenko	Night Watch series, starting with *Night Watch*
Gregory Maguire	Wicked Years, starting with *Wicked*
George R. R. Martin	A Song of Ice and Fire, starting with *The Game of Thrones*
Patricia A. McKillip	*Ombria in Shadow*
Tim Powers	*Last Call*
Philip Pullman	His Dark Materials, starting with *The Golden Compass*
Jenna Rhodes	The Elven Ways, starting with *The Four Forges*
J. K. Rowling	Harry Potter, starting with *Harry Potter and the Sorcerer's Stone*
Brian Ruckley	Godless World, starting with *Winterbirth*
Salman Rushdie	*The Satanic Verses*
Mary Doria Russell	*The Sparrow*; *Children of God*
R. A. Salvatore	Most novels, such as the DemonWars trilogy, starting with *The Demon Awakens*
Brandon Sanderson	*Elantris*
Brandon Sanderson	Mistborn series, starting with *The Final Empire*
Dan Simmons	Hyperion Cantos, starting with *Hyperion*
J. R. R. Tolkien	*The Lord of the Rings*
Karen Traviss	Wess'Har Wars, starting with *City of Pearl*

THEMATIC QUESTIONS

- What are the central moral conflicts in the book that you chose? Do you find them compelling? Are their answers or resolutions obvious, or is it difficult to identify the right path?

- Is good behavior rewarded with good results in the book that you read? Is it rewarded in real life?
- Did the villains in the book that you read intend to do evil, or did they have good intentions? How would the book change if told from their perspective?
- Do you prefer a clear division between good and evil, or do you favor morality drawn with shades of gray? Or does your preference depend on your mood?
- Was corruption a theme in the novel that you selected? Were the pressures or temptations brought to bear on the forces of good convincing? Would you, or most of the people you know, have withstood them?
- Has turning from the purely heroic toward more use of irony, realism bordering on cynicism, and complex approaches to good and evil improved fantasy and science fiction?

GRAPHIC NOVELS: STAND-UP COMICS IN SCIENCE FICTION AND FANTASY

The comic book is the marijuana of the nursery, the bane of the bassinet, the horror of the home, the curse of the kids, and a threat to the future.
—John Mason Brown

Badly drawn, badly written and badly printed—a strain on the young eyes and young nervous systems—the effect of these pulp-paper nightmares is that of a violent stimulant. Their crude blacks and reds spoil a child's natural sense of color; their hypodermic injection of sex and murder make the child impatient with better, quieter stories. Unless we want a coming generation even more ferocious than the present one, parents and teachers throughout America must band together to break the comic magazine.
—Dr. Frederic Wertham

Once considered a threat to America's youth by members of Congress and the FBI, comics—particularly when grouped into longer narratives euphemistically called "graphic novels"—are now viewed as a gateway to literacy for young readers and a serious artistic format by most critics. Regardless of what you call them or how important you think they are, graphic novels make a diverting theme, a step outside the ordinary, for book groups. Make sure that you pass around copies. Looking at all of the artistic styles is at least half the fun!

SUGGESTED WORKS

Hiromu Arakawa	Full Metal Alchemist series
Darren Aronofsky and Kent Williams	*The Fountain*
Chris Bachalo and Joe Kelly	Steampunk series
Holly Black and Ted Naifeh	*The Good Neighbors*
Jim Butcher, Ardian Syaf, et al.	The Dresden Files series
Nicholas De Crécy	*Glacial Period*
J. M. De Matteis et al.	*The Compleat Moonshadow*

J. M. De Matteis and Mike Ploog	Abadazad series
Ian Edginton and D'Israeli	Scarlet Traces series
Warren Ellis et al.	Transmetropolitan series
Warren Ellis et al.	Global Frequency series
Garth Ennis et al.	Preacher series
Phil Foglio, Kaja Foglio and Cheyenne Wright	Girl Genius series
Neil Gaiman et al.	The Sandman series
Neil Gaiman et al.	Death: The High Cost of Living series
Neil Gaiman and P. Craig Russell	*Coraline*
Neil Gaiman et al.	The Books of Magic series
René Goscinny and Albert Uderzo	Asterix series
Kazu Kibuishi, ed.	Flight series
Stephen King, Peter David, et al.	Dark Tower series
Robert Kirkman et al.	The Walking Dead series
Yukito Kishiro	Battle Angle Alita series
Many contributors	Star Wars series
George R. R. Martin et al.	*The Hedge Knight*
Winsor McCay	*Little Nemo in Slumberland*
Linda Medley	*Castle Waiting*
Frank Miller and Geoff Darrow	*Hard Boiled*
Tony Millionaire	Billy Hazelnuts series
Pat Mills et al.	Slaine series, starting with *Warrior's Dawn*
Hayao Miyazaki	*Nausicaä of the Valley of the Wind*
Walter Moers	*The 13? Lives of Captain Bluebear*
Walter Moers	*Rumo: and His Miraculous Adventures*
Alan Moore and Dave Gibbons	*Watchmen*
Alan Moore and David Lloyd	*V for Vendetta*
Alan Moore and Kevin O'Neill	The League of Extraordinary Gentlemen series
Alan Moore and J. H. Williams	Promethea series
Grant Morrison et al.	The Invisibles series
Dean Motter et al.	Mister X series
Katsuhiro Otomo	Akira series
David Petersen	Mouse Guard series
Wendy Pini and Richard Pini	Elfquest
Terry Pratchett et al.	The Discworld graphic novels series
Yoshiyuki Sadamoto et al.	Neon Genesis Evangelion series

Masamune Shirow	Ghost in the Shell series
Masamune Shirow	Appleseed series
Jeff Smith	Bone series
Andrew Stephenson and Trevor Goring	*Waterloo Sunset*
Koushun Takami and Masayuki Taguchi	Battle Royale series
Rumiko Takahashi	InuYasha series
Bryan Talbot	*Alice in Sunderland*
Bryan Talbot	Luther Arkwright, starting with *The Adventures of Luther Arkwright*
Osamu Tezuka	Astro Boy series
Roy Thomas et al.	The Chronicles of Conan series
Jean Van Hamme et al.	Thorgal series
Brian K. Vaughan et al.	Y: The Last Man series
Brian K. Vaughan and Tony Harris	Ex Machina series
Mark Verheiden et al.	*Aliens Omnibus*
John Wagner et al.	Judge Dredd series
Yuu Watase	Fushigi Yugi series
Gerard Way and Gabriel Ba	The Umbrella Academy
Joss Whedon et al.	Buffy the Vampire Slayer series
Joss Whedon, Brett Matthews and Will Conrad	Serenity series
Bill Willingham et al.	Fables series
Bill Willingham et al.	Jack of Fables series

Graphic novels featuring superheroes—such as Batman, Captain America, Daredevil, The Fantastic Four, Green Lantern, Hellboy, The Incredible Hulk, Iron Man, the Justice League of America, Spawn, Spiderman, The Spirit, Superman, and X-Men—are also appropriate for this theme, as are most manga, comics published in Japan or influenced by the Japanese style.

THEMATIC QUESTIONS

- How does the artist's style contribute to the mood, tone, or content of the storytelling?
- Would the book that you selected work if it were rewritten as a print-only novel?
- What's the best graphic novel with a fantasy theme? With a science fiction theme?
- What's the difference between a graphic novel and a comic book?
- Do you like adaptation of existing works of fiction to graphic formats, or do you prefer for these works to be left in their original formats?

RESOURCES

Graphic Novel Reporter

http://www.graphicnovelreporter.com

HARD SF: PUTTING THE SCIENCE IN SCIENCE FICTION

These wild ideas are more than just window dressing; they're the inventions of writers who look at the stuff our lives are made of, from toaster ovens to string theory, and say: what if? If you're a true hard SF fan, you thrill to these ideas . . .

—Chris Moriarty

It is as though everybody in the field pretends not to notice how really depressed most hard SF is, how seriously lacking in affect are most of its protagonists, how lassitudinous are the worlds these protagonists inhabit and transform.

—John Clute

There are two kinds of science fiction reader, who in their extreme forms constitute disjoint reading populations. A pure Population One reader wants scientific ideas and will be tolerant of other flaws provided those ideas are present. A pure Population Two reader will tolerate (or fail to notice) scientific errors but insist on literary virtues.

—Charles Sheffield

Inclusion of solid scientific theory draws some readers to science fiction and scares others away. Perhaps that has something to do with the reputation of hard SF for being high in ideas but low in quality characters or authorial style. But is that reputation fair? That's one of the questions that your group should explore if you take on the theme of hard SF. Another is the surprisingly tricky question of what accurate "science" is exactly, especially when speculation about the future is involved. White lab coats are optional.

SUGGESTED WORKS

Stephen Baxter	<u>Manifold</u> series, starting with *Manifold: Time*
Stephen Baxter	*The Time Ships*
Greg Bear	*Blood Music*
Greg Bear	*Eon*
Greg Bear	*The Forge of God*
Greg Bear	*Moving Mars*
Gregory Benford	*Timescape*
David Brin	<u>Uplift Saga</u>, starting with *Sundiver*
Mike Brotherton	*Star Dragon*
Mike Brotherton	*Spider Star*
Arthur C. Clarke	*Rendezvous with Rama*
Arthur C. Clarke	*Fountains of Paradise*
Hal Clement	*Heavy Planet: The Classic Mesklin Stories*
Greg Egan	*Incandescence*
Robert Forward	*Dragon's Egg*
Peter F. Hamilton	<u>Night's Dawn</u>, starting with *The Reality Dysfunction*
Peter F. Hamilton	<u>Commonwealth Saga</u>, starting with *Pandora's Star*
Peter F. Hamilton	<u>The Void Trilogy</u>, starting with *The Dreaming Void*
David Hartwell and Kathryn Cramer, eds.	*The Hard SF Renaissance*

Matthew Jarpe	*Radio Freefall*
Wil McCarthy	<u>The Queendom of Sol</u>, starting with *Collapsium*
Jack McDevitt	<u>Alex Benedict</u> series, starting with *The Engines of God*
Chris Moriarty	*Spin State*; *Spin Control*
Larry Niven	<u>Ringworld</u> series, starting with *Ringworld*
Larry Niven and Jerry Pournelle	*The Mote in God's Eye*
Alastair Reynolds	<u>Revelation Space</u> series, starting with *Revelation Space*
Kim Stanley Robinson	<u>Mars</u> trilogy, starting with *Red Mars*
Robert J. Sawyer	*Factoring Humanity*
Charles Stross	*Accelerando*
Vernor Vinge	*A Deepness in the Sky*; *A Fire upon the Deep*
Vernor Vinge	*Rainbows End*
Peter Watts	*Blindsight*
Peter Watts	<u>Rifters</u> series, starting with *Starfish*
Robert Charles Wilson	*Darwinia*

Authors whose works are considered "hard science fiction" by some

- Poul Anderson
- Neal Asher
- Isaac Asimov
- Iain M. Banks
- Ben Bova
- Joe Haldeman
- Robert A. Heinlein
- Frank Herbert
- Ian McDonald
- Richard Morgan
- Frederik Pohl
- Charles Sheffield
- Dan Simmons
- Neal Stephenson
- Scott Westerfeld

THEMATIC QUESTIONS

- Hard science fiction has many definitions. Broad definitions include any book featuring science that doesn't violate scientific laws as understood at the time that the book was written. Narrow definitions stipulate that scientific content has to be extensive and integral to the plot of the book, that it must continue to be accurate based on current knowledge, or that it must be from "hard" sciences, not "soft" sciences such as the social sciences. Does the book that you read fit the subgenre under all of these definitions or only according to some of them?

- Which definition of hard science fiction do you prefer? Which is most useful in identifying it to the readers who are the most likely to enjoy it?

- Does writing with scientific accuracy conflict somehow with writing with good style or with building good characters, or is it simply hard for an author to do all of those things well? What writers have this combination of skills?

- How important is accurate science to science fiction? Can a great science fiction book be written that has inaccurate science?
- Which goal should take priority: to write science fiction that can be understood by the lay reader, or to explore the full extent of science and its applications in fiction?

RESOURCES

Hard SF.org

http://hardsf.org

HEALTH, MEDICINE, BIOLOGY, AND GENETICS: SCIENCE FICTION GETS UP CLOSE AND PHYSICAL

There is no medicine like hope, no incentive so great, and no tonic so powerful as expectation of something better tomorrow.

—Orison Swett Marsden

Mankind has survived all catastrophes. It will also survive modern medicine.

—Gerhard Kocher

They've mapped the entire human genome. But the bad news is that the audio version will be narrated by William Shatner.

—Bill Maher

What's the future of the human body (besides sagging and wrinkles)? It's probably the science fiction question that preoccupies us the most as we go about our everyday lives. Major medical advances are a double-edged sword that excite the imagination of some writers and raise worries among others. Are we headed toward immortality or plague? Stronger more durable bodies or polluted shells? This theme is sure to raise attention because every reader has a personal interest in the outcome.

SUGGESTED WORKS

Chris Adrian	*A Better Angel: Stories*
Margaret Atwood	*Oryx & Crake*
Scott Bakker	*Neuropath*
Stephen Baxter	*Evolution*
Greg Bear	*Blood Music*
Greg Bear	*Darwin's Radio; Darwin's Children*
M. D. Benoit	*Synergy*
David Brin	*Glory Season*
Keith Brooke	*Genetopia*
Lois McMaster Bujold	*Barrayar*
Octavia Butler	*Lilith's Brood*
Octavia Butler	*Fledgling*

C. J. Cherryh	*Cyteen*
Michael Crichton	*The Andromeda Strain*
Michael Crichton	*Prey*
Michael Crichton	*Next*
Julie Czerneda	<u>Web Shifters</u> series, starting with *Beholder's Eye*
Philip K. Dick	*The Scanner Darkly*
Cory Doctorow	*Down and Out in the Magic Kingdom*
Nicola Griffith	*Slow River*
Frank Herbert	*The White Plague*
Eva Hoffman	*The Secret*
Aldous Huxley	*Brave New World*
Kazuo Ishiguro	*Never Let Me Go*
P. D. James	*The Children of Men*
Daniel Keyes	*Flowers for Algernon*
Stephen King	*The Stand*
Nancy Kress	<u>Sleepless</u> series, starting with *Beggars in Spain*
Nancy Kress	*Nothing Human*
Nancy Kress	*Dogs*
Karen Krossing	*Pure*
Paul Levinson	<u>Dr. Phil D'Amato</u> series, starting with *The Silk Code*
David Marusek	*Counting Heads*
Richard Matheson	*I Am Legend*
Paul McAuley	*White Devils*
Anne McCaffrey and Elizabeth Ann Scarborough	<u>Petaybee</u> series, starting with *Powers That Be*
China Miéville	*Perdido Street Station*
Elizabeth Moon	*The Speed of Dark*
Elizabeth Moon	<u>*The Deed of Paksenarrion*</u>
Richard K. Morgan	<u>Takeshi Kovacs</u> series, starting with *Altered Carbon*
Richard K. Morgan	*Thirteen* (aka *Black Man*)
Craig Nova	*Wetware*
Jennifer Pelland	*Unwelcome Bodies*
Justina Robson	*Natural History*
Jennifer L. Rohn	*Experimental Heart*
Rudy Rucker	*Frek and the Elixir*
Nick Sagan	<u>Post Human</u> trilogy, starting with *Idlewild*
Robert J. Sawyer	<u>Neanderthal Parallax</u>, starting with *Hominids*
Robert J. Sawyer	*Mindscan*
Robert J. Sawyer	*Rollback*
John Scalzi	*Old Man's War*; *The Ghost Brigades*
Mary Shelley	*Frankenstein*
Scott Sigler	*Infected*; *Contagious*
Brian Stableford	<u>Emortals</u>, starting with *Inherit the Earth*
Charles Stross	*Accelerando*
Sheri S. Tepper	*Grass*
Karen Traviss	<u>Wess'har</u> series starting with *City of Pearl*

Jeff VanderMeer and Mark Roberts	*The Thackery T. Lambshead Pocket Guide to Eccentric & Discredited Diseases*
S. L. Viehl	<u>Stardoc</u> series, starting with *Stardoc*
Peter Watts	*Blindsight*
H. G. Wells	*The Island of Dr. Moreau*
James White	<u>Sector General</u> series, starting with *Beginning Operations*
Connie Willis	*Doomsday Book*

THEMATIC QUESTIONS

- What are the dangers or costs of medical or genetic advancement in the novel that you read? Do you find these dangers believable?

- What single potential advancement in biology or genetics excites you the most? What change worries you the most?

- Equal access can be just as crucial to health care as advancements themselves. Was access a concern in the book that you read? If major advancements come in the future, what will happen if they are only available to a select population?

- If it were available, would you consider gene therapy? Cybernetic enhancements? Having your consciousness transplanted into another body? Cloning yourself?

- Will medicine advance as quickly in the real world as it did in your book? Why or why not?

- Which health problems will be eliminated in the future? On which will we make little progress?

RESOURCES

Medical Innovations in Science Fiction

http://www.technovelgy.com/ct/Science_List_Detail.asp?BT=Medical

---

HORROR CROSSOVERS: SPECULATIVE FICTION SO SCARY IT'S GOOD

It is not so much the things we know that terrify us as it is the things we do not know, the things that break all known laws and rules, the things that come upon us unaware and shatter the pleasant dream of our little world.

—Donald A. Wandrei

However selective the conscious mind may be, most biological memories are unpleasant ones, echoes of danger and terror. Nothing endures for so long as fear.

—J. G. Ballard

I must not fear. Fear is the mind-killer. Fear is the little death that brings total obliteration. I will face my fear. I will permit it to pass over me and through me. And when it has gone past I will turn the inner eye to see its path. Where the fear has gone there will be nothing. Only I will remain.

—Frank Herbert

It's difficult to draw a bright line distinction between horror and fantasy. At one point in history, the term "dark fantasy" was more common in usage than "horror." Some book group members may have limited thresholds for fear, so check with your readers before you try this theme. The recent trend is toward making characters such as vampires and werewolves sympathetic instead of truly scary, so that even the faint of heart can probably find a book that pleases them with a little haunting . . . er, make that a little hunting.

SUGGESTED WORKS

Kelley Armstrong	Women of the Otherworld, starting with *Bitten*
Clive Barker	*Weaveworld*
Clive Barker	*Imajica*
Clive Barker	The Art, starting with *The Great and Secret Show*
Anne Bishop	Black Jewels Trilogy, starting with *Daughter of the Blood*
K. J. Bishop	*The Etched City*
Ray Bradbury	*Something Wicked This Way Comes*
Jim Butcher	The Dresden Files, starting with *Storm Front*
Alan Campbell	Deepgate Codex, starting with *Scar Night*
Angela Carter	*Burning Your Boats: The Collected Stories*
Ellen Datlow, ed.	*Poe*
Charles de Lint	*The Riddle of the Wren*
Hal Duncan	The Book of All Hours, starting with *Vellum*
Raymond Feist	*Faerie Tale*
Neil Gaiman	*Neverwhere*
Neil Gaiman	Sandman graphic novels
Christopher Golden and Tim Lebbon	Hidden Cities series, starting with *Mind the Gap*
Christopher Golden	Veil series, starting with *The Myth Hunters*
Simon R. Green	Nightside series, starting with *Something from the Nightside*
Barb and J. C. Hendee	Noble Dead series, starting with *Dhampir*
Graham Joyce	*The Tooth Fairy*
Graham Joyce	*Requiem*
Caitlin R. Kiernan	*Silk*; *Murder of Angels*
Caitlin R. Kiernan	*Threshold*; *Low Red Moon*; *Daughter of Hounds*
Stephen King	*The Stand*
Stephen King	The Dark Tower series, starting with *The Gunslinger*
Tim Lebbon	Noreela series, starting with *Dusk*
Tanith Lee	*Secret Books of Paradys*
H. P. Lovecraft	*The Dunwich Horror and Others*
H. P. Lovecraft	*At the Mountains of Madness and Other Macabre Tales*
Sergei Lukyanenko	Watch series, starting with *Night Watch*
George R. R. Martin	*Dreamsongs* anthologies
George R. R. Martin	*Fevre Dream*
Richard Matheson	*I Am Legend*
Robert McCammon	*Swan Song*

Robin McKinley	*Sunshine*
John Meaney	*Bone Song; Black Blood*
China Miéville	New Crobuzon, starting with *Perdido Street Station*
Norman Partridge	*Dark Harvest*
S. M. Peters	*Whitechapel Gods*
Tim Powers	*Last Call*
Mary Shelley	*Frankenstein*
Dan Simmons	*Drood*
Ann and Jeff VanderMeer, eds.	*The New Weird*
Chelsea Quinn Yarbro	Saint-Germain series, starting with *Hotel Transylvania*

THEMATIC QUESTIONS

- Is the book that you read truly frightening? Why or why not?
- Why do some people like to be scared? Conversely, why can't some people handle fear?
- What's the difference between horror and fantasy?
- Is the threat of violence, pain, and death the most horrifying for you as a reader? Or is something else scarier? Can you give examples of other horrors from the novel that you read?
- Much of recent fantasy and horror has been marketed as "paranormal" and is more sympathetic to the occult than frightened by it. What are the reasons for this trend? Did the book that you read fit into this trend?

IMMORTALS, LONGEVITY, AND REJUVENATION: THE DOOR TO FOREVER

The first ten million years were the worst. And the second ten million years, they were the worst too. The third ten million I didn't enjoy at all. After that I went into a bit of a decline.

—Douglas Adams

When I die, I'm leaving my body to science fiction.

—Steven Wright

Readers know something about the search for eternal life: Reading itself is an attempt to squeeze many lifetimes of experience into one brief span. Perhaps that is why immortality is such a popular theme in fantasy and why rejuvenation and life extension are such a mainstay of science fiction. At the core of this theme are two fascinating questions: Would living forever be a blessing or a curse? And if one were to live forever, what would be the proper way to conduct that life?

Suggested Works

Poul Anderson	*The Boat of a Million Years*
Neal Asher	*The Skinner*

Kage Baker	<u>The Company</u> series, starting with *In the Garden of Iden*
Greg Bear	*Vitals*
Ben Bova	*The Immortality Factor*
M. M. Buckner	*War Surf*
Octavia Butler	*Wild Seed*
Steve Cash	*The Meq*
Arthur C. Clarke	*The City and the Stars*
Peter David	<u>Modern Arthur</u> series, starting with *Knight Life*
Cory Doctorow	*Down and Out in the Magic Kingdom*
Sara Douglass	<u>Troy Game</u> series, starting with *Hades' Daughter*
Tananarive Due	*My Soul to Keep*
Jon Fasman	*The Geographer's Library*
Minister Faust	*Coyote Kings of the Space-Age Bachelor Pad*
C. S. Friedman	*The Madness Season*
C. S. Friedman	<u>Magister</u> series, starting with *Feast of Souls*
Andrew Sean Greer	*The Confessions of Max Tivoli*
James Gunn	*The Immortals*
Pete Hamill	*Forever*
Laurell K. Hamilton	<u>Meredith Gentry</u> series, starting with *A Kiss of Shadows*
Robert A. Heinlein	<u>Lazarus Long</u>, starting with *Methuselah's Children*
Mark Helprin	*Winter's Tale*
William Kotzwinkle	*The Amphora Project*
Jane Lindskold	*Changer*
Holly Lisle	<u>World Gates</u> series, starting with *Memory of Fire*
Ken Macleod	*Engine City*
Louise Marley	*The Child Goddess*
David Marusek	*Counting Heads*
Vonda N. McIntyre	*The Moon and the Sun*
Syne Mitchell	<u>Deathless</u> series, starting with *The Last Mortal Man*
L. E. Modesitt	*Timegods' World*
Christopher Moore	*Practical Demonkeeping*
Richard K. Morgan	<u>Takeshi Kovacs</u>, starting with *Altered Carbon*
Stan Nicholls	<u>Dreamtime</u>, starting with *The Covenant Rising*
Patrick O'Leary	*The Impossible Bird*
Tim Powers	*Expiration Date*
Douglas Preston and Lincoln Child	*The Cabinet of Curiosities*
Robert Reed	*Marrow; The Well of Stars*
Anne Rice	<u>Vampire Lestadt</u>, starting with *Interview with a Vampire*
Kim Stanley Robinson	<u>Mars</u> trilogy, starting with *Red Mars*
Robert J. Sawyer	*Rollback*
Robert J. Sawyer	*The Terminal Experiment*
John Scalzi	*Old Man's War; The Ghost Brigades*
Michael Dylan Scott	<u>Secrets of the Immortal Nicholas Flamel</u>, starting with *The Alchemyst*
Dan Simmons	<u>Hyperion Cantos</u>, starting with *Hyperion*

Brian Stableford	*The Omega Expedition*
Brian Stableford	*Architects of Emortality*
Steph Swainston	*The Year of Our War*
Judith Tarr	*The Hound and the Falcon*
J. R. R. Tolkien	<u>*The Lord of the Rings*</u>
Karen Traviss	<u>Wess'har Wars</u>, starting with *City of Pearl*
Lawrence Watt-Evans	<u>Obsidian Chronicles</u>, starting with *Dragon Weather*
Scott Westerfeld	<u>Succession</u>, starting with *The Risen Empire*
Liz Williams	<u>Detective Inspector Chen</u>, starting with *Snake Agent*
Tad Williams	<u>Otherland</u> series, starting with *City of Golden Shadow*
John C. Wright	<u>The Golden Age</u> series, starting with *The Golden Age*
John C. Wright	<u>Chaos</u> series, starting with *Orphans of Chaos*
Chelsea Quinn Yarbro	<u>St. Germain</u> series, starting with *Hotel Transylvania*
Roger Zelazny	<u>*The Great Book of Amber*</u>
Roger Zelazny	*Lord of Light*

THEMATIC QUESTIONS

- Does the search for or existence of immortality cause problems in the novel that you read?

- What sacrifices would you make to obtain eternal life? Would you choose to be immortal even if those who you knew and loved could not join you?

- Is the extreme extension of life (to 150 years or more, for instance) possible? Do you believe we will ever achieve immortality?

- How would the extension of human life or the attainment of immortality change the world? How is this reflected in the book that you read?

- In the novel that you read, how does immortality or long life affect the attitude of those who have it toward those who do not?

JOKERS WILD: HUMOR IN SPECULATIVE FICTION

Laughter and tears are both responses to frustration and exhaustion. I myself prefer to laugh, since there is less cleaning up to do afterward.

—Kurt Vonnegut

At the height of laughter, the universe is flung into a kaleidoscope of new possibilities.

—Jean Houston

Sometimes laughs are needed in book groups. Lighthearted books can help a group recover from a streak of bad meetings, an especially challenging work, a dreary winter, or a tighter-than-usual time frame. But talking about a single work of humor can be a challenge. First comes finding a book that satisfies everyone's sense of humor, a very tricky task indeed. Even if you surmount this problem of subjectivity, you may not find much to discuss: you can only spend so much time repeating one author's jokes. Addressing humor as a theme instead of sharing a book mitigates the problem: each member selects a book tuned to his or her own funny bone and shares a few choice bits with the group. SF & F readers can tackle the whole gamut of humor or select one of the genre's specialties: British humor, puns, comic characters, satire, or parody, to name a few.

SUGGESTED WORKS

Douglas Adams	Hitchhiker's Guide to the Galaxy series, starting with *The Hitchhiker's Guide to the Galaxy*
Douglas Adams	Dirk Gently, starting with *Dirk Gently's Holistic Detective Agency*
Piers Anthony	Xanth series, starting with *A Spell for Chameleon*
Robert Aspirin	Myth series, starting with *Another Fine Myth*
Kage Baker	*The Anvil of the World*
John Barnes	*Gaudeamus*
Max Barry	*Jennifer Government*
Terry Bisson	*Bears Discover Fire and Other Stories*
Terry Brooks	Magic Kingdom of Landover, starting with *Magic Kingdom for Sale—Sold!*
S. G. Browne	*Breathers: A Zombie's Lament*
Steven Brust	Vlad Taltos series, starting with *The Book of Jhereg*
Jim Butcher	The Dresden Files, starting with *Storm Front*
Eoin Colfer	Artemis Fowl series, starting with *Artemis Fowl*
Glen Cook	Garrett, P. I., starting with *Sweet Silver Blues*
Peter David	Apropos of Nothing, starting with *Sir Apropos of Nothing*
Peter David	Modern Arthur series, starting with *Knight Life*
Gordon R. Dickson	Dragon series, starting with *The Dragon and the George*
Cory Doctorow	*Down and Out in the Magic Kingdom*
Jasper Fforde	Thursday Next series, starting with *The Eyre Affair*
Jasper Fforde	Nursery Crimes series, starting with *The Big Over Easy*
Dave Freer and Eric Flint	Pyramid series, starting with *Pyramid Scheme*
Esther Friesner	Chicks in Chainmail series, starting with *Chicks in Chainmail*
Neil Gaiman and Terry Pratchett	*Good Omens*
Mary Gentle	*Grunts!*
William Goldman	*The Princess Bride*
Austin Grossman	*Soon I Will Be Invincible*
Harry Harrison	*Bill, the Galactic Hero*
Harry Harrison	Stainless Steel Rat series, starting with *The Stainless Steel Rat*
Jim Hines	Jig the Goblin, starting with *Goblin Quest*
Tom Holt	*Tall Stories*
Tom Holt	*The Portable Door*
Tom Holt	*You Don't Have to Be Evil to Work Here, But It Helps*
Tom Holt	*Expecting Beowulf*

Tanya Huff	<u>Keeper</u> series, starting with *Summon the Keeper*
Barry Hughart	<u>Master Li</u> series, starting with *Bridge of Birds*
Diana Wynne Jones	*The Tough Guide to Fantasyland*
A. Lee Martinez	*Gil's All-Fright Diner*
A. Lee Martinez	*In the Company of Ogres*
A. Lee Martinez	*A Nameless Witch*
Christopher Miller	*The Cardboard Universe*
Christopher Moore	*Fluke*
Christopher Moore	*Practical Demonkeeping*
Christopher Moore	*Fool*
Terry Pratchett	<u>Discworld: Wizards</u>, starting with *The Colour of Magic*
Terry Pratchett	<u>Discworld: Death</u>, starting with *Mort*
Terry Pratchett	<u>Discworld: Witches</u>, starting with *Equal Rites*
Terry Pratchett	<u>Discworld: The Watch</u>, starting with *Guards! Guards!*
Terry Pratchett	<u>Discworld: Tiffany Aching</u>, starting with *Wee Free Men*
Robert Rankin	*The Hollow Chocolate Bunnies of the Apocalypse*
Robert Rankin	<u>Brentford</u> series, starting with *The Antipope*
Spider Robinson	<u>Callahan's</u> series, starting with *Callahan's Crosstime Saloon*
Rudy Rucker	*Frek and the Elixir*
Rudy Rucker	*Mathematicians in Love*
John Scalzi	*Agent to the Stars*
John Scalzi	*The Android's Dream*
Robert Sheckley	*Dimensions of Sheckley: The Selected Novels of Robert Sheckley*
Jeff Smith	<u>Bone</u> graphic novels
Lemony Snicket	<u>A Series of Unfortunate Events</u>, starting with *The Bad Beginning*
Jonathan Stroud	<u>Bartimaeus Trilogy</u>, starting with *The Amulet of Samarkand*
Kurt Vonnegut	*Galapagos*
Lawrence Watt Evans	<u>Ethshar</u> series, starting with *The Misenchanted Sword*
Leslie What	*Olympic Games*
Leslie What	*Crazy Love*
Connie Willis	*To Say Nothing of the Dog*
Patricia Wrede	<u>Enchanted Forest Chronicles</u>, starting with *Dealing with Dragons*
John Zakour and Lawrence Ganem	<u>Zach Johnson</u> series, starting with *The Plutonium Blonde*
Roger Zelazny and Robert Sheckley	<u>Millennial Contest</u>, starting with *Bring Me the Head of Prince Charming*

THEMATIC QUESTIONS

- What kind of reader finds the book that you read humorous? What kind does not?
- Who is the funniest science fiction or fantasy writer? What is the funniest book? The funniest science fiction or fantasy movie?

- Does the book that you read have any funny lines or scenes that you want to share?
- Does humor age well?
- As a reader, do you select books with the intention of finding good laughs, or is the humor incidental to books that you select for other reasons?
- Does your book feature satire or parody? If so, is it a satire or parody of fantasy and science fiction, or does it address other themes in a science fiction or fantasy setting?

LITERARY CROSSOVERS: GENTRIFYING GENRE FICTION

The demand for absolute purity of genres is becoming nowadays an anachronism in literature.

—Stanislaw Lem

I have been a sore-headed occupant of a file drawer labeled "science fiction" ever since, and I would like out, particularly since so many serious critics regularly mistake the drawer for a urinal.

—Kurt Vonnegut

Although some booksellers or libraries try to stuff each book in a pigeonhole, many of the most interesting books don't conveniently fit any convention. This is especially true today, because many writers deliberately pursue "interstitial" fiction, intentionally blurring genre lines. The list for this theme is divided into two parts: works of science fiction/fantasy that you probably can find in the bookstore or library's "literature," "literary fiction," or "mainstream" section and works that are conscripted to the science fiction/fantasy section that also please literary readers. Whether your group tackles these works as one theme or two, you can certainly find some wonderful books.

SUGGESTED WORKS: MARKETED AS LITERARY FICTION

Edwin Abbott	*Flatland*
Chris Adrian	*Children's Hospital*; *A Better Angel*
Sarah Addison Allen	*Garden Spells*; *The Sugar Queen*
Isabel Allende	*The House of the Spirits*
Margaret Atwood	*The Handmaid's Tale*; *Oryx & Crake*
Jorge Luis Borges	*Ficciones*
Kevin Brockmeier	*A Brief History of the Dead*; *A View from the Seventh Layer*
Mikhail Bulgakov	*The Master and Margarita*
Anthony Burgess	*A Clockwork Orange*
Italo Calvino	*Invisible Cities*; *If on a Winter's Night a Traveler*
Jonathan Carroll	*The Ghost in Love*; *The Land of Laughs*; *The Marriage of Sticks*
Lewis Carroll	*Alice's Adventures in Wonderland*; *Through the Looking Glass*
Angela Carter	*Burning Your Boats: The Collected Short Stories*
Michael Chabon	*The Yiddish Policeman's Union*

Patrick Chamoiseau	*Texaco*
Susanna Clarke	*Jonathan Strange & Mr. Norrell*
Paulo Coelho	*The Alchemist*
John Connolly	*The Book of Lost Things*
Jim Crace	*The Pesthouse*
John Crowley	*Little, Big*
Mark Z. Danielewski	*House of Leaves*
Keith Donohue	*The Stolen Child*
Umberto Eco	*Baudolino*
Gabriel Garcia-Marquez	*One Hundred Years of Solitude*
Lisa Goldstein	*The Red Magician*
Gunter Grass	*The Tin Drum*
Andrew Sean Greer	*The Confessions of Max Tivoli*
Steven Hall	*The Raw Shark Texts*
Mark Helprin	*A Winter's Tale*
Alice Hoffman	*Practical Magic*
Aldous Huxley	*Brave New World*
Kazuo Ishiguro	*Never Let Me Go*
Franz Kafka	*The Metamorphosis*; *The Trial*
Thomas King	*Green Grass, Running Water*
Elizabeth Kostova	*The Historian*
Jonathan Lethem	*Gun, with Occasional Music*; *Fortress of Solitude*
William Kotzwinkle	*The Bear Went over the Mountain*
Yann Martel	*The Life of Pi*
Cormac McCarthy	*The Road*
Toni Morrison	*Beloved*
Haruki Murakami	*Hard-Boiled Wonderland and the End of the World*
Audrey Niffenegger	*The Time Traveler's Wife*
Carlos Ruiz Zafon	*The Shadow of the Wind*
Salman Rushdie	*Midnight's Children*; *The Satanic Verses*
Mary Doria Russell	*The Sparrow*; *Children of God*
Jose Saramago	*Blindness*
William Shakespeare	*The Tempest*; *A Midsummer Night's Dream*
Mary Shelley	*Frankenstein*
Nevil Shute	*On the Beach*
Johanna Sinisalo	*Troll: A Love Story*
Patrick Susskind	*Perfume*
Jonathan Swift	*Gulliver's Travels*
John Updike	*The Witches of Eastwick*; *The Widows of Eastwick*
Virginia Woolf	*Orlando*

SUGGESTED WORKS: MARKETED AS FANTASY AND SCIENCE FICTION

Richard Adams	*Watership Down*
James P. Blaylock	*The Adventures of Langdon St. Ives*
Ray Bradbury	*Bradbury Stories: 100 of His Most Celebrated Tales*

Lois McMaster Bujold	*The Curse of Chalion*; *Paladin of Souls*
Samuel Delany	*Dhalgren*
Charles de Lint	Newford, starting with *Dreams Underfoot*
Neil Gaiman	*American Gods*
Greer Gilman	*Moonwise*; *Cloud & Ashes: Three Winter's Tales*
Guy Gavriel Kay	*The Lions of Al-Rassan*; *Tigana*
Ursula K. Le Guin	*The Dispossessed*
Ursula K. Le Guin	Earthsea Chronicles, starting with *The Wizard of Earthsea*
Jonathan Lethem	*Gun, with Occasional Music*
Ian R. MacLeod	*The Light Ages*; *House of Storms*
George R. R. Martin	A Song of Ice and Fire, starting with *A Game of Thrones*
James Morrow	*The Last Witchfinder*
Mervyn Peake	Gormenghast trilogy, starting with *Titus Groan*
Philip Pullman	His Dark Materials, starting with *The Golden Compass*
Michael Swanwick	*The Iron Dragon's Daughter*; *Dragons of Babel*
J. R. R. Tolkien	*The Lord of the Rings*
Jack Vance	*Tales of the Dying Earth*
Gene Wolfe	The Book of the New Sun, starting with *Shadow & Claw*

THEMATIC QUESTIONS

- What kind of readers are the primary audience for the book that you selected?
- Did you find the book that you read to be "literary"? If so, what are the elements that make it so?
- What are the advantages of dividing books into genre categories? The disadvantages?
- Some readers avoid books with any fantastic or speculative content. Why do they make this decision? Is it a mistake?
- Which genre writers would you recommend to friends who think of themselves as "literary" or "highbrow"?
- There is a trend for literary writers to use fantasy and science fiction themes. Why is such "interstitial" writing popular now?

MILITARY SPECULATIVE FICTION: GENRE GET YOUR GUN

"The key to strategy, little Vor," she explained kindly, "is not to choose a path to victory, but to choose so that all paths lead to a victory."

—Lois McMaster Bujold

Of course a war is entertaining. The immediate fear and suffering of the humans is a legitimate and pleasing refreshment for our myriads of toiling workers.

—C. S. Lewis

There are many reasons to read military science fiction and fantasy. Some like to study military strategy. Others like to read about courage, heroism, and valor in difficult circumstances.

Some enjoy the adrenaline rush they get from high-action, high-violence fiction; others may be looking for anti-war messages or for darkly comic looks at the foolishness of sacrificing lives in a greedy pursuit for empire. Some find catharsis in the tragedies of war. This seething stew of sometimes contradictory reading motivations makes this a juicy discussion theme.

SUGGESTED WORKS

Joe Abercrombie	The First Law series, starting with *The Blade Itself*
Taylor Anderson	Destroyermen series, starting with *Into the Storm*
John Birmingham	Axis of Time trilogy, starting with *Weapons of Choice*
Max Brooks	*World War Z*
Robert Buettner	Jason Wander series, starting with *Orphanage*
Lois McMaster Bujold	Vorkosigan Saga, starting with *Young Miles*
Jack Campbell	The Lost Fleet, starting with *Dauntless*
Orson Scott Card	*Ender's Game*
Glen Cook	Black Company series, starting with *The Black Company*
John Dalmas	*The Regiment: A Trilogy*
Gordon R. Dickson	Dorsai series, starting with *Dorsai Spirit* omnibus
William C. Dietz	Legion of the Damned series, starting with *Legion of the Damned*
Ian Douglas	Heritage Trilogy, starting with *Semper Mars*
Ian Douglas	Inheritance trilogy, starting with *Star Strike*
David Drake	*The Complete Hammer's Slammers Vols. 1–3*
David Drake	RCN series, starting with *With the Lightnings*
Steven Erikson	Malazan Book of the Fallen, starting with *Gardens of the Moon*
Chris Evans	The Iron Elves, starting with *A Darkness Forged in Fire*
David Gemmell	Drenai Tales, starting with *Legend*
David Gemmell	Rigante series, starting with *Sword in the Storm*
David Gemmell	*Lion of Macedon; Dark Prince*
David Gemmell	Troy series, starting with *Lord of the Silver Bow*
Mary Gentle	Ash series, starting with *A Secret History*
Mary Gentle	*Grunts!*
David Golemon	*Event*
Simon R. Green	Deathstalker series, starting with *Deathstalker*
Joe Haldeman	*The Forever War*
Joe Haldeman and Martin Greenberg, eds.	*Future Weapons of War*
Robert A. Heinlein	*Starship Troopers*
Tanya Huff	Valor series, starting with *A Confederation of Valor*
Stephen L. Kent	Clone series, starting with *The Clone Republic*
Tom Kratman	*A Desert Called Peace*
John Marco	Tyrants and Kings series, starting with *The Jackal of Nar*
George R. R. Martin	A Song of Ice and Fire, starting with *A Game of Thrones*
Sandra McDonald	*The Outback Stars; The Stars Down Under; The Stars Blue Yonder*

R. M. Meluch	Tour of the Merrimack series, starting with *The Myriad*
Elizabeth Moon	*The Deed of Paksenarrion*
Elizabeth Moon	Vatta's War, starting with *Trading in Danger*
Naomi Novik	Dragon Temeraire, starting with *His Majesty's Dragon*
Eric Nylund, et al.	Halo series, starting with *The Fall of Reach*
K. J. Parker	*The Company*
Graham Sharp Paul	Hellfort's War, starting with *The Battle at Moons of Hell*
John Ringo and Travis Taylor	Looking Glass, starting with *Into the Looking Glass*
John Ringo	Posleen War series, starting with *A Hymn before Battle*
John Ringo	Council Wars series, starting with *There Will Be Dragons*
Brian Ruckley	Godless World series, starting with *Winterbirth*
John Scalzi	Old Man's War series, starting with *Old Man's War*
Mike Shepherd	Kris Longknife series, starting with *Deserter*
David Sherman and Dan Cragg	Starfist series, starting with *First to Fight*
John Steakley	*Armor*
Harry Turtledove	Videssos Cycle, starting with *The Misplaced Legion*
Harry Turtledove	Worldwar series, starting with *In the Balance*
Harry Turtledove	Great War series, starting with *How Few Remain*
Harry Turtledove	Darkness series, starting with *Into the Darkness*
Harry Turtledove and Martin Greenberg, eds.	*The Best Military Science Fiction of the 20th Century*
Mark L. Van Name	Jon & Lobo series, starting with *One Jump Ahead*
David Weber	Honor Harrington series, starting with *On Basilisk Station*
David Weber and John Ringo	Empire of Man series, starting with *March Upcountry*
Michael Z. Williamson	*Better to Beg Forgiveness*

THEMATIC QUESTIONS

- Do you enjoy military fiction? If so, what draws you to it? If not, what turns you away?
- Is the military action in the book that you read believable?
- Did you learn anything about military strategy from the book that you read?
- Are the wars waged in the book that you read justified?
- What is the future of battle and war? How have advances in technology changed war? How will future advances change it further?
- Do you prefer to read about military actions of the past or of the future? Why?

RESOURCES

MilSciFi.Com

http://www.milscifi.com

MONSTER MASH: READING WHERE THE WILD THINGS ARE

Some things deserve to be called "it."

—Octavia Butler

Monsters are made, not born.

—Greg Bear

This theme looks at vampires, werewolves, sea monsters, trolls, ogres, zombies, demons, and other less familiar monsters. These mythical creatures embody our fears, turning the emotions that scare us into something corporeal. Your group can discuss what kinds of fears underlie the physical being of these famous creatures. Then again, monsters can be sympathetic, make us think about ways in which we feel isolated from the world. If none of that works, let go of the psychology and just read for the thrill of it!

SUGGESTED WORKS

John Joseph Adams, ed.	*The Living Dead*
Joan Aiken	*The Cockatrice Boys*
David Almond	*Clay*
Steve Alten	Meg series, starting with *Meg*
M. T. Anderson	*Thirsty*
Kelley Armstrong	Women of the Underworld series, starting with *Bitten*
Neal Asher	*The Skinner; The Voyage of the Sable Keech*
Jane Austen and Seth Grahame-Smith	*Pride and Prejudice and Zombies*
L. A. Banks	Vampire Huntress Legends, starting with *Minion*
Alice Borchardt	Legends of the Wolves, starting with *Silver Wolf*
J. L. Bourne	*Day by Day Armageddon*
Patricia Briggs	Mercy Thompson series, starting with *Moon Called*
Max Brooks	*World War Z*
S. G. Browne	*Breathers: A Zombie's Lament*
Jim Butcher	Dresden Files, starting with *Storm Front*
Octavia Butler	*Fledgling*
Cassandra Clare	Mortal Instruments, starting with *City of Bones*
D. M. Cornish	Monster Blood Tattoo series, starting with *Foundling*
Nancy Farmer	*The Sea of Trolls*
John Gardner	*Grendel*
Molly Gloss	*Wild Life*
Christopher Golden	The Veil, starting with *The Myth Hunters*
Joe Haldeman	*Camouflage*
Laurell K. Hamilton	Anita Blake series, starting with *Guilty Pleasures*
Charlaine Harris	Sookie Stackhouse series, starting with *Dead until Dark*
Kim Harrison	The Hollows, starting with *Dead Witch Walking*
Barb and J. C. Hendee	Noble Dead Saga, starting with *Dhampir*
Charlie Huston	Joe Pitt series, starting with *Already Dead*

Stephen King	*It*
Stephen King	*Salem's Lot*
E. E. Knight	<u>Vampire Earth</u> series, starting with *The Way of the Wolf*
Dean Koontz	<u>Dean Koontz's Frankenstein</u>, starting with *Prodigal Son*
A. Lee Martinez	*Gil's All Fright Diner*
Robin McKinley	*Sunshine*
Stephenie Meyer	<u>Twilight</u> series, starting with *Twilight*
China Miéville	*Perdido Street Station*
James Morrow	*Shambling towards Hiroshima*
Terry Pratchett	*Carpe Jugulum*
Douglas Preston and Lincoln Child	*Relic*; *Reliquary*
Anne Rice	<u>The Vampire Chronicles</u>, starting with *Interview with the Vampire*
Cameron Rogers	*The Music of Razors*
Mary Shelley	*Frankenstein*
Neal Shusterman	*Everlost*
Dan Simmons	*The Terror*
Dan Simmons	<u>Hyperion Cantos</u>, starting with *Hyperion*
Bram Stoker	*Dracula*
Charles Stross	*The Atrocity Archives*
Rob Thurman	<u>Cal Leandros</u> series, starting with *Nightlife*
J. R. Ward	<u>Black Dagger Brotherhood</u>, starting with *Dark Lover*
Peter Watts	<u>Rifters</u> trilogy, starting with *Starfish*
David Wellington	<u>Zombie</u> trilogy, starting with *Monster Island*
John Wyndham	*The Day of the Triffids*
Chelsea Quinn Yarbro	<u>St. Germain</u> series, starting with *Hotel Transylvania*

THEMATIC QUESTIONS

- Is the monster in the book that you selected scary? What kind of fears does it tap into?
- Is there anything sympathetic or charismatic about the monster in the book that you read?
- What kind of monsters do you find the most terrifying? Which do you find kind of silly?
- Would the book that you read make a good film? What is your favorite monster film of all time?
- Is the book that you read appropriate for all ages? Should children be exposed to stories about monsters? If so, should some kind of limits be placed?

MUSICAL EXTRAVAGANZA: SONG BOOKS THE SPECULATIVE FICTION WAY

Ah, music. A magic beyond all we do here!
                    —J. K. Rowling, *Harry Potter and the Sorcerer's Stone*

Look at the stars sometime. They are only notes. They are music.

—Pat Conroy

It had never occurred to me before that music and thinking are so much alike. In fact, you could say music is another way of thinking, or maybe thinking is another kind of music.

—Ursula K. Le Guin

Many of the most perceptive fictional treatments of the passion for music and for the act of performing it occur in speculative fiction. Fantasy, in particular, is full of examples of the magical power of music. If you tackle this theme, it can be a good chance for group members to get to know each other better. Leave a little time to talk about your own musical preferences or to spin a few discs.

SUGGESTED WORKS

Piers Anthony	*Being a Green Mother*
Catherine Asaro	*Diamond Star*
Sarah Ash	*Tracing the Shadow*
Peter S. Beagle	*The Unicorn Sonata*
Greg Bear	*Songs of Earth and Power*
Carol Berg	*Song of the Beast*
Paul Brandon	*Swim the Moon*
Paul Brandon	*The Wild Reel*
Emma Bull	*War for the Oaks*
Kate Constable	Chanters of Tremaris, starting with *The Singer of All Songs*
Charles de Lint	*Jack of Kinrowan*
Charles de Lint	*Into the Green*
Charles de Lint	*Trader*
Keith Donohue	*The Stolen Child*
Tananarive Due	*Joplin's Ghost*
Michael Flynn	*The January Dancer*
Gregory Frost	*Shadowbridge*
William Goldman	*The Silent Gondoliers*
Kathleen Ann Goonan	*In War Times*
Simon R. Green	*Nightingale's Lament*
Shannon Hale	*Book of a Thousand Days*
Elizabeth Haydon	Symphony of Ages series, starting with *Rhapsody*
Tanya Huff	Quarters series, starting with *Sing the Four Quarters*
Elaine Isaak	*The Singer's Crown*
Matthew Jarpe	*Radio Freefall*
Diana Wynne Jones	Dalemark Quartet, starting with *Cart and Cwidder*
Guy Gavriel Kay	*A Song for Arbonne*
Guy Gavriel Kay	*Tigana*
Greg Keyes	*The Charnal Prince*
Ellen Kushner	*Thomas the Rhymer*

Mercedes Lackey	Bardic Voices, starting with *Lark and the Wren*
Mercedes Lackey and Ellen Guon	Eric Banyon series, starting with *Bedlam's Bard*
Gaston Leroux	*The Phantom of the Opera*
Louise Marley	*The Glass Harmonica*
Louise Marley	Singers of Nevya series, starting with *Sing the Light*
Anne McCaffrey	Harper Hall trilogy, starting with *Dragonsong*
Anne McCaffrey	Crystal Singer series, starting with *Crystal Singer*
Patricia McKillip	*Song for the Basilisk*
China Miéville	*King Rat*
L. E. Modesitt	The Spellsong Cycle, starting with *The Soprano Sorceress*
L. E. Modesitt	*Archform: Beauty*
Robin D. Owens	Summoning series, starting with *Guardian of Honor*
Terry Pratchett	*Soul Music*
Terry Pratchett	*Maskerade*
Terry Pratchett	*The Amazing Maurice and His Educated Rodents*
Katherine Roberts	Echorium Sequence, starting with *Song Quest*
Justina Robson	Quantum Gravity series, starting with *Keeping It Real*
Patrick Rothfuss	*The Name of the Wind*
Mary Doria Russell	*The Sparrow*
Michael Scott	*The Magician: The Secrets of the Immortal Nicholas Flamel*
Adam Stemple	*Singer of Souls*; *Steward of Song*
Bruce Sterling	*Zeitgeist*
Kate Thompson	*The New Policeman*
John Varley	*Rolling Thunder*
Scott Westerfeld	*The Last Days*
Tad Williams	*War of the Flowers*
Jack Womack	*Elvissey*
Jane Yolen and Adam Stemple	*Pay the Piper*; *Troll Bridge*

THEMATIC QUESTIONS

- Is music well integrated into the plot of the book that you read? Does the author seem to understand what it is like to compose, perform, or appreciate music?

- Are there particular performers or musical styles that you associate with fantasy or science fiction? Does this influence how you feel about this music?

- Music and musical characters are common in fantasy fiction, more rare in science fiction. Is this a function of the subject matter, the background of the writers, or something else?

- Is there a stereotypical musical character in fantasy? If so, what role does this character usually play?

- How might music change in the future? What music is most likely to stand the test of time?

- What place does music have in your life? What are some of your favorite performers and styles?

MYSTERY CROSSOVERS: CRIMES OF THE IMAGINATION

There will be time to murder and create.

—T. S. Eliot

Murder most foul, as in the best it is; But this most foul, strange and unnatural.

—William Shakespeare

The genres of science fiction, fantasy, and mystery each have so many distinct conventions that it takes a skilled writer to meld them. Despite this challenge, there is a significant tradition of blending science fiction and crime and a growing number of successful combinations of fantasy and crime. Taken by themselves, these novels may be difficult to discuss because they are strongly plot-driven. Treat them, however, as a theme (warning participants not to give away the murderer), and you can have a great discussion.

SUGGESTED WORKS

Douglas Adams	*Dirk Gently's Holistic Detective Agency*
Lou Anders, ed.	*Sideways in Crime*
Neal Asher	*Gridlinked*
Isaac Asimov	*Caves of Steel; The Naked Sun*
Jonathan Barnes	*The Somnambulist*
Elizabeth Bear	*New Amsterdam*
Jedediah Berry	*The Manual of Detection*
Alfred Bester	*The Demolished Man*
Alex Bledsoe	*The Sword-Edged Blonde*
David Brin	*Sundiver*
Jim Butcher	Dresden Files, starting with *Storm Front*
Mike Carey	Felix Castor series, starting with *The Devil You Know*
Adam-Troy Castro	Andrea Cort series, starting with *Emissaries from the Dead*
Michael Chabon	*The Yiddish Policeman's Union*
G. K. Chesterton	*The Man Who Was Thursday*
Glen Cook	Garrett, P.I. series, starting with *Sweet Silver Blues*
Philip K. Dick	*Do Androids Dream of Electric Sheep?*
Warren Ellis	*Crooked Little Vein*
P. N. Elrod	*The Vampire Files*
Jasper Fforde	Thursday Next series, starting with *The Eyre Affair*
Jasper Fforde	Nursery Crimes, starting with *The Big Over Easy*
Eric Garcia	Tyrannosaurus Rex series, starting with *Anonymous Rex*
Randall Garrett	*Lord Darcy*
William Gibson	*Neuromancer; Virtual Light*
Simon R. Green	Nightside, starting with *Something from the Nightside*
Jon Courtenay Grimwood	Arabesk series, starting with *Pashazade*
Jon Courtenay Grimwood	*9 Tail Fox*
Laurell K. Hamilton	Anita Blake series, starting with *Guilty Pleasures*
Peter F. Hamilton	Greg Mandel series, starting with *Mindstar Rising*

Charlaine Harris	Southern Vampire series, starting with *Dead until Dark*
Kim Harrison	Rachel Morgan series, starting with *Dead Witch Walking*
Tanya Huff	Vicky Nelson series, starting with *Blood Price*
Barry Hughart	Master Li series, starting with *Bridge of Birds*
Matthew Hughes	Henghis Hapthorn series, starting with *Majestrum*
Charlie Huston	Joe Pitt series, starting with *Already Dead*
Alexander Irvine	*Buyout*
K. W. Jeter	*Noir*
Tamara Siler Jones	Dubric Bryerly series, starting with *Ghosts in the Snow*
Jonathan Lethem	*Gun with Occasional Music*
Paul Levinson	Phil D'Amato series, starting with *The Silk Code*
China Miéville	*The City and the City*
Richard K. Morgan	Takeshi Kovacs series, starting with *Altered Carbon*
Richard K. Morgan	*Thirteen* (published in the United Kingdom as *Black Man*)
Haruki Murakami	*Hard-Boiled Wonderland and the End of the World*
Terry Pratchett	Discworld: The Watch, starting with *Guards! Guards!*
Philip Pullman	Sally Lockhart novels, starting with *The Ruby in the Smoke*
Alastair Reynolds	*The Prefect*
Kat Richardson	Greywalker series, starting with *Greywalker*
J. D. Robb	Eve Dallas series, starting with *Naked in Death*
Kristine Kathryn Rusch	The Retrieval Artist, starting with *The Disappeared*
Robert J. Sawyer	*Flashforward*
Dan Simmons	Hyperion Cantos, starting with *Hyperion*
Wen Spencer	Ukiah Oregon, starting with *Alien Taste*
Dana Stabenow, ed.	*Unusual Suspects: Stories of Mystery and Fantasy*
Charles Stross	*Halting State*
Rob Thurman	Cal Leandros series, starting with *Nightlife*
Phaedra Weldon	Zoë Martinique series, starting with *Wraith*
Colson Whitehead	*The Intuitionist*
Liz Williams	Detective Inspector Chen series, starting with *Snake Agent*
Walter Jon Williams	*This Is Not a Game*
Timothy Zahn	Frank Compton series, starting with *Night Train to Rigel*
John Zakour and Lawrence Ganem	Zach Johnson series, starting with *The Plutonium Blonde*

THEMATIC QUESTIONS

- Does the mystery genre combine more easily with science fiction or fantasy?
- Is the mystery in the speculative fiction that you read handled in the same way that it would be in a traditional mystery novel?
- What kind of mystery did the novel that you read most closely resemble? Hard-boiled? Cozy?
- What characteristics does the detective have in the novel that you read? Do certain character types in science fiction or fantasy lend themselves well to the role of detective?

- Arthur Conan Doyle had Sherlock Holmes famously note, "Once you eliminate the impossible, whatever remains, no matter how improbable, must be the truth." If this is true, does it create a dilemma for writers trying to blend speculative fiction with mystery?

  Are you a reader of mysteries as well as speculative fiction? Why or why not?

MYTHS, FABLES, AND LEGENDS: THE LURE OF LORE

Myth is, after all, the neverending story.

—Joan D. Vinge

Over the centuries we have transformed the ancient myths and folk tales and made them into the fabric of our lives. Consciously and unconsciously we weave the narratives of myth and folk tale into our daily existence.

—Jack Zipes

Myths, fables, and legends are the roots of fantasy fiction, and if we classify them as fantasy, it is the oldest of genres. Books based on myth create an air of mystery, an aura difficult to penetrate, harder still to analyze, but in attempting to do so, your discussion may touch archetypes that are central to human nature. You may handle books based on fables—often (but not always) simpler and aimed at younger readers—separately from those based on myth, which are more complex, but the two forms share common ground and can work together as well. You might also choose to include original folklore in your discussion.

SUGGESTED WORKS

Richard Adams	*Watership Down*
Piers Anthony	<u>Incarnations of Immortality</u>, starting with *On a Pale Horse*
Marion Zimmer Bradley	<u>Avalon</u> series, starting with *The Mists of Avalon*
Michael Cadnum	*Can't Catch Me and Other Twice-Told Tales*
Orson Scott Card	*Enchantment*
Angela Carter	*The Bloody Chamber*; *Burning Your Boats: Collected Short Stories*
John Connolly	*The Book of Lost Things*
Bernard Cornwell	<u>Warlord Chronicles</u>, starting with *The Winter King*
John Crowley	*Little, Big*
Ellen Datlow and Terri Windling, eds.	*Snow White, Blood Red*; *Black Thorn, White Rose*; *Ruby Slippers, Golden Tears*; *Black Swan, White Raven*; *Silver Birch, Blood Moon*; *Black Heart, Ivory Bones*
Ellen Datlow and Terri Windling, eds.	*The Coyote Road*; *The Green Man: Tales from the Mythic Forest*
Pamela Dean	*Tam Lin*
Charles de Lint	*Jack of Kinrowan*
Charles de Lint	<u>Newford</u>, starting with *Dreams Underfoot*
Keith Donohue	*The Stolen Child*
Hal Duncan	*Vellum*; *Ink*

Alex Flinn	*Beastly*
Gregory Frost	*Shadowbridge*; *Lord Tophet*
Cornelia Funke	<u>Inkheart</u> series, starting with *Inkheart*
Neil Gaiman	*American Gods*; *Anansi Boys*; *Coraline*
R. Garcia y Robertson	*Firebird*
Jessica Day George	*Princess of the Midnight Ball*
Christopher Golden	<u>The Veil</u>, starting with *The Myth Hunters*
Theodora Goss	*In the Forest of Forgetting*
Michael Gruber	*The Witch's Boy*
Shannon Hale	<u>Bayern</u> series, starting with *The Goose Girl*
Shannon Hale	*Book of a Thousand Days*
M. John Harrison	*Viriconium*
Nina Kiriki Hoffman	*Spirits That Walk in Shadow*
Robert Holdstock	<u>Ryhope Wood</u> series, starting with *Mythago Wood*
Robert Holdstock	<u>Merlin Codex</u>, starting with *Celtika*
Kij Johnson	*Fudoki*; *The Fox Woman*
Guy Gavriel Kay	<u>The Fionovar Tapestry</u>, starting with *The Summer Tree*
Mercedes Lackey	<u>Five Hundred Kingdoms</u>, starting with *The Fairy Godmother*
Stephen R. Lawhead	*Hood*
Ursula K. Le Guin	<u>Earthsea Chronicles</u>, starting with *A Wizard of Earthsea*
Gail Carson Levine	*Ella Enchanted*
Gregory Maguire	*Confessions of an Ugly Stepsister*; *Mirror, Mirror*
Gregory Maguire	*Wicked*; *Son of a Witch*; *A Lion Among Men*
Juliet Marillier	<u>Sevenwaters</u> series, starting with *Daughter of the Forest*
Dennis McKiernan	<u>Once Upon</u> series, starting with *Once Upon a Summer Day*
Patricia A. McKillip	<u>Riddle-Master</u>, starting with *The Riddle-Master of Hed*
Patricia A. McKillip	*The Book of Atrix Wolfe*; *Alphabet of Thorn*; *The Changeling Sea*; *In the Forests of Serre*; *Solstice Wood*; *Od Magic*
Robin McKinley	*Beauty*; *Deerskin*; *Rose Daughter*; *Spindle's End*
Linda Medley	*Castle Waiting*
China Miéville	*King Rat*
John Myers Myers	*Silverlock*
Donna Jo Napoli	*Zel*; *Sirena*; *Spinners*
Eric Nylund	*Mortal Coils*
Edith Pattou	*East*
Mary Renault	*The King Must Die*; *The Bull from the Sea*
Ekaterina Sedia	*The Secret History of Moscow*
Mary Stewart	*Merlin Trilogy*
J. R. R. Tolkien	*The Silmarillion*; *The Children of Hurin*
Lisa Tuttle	*Silver Bough*; *The Mysteries*
M. Catherynne Valente	<u>The Orphan's Tales</u>, starting with *In the Night Garden*
T. H. White	*The Once and Future King*
Kim Wilkins	*Veil of Gold*
Bill Willingham	<u>Fables</u> graphic novels

Terri Windling	*The Wood Wife*
Gene Wolfe	*The Knight*; *The Wizard*
John C. Wright	Everness, starting with *The Last Guardian of Everness*
John C. Wright	Chaos series, starting with *Orphans of Chaos*
Jane Yolen	*Briar Rose*

THEMATIC QUESTIONS

- Is there a difference between a fable, a myth, and a legend? If so, how would you define each of them?

- Do you believe in the ideas behind Jungian psychology—that there are shared archetypes of human consciousness and that these ideas often find expression in our myths and legends?

- Does the work that you read derive from older myths and fables? If you've read those as well, how loyal is your book to this source material? What kinds of changes does it make?

- What do we mean when we say that a story or book has a "mythic" feel or style?

- What myths, fables, and legends have been overworked in speculative fiction? Which deserve further exploration?

PARANORMAL ADVENTURES: HEX AND THE CITY

It's one of those lessons that every child should learn: Don't play with fire, sharp objects, or ancient artifacts.

—Patricia Briggs

Paranoid? Probably. But just because you're paranoid doesn't mean there isn't an invisible demon about to eat your face.

—Jim Butcher

The hottest corner of the fantasy marketplace right now is "paranormal" literature. First fueled by the popularity of *Buffy the Vampire Slayer*, then by breakout authors such as Jim Butcher, Charlaine Harris, Laurell K. Hamilton, and most recently, Stephenie Meyer, paranormal fantasy straddles the line between fantasy and thriller, often with a hearty dose of romance thrown in. These books are not complex: discussing a shared book makes for a short meeting, but taken as a theme, this subgenre can provide an enjoyable evening in a month when the group needs light reading.

SUGGESTED WORKS

Mario Acevedo	Felix Gomez, starting with *The Nymphos of Rocky Flats*
Ilona Andrews	Kate Daniels series, starting with *Magic Bites*
Kelley Armstrong	Women of the Underworld, starting with *Bitten*
Kelley Armstrong	Darkest Powers, starting with *The Summoning*

Patricia Briggs	Mercy Thompson series, starting with *Moon Called*
Patricia Briggs	Alpha and Omega, starting with *Cry Wolf*
Emma Bull	*Finder*
Emma Bull	*War for the Oaks*
Jim Butcher	The Dresden Files, starting with *Storm Front*
Rachel Caine	Weather Warden series, starting with *Ill Wind*
Mike Carey	Felix Castor series, starting with *The Devil You Know*
Jonathan Carroll	*The Ghost in Love*
Karen Chance	Cassandra Palmer series, starting with *Touch the Dark*
Cassandra Clare	Mortal Instruments, starting with *City of Bones*
MaryJanice Davidson	Betsy the Vampire Queen, starting with *Undead and Unwed*
Charles de Lint	Newford books, starting with *Dreams Underfoot*
Charles de Lint	*The Mystery of Grace*
Mark Del Franco	Connor Grey series, starting with *Unshapely Things*
Andrew Fox	Fat White Vampire, starting with *Fat White Vampire Blues*
Jeaniene Frost	Night Huntress series, starting with *Halfway to the Grave*
Yasmine Galenorn	Sisters of the Moon, starting with *Witchling*
Laura Anne Gilman	The Retrievers, starting with *Staying Dead*
Christopher Golden	The Veil, starting with *The Myth Hunters*
Christopher Golden and Tim Lebbon	The Hidden Cities, starting with *Mind the Gap*
Christopher Golden and Tom Sniegoski	The Menagerie, starting with *The Nimble Man*
Simon R. Green	Nightside, starting with *Something from the Nightside*
Justin Gustainis	Quincy Morgan, Supernatural Investigation, starting with *Black Magic Woman*
Laurell K. Hamilton	Anita Blake, starting with *Guilty Pleasures*
Laurell K. Hamilton	Meredith Gentry series, starting with *A Kiss of Shadows*
Charlaine Harris	Southern Vampire series, starting with *Dead until Dark*
Kim Harrison	The Hollows, starting with *Dead Witch Walking*
Barb and J. C. Hendee	Noble Dead series, starting with *Dhampir*
Charlie Huston	Joe Pitt series, starting with *Already Dead*
John Levitt	Dog Days series, starting with *Dog Days*
Marjorie Liu	Hunter Kiss, starting with *The Iron Hunt*
Sergei Lukyanenko	Watch series, starting with *Night Watch*
A. Lee Martinez	*Gil's All Fright Diner*
Richelle Mead	Georgina Kincaid series, starting with *Succubus Blues*
Richelle Mead	Dark Swan series, starting with *Storm Born*
Stephenie Meyer	Twilight Saga, starting with *Twilight*
Mike Mignola et al.	Hellboy graphic novels
C. E. Murphy	The Negotiator, starting with *Heart of Stone*
Vicki Pettersson	Sign of the Zodiac, starting with *The Scent of Shadows*
T. A. Pratt	Marla Mason series, starting with *Blood Engines*
Mike Resnick	Fables of Tonight, starting with *Stalking the Unicorn*
Kat Richardson	Greywalker series, starting with *Greywalker*

Lilith Saintcrow	Dante Valentine series, starting with *Working for the Devil*
Will Shetterly	*Elsewhere*; *NeverNever*
Jeanne C. Stein	Anna Strong Chronicles, starting with *The Becoming*
Rob Thurman	Cal Leandros, starting with *Nightlife*
Carrie Vaughan	Kitty Norville, starting with *Kitty and the Midnight Hour*
J. R. Ward	Black Dagger Brotherhood, starting with *Dark Lover*
Marc Zicree et al.	Magic Time series, starting with *Magic Time*

THEMATIC QUESTIONS

- Do paranormal adventures fit most closely with the romance genre, the fantasy genre, or the horror genre?

- Do you find it easier or more difficult to overcome disbelief when reading fantasy in a contemporary setting? Is it difficult to overcome in the novel that you selected?

- Sexuality is more common in paranormal fantasy than in any other subgenre. What is it about paranormal fiction that makes it popular with writers of the romantic and erotic? How strong is the sexuality in the novel you read?

- Not long ago, fantastic fiction was mostly set in the medieval period (or somewhere in early historical times). Why has the urban contemporary setting of paranormal fantasy become so popular? Is the literature deserving of this popularity? Will it last?

- Most of the authors on this list only began publishing in the last decade. Which have staying power? Do the established writers in this list (Emma Bull, Charles De Lint, Will Shetterly) fit within the category or is their style somewhat different?

- The publishing industry has chosen "paranormal" as the name for this subgenre of writing. Why was this term chosen? Has the meaning of "paranormal" shifted over time? Under what other names has this kind of fantasy been marketed in the past?

PLANETARY ROMANCE: SEEKING OUT STRANGE NEW WORLDS, RED SHIRT OPTIONAL

Wonder if there is life on another planet? Let's suppose there is. Suppose further, that only one star in a trillion has a planet that could support life. If that were the case, then there would be at least 100 million planets that harbored life.
—Ben Sweetland

Oh man! There is no planet, sun, or star could hold you, if you but knew what you are.
—Ralph Waldo Emerson

"Planetary romance" is an old term, referring to a subset of space opera: romantic adventures on an exotic planet, usually told from the point of view of a character who is relatively new to that planet. Think *Dune*, for a well-known literary example, or most episodes of the original *Star Trek*, for an example from television. It's easy and fun to get caught up in the adventure of these novels, asking yourself how you would handle the situations encountered by the protagonists.

SUGGESTED WORKS

Neal Asher	*The Skinner*
Iain M. Banks	*Consider Phlebas*
C. F. Bentley	*Harmony*; *Enigma*
Marion Zimmer Bradley	<u>Darkover</u> series, starting with *Darkover: First Contact*
Mike Brotherton	*Spider Star*
Tobias Buckell	<u>Xenowealth Saga</u>, starting with *Crystal Rain*
Edgar Rice Burroughs	<u>Barsoom</u> series, starting with *A Princess of Mars*
C. J. Cherryh	<u>Foreigner Universe</u>, starting with *Foreigner*
Brenda Cooper	<u>Silver Ship</u> series, starting with *The Silver Ship and the Sea*
Julie E. Czerneda	<u>Trade Pact</u> trilogy, starting with *A Thousand Words for Stranger*
Julie E. Czerneda	<u>Webshifters</u> series, starting with *Beholder's Eye*
Alan Dean Foster	<u>Pip & Flinx</u> series, starting with *The Tar-Aiym Krang*
Thomas Harlan	*House of Reeds*
Robert A. Heinlein	*Tunnel in the Sky*
Frank Herbert	<u>Dune</u> series, starting with *Dune*
James Patrick Kelly	*Burn*
Kay Kenyon	<u>The Entire and the Rose</u>, starting with *Bright of the Sky*
Nancy Kress	<u>Cosmic Crossfire</u> series, starting with *Crossfire*
Ursula K. Le Guin	*World of Exile and Illusion*
C. S. Lewis	<u>Space Trilogy</u>, starting with *Out of the Silent Planet*
Ken MacLeod	*Learning the World*
George R. R. Martin, Gardner Dozois and Daniel Abraham	*Hunter's Run*
Julian May	<u>Rampart Worlds</u>, starting with *Perseus Spur*
Anne McCaffrey	<u>Pern</u> series, starting with *Dragonflight*
Anne McCaffrey	<u>Freedom</u> series, starting with *Freedom's Landing*
Larry Niven	<u>Ringworld</u> series, starting with *Ringworld*
Andre Norton	<u>Solar Queen</u> series, starting with <u>*The Solar Queen*</u> omnibus
Andre Norton	<u>Hosteen Storm</u> series, starting with *Beast Master's Planet*
Andre Norton	<u>Moonsinger</u> omnibus
Chris Roberson	*Paragaea: A Planetary Romance*
Mary Doria Russell	*The Sparrow*; *Children of God*
Pamela Sargent	*Earthseed*; *Farseed*
Karl Schroeder	<u>Virga</u> series, starting with *Sun of Suns*
Dan Simmons	<u>Hyperion Cantos</u>, starting with *Hyperion*
S. M. Stirling	*The Sky People*; *In the Courts of the Crimson Kings*
Sheri Tepper	*Grass*
Sheri Tepper	*Sideshow*
Sheri Tepper	*Shadow's End*
Karen Traviss	<u>Wess'har</u> series, starting with *City of Pearl*
Jack Vance	*Planet of Adventure*

THEMATIC QUESTIONS

- Describe the planet or planets in the novel that you read. Do you find the setting original? Believable? Would you want to visit?

- In what sense is the word *romance* to be taken in the term *planetary romance*?

- Are outsiders welcome on the planet they visit in the novel that you read? Do they understand everything that they experience there?

- If humans were to discover life on another world, who should we send to visit or explore? How should we represent ourselves upon first contact?

- Will we find life on other planets? Will it find us? If yes, do you think it will be in your lifetime or later?

––––––––––––––––––––––

POLITICAL FANTASY AND SCIENCE FICTION: GOVERNING PLEASURES

"Ideology," growled one of his new friends. "It's a virus. The world is dying of it."
—Brian Aldiss

I think you'd like politics, at least on Barrayar. Maybe because it's so similar to what we call war elsewhere.
—Lois McMaster Bujold

Some of the best political fiction written is speculative fiction. By devising political and sociological systems in alternate worlds or by hypothesizing alternative events in our own world, authors can create a fictional laboratory in which to explore any political question. Lessons derived from such reading may subtly shape our viewpoints of how politics should be conducted in the real world. It's a good example of how speculative reading helps us see beyond the quagmire of what is and consider what might be—if we find the will to change it.

SUGGESTED WORKS

Daniel Abraham	The Long Price Quartet, starting with *A Shadow in Summer*
Isaac Asimov	Foundation series, starting with *Foundation*
Margaret Atwood	*The Handmaid's Tale*
R. Scott Bakker	The Prince of Nothing, starting with *The Darkness That Comes Before*
Max Barry	*Jennifer Government*
Marion Zimmer Bradley	*The Mists of Avalon*
Max Brooks	*World War Z*
Lois McMaster Bujold	Vorkosigan Saga, starting with *Cordelia's Honor*
Lois McMaster Bujold	*The Curse of Chalion*
Jim Butcher	Codex Alera, starting with *Furies of Calderon*
Ernest Callenbach	*Ecotopia*
Jacqueline Carey	Kushiel series, starting with *Kushiel's Dart*
C. J. Cherryh	Chanur series, starting with *The Chanur Saga*

C. J. Cherryh	<u>Foreigner</u> series, starting with *Foreigner*
Philip K. Dick	*The Man in the High Castle*
Kate Elliott	<u>Crown of Stars</u>, starting with *King's Dragon*
Jennifer Fallon	<u>Hythrun Chronicles</u>, starting with *Medalon*
Jennifer Fallon	<u>Wolfblade Trilogy</u>, starting with *Wolfblade*
S. L. Farrell	<u>Nessantico</u> series, starting with *A Magic of Twilight*
Raymond Feist and Janny Wurts	<u>Empire</u> series, starting with *Daughter of the Empire*
Harry Harrison	*Make Room! Make Room!*
Robert A. Heinlein	*The Moon Is a Harsh Mistress*
Frank Herbert	<u>Dune</u> series, starting with *Dune*
Robin Hobb	<u>Farseer</u> trilogy, starting with *Assassin's Apprentice*
Aldous Huxley	*Brave New World*
Alexander C. Irvine	*Buyout*
Guy Gavriel Kay	*The Lions of al-Rassan*
Ursula K. Le Guin	*The Dispossessed*
Ken MacLeod	*The Execution Channel*
Gregory Maguire	*Wicked*
George R. R. Martin	<u>A Song of Ice and Fire</u>, starting with *A Game of Thrones*
L. E. Modesitt	<u>Saga of Recluce</u>, starting with *The Magic of Recluce*
Alan Moore	*V for Vendetta*
George Orwell	*Animal Farm*
George Orwell	*1984*
Paul Park	<u>Roumania</u> series, starting with *A Princess of Roumania*
Terry Pratchett	*The Truth*
Terry Pratchett	*Jingo*
Terry Pratchett	*Nation*
Kim Stanley Robinson	<u>Mars</u> trilogy, starting with *Red Mars*
Kim Stanley Robinson	<u>Science in the Capital</u>, starting with *Forty Signs of Rain*
Mary Rosenblum	*Horizons*
Brandon Sanderson	*Elantris*
Maria V. Snyder	<u>Yelena</u> series, starting with *Poison Study*
Allen Steele	<u>Coyote</u> series, starting with *Coyote*
Jonathan Swift	*Gulliver's Travels*
Megan Whalen Turner	<u>Queen's Thief</u> series, starting with *The Thief*
Jo Walton	<u>Alternate Britain</u> series, starting with *Farthing*
Yevgeny Zamyatin	*We*

THEMATIC QUESTIONS

- What kind of political systems are represented in the book that you read?
- Can you derive any lessons from the book that you read that would be applicable to our own political landscape?
- Where would you speculate that the author of the book that you read falls on the political spectrum? How does this compare with other authors read by your group?

- What does speculative fiction have to say about the role of the individual in political systems? What about the book that you read in particular?

- How might politics change in the future? Is this reflected by any of the science fiction novels read by your group?

- Do fantasy readers tend to be liberal or conservative? What about science fiction readers?

QUESTS: SEARCHING FOR THE BEST IN SPECULATIVE FICTION

He liked the steady sway and rhythms of voyaging, of movement of the perpetual mystery that lurked beyond the far horizon. This was humanity's role.

—Gregory Benford

We are plain quiet folk and have no use for adventures. Nasty disturbing uncomfortable things! Make you late for dinner! I can't think what anybody sees in them.

—J. R. R. Tolkien

We're all searching for something. Science fiction and fantasy make these searches tangible through the familiar quest plot. Sometimes this quest is all important, but often it's what Hitchcock called the *MacGuffin*, a device to get the plot rolling. What characters learn about their worlds and themselves during quests often becomes more important than their original objectives. Readers enjoy the vicarious experience of joining in the adventure in one of genre fiction's evergreen motifs.

SUGGESTED WORKS

Richard Adams	*Watership Down*
Lloyd Alexander	The Chronicles of Prydain, starting with *The Book of Three*
Piers Anthony	Xanth series, starting with *A Spell for Chameleon*
Iain M. Banks	*Consider Phlebas*; *The Algebraist*
Peter S. Beagle	*The Last Unicorn*
Peter S. Beagle	*The Innkeeper's Song*
Carol Berg	Lighthouse duet, starting with *Flesh and Spirit*
Kristen Britain	Green Rider series, starting with *The Green Rider*
Keith Brooke	*Genetopia*
Terry Brooks	Shannara series, starting with *The Sword of Shannara*
Dan Chernenko	Scepter of Mercy series, starting with *The Bastard King*
James Clemens	Godslayer Chronicles, starting with *Shadowfall*
Alison Croggon	The Book of Pellinor, starting with *The Naming*
Stephen R. Donaldson	Chronicles of Thomas Covenant, starting with *Lord Foul's Bane*
Dave Duncan	*Paragon Lost*; *The Jaguar Knights*
David Eddings	The Belgariad, starting with *Pawn of Prophecy*
Nancy Farmer	*The Sea of Trolls*; *The Land of the Silver Apples*
Raymond Feist	*Silverthorn*
Michael Flynn	*The January Dancer*

Neil Gaiman	*American Gods*
Neil Gaiman	*Stardust*
Jo Graham	*Black Ships*
Elizabeth Haydon	Symphony of Ages, starting with *Rhapsody*
Robert A. Heinlein	*Glory Road*
Amanda Hemingway	Sangreal trilogy, starting with *The Greenstone Grail*
Robert Howard	Conan, starting with *The Coming of Conan the Cimmerian*
Jim C. Hines	Jig the Goblin, starting with *Goblin Quest*
Barry Hughart	*Bridge of Birds*
J. V. Jones	Sword of Shadows, starting with *A Cavern of Black Ice*
Robert Jordan	The Wheel of Time, starting with *The Eye of the World*
Stephen King	The Dark Tower, starting with *The Gunslinger*
Stephen King and Peter Straub	*The Talisman*
E. E. Knight	Age of Fire series, starting with *Dragon Champion*
Jay Lake	*Mainspring; Escapement*
Ursula K. Le Guin	Earthsea Chronicles, starting with *A Wizard of Earthsea*
Doris Lessing	*Mara and Dann: an Adventure*
Robert Low	Oathsworn, starting with *The Whale Road*
David Marusek	*Counting Heads*
Dennis McKiernan	Mithgar series, such as *The Eye of the Hunter*; *City of Jade*
Garth Nix	Abhorsen trilogy, starting with *Sabriel*
Mel Odom	The Rover series, starting with *The Rover*
Nnedi Okorafor-Mbachu	*Zahrah the Windseeker*
Christopher Paolini	Inheritance, starting with *Eragon*
Philip Pullman	His Dark Materials, starting with *The Golden Compass*
J. K. Rowling	Harry Potter, starting with *Harry Potter and the Sorcerer's Stone*
Rudy Rucker	*Frek and the Elixir*
Mary Doria Russell	*The Sparrow*
Kris Saknussemm	*Zanesville*
John Scalzi	*The Android's Dream*
Robert Silverberg	*Lord Valentine's Castle*
Dan Simmons	*Hyperion*
Michael Stackpole	DragonCrown War Cycle, starting with *Fortress Draconis*
S. M. Stirling	*In the Courts of the Crimson Kings*
Eldon Thompson	The Legend of Asahiel, starting with *The Crimson Sword*
J. R. R. Tolkien	*The Hobbit*
J. R. R. Tolkien	*The Lord of the Rings*
Tad Williams	Memory, Sorrow, and Thorn, starting with *The Dragonbone Chair*
Gene Wolfe	The Book of the Short Sun, starting with *On Blue's Waters*
Gene Wolfe	*The Knight; The Wizard*
David Zindell	*The Lightstone; The Silver Sword; Lord of Lies*

THEMATIC QUESTIONS

- What is the most prominent objective of the quest in the book that you read? An object? A task? Personal growth?
- Does the goal of the characters change at all in the course of the book that you read? Does their quest succeed in the terms that they originally envision?
- Quests have been a common plot in fantasy and science fiction for many years. Why is this plot so popular? Is there anything dated about this part of speculative fiction?
- The majority of characters who undertake quests in fiction are young. Why is this so? Do you still relate to the quest motif as an adult reader?
- Travel is often an important element of the quest novel. How does travel in the typical speculative fiction novel compare to travel in the real world?

REBELLION IN SPECULATIVE FICTION: YOU SAY YOU WANT A REVOLUTION

"What are you rebelling against, Johnny?"
"Whaddya got?"

—*The Wild One*

Everything ought to be turned upside down occasionally; it lets in air and light.
—Robert Heinlein

You cannot buy the Revolution. You cannot make the Revolution. You can only be the Revolution. It is in your spirit, or it is nowhere.
—Ursula K. Le Guin

Viva la reading group! Mount the barricades! Destroy the Death Star! There are more instances of revolution in speculative fiction than in any other genre of literature, so sign on with the underdogs and spend a month doing metaphysical battle with everything that oppresses you. This is genre fiction, so you'll probably win. But you might lose a few comrades along the way. So it goes; the book group was getting too big anyway.

SUGGESTED WORKS

Isaac Asimov	*Foundation's Edge*
Elizabeth Bear	*Undertow*
Greg Bear	*Moving Mars*
Marion Zimmer Bradley	*The Heritage of Hastur*
Patricia Briggs	*Dragon Bones*; *Dragon Blood*
Tobias Buckell	*Ragamuffin*
Mark Budz	*Clade*
Jim Butcher	Codex Alera, starting with *Furies of Calderon*
Ernst Callenbach	*Ecotopia*
David B. Coe	Winds of the Forelands, starting with *Rules of Ascension*

Cory Doctorow	*Down and Out in the Magic Kingdom*
Cory Doctorow	*Little Brother*
David Anthony Durham	<u>Acacia</u>, starting with *The War with the Mein*
Jennifer Fallon	<u>Second Sons</u> trilogy, starting with *The Lion of Senet*
Jennifer Fallon	<u>Demon Child</u> trilogy, starting with *Medalon*
S. L. Farrell	*A Magic of Twilight*
Raymond Feist and Janny Wurts	<u>Empire</u> series, starting with *Daughter of the Empire*
David Gemmell	<u>The Rigante</u>, starting with *Sword in the Storm*
Simon R. Green	*Deathstalker Rebellion*
Joe Haldeman	*The Forever War*
Robert A. Heinlein	*The Moon Is a Harsh Mistress*
Robert A. Heinlein	*Red Planet*
Robert A. Heinlein	*Revolt in 2100*
Frank Herbert	*Dune*
Robin Hobb	<u>Farseer</u> trilogy, starting with *Assassin's Apprentice*
Guy Gavriel Kay	*Tigana*
Guy Gavriel Kay	*A Song for Arbonne*
Tom Kratman	*A State of Disobedience*
Naomi Kritzer	<u>Dead Rivers</u> trilogy, starting with *Freedom's Gate*
Katherine Kurtz	*Deryni Rising*
Ursula K. Le Guin	*The Dispossessed*
C. S. Lewis	*Prince Caspian*
Lois Lowry	*The Giver*
Ken MacLeod	<u>The Fall Revolution</u>, starting with *The Star Fraction*
J. Laurie Marks	<u>Elemental Logic</u> series, starting with *Fire Logic*
George R. R. Martin	<u>A Song of Ice and Fire</u>, starting with *The Game of Thrones*
James Maxey	<u>The Dragon Age</u>, starting with *Bitterwood*
Anne McCaffrey	<u>Catteni</u> series, starting with *Freedom's Landing*
Anne McCaffrey and Elizabeth Ann Scarborough	<u>Petaybee</u> series, starting with *Powers That Be*
John Meaney	<u>Nulapeiron</u> sequence, starting with *Paradox*
China Miéville	*Iron Council*
L. E. Modesitt	*Empire & Ecolitan*
Alan Moore and David Lloyd	*V for Vendetta*
Richard K. Morgan	*Broken Angels*
George Orwell	*Animal Farm*
Christopher Paolini	<u>Inheritance</u> series, starting with *Eragon*
Tamora Pierce	*Trickster's Queen*
Terry Pratchett	*Night Watch*
Kim Stanley Robinson	<u>Mars</u> trilogy, starting with *Red Mars*
J. K. Rowling	*Harry Potter and the Order of the Phoenix*
J. K. Rowling	*Harry Potter and the Deathly Hallows*
Mary Doria Russell	*Children of God*
Brandon Sanderson	*Elantris*

Brandon Sanderson	*Mistborn: The Final Empire*
<u>Star Wars</u> series	
Allen Steele	<u>Coyote</u> series, starting with *Coyote*
Jonathan Stroud	<u>Bartimaeus</u> trilogy, starting with *The Amulet of Samarkand*
S. Andrew Swann	<u>Hostile Takeover Trilogy</u>
Paula Volsky	*The Gates of Twilight*
Scott Westerfeld	<u>Uglies</u> series, starting with *Uglies*
Yevgeny Zamyatin	*We*
Roger Zelazny	*Lord of Light*

THEMATIC QUESTIONS

- Stories of rebellion, particularly within speculative fiction, are nearly always sympathetic to the rebels and told from their point of view. Is your book an exception? Why do you suppose that fiction favors the rebels?

- Is the rebellion that occurs in the book that you read justified?

- Compare real-world rebellions and revolutions with those portrayed in fiction. In which case is rebellion more often justified? In which case is it more often successful?

- Are there downsides to the act of revolution or rebellion in the book that you read? Are the costs worth the result? If the rebels were to win and if they conduct their government as they conduct their revolt, will the regime change be an improvement?

- Compare oppressors in books that your group members chose. Where do these leaders and systems fall on the political spectrum (left to right)? Does the manner in which they oppress vary according to whether they are left- or right-wing, or is all oppression similar?

ROBOTS, CYBORGS, ANDROIDS, AND AI: BREATHING ARTIFICIAL LIFE INTO SCIENCE FICTION

A robot may not injure a human being, or, through inaction, allow a human being to come to harm.
A robot must obey the orders given it by human beings except where such orders would conflict with the First Law.
A robot must protect its own existence as long as such protection does not conflict with the First or Second law.

—Isaac Asimov

In the beginning I was made. I didn't ask to be made; no one consulted me or considered my feelings in the matter. I don't think it even occurred to them that I might have feelings, but if it brought some passing sadistic pleasure to some mentally benighted humans as they pranced their haphazard way through life's mournful jungle then so be it.
—Marvin the Paranoid Android, in *The Hitch-Hiker's Guide to the Galaxy*

Artificially created life forms are a staple of the science fiction genre. Their existence begs some fundamental questions: What is it to be human? If we create something better than us, will we later have reason to fear it? Can we accelerate the evolution of our species into over-drive? These are big questions indeed, certainly enough to keep your circle of readers entertained for an evening. If not, you can always put on "Mr. Roboto" and see who can do "The Robot" the best.

SUGGESTED WORKS

Douglas Adams	<u>Hitchhiker's Guide</u>, starting with *The Hitchhiker's Guide to the Galaxy*
Piers Anthony	*Pet Peeve*
Catherine Asaro	*The Phoenix Code*
Neal Asher	*The Skinner*
Neal Asher	<u>Ian Cormac</u> series, starting with *Gridlinked*
Isaac Asimov	<u>Daneel Olivaw</u> series, starting with *The Caves of Steel*
Isaac Asimov	<u>Robot</u> series, starting with *I, Robot*
Kage Baker	<u>The Company</u> series, starting with *In the Garden of Iden*
Tony Ballantyne	*Recursion*; *Capacity*; *Divergence*
Iain M. Banks	*Matter*
Elizabeth Bear	<u>Jenny Casey</u> series, starting with *Hammered*
Greg Bear	*The Forge of God*
Margaret Bechard	*Spacer and Rat*
K. A. Bedford	*Orbital Burn*
M. M. Buckner	*Watermind*
Lincoln Child	*Utopia*
Peter Crowther, ed.	*We Think Therefore We Are*
Philip K. Dick	*Do Androids Dream of Electric Sheep?*
Philip K. Dick	*The Simulacra*
Philip K. Dick	*We Can Build You*
Dave Diotalevi	*Miracle Myx*
Hiroki Endo	<u>Eden</u> graphic novels, starting with *It's an Endless World*
Austin Grossman	*Soon I Will Be Invincible*
David Gunn	<u>Death's Head</u> series, starting with *Death's Head*
John Helfers and Martin Greenberg, eds.	*Man vs. Machine*
Brian Herbert and Kevin J. Anderson	<u>Legends of Dune</u> series, starting with *The Butlerian Jihad*
James P. Hogan	*The Two Faces of Tomorrow*
Matthew Hughes	<u>Henghis Hapthorn</u> series, starting with *Majestrum*
Yukito Kishiro	<u>Battle Angel Alita</u> graphic novels
Keith Laumer, et al.	<u>Bolo</u> series, starting with *Honor of the Regiment: Bolos 1*
Tanith Lee	*The Silver Metal Lover*; *Metallic Love*
Edward Lerner	*Fools' Experiments*
Ken MacLeod	<u>Fall Revolution</u>, starting with *Fractions*
A. Lee Martinez	*The Automatic Detective*
Anne McCaffrey et al.	<u>Brainship</u> series, starting with *The Ship Who Sang*

Sandra McDonald	*The Outback Stars*
Chris Moriarty	*Spin State*; *Spin Control*
Craig Nova	*Wetware*
S. M. Peters	*Whitechapel Gods*
Marge Piercy	*He, She, and It*
Alastair Reynolds	Revelation Space series, starting with *Revelation Space*
Justina Robson	*Natural History*
Justina Robson	Quantum Gravity series, starting with *Keeping It Real*
Rudy Rucker	*Postsingular*
Robert J. Sawyer	*Mindscan*
Ken Scholes	The Psalms of Isaak, starting with *Lamentation*
Karl Schroeder	*Lady of Mazes*
Ekaterina Sedia	*The Alchemy of Stone*
Mary Shelley	*Frankenstein*
Joel Shepherd	Cassandra Kresnov series, starting with *Crossover*
Dan Simmons	Hyperion Cantos, starting with *Hyperion*
Dan Simmons	*Ilium*; *Olympos*
Jeff Somers	*The Electric Church*
S. M. Stirling	T2 series, starting with *Infiltrator*
Charles Stross	Singularity series, starting with *Singularity Sky*
Charles Stross	*Saturn's Children*
The Terminator Omnibus graphic novels	
Osamu Tezuka	Astro Boy graphic novels
Jeffrey Thomas	Punktown series, starting with *Punktown*
Peter Watts	Rifters series, starting with *Starfish*
David Weber	*Bolo!*
David Weber	Safehold series, starting with *Off Armageddon Reef*
Scott Westerfeld	Succession series, starting with *The Risen Empire*
Sean Williams	Astropolis series, starting with *Saturn Returns*
Jeanette Winterson	*The Stone Gods*
John Zakour and Lawrence Ganem	Zach Johnson series, starting with *The Plutonium Blonde*

THEMATIC QUESTIONS

- Are the robots, cyborgs, androids, or artificial intelligences in the novel that you read friendly or hostile to humans?

- What advancements in technology are described in the novel that you read? Will technology really develop in this way? If so, how far in the future will such developments occur?

- Do you fear the development of artificial life forms in the future? Why or why not?

- What is the difference between a human and an intelligent machine? How much of a human can be replaced with artificial components before that person ceases to be human? Before that person becomes someone else?

- Under what conditions would you accept implants to your body? Which parts would you be willing to replace? What implants would you refuse? If it would extend your life or somehow improve you, would you consider having your consciousness implanted in another body?

SCIENCE FANTASY: TWO GENRES FOR THE PRICE OF ONE

Any sufficiently advanced technology is indistinguishable from magic.
—Arthur C. Clarke

Fantasy has trees, and science fiction has rivets. That's it, that's all the difference there is, the difference of feel, perception.
—Orson Scott Card

Where does the border lie between fantasy and science fiction? Is imagined or speculative science still in the realm of science fiction or is it fantasy? Is a fantasy novel that is set in the future and contains some technology also science fiction? If your book group can't get a successful discussion out of this topic, they just aren't fans! Just take care that this borderlands theme doesn't warp into a session where fans of one genre degrade the other. After all, one of the reasons for thematic groups is to help disparate genre readers get along.

SUGGESTED WORKS

Piers Anthony	<u>Apprentice Adept</u> series, starting with *Split Infinity*
Alison Baird	<u>The Dragon Throne</u>, starting with *The Stone of the Stars*
Marion Zimmer Bradley	<u>Darkover</u>, starting with *Darkover: First Contact* omnibus
Terry Brooks	<u>Genesis of Shannara</u>, starting with *Armageddon's Children*
Terry Brooks et al.	*Star Wars: The Prequel Trilogy*
Edgar Rice Burroughs	<u>Barsoom</u> series, starting with *A Princess of Mars*
C. J. Cherryh	*<u>The Morgaine Saga</u>*
Eoin Colfer	<u>Artemis Fowl</u> series, starting with *Artemis Fowl*
Storm Constantine	*<u>Wraeththu</u>* omnibus
Rick Cook	<u>Wiz Zumwalt</u> series, starting with *The Wiz Biz* omnibus
Peter David	<u>Hidden Earth Chronicles</u>, starting with *Darkness of the Light*
L. Sprague de Camp and Fletcher Pratt	*The Mathematic of Magic: The Enchanter Stories*
Charles de Lint	*Svaha*
Philip Jose Farmer	<u>Riverworld</u> series, starting with *To Your Scattered Bodies Go*
Jasper Fforde	<u>Thursday Next</u> series, starting with *The Eyre Affair*
Eric Flint et al.	<u>Assiti Shards</u> series, starting with *1632*
C. S. Friedman	<u>Coldfire Trilogy</u>, starting with *Black Sun Rising*
Jim Grimsley	*The Ordinary*; *The Last Green Tree*
Austin Grossman	*Soon I Will Be Invincible*

Frank Herbert	<u>Dune</u> series, starting with *Dune*
Kay Kenyon	<u>The Rose and the Entire</u>, starting with *Bright of the Sky*
J. Gregory Keyes	<u>The Age of Unreason</u>, starting with *Newton's Cannon*
Stephen King	*The Stand*
Rosemary Kirstein	<u>Steerswoman</u> series, starting with *The Steerswoman's Road*
Jay Lake	*Mainspring*; *Escapement*
Madeleine L'Engle	<u>Time Quartet</u>, starting with *A Wrinkle in Time*
George Lucas et al.	<u>*Star Wars Trilogy*</u>
Anne McCaffrey	<u>Pern</u> series, starting with *Dragonflight*
Anne McCaffrey et al.	<u>Acorna</u> series, starting with *Acorna: The Unicorn Girl*
Kelly McCullough	<u>Ravirn</u> series, starting with *WebMage*
China Miéville	<u>Bas Lag</u> novels, starting with *Perdido Street Station*
Larry Niven, ed.	<u>*The Magic Goes Away Collection*</u>
Andre Norton	<u>Witch World</u> series, starting with *The Gates to Witch World*
Nnedi Okorafor-Mbachu	*The Shadow Speaker*
S. M. Peters	*Whitechapel Gods*
Philip Pullman	<u>His Dark Materials</u>, starting with *The Golden Compass*
John Ringo	<u>Council Wars</u> series, starting with *There Will Be Dragons*
Justina Robson	<u>Quantum Gravity</u> series, starting with *Keeping It Real*
Ken Scholes	<u>The Psalms of Isaak</u>, starting with *Lamentation*
Sharon Shinn	<u>Samaria</u> series, starting with *Archangel*
Robert Silverberg	<u>Majipoor</u> series, starting with *Lord Valentine's Castle*
Dan Simmons	*Ilium*; *Olympos*
Wen Spencer	<u>Tinker</u> series, starting with *Tinker*
S. M. Stirling	<u>The Change</u>, starting with *Dies the Fire*
Charles Stross	<u>The Merchants' War</u>, starting with *The Family Trade*
Michael Swanwick	*The Iron Dragon's Daughter*; *The Dragons of Babel*
Harry Turtledove	<u>Darkness</u> series, starting with *Into the Darkness*
Matthew Woodring Stover	<u>Overworld</u> series, starting with *Heroes Die*
Jack Vance	*Tales of the Dying Earth*
John Varley	<u>Gaea</u> series, starting with *Titan*
Liz Williams	*Nine Layers of Sky*
Liz Williams	<u>Detective Inspector Chen</u> series, starting with *Snake Agent*
Tad Williams	<u>Otherland</u> saga, starting with *City of Golden Shadow*
Gene Wolfe	<u>Book of the New Sun</u>, starting with <u>*Shadow & Claw*</u> omnibus
Roger Zelazny	*Lord of Light*

THEMATIC QUESTIONS

- Is the book that you read equal parts science and fantasy, or does it fit mainly in one of the two genres?
- What is the difference between science fiction and fantasy? Do both genres appeal to readers for the same reasons?

- Do you enjoy both genres equally? Is there a difference between fans of the two genres?
- Can there be magic in a true science fiction novel? What about religion?
- Which writer combines science fiction and fantasy the best? Which writers can write both genres with equal skill?

SHORT STORIES: QUICK READS, BIG IDEAS

The universe is made of stories, not atoms.

—Muriel Rukeyser

If you've heard this story before, don't stop me, because I'd like to hear it again.

—Groucho Marx

Because of the importance of pulp magazines to the development of science fiction and fantasy, short stories are more integral to speculative fiction than any other genre. Preference for stories is common among readers who started during the magazine era, but there are young readers as well who prefer shorter formats. This works fine in a thematic group, where the length of the work doesn't matter. You should, in fact, encourage readers to squeeze a story into their schedule and attend the meeting, even if they don't have time for a full-length work. If you have many story fans in your group, divide this theme into at least two topics: single-author collections and anthologies.

SUGGESTED WORKS: SINGLE-AUTHOR COLLECTIONS

Poul Anderson	*To Outlive Eternity and Other Stories*; *The Collected Short Works of Poul Anderson: Vol. 1, Call Me Joe*
Isaac Asimov	*The Complete Stories*
Paolo Bacigalupi	*Pump Six and Other Stories*
J. G. Ballard	*The Best Short Stories of J. G. Ballard*
Iain M. Banks	*The State of the Art*
Peter S. Beagle	*The Line Between*; *We Never Talk about My Brother*
Greg Bear	*The Collected Stories of Greg Bear*
Terry Bisson	*Bears Discover Fire & Other Stories*; *Greetings and Other Stories*
James Blish	*Works of Art*
Jorge Luis Borges	*Colleciones*
Ray Bradbury	*Bradbury Stories: One Hundred of His Most Celebrated Tales*
Fredric Brown	*From These Ashes: The Complete Short SF of Fredric Brown*
Orson Scott Card	*Maps in a Mirror: The Short Fiction of Orson Scott Card*
Angela Carter	*Burning Your Boats: The Collected Short Stories*
Ted Chiang	*Stories of Your Life and Others*
Arthur C. Clarke	*The Collected Short Stories of Arthur C. Clarke*
Susanna Clarke	*The Ladies of Grace Adieu and Other Stories*
L. Sprague de Camp and Fletcher Pratt	*The Mathematics of Magic*

Charles de Lint	*Dreams Underfoot*; *Moonlight & Vines*; *The Ivory & the Horn*
Philip K. Dick	*The Philip K. Dick Reader*
Paul De Filippo	*Harsh Oases*
Cory Doctorow	*Overclocked: Stories of the Future Present*
David Drake	*The Complete Hammer's Slammers Volumes 1–3*
Lord Dunsany	*In the Land of Time and Other Fantasy Tales*
Harlan Ellison	*The Essential Ellison*
Jack Finney	*About Time*
Eric Flint	*Worlds*
Neil Gaiman	*Fragile Things*
Elizabeth Hand	*Saffron and Brimstone: Strange Stories*
Zenna Henderson	*Ingathering: The Complete People Stories of Zenna Henderson*
Robert E. Howard	*The Coming of Conan the Cimmerian*; *The Bloody Crown of Conan*; *The Conquering Sword of Conan*
John Kessel	*The Baum Plan for Financial Independence and Other Stories*
Ellen Klages	*Portable Childhoods*
C. M. Kornbluth	*His Share of Glory: The Complete Short Science Fiction of C. M. Kornbluth*
Nancy Kress	*Nano Comes to Clifford Falls and Other Stories*
Margo Lanagan	*White Time*; *Black Juice*; *Red Spikes*
Ursula K. Le Guin	*A Fisherman of the Inland Sea*; *Four Ways to Forgiveness*; *Tales from Earthsea*; *The Birthday of the World and Other Stories*
Fritz Leiber	<u>Lankhmar</u>, starting with *Lankhmar Book 1: Swords and Deviltry*
Murray Leinster	*First Contacts: The Essential Murray Leinster*
Kelly Link	*Stranger Things Happen*; *Magic for Beginners*; *Pretty Monsters*
George R. R. Martin	*Dreamsongs, Volumes 1 and 2*
Richard Matheson	*Collected Stories, Volumes 1–3*
China Miéville	*Looking for Jake and Other Stories*
C. L. Moore	*Miracle in Three Dimensions and Other Stories by C. L. Moore*
Susan Palwick	*The Fate of Mice*
Frederik Pohl	*Platinum Pohl: The Collected Best Stories*
Alastair Reynolds	*Zima Blue and Other Stories*
Benjamin Rosenbaum	*The Ant King and Other Stories*
Lucius Shepard	*The Best of Lucius Shepard*; *Beast of the Heartland*; *The Jaguar Hunter*
Robert Silverberg	*Phases of the Moon: Six Decades of Masterpieces*
Cordwainer Smith	*The Rediscovery of Man: The Complete Short Science Fiction of Cordwainer Smith*
Theodore Sturgeon	*Selected Stories*

Michael Swanwick	*The Dog Said Bow-Wow*; *The Best of Michael Swanwick*
William Tenn	*Immodest Proposals*; *Here Comes Civilization*
James Tiptree, Jr.	*Her Smoke Rose Up Forever*
Vernor Vinge	*The Collected Stories of Vernor Vinge*
Connie Willis	*The Winds of Marble Arch*
Gene Wolfe	*The Best of Gene Wolfe: A Definitive Retrospective*
Roger Zelazny	*The Collected Short Works of Roger Zelazny: Volume 1, Threshold*; *Volume 2, Power & Light*

SUGGESTED WORKS: ANTHOLOGIES

Editor	Title
John Joseph Adams	*Wastelands: Stories of the Apocalypse*
Lou Anders	*Fast Forward*; *Fast Forward 2*
Lou Anders	*Sideways in Crime*
Isaac Asimov	*50 Short Science Fiction Tales*
Orson Scott Card	*Masterpieces: The Best Science Fiction of the 20th Century*
F. Brett Cox and Andy Duncan	*Crossroads: Tales of the Southern Literary Fantastic*
Peter Crowther	*We Think Therefore We Are*
Ellen Datlow et al.	*The Year's Best Fantasy and Horror* annual collections
Ellen Datlow and Terri Windling	*Ruby Slippers, Golden Tears*; *Black Swan, White Raven*; *Silver Birch, Blood Moon*; *Black Heart, Ivory Bones*; *The Faery Reel*; *Coyote Road*
Ellen Datlow	*The Del Rey Book of Science Fiction and Fantasy*
Gardner Dozois	*The Year's Best Science Fiction* annual collections
Gardner Dozois and Jonathan Strahan	*The New Space Opera*
David Drake et al.	*The World Turned Upside Down*
Karen Joy Fowler, et al.	*The James Tiptree Award Anthology 1–3*
Nick Gevers	*Extraordinary Engines: The Definitive Steampunk*
David Hartwell and Kathryn Cramer	*The Hard SF Renaissance*
David Hartwell and Kathryn Cramer	*The Space Opera Renaissance*
James Patrick Kelly and John Kessel	*Feeling Very Strange: The Slipstream Anthology*
Justine Larbalestier	*Feminist Science Fiction in the Twentieth Century*
Ursula K. Le Guin and Brian Attebery	*The Norton Book of Science Fiction*
George Mann	*The Solaris Book of New Science Fiction* (volumes 1–3)
Rusty Morrison and Ken Keegan	*ParaSpheres*
Pamela Sargent	*Women of Wonder*
Ekaterina Sedia	*Paper Cities: An Anthology of Urban Fantasy*

Delia Sherman and Theodora Goss	*Interfictions: An Anthology of Interstitial Writing*
Tom Shippey	*The Oxford Book of Science Fiction Stories*
Robert Silverberg	*The Science Fiction Hall of Fame, Volume One*
Jonathan Strahan	*The Best Science Fiction and Fantasy of the Year* annual collections
Jonathan Strahan	*Eclipse: New Science Fiction and Fantasy; Eclipse Two*
Jonathan Strahan	*The Starry Rift*
Harry Turtledove and Martin Greenberg	*The Best Time Travel Stories of the 20th Century*
Harry Turtledove and Martin Greenberg	*The Best Alternative History Stories of the 20th Century*
Ann and Jeff VanderMeer	*The New Weird*
Ann and Jeff VanderMeer	*Steampunk*
Ann and Jeff VanderMeer	*Fast Ships, Black Sails*

THEMATIC QUESTIONS

- Are the short story magazines, and the story format in general, in permanent decline, or will they become more popular again?

- Do you prefer stories or novels? Did you begin reading science fiction and fantasy in short stories or long formats?

- How does storytelling differ in short works compared to long works? What gets cut? With extra material, would the stories you chose for this meeting make good novels?

- Is the short story more suited to science fiction writing or fantasy writing?

- Which speculative fiction writers do you consider to be short story specialists? Who are the best contemporary story writers?

SLIPSTREAM AND THE NEW WEIRD: FRONTIERS OF THE IMAGINATION

"Your story is impossible, ridiculous, fantastic, mad, and obviously the ravings of a disordered mind," Hermann said. "And I believe every word of it."

—Keith Laumer

It's not so much what you have to learn if you accept weird theories, it's what you have to unlearn.

—Isaac Asimov

Slipstream and the New Weird are movements within speculative fiction. Each has been defined in many ways. There is no agreed definition of which authors, works, or styles fit either school, but Slipstream and the New Weird share the trait of deliberately subverting genre conventions to make something new. Because of this attempt to keep speculative fiction atypical and unusual, resulting works are often challenging: both movements appeal to readers of a more literary bent. Muster your courage, and dive into some truly strange waters: you may find a real pearl!

SUGGESTED WORKS

Iain Banks	*The Wasp Factory*
K. J. Bishop	*The Etched City*
Alan Campbell	Deepgate Codex, starting with *Scar Night*
Paul Di Filippo	*Ribofunk*; *Harsh Oases*
Hal Duncan	The Book of All Hours, starting with *Vellum*
Carol Emshwiller	*The Mount*
Jeffrey Ford	*The Emperor of Ice Cream*; *The Portrait of Mrs. Charbuque*
Nick Gevers and Jay Lake, eds.	*Other Earths*
Felix Gilman	*Thunderer*; *Gears of the City*
Theodora Goss	*In the Forest of Forgetting*
Elizabeth Hand	*Saffron and Brimstone: Strange Stories*
M. John Harrison	*Viriconium*; *Light*; *Nova Swing*
James Patrick Kelly and John Kessel, eds.	*Feeling Very Strange: The Slipstream Anthology*
Ellen Klages	*Portable Childhoods*
Jay Lake	*Mainspring*; *Escapement*
Kelly Link	*Stranger Things Happen*; *Magic for Beginners*
Ian R. MacLeod	*The Light Ages*; *House of Storms*
China Miéville	Bas Lag novels, starting with *Perdido Street Station*
China Miéville	*Looking for Jake*
Rusty Morrison and Ken Keegan, eds.	*ParaSpheres: Extending Beyond the Spheres of Literary and Genre Fiction*
Jeff Noon	*Vurt*
Holly Phillips	*The Engine's Child*
Geoff Ryman	*Was*; *Lust*; *Air*
Lucius Shepard	*The Best of Lucius Shepard*; *Beast of the Heartland*
Delia Sherman and Theodora Goss, eds.	*Interfictions: An Anthology of Interstitial Writing*
Neal Stephenson	*Cryptonomicon*
Peter Straub, ed.	*Conjunctions: 39, The New Wave Fabulists*
Steph Swainston	*The Year of Our War*
Catherynne M. Valente	The Orphan's Tales, starting with *In the Night Garden*
Ann and Jeff VanderMeer, eds.	*The New Weird*
Jeff VanderMeer	*Veniss Underground*; *City of Saints and Madmen*
Barry Yourgrau	*A Man Jumps out of a Plane*; *Wearing Dad's Head*

Older writers whose works fit the conceptual definition of new weird:

J. G. Ballard
Jorge Luis Borges
Italo Calvino
Jonathan Carroll
John Crowley
Samuel Delany
Philip K. Dick

H. P. Lovecraft
Michael Moorcock
Mervyn Peake
Tim Powers
Christopher Priest
Thomas Pynchon
Michael Swanwick
Gene Wolfe

THEMATIC QUESTIONS

- How is the book that you chose different from other genre fiction that you have read? Does the author succeed in creating something truly new?

- Do you prefer works that are challenging and unique, or would you prefer for authors to stick to the genre's tried-and-true conventions?

- Do you prefer a different definition of either of these subgenres? Are their authors whom you would remove from or add to this list?

- Is there anything truly new about the New Weird, or have works of this type been available throughout the history of fantasy and science fiction?

- Who is most likely to appreciate these works: those who prefer literary fiction, those who prefer fantasy, or those who prefer science fiction?

SPACE OPERA: READING THE MASTERS OF THE UNIVERSE

Overhead wheeled the stars, the million suns of space, fire and ice and the giant sprawl of constellations, the Milky Way a rush of curdled silver, the far, mysterious glow of nebulae, hugeness and loneliness to break a human heart.

—Poul Anderson

"It is good to renew one's wonder," said the philosopher. "Space travel has again made children of us all."

—Ray Bradbury

Space opera was originally a derogatory term, applied to overly melodramatic science fiction in the same way that "horse opera" is applied derisively to Westerns. But over time, genre lovers embraced the term, coming to the defense of sagas and epics with large casts, multiplanet settings, emotional scope, and dramatic story lines. It's a big universe, so why not fill it with big stories? Most of these are long books, often part of long series, but they are first-class page-turners as well.

SUGGESTED WORKS

Kevin J. Anderson	Saga of Seven Suns, starting with *Hidden Empire*
Catherine Asaro	Saga of the Skolian Empire, starting with *Primary Inversion*
Neal Asher	Cormac/Polity series, starting with *Gridlinked*

Isaac Asimov	<u>Foundation</u> series, starting with *Foundation*
Iain M. Banks	<u>The Culture</u>, starting with *Consider Phlebas*
Gregory Benford	<u>Galactic Center</u>, starting with *In the Ocean of Night*
Ben Bova	<u>Grand Tour</u> series, starting with *Venus*
Ben Bova	<u>Asteroid Wars</u>, starting with *The Precipice*
David Brin	<u>Uplift Saga</u>, starting with *Sundiver*
Tobias Buckell	*Crystal Rain*; *Ragamuffin*
Lois McMaster Bujold	<u>Vorkosigan Saga</u>, starting with *Cordelia's Honor*
Jack Campbell	<u>The Lost Fleet</u>, starting with *Dauntless*
Orson Scott Card	<u>Ender</u> series, starting with *Ender's Game*
C. J. Cherryh	<u>The Company Wars</u>, starting with *Downbelow Station*
C. J. Cherryh	<u>Foreigner</u> series, starting with *Foreigner*
Michael Cobley	<u>Humanity's Fire</u>, starting with *Seeds of Earth*
Julie E. Czerneda	<u>Trade Pact Universe</u>, starting with *A Thousand Words for Stranger*
Julie E. Czerneda	<u>Webshifters</u>, starting with *Beholder's Eye*
Stephen R. Donaldson	<u>Gap</u> series, starting with *The Real Story: The Gap Into Conflict*
Gardner Dozois and Jonathan Strahan, eds.	*The New Space Opera*
Michael Flynn	*The January Dancer*
Simon R. Green	<u>Deathstalker</u> series, starting with *Deathstalker*
Joe Haldeman	<u>Forever</u> series, starting with *The Forever War*
Peter F. Hamilton	<u>Night's Dawn</u>, starting with *The Reality Dysfunction*
Peter F. Hamilton	<u>Commonwealth Saga</u>, starting with *Pandora's Star*
Peter F. Hamilton	<u>The Void</u> trilogy, starting with *The Dreaming Void*
David G. Hartwell and Kathryn Cramer, eds.	*The Space Opera Renaissance*
Robert A. Heinlein	*Red Planet*
Robert A. Heinlein	*Between Planets*
Robert A. Heinlein	*Citizen of the Galaxy*
Robert A. Heinlein	*Have Spacesuit—Will Travel*
Robert A. Heinlein	*Starship Troopers*
George Lucas, et al.	<u>Star Wars</u> series, starting with <u>*Star Wars Trilogy*</u> omnibus
Ken MacLeod	<u>Fall Revolution</u>, starting with <u>*Fractions*</u> omnibus
Jack McDevitt	<u>Priscilla "Hutch" Hutchins</u>, starting with *The Engines of God*
John Meaney	<u>Nulapeiron Sequence</u>, starting with *Paradox*
Elizabeth Moon	<u>Serrano Legacy</u>, starting with *Hunting Party*
Elizabeth Moon	<u>Vatta's War</u>, starting with *Trading in Danger*
Larry Niven	<u>Ringworld</u> series, starting with *Ringworld*
Mike Resnick	<u>Starship</u> series, starting with *Starship: Mutiny*
Alastair Reynolds	<u>Revelation Space</u> series, starting with *Revelation: Space*
Justina Robson	*Natural History*
John Scalzi	<u>Old Man's War</u> series, starting with *Old Man's War*
Karl Schroeder	<u>Virga</u> series, starting with *Sun of Suns*
Dan Simmons	<u>Hyperion Cantos</u>, starting with *Hyperion*
Dan Simmons	<u>Endymion Saga</u>, starting with *Endymion*

Wen Spencer	*Endless Blue*
Allen Steele	<u>Coyote</u> series, starting with *Coyote*
Charles Stross	*Singularity Sky*; *Iron Sunrise*
S. Andrew Swann	<u>Hostile Takeover</u> omnibus
Karen Traviss	<u>Wess'har</u> series, starting with *City of Pearl*
Jack Vance	*Tales of the Dying Earth*
Vernor Vinge	<u>Queng Ho</u> series, starting with *A Deepness in the Sky*
David Weber	<u>Honor Harrington</u> series, starting with *On Basilisk Station*
David Weber	<u>Safehold</u> series, starting with *Off Armageddon Reef*
Scott Westerfeld	<u>Succession</u>, starting with *The Risen Empire*
Walter Jon Williams	<u>Dread Empire's Fall</u>, starting with *Praxis*
John C. Wright	<u>The Golden Age</u> series, starting with *The Golden Age*

THEMATIC QUESTIONS

- What elements are required to make a space opera? Are these all present in the book that you chose?
- Do you have any derogatory associations with the idea of space opera?
- Can a true space opera be contained in a single book? In a short book?
- What are your favorite space operas? In hindsight, how much did your appreciation for these works contribute to your love of the genre?
- Is there a difference between the way the British write space opera and the way that Americans write it? Is there a "new space opera" or "space opera renaissance," as the titles of some story collections claim?

STEAMPUNK AND VICTORIANA: HIGH ADVENTURE, HIGH ATTITUDE, HIGH TEA

The history of the Victorian age will never be written: We know too much about it.
—Lytton Strachey

We are not amused.

—Queen Victoria

The term *steampunk* can be applied to any work of science fiction or fantasy that combines early industrial-age technologies (such as the steam engine) with an anti-authority (punk) attitude. It's a highly visual subgenre, beloved of audiophiles and graphic novelists because it combines grandiose historic get-up, shiny, extravagant contraptions, and a bit of grit and grime. Try a high tea with tea, cakes, and finger sandwiches for refreshments at this meeting.

SUGGESTED WORKS

Jonathan Barnes	*The Somnambulist*
Elizabeth Bear	*New Amsterdam*
James P. Blaylock	*The Digging Leviathan*

James P. Blaylock	*Homunculus*
Libba Bray	<u>Gemma Doyle</u> trilogy, starting with *A Great and Terrible Beauty*
Alan Campbell	<u>Deepgate Codex</u>, starting with *Scar Night*
Susanna Clarke	*Jonathan Strange & Mr Norrell*
Eoin Colfer	*Airmen*
Gordon Dahlquist	*The Glass Books of the Dream Eaters*
Paul di Filippo	*The Steampunk Trilogy*
Kaja and Phil Foglio	<u>Girl Genius</u> graphic novels
Matt Fraction	*Five Fists of Science*
Mark Frost	*The List of Seven*
Nick Gevers, ed.	*Extraordinary Engines*
William Gibson and Bruce Sterling	*The Difference Engine*
Stephen Hunt	<u>Kingdom of Jackals</u>, starting with *The Court of the Air*
K. W. Jeter	*Infernal Devices*
Gregory Keyes	<u>The Age of Unreason</u>, starting with *Newton's Cannon*
Jay Lake	*Mainspring*; *Escapement*
Ian R. MacLeod	*The Light Ages*; *House of Storms*
China Miéville	<u>Bas-Lag</u> novels, starting with *Perdido Street Station*
Alan Moore and Kevin O'Neill	<u>The League of Extraordinary Gentlemen</u> graphic novels
Kim Newman	*The Secret Files of the Diogenes Club*
Kenneth Oppel	<u>Matt Cruse & Kate de Vries</u> series, starting with *Airborn*
Dru Pagliassotti	*Clockwork Heart*
S. M. Peters	*Whitechapel Gods*
Tim Powers	*Anubis Gates*
Christopher Priest	*The Prestige*
Philip Pullman	<u>His Dark Materials</u>, starting with *The Golden Compass*
Philip Pullman	<u>Sally Lockhart</u> trilogy, starting with *The Ruby in the Smoke*
Philip Reeve	<u>Hungry City Chronicles</u>, starting with *Mortal Engines*
Ekaterina Sedia	*The Alchemy of Stone*
Neal Stephenson	*Diamond Age*
S. M. Stirling	*The Peshawar Lancers*
Bryan Talbot	*The Adventures of Luther Arkwright*
Ann and Jeff VanderMeer, eds.	*Steampunk*
Paula Volsky	*The Grand Ellipse*
Martha Wells	*Death of the Necromancer*
Connie Willis	*To Say Nothing of the Dog*
Robert Charles Wilson	*Darwinia*
Patricia C. Wrede and Caroline Stevermer	<u>Cecelia and Kate</u>, starting with *Sorcery and Cecelia*

And writers of the period, whose work now has a steampunk appeal:

Edwin Abbott
H. Rider Haggard

Lord Dunsany
Jules Verne
H. G. Wells

THEMATIC QUESTIONS

- Is steampunk at a zenith now? Is it just a fad? Or is there something about the Victorian era with permanent appeal to contemporary readers?
- What kinds of characters are typical of the steampunk genre or the Victorian era? What kinds of objects? What settings?
- Does the work that you read have all of the elements of steampunk or only some of them?
- What films and television shows can be classified as steampunk?
- Other terms—such as *cyberpunk*, *splatterpunk*, *dieselpunk*, and even *sandalpunk*—are applied to other parts of the science fiction/fantasy genre. Do the so-described works have a *punk* quality, or do writers and publishers just use the suffix because it sounds cool?

RESOURCES

Steampunkopedia

http://www.steampunk.republika.pl/opedia.html

Steampunk Workshop

http://steampunkworkshop.com

TIME TRAVEL: ACROSS THE SPACE-TIME CONTINUUM IN SPECULATIVE FICTION

> *Your ancestor did not believe in a uniform, absolute time. He believed in an infinite series of times, in a growing, dizzying net of divergent, convergent, and parallel times. This network of times, which approached one another, forked, broke off, or were unaware of one another for centuries, embraces all possibilities of time.*
>
> —Jorge Luis Borges

> *In grasping the present, he felt for the first time the massive steadiness of time's movement everywhere complicated by shifting currents, waves, surges, and countersurges, like surf against rocky cliffs.*
>
> —Frank Herbert

What author can resist adding a fourth dimension to his or her storytelling? Time travel, although viewed by many as scientifically dubious, opens fascinating realms of possibility to writers and readers. As such, it has been one of science fiction/fantasy's most popular tropes from the very beginning. Combining past and future, fantasy and logic puzzles, this theme is a popular choice to which your group can return repeatedly.

SUGGESTED WORKS

Douglas Adams	*Dirk Gently's Holistic Detective Agency*; *The Long Dark Tea-Time of the Soul*
Poul Anderson	*Time Patrol*; *The Shield of Time*
Taylor Anderson	Destoyermen series, starting with *Into the Storm*
Isaac Asimov	*Pebble in the Sky*
Kage Baker	The Company series, starting with *In the Garden of Iden*
Stephen Baxter	*The Time Ships*
Stephen Baxter	Time's Tapestry series, starting with *Emperor*
Greg Bear	*City at the End of Time*
Edward Bellamy	*Looking Backward: 2000–1887*
Gregory Benford	*Timescape*
John Birmingham	Axis of Time series, starting with *Weapons of Choice*
Octavia Butler	*Kindred*
Orson Scott Card	*Pastwatch*
Arthur C. Clarke and Stephen Baxter	Time Odyssey series, starting with *Time's Eye*
Michael Crichton	*Timeline*
L. Sprague de Camp and Fletcher Pratt	*The Mathematics of Magic*
Charles Dickinson	*A Shortcut in Time*
Daphne du Maurier	*The House on the Strand*
Jasper Fforde	Thursday Next series, starting with *The Eyre Affair*
Jack Finney	*Time and Again*; *From Time to Time*
Eric Flint and others	Ring of Fire series, starting with *1632*
Diana Gabaldon	Outlander series, starting with *Outlander*
David Gerrold	*The Man Who Folded Himself*
Kathleen Ann Goonan	*In War Times*
Ken Grimwood	*Replay*
Joe Haldeman	*The Accidental Time Machine*
Pete Hautman	*Mr. Was*
Robert Heinlein	*The Door into Summer*
Ben Jeapes	*Time's Chariot*
Dean Koontz	*Lightning*
Paul Levinson	*The Plot to Save Socrates*
Richard Matheson	*Somewhere in Time*
Sean McMullen	*The Time Engine*
Audrey Niffenegger	*The Time Traveler's Wife*
Andre Norton	Time Traders, starting with *The Time Traders* omnibus
Marge Piercy	*Woman on the Edge of Time*

Tim Powers	*The Anubis Gates*
Alastair Reynolds	*Century Rain*
Chris Roberson	*Here, There & Everywhere*
Spider Robinson	*Callahan's Crosstime Saloon*
Robert J. Sawyer	*Flashforward*
S. M. Stirling	Nantucket series, starting with *Island in the Sea of Time*
Judith Tarr	*Household Gods*
Harry Turtledove	Crosstime Traffic series, starting with *Gunpowder Empire*
Harry Turtledove and Martin Greenberg, eds.	*The Best Time Travel Stories of the 20th Century*
John Varley	*Mammoth*
Kurt Vonnegut	*Slaughterhouse-Five*
Kurt Vonnegut	*Timequake*
H. G. Wells	*The Time Machine*
Connie Willis	*The Doomsday Book*
Connie Willis	*To Say Nothing of the Dog*

THEMATIC QUESTIONS

- What kind of paradoxes does time travel create in the novel that you read?
- If you could travel in time, would you go forward or backward? Is there anyone in particular you would like to meet? If you could travel backward, what era would you visit?
- Can history be changed by time travelers in the novel that you read? In the novel, is it beneficial, dangerous, or just plain disastrous to make changes in history?
- Is the explanation for time travel in your novel satisfying, or do you find it hard to suspend disbelief? Is the explanation fantastic or scientific?
- Do you think that time travel is scientifically possible? If the means for such travel is ever devised, do you think that time travel is a good idea?
- Are the time travelers in your novel interested mostly in their own lives or in history on a broad scale?

RESOURCES

Wikipedia on Time Travel

http://en.wikipedia.org/wiki/Time_travel

WATERY WORLDS: SPECULATIVE FICTION ON THE HIGH SEAS

The sea is everything. It covers seven-tenths of the planet. Its breath is pure and healthful. It's an immense wilderness where a man never feels lonely for he feels life astir on every side. The sea fosters a wondrous, supernatural existence.

—Jules Verne

Ocean is more ancient than the mountains, and freighted with the memories and the dreams of Time.

—H. P. Lovecraft

Duh-dum . . . Duh-dum . . .

—*Jaws*

The deep sea is as much a mystery as the far reaches of space, and thus makes a marvelous setting for fantasy and science fiction. Whether the book rides the waves in boats or dives beneath to find submerged kingdoms and unimagined monsters, there's fun to be had exploring these watery worlds. Just don't drink too much rum at this meeting. If you start to talk like a pirate, it's time to go home.

SUGGESTED WORKS

Neal Asher	Spatterjay series, starting with *The Skinner*
Peter David	*Tigerheart*
Daniel Fox	*Dragon in Chains*
Diana Pharaoh Francis	Crosspointe series, starting with *The Cipher*
Dave Freedman	*Natural Selection*
David Gemmell	*Troy: Lord of the Silver Bow*
Jo Graham	*Black Ships*
Joe W. Haldeman	*Camouflage*
Robin Hobb	Liveship Traders series, starting with *Ship of Magic*
Paul Kearney	Sea Beggars, starting with *The Mark of Ran*
Tanith Lee	*Venus Preserved*
Ursula K. Le Guin	Earthsea Chronicles, starting with *A Wizard of Earthsea*
Scott Lynch	*Red Seas under Red Skies*
Scott Mackay	*Tides*
Misty Massey	*Mad Kestrel*
Patricia McKillip	*Something Rich and Strange*
Patricia McKillip	*The Changeling Sea*
Robin McKinley and Peter Dickinson	*Water: Tales of Elemental Spirits*
Sean McMullen	*Voyage of the Shadowmoon*
China Miéville	*The Scar*
Walters Moers	*The 13 1/2 Lives of Captain Bluebear*
Christopher Moore	*Fluke*
Garth Nix	*Drowned Wednesday*
Naomi Novik	Temeraire series, starting with *His Majesty's Dragon*
George Bryan Polivka	Trophy Chase, starting with *The Legend of the Firefish*
Tim Powers	*On Stranger Tides*
Alastair Reynolds	*Turquoise Days* in *Diamond Days, Turquoise Days*
James Rollins	*Deep Fathom*
Frank Schatzing	*The Storm*
Dan Simmons	*The Terror*

Wm. Mark Simmons	*Dead Easy*
Justin Somper	<u>Vampirates</u> series, starting with *Vampirates*
Michael A. Stackpole	<u>The Age of Discovery</u>, starting with *A Secret Atlas*
Allen Steele	*OceanSpace*
William R. Trotter	*Warrener's Beastie*
Anne and Jeff VanderMeer, eds.	*Fast Ships, Black Sails*
Jules Verne	*Twenty Thousand Leagues under the Sea*
Jules Verne	*The Mysterious Island*
James M. Ward	<u>Halcyon Blithe</u>, starting with *Midshipwizard Halcyon Blithe*
Peter Watts	<u>Rifters</u> series, starting with *Starfish*
David Weber and John Ringo	*March to the Stars*
Edward Willett	*Marseguro*
Gene Wolfe	*On Blue's Waters*
Gene Wolfe	*Pirate Freedom*

THEMATIC QUESTIONS

- Do you find the sea exciting or intimidating? In the book that you read, which description does it deserve most?
- When it comes to nautical fiction, do you like science fiction/fantasy settings, or would you prefer to read historical fiction?
- Which is more important to the future of humanity, the depths of space or the depths of the oceans? How do sea travel and space travel compare?
- Are pirates daring individualists or evil villains? How are they portrayed in the book that you read?
- Which watery world from fiction or film do you find the most convincing? The most intriguing?
- Are there still major mysteries to be found under the seas?

WORMHOLES AND WARDROBES: THE WORLD NEXT DOOR

Toto, I have a feeling we're not in Kansas anymore.

—L. Frank Baum

"Yes," said Peter, "I suppose what makes it feel so queer is that in the stories it's always someone from our world who does the calling. One doesn't really think about where the Jinn's coming from."
"And now we know what it feels like for the Jinn," said Edmond with a chuckle. "Golly! It's a bit uncomfortable to know that we can be whistled for like that."

—C. S. Lewis

As a child, did you ever search for a way into another world? For now, you may have to settle for a trip to your book group. This theme is devoted to those alternate dimensions or magical lands next door. Whether in science fiction or fantasy, in a faster-than-light ship or a tornado-borne farmhouse, the key questions with this theme are how one crosses over and how one returns home again.

SUGGESTED WORKS

Taylor Anderson	Destroyermen series, starting with *Into the Storm*
L. Frank Baum	Oz series, starting with *The Wonderful Wizard of Oz*
Greg Bear	*City at the End of Time*
Lewis Carroll	*Alice's Adventures in Wonderland*; *Through the Looking Glass*
John Connolly	*The Book of Lost Things*
Charles de Lint	Newford series, starting with *Dreams Underfoot*
Gordon R. Dickson	*The Dragon and the George*
Stephen R. Donaldson	Chronicles of Thomas Covenant, starting with *Lord Foul's Bane*
Sara Douglass	Crucible series, starting with *The Nameless Day*
Hal Duncan	The Book of All Hours, starting with *Vellum*
Neil Gaiman	*Neverwhere*
Neil Gaiman	*Coraline*
Christopher Golden	The Veil, starting with *The Myth Hunters*
Simon R. Green	Nightside, starting with *Something from the Nightside*
Amanda Hemingway	Sangreal series, starting with *The Greenstone Grail*
Guy Gavriel Kay	Fionovar Tapestry series, starting with *The Summer Tree*
Kay Kenyon	The Entire and the Rose, starting with *Bright of the Sky*
Stephen King	Dark Tower series, starting with *The Gunslinger*
Ursula K. Le Guin	*Changing Planes*
Madeleine L'Engle	Time Quintet, starting with *A Wrinkle in Time*
H. P. Lovecraft	*Tales*
C. S. Lewis	Chronicles of Narnia, starting with *The Lion, The Witch & The Wardrobe*
Paul Melko	*The Walls of the Universe*
China Miéville	*Un Lun Dun*
China Miéville	*The City and the City*
Hayao Miyazaki	Spirited Away graphic novels
John Myers Myers	*Silverlock*
Paul Park	Roumania series, starting with *A Princess of Roumania*
Philip Pullman	His Dark Materials, starting with *The Golden Compass*
Justina Robson	Quantum Gravity series, starting with *Keeping It Real*
J. K. Rowling	Harry Potter, starting with *Harry Potter and the Sorcerer's Stone*
Robert J. Sawyer	Neanderthal Parallax, starting with *Hominids*
Ekaterina Sedia	*The Secret History of Moscow*
Wen Spencer	Elf Home, starting with *Tinker*
Charles Stross	Merchant Princes series, starting with *The Family Trade*
Charles Stross	*The Atrocity Archives*; *The Jennifer Morgue*

Scott Westerfeld	<u>Midnighters</u>, starting with *The Secret Hour*
Kim Wilkins	*The Veil of Gold*
Sean Williams	<u>Books of the Cataclysm</u>, starting with *The Crooked Letter*
Tad Williams	<u>Otherland</u>, starting with *City of Golden Shadow*
John C. Wright	<u>War of the Dreaming</u>, starting with *The Last Guardians of Everness*
Roger Zelazny	*The Great Book of Amber: The Complete Amber Chronicles*

THEMATIC QUESTIONS

- How do characters travel between this world and others in the book that you chose?

- In reality, do you rule out the possibility of travel between dimensions or of alternate worlds?

- If you could travel to an alternate dimension, would you? What if there were no guarantee of your ability to return?

- In the book that you read, does it become important to the characters to return home? Do they prefer this world or the other worlds that they visit?

- What are the parallels between alternate worlds and religious interpretations of the afterlife? What are the differences?

- Can one "go home again," or does visiting other places permanently change one's experience of home? How do the views of characters about their homes change after journeying in the book that you read?

- Do you find it easier to suspend disbelief in a work where characters travel between this world and the imagined world or in works set in an independent world or universe?

YOUNG ADULT FANTASY: NOT JUST FOR TEENS

There were dreams once upon a time, dreams all but now forgotten. On sad days, I dust them off and fondle them nostalgically, with a patronizing wonder at the naiveté of the youth who dreamed them.

—Glen Cook

You can only be young once. But you can always be immature.

—Dave Barry

Fantasy fans are more willing than any other readers to cross the gulf (okay, it's really just an aisle) between the young adult and adult sections in the library or bookstore. That's a good thing; there's little reason for members of either group to limit themselves, and <u>Harry Potter</u>, although great fun, is hardly the only series for adults to find. This list also includes a few of the best children's fantasy books, many of which also appeal to adult readers. For a book group, this theme is a triple joy: an exercise in nostalgia, a chance to find excellent new authors and books, and an opportunity to stock up on recommendations and gift ideas for young relatives.

SUGGESTED WORKS

Lloyd Alexander	Chronicles of Prydain, starting with *The Book of Three*
David Almond	*Skellig*
Clive Barker	Abarat, starting with *Abarat*
T. A. Barron	The Lost Years of Merlin, starting with *The Lost Years of Merlin*
T. A. Barron	Great Tree of Avalon, starting with *Child of the Dark Prophecy*
Dave Barry and Ridley Pearson	The Starcatchers, starting with *Peter and the Starcatchers*
Hilari Bell	Farsala trilogy, starting with *Fall of a Kingdom*
Holly Black	Modern Tales of Faerie, starting with *Tithe*
Libba Bray	Gemma Doyle series, starting with *A Great and Terrible Beauty*
Linda Buckley-Archer	Gideon trilogy, starting with *Gideon the Cutpurse*
Elizabeth C. Bunce	*A Curse Dark as Gold*
Kristin Cashore	*Graceling*; *Fire*
Cinda Williams Chima	Heir series, starting with *The Warrior Heir*
David Clement-Davies	*Firebringer*; *The Sight*; *Fell*
Eoin Colfer	Artemis Fowl series, starting with *Artemis Fowl*
Kate Constable	Chanters of Tremaris, starting with *The Singer of All Songs*
Susan Cooper	The Dark Is Rising, starting with *The Dark Is Rising*
Charles de Lint	*The Blue Girl*; *Little (grrl) Lost*
Toni diTerlizzi and Holly Black	The Spiderwick Chronicles, starting with *The Field Guide*
Diane Duane	Young Wizards, starting with *So You Want to Be a Wizard*
Nancy Farmer	*Sea of Trolls*; *The Land of the Silver Apples*
John Flanagan	Ranger's Apprentice, starting with *The Ruins of Gorlan*
Cornelia Funke	Inkheart series, starting with *Inkheart*
Neil Gaiman	*Coraline*; *The Graveyard Book*
Shannon Hale	Bayern series, starting with *The Goose Girl*
Shannon Hale	*Book of a Thousand Days*
Brian Jacques	Redwall series, starting with *Redwall*
Diana Wynne Jones	Chronicles of Chrestomanci, starting with *Charmed Life*
Diana Wynne Jones	Howl's Castle series, starting with *Howl's Moving Castle*
Diana Wynne Jones	*Deep Secret*; *The Merlin Conspiracy*
Diana Wynne Jones	*Dark Lord of Derkholm*; *Year of the Griffin*
Annette Curtis Klause	*Blood and Chocolate*; *The Silver Kiss*
Margo Lanagan	*Tender Morsels*
Justine Larbalestier	Magic or Madness, starting with *Magic or Madness*
Ursula K. Le Guin	Annals of the Western Shore, starting with *Gifts*
C. S. Lewis	Chronicles of Narnia, starting with *The Lion, the Witch, and the Wardrobe*
Kelly Link	*Pretty Monsters*
D. J. MacHale	Pendragon series, starting with *The Merchant of Death*
Juliet Marillier	Wildwood Dancing series, starting with *Wildwood Dancing*

Robin McKinley	<u>Damar</u> series, starting with *The Blue Sword*
Robin McKinley	*Beauty; Rose Daughter*
Stephenie Meyer	<u>Twilight Saga</u>, starting with *Twilight*
China Miéville	*Un Lun Dun*
Brandon Mull	<u>Fablehaven</u> series, starting with *Fablehaven*
Catherine Murdock	*Princess Ben*
Donna Jo Napoli	*Beast*
Henry H. Neff	<u>The Tapestry</u>, starting with *The Hound of Rowan*
Jenny Nimmo	<u>Charlie Bone</u>, starting with *Midnight for Charlie Bone*
Garth Nix	<u>Abhorsen</u> trilogy, starting with *Sabriel*
Garth Nix	<u>Keys to the Kingdom</u>, starting with *Mister Monday*
Christopher Paolini	<u>Inheritance</u>, starting with *Eragon*
Tamora Pierce	<u>Song of the Lioness</u>, starting with *Alanna: The First Adventure*
Tamora Pierce	<u>The Immortals</u>, starting with *Wild Magic*
Tamora Pierce	<u>The Legend of Beka Cooper</u>, starting with *Terrier*
Terry Pratchett	*The Bromeliad Trilogy*
Terry Pratchett	<u>Tiffany Aching</u> series, starting with *Wee Free Men*
Terry Pratchett	*Nation*
Philip Pullman	<u>His Dark Materials</u>, starting with *The Golden Compass*
Amelia Atwater-Rhodes	<u>The Kiesha'ra</u>, starting with *Hawksong*
Rick Riordan	<u>Percy Jackson and the Olympians</u>, starting with *The Lightning Thief*
J. K. Rowling	<u>Harry Potter</u>, starting with *Harry Potter and the Sorcerer's Stone*
Angie Sage	<u>Septimus Heap</u>, starting with *Magyk*
Michael Scott	<u>Secrets of the Immortal Nicholas Flamel</u>, starting with *The Alchemyst*
Nancy Springer	*I Am Mordred; I Am Morgan le Fay*
Jonathan Stroud	<u>Bartimaeus Trilogy</u>, starting with *The Amulet of Samarkand*
Kate Thompson	*The New Policeman*
J. R. R. Tolkien	*The Hobbit*
Megan Whalen Turner	<u>Queen's Thief</u> series, starting with *The Thief*
Nancy Werlin	*Impossible*
Scott Westerfeld	<u>Midnighters</u>, starting with *The Secret Hour*
Ysabeau Wilce	<u>Flora Segunda</u>, starting with *Flora Segunda*
Patricia Wrede	<u>Enchanted Forest Chronicles</u>, starting with *Dealing with Dragons*
Jane Yolen	<u>The Pit Dragon Chronicles</u>, starting with *Dragon's Blood*

THEMATIC QUESTIONS

- What makes a work fit into the "young adult" category? Do publishers apply this label consistently? What books are found in the adult section of the library or bookstore that should be in the young adult section? Which young adult works are most appropriate to adults?

- What's the difference between children's literature and young adult literature? Into which category does the book that you read fit?
- What books introduced you to fantasy fiction as a young reader?
- Is young adult fantasy better now than it was when you were growing up?
- Who are the top five writers of fantasy for children and young adults? Are they as good as the best writers for adults?
- As an adult, do you ever seek out young adult works? Do you do this to share them with young people or for your own pleasure?
- Are you more likely to find controversial content in works for young adults or in works for adults? Should any subjects be taboo in this literature?
- Is young adult fantasy better than young adult literature on the whole?

YOUNG ADULT SCIENCE FICTION: NOT JUST FOR TEENS

What a distressing contrast there is between the radiant intelligence of the child and the feeble mentality of the average adult.

—Sigmund Freud

You're never too old to become younger.

—Mae West

Young adult science fiction is excellent, although perhaps not as common as young adult fantasy fiction. That's likely to change, however, because authors such as Cory Doctorow, John Scalzi, and Scott Westerfeld have recently published books for the young adult market and found better sales and more readers there than they get in the adult market. As science fiction fans are aging and as authors are looking for more readers, the young adult market seems a likely place for a genre renaissance. Try this theme with your group and see if they can find signs of this new beginning.

SUGGESTED WORKS

L. J. Adlington	*The Diary of Pelly D*
M. T. Anderson	*Feed*
Margaret Bechard	*Spacer and Rat*
Julie Bertagna	*Exodus*
Orson Scott Card	Ender series, starting with *Ender's Game*
John Christopher	The Tripods, starting with *When the Tripods Came*
Troy Cle	Marvelous World, starting with *The Marvelous Effect*
Eoin Colfer	*The Supernaturalist*
Suzanne Collins	*The Hunger Games*; *Catching Fire*
Peter Dickinson	*Eva*
Cory Doctorow	*Little Brother*
Jeanne DuPrau	Books of Ember, starting with *The City of Ember*
Sylvia Louise Engdahl	*Enchantress from the Stars*

Nancy Farmer	*The House of the Scorpion*
Phil and Kaja Foglio	<u>Girl Genius</u> graphic novels
Neil Gaiman and Michael Reaves	*InterWorld*
Steven Gould	*Jumper*
Margaret Peterson Haddix	<u>Shadow Children</u> series, starting with *Among the Hidden*
Margaret Peterson Haddix	*Turnabout*
Ann Halam	*Dr. Franklin's Island*
Pete Hautman	*Hole in the Sky; Rash*
Robert Heinlein	*Red Planet; Farmer in the Sky; Starman Jones; The Star Beast; Tunnel in the Sky; Citizen of the Galaxy; Have Spacesuit—Will Travel*
Monica Hughes	*Invitation to the Game; Keeper of the Isis Light*
Ben Jeapes	*The Xenocide Mission*
Catherine Jinks	*Evil Genius; Genius Squad*
David Klass	<u>The Caretaker Trilogy</u>, starting with *Firestorm*
Conor Kostick	*Epic; Saga*
Madeleine L'Engle	<u>Time Quintet</u>, starting with *A Wrinkle in Time*
Lois Lowry	*The Giver; Gathering Blue; Messenger*
Gemma Malley	*The Declaration*
Janet Elizabeth McNaughton	*The Secret Under My Skin*
Rune Michaels	*Genesis Alpha*
Patrick Ness	<u>Chaos Walking</u>, starting with *The Knife of Never Letting Go*
Garth Nix	*Shade's Children*
Robert C. O'Brien	*Z for Zachariah*
Kenneth Oppel	<u>Matt Cruse</u> series, starting with *Airborn*
James Patterson	<u>Maximum Ride</u>, starting with *The Angel Experiment*
Gary Paulsen	*The Transall Saga*
Mary E. Pearson	*The Adoration of Jenna Fox*
Susan Beth Pfeffer	*Life as We Knew It; The Dead and the Gone*
Rodman Philbrick	*The Last Book in the Universe*
Terry Pratchett	<u>Johnny Maxwell</u> trilogy, starting with *Only You Can Save Mankind*
Philip Reeve	<u>The Hungry City Chronicles</u>, starting with *Mortal Engines*
Philip Reeve	<u>Larklight</u> series, starting with *Larklight*
Pamela Sargent	<u>Seed</u> trilogy, starting with *Earthseed*
John Scalzi	*Zoe's Tale*
Neal Shusterman	*The Dark Side of Nowhere; Unwind*
Gloria Skurzynski	<u>The Virtual War Chronologs</u>, starting with *Virtual War*
William Sleator	*House of Stairs; Interstellar Pig; Singularity*
Kate Thompson	<u>Missing Link Trilogy</u> starting with *Fourth World*
Vivian Vande Velde	*Heir Apparent*
Ned Vizzini	*Be More Chill*
Nancy Werlin	*Double Helix*
Scott Westerfeld	<u>Uglies</u> series, starting with *Uglies*
Andrea White	*Surviving Antarctica: Reality TV 2083*

THEMATIC QUESTIONS

- The young adult market currently has more offerings in fantasy fiction than in science fiction. Can you identify the reasons that have led to this disparity?
- What makes a work fit into the "young adult" category? What books are found in the adult section of the library or bookstore that should be in the young adult section? Which young adult works are most appropriate to adults?
- What's the difference between children's literature and young adult literature? Which category does the book that you read fit into?
- What books introduced you to science fiction as a young reader?
- Is the science fiction for young adults better now than it was when you were growing up?
- Who are the top five writers of science fiction for children and young adults? Are they as good as the best writers for adults?

100 MORE THEMES TO EXPLORE

Alien artifacts and big dumb objects
Alien wars
American settings
Amnesia and memory
Arthurian fantasy
Asian settings
Asteroids and comets
Australian SF & F
Black holes
Black magic
British SF & F
Campbell Award winners
Children's literature
Cities
Classics with SF & F elements
Cloning
Colonizing and terraforming
Coming-of-age tales
Cosmological SF
Courage
Cyberpunk
Dark and gritty
Dinosaurs and paleontology
Diplomatic missions
Doppelgangers
Dragons
Dual authors
Dwarves
Elves

Evolution and mutations
Experimental science
Extreme settings
Far futures
Faster-than-light travel
Female lead characters
First contact and SETI
First-person point of view
First novels
Folklore
Future histories
Gaming connections
Ghosts and hauntings
Hero fantasy
Homosexuality
Hugo Award winners
In our own galaxy or solar system
Intelligence
Invasions
Invisibility
Locus Poll winners
Lost civilizations and worlds
Low fantasy
Magic systems
Magical creatures
Mental powers
Multiple narrators
Mythology: Primary sources
Mythopoeic Award winners
Nanotechnology
Near future thrillers
Nebula Award winners
Nonfiction about science fiction and fantasy
Novellas
Optimistic
Pastoral settings
Pessimistic
Plagues and diseases
Prophecies and fate
Psychic powers
Psychology
Published in the reader's birth year
Published this year
Pulp magazine origins
Rereading a favorite
Recursive fiction

Revenge
Road stories
Romance crossovers
Royalty/secession battles
Satire
School settings
Secret histories
Settlers and colonizers
Sexuality
SFWA grandmasters
Shapeshifters
Shared worlds
Space habitats and long flights
Superpowers
Survival
Suspended animation and long sleeps
Technothrillers
Transportation
Unlikely heroes
Utopias and dystopias
Vampires
Villains
Witches
Wizards
Writers by decade

Appendix A
A Chronology of Science Fiction/Fantasy History

ca. 2000 B.C.
- The earliest versions of the *Epic of Gilgamesh* originate.

ca. 750 B.C.
- *The Iliad* and *The Odyssey,* traditionally ascribed to Homer, are composed.

ca. 600 B.C.
- Aesop's *Fables* are written, a prototype for animal fantasy, humorous fantasy, and fable writing.

414–405 B.C.
- Aristophanes writes comic plays of fantasy, including *The Birds* and *The Frogs*

ca. 400 B.C.
- The Sanskrit epics, the *Mahabharata* and the *Ramayana*, are composed.

19 B.C.
- Virgil writes *The Aeneid.*

125 A.D.
- Lucian of Samosata writes satires that contain elements of science fiction.

ca. 725–800 A.D.
- *Beowulf* is written.

ca. 800 A.D.
- *The Thousand and One Arabian Nights* is written. For the Western world, its most influential form does not appear until 1704–1717, when Antoine Galland translates it, adding many stories that are probably of his own creation.

1136
- Geoffrey of Monmouth's *The History of the Kings of Britain* compiles the Arthurian tales.

ca. 1150
- *The Song of Roland* originates in France.

1170–1182
- Chretien de Troyes adds to the Arthurian legends with *Lancelot* and *Perceval*.

ca. 1200
- The *Nibelungenlied*, an epic poem recounting the Germanic version of the adventures of Siegfried, is composed. It's based on historical events from the fifth and sixth centuries.

ca. 1220
- Snorri Sturluson writes the *Prose Edda*, an Icelandic saga and account of Norse mythology.

1321
- Dante publishes his fantastic conception of Hell in the *Divine Comedy*.

ca. 1400
- The Welsh folklore collection, the *Mabinogion*, is composed. It includes stories that influence the Arthurian legends and writers such as Lloyd Alexander.

1470
- Sir Thomas Malory writes *Le Morte d'Arthur*, an influential compilation of Arthurian legend.

1516
- Sir Thomas More publishes his *Utopia*.

1589–1596
- Edmund Spenser composes his epic poem, *The Faerie Queen*.

1595
- The first of Shakespeare's major fantasies, *A Midsummer Night's Dream*, is completed.

1611
- William Shakespeare writes *The Tempest*.

1667
- John Milton composes *Paradise Lost*.

1697
- Charles Perrault publishes *Histoires ou Contes du Temps Passé*. In English, it's known as *Mother Goose Tales*.

1726
- Jonathan Swift writes *Gulliver's Travels*, a literary classic and important prototype for speculative writing.

1752
- Voltaire publishes *Micromegas*, the first book about aliens on Earth.

1812–1815

- The Brothers Grimm first publish their *Fairy Tales*.

1818

- Mary Shelley publishes *Frankenstein*, a book that many consider to be the first modern science fiction novel.

1835

- Hans Christian Anderson publishes his first anthology, *Tales for Children*.
- Edgar Allan Poe publishes "Hans Pfaall," a story featuring a voyage to the moon.
- Elias Lönnrot begins publishing his compilation of the *Kalevala*, an influential Finnish epic.

1858

- George MacDonald's *Phantastes* is published.

1864–1875

- Jules Verne publishes *Journey to the Center of the Earth*, *From the Earth to the Moon*, *20,000 Leagues Under the Sea*, and *The Mysterious Island*. Verne is the first to make a career writing mostly science fiction.

1865–1871

- Lewis Carroll publishes *Alice's Adventures in Wonderland* and *Through the Looking Glass*.

1885–1887

- H. Rider Haggard writes *King Solomon's Mines* and *She*, starting a trend of lost-race fantasy.

1888

- Edward Bellamy publishes his utopian novel *Looking Backwards*.

1889

- Mark Twain's *A Connecticut Yankee in King Arthur's Court*, arguably the first American science fiction novel, is published.

1890

- James Frazer publishes the first edition of *The Golden Bough*. A major work of comparative mythology and religion, the archetypes to which it points become a major inspiration for fantasy writers in developing systems of magical belief.

1890s

- *The Strand* and *The Black Cat*, fiction magazines that include some fantasy and science fiction stories, appear in Britain, launching the rise of the magazine era.

1895

- William Morris writes *The Wood beyond the World* and *The Well at World's End*, early works of epic fantasy.

1895–1898

- H. G. Wells publishes works including *The Time Machine*, *The Island of Dr. Moreau*, *The Invisible Man*, and *The War of the Worlds*.

1897
- Bram Stoker's *Dracula* is published.

1900
- L. Frank Baum, one of the first great American fantasists, publishes *The Wonderful Wizard of Oz*.

1902
- E. Nesbit writes the first of her classic fantasies, *Five Children & It*.

1904
- J. M. Barrie's play *Peter Pan* arrives.

1912
- Edgar Rice Burroughs publishes his first <u>Barsoom</u> story, *A Princess of Mars*. It was made into a novel five years later.

1915
- Charlotte Perkins Gilman brings a feminist take to science fiction in *Herland*.

1919
- James Branch Cabell publishes the controversial fantasy *Jurgen*.

1920s
- H. P. Lovecraft develops his Cthulhu Mythos. Although finding little success in his own life, Lovecraft had great influence on horror and dark fantasy writers in the future.

1921
- Karel Capek, a Czech playwright, coins the word "robot" in his *R.U.R.*

1922
- E. R. Eddison publishes his epic fantasy, *The Worm Ouroboros*.

1924
- *The Thief of Baghdad*, featuring Douglas Fairbanks, is Hollywood's first major fantasy film.
- Lord Dunsany writes *The King of Elfland's Daughter*, establishing many tropes of the fairy world fantasy.

1926
- Hugo Gernsback starts *Amazing Stories*, beginning the era of U.S. pulp magazines.
- Fritz Lang's *Metropolis* depicts a dystopian future on film.

1928
- "Doc" Smith publishes "The Skylark of Space," the first epic story of humans going to space.

1930s
- Films such as *Frankenstein, King Kong, Dracula, Snow White and the Seven Dwarves, The Wizard of Oz, King Solomon's Mines, Lost Horizon*, and *Topper* establish the long-running importance of speculative work to the cinema.

1930s and 1940s

- The Inklings, an Oxford study group that espouses the cause of fantasy fiction forms. It includes J. R. R. Tolkien and C. S. Lewis.
- Serial films such as *Flash Gordon* and *Buck Rogers* have their heyday in the cinema.

1930

- *Astounding Stories* magazine begins publication.

1932

- Robert E. Howard publishes his first <u>Conan</u> story, "The Dragon and the Sword."
- Aldous Huxley's influential dystopia, *Brave New World*, is written.

1934

- Stanley Weinbaum publishes "A Martian Odyssey," the first prominent story to feature sympathetic aliens.
- A Los Angeles group joins Gernsback's Science Fiction League. In 1940 it becomes the Los Angeles Science Fantasy Society. Still active today, the club is the longest running group of its kind.

1937

- J. R. R. Tolkien publishes *The Hobbit*.
- John Campbell takes over editorship of *Astounding Stories* and renames it *Astounding Science Fiction*. Under his leadership, the magazine sets the style of writing for what is called the Golden Age of Science Fiction.
- Olaf Stapledon writes *Star Maker*.
- Frederik Pohl publishes a poem in *Amazing Stories*, beginning a 70-year publishing career.

1937–1945

- The Futurians, a group of writers and fans including Isaac Asimov, James Blish, Damon Knight, C. M. Kornbluth, Judith Merril, Frederik Pohl, and Donald A. Wollheim, are active in New York City, greatly influencing the future of science fiction and fandom.

1937–1949

- Tolkien writes <u>*The Lord of the Rings*</u>. It doesn't see publication until 1954–1955.

1938

- T. H. White publishes *The Sword in the Stone*, the first book in <u>*The Once and Future King*</u>, which repopularizes the Arthurian legends.

1939

- New York City hosts the first World Science Fiction Convention (now World Con), the first to bring together fans and authors from a large number of locations.
- Fritz Leiber publishes his first <u>Fafhrd & the Grey Mouser</u> sword and sorcery story.

1941

- *The Other Worlds* is the first anthology of reprinted science fiction stories. It is followed in 1943 by an even more influential collection, *The Pocket Book of Science Fiction*, edited by Donald A. Wollheim.

1941–1942
- L. Sprague de Camp explores time travel in *Lest Darkness Fall* and comic fantasy with Fletcher Pratt in *The Incompleat Enchanter*.

1946
- A. E. van Vogt's novel *Slan*, an expansion of an earlier story, arrives.
- Mervyn Peake publishes *Titus Groan*, the first work in his <u>Gormenghast</u> trilogy.

1947
- Poul Anderson publishes his first story, beginning a prolific and popular career writing both fantasy and science fiction.

1949
- George Orwell publishes *1984*.
- Doubleday begins publication of a line of hardcover science fiction, speeding the popularity of the genre and the growth of novels, as opposed to short stories.

1950s
- Ray Bradbury begins a 60-year publishing career with his works of greatest influence on science fiction and fantasy, including *The Martian Chronicles*, *The Illustrated Man*, *Fahrenheit 451*, and *Dandelion Wine*.

1950
- *Galaxy Science Fiction* magazine, which features a more literary kind of science fiction story, begins publication.
- Publication of *The Dying Earth*, a collection of stories, marks the arrival of writer Jack Vance.

1950–1956
- C. S. Lewis publishes his <u>Narnia</u> chronicles.

1951
- John Wyndham, Britain's most popular 1950s SF writer, publishes *The Day of the Triffids*.
- The first book of Isaac Asimov's <u>Foundation</u> series is published.

1953
- The first Hugo Awards (named for editor Hugo Gernsback) are given at World Con in Philadelphia. Alfred Bester's *The Demolished Man* is the first novel to win. After a one-year hiatus, the awards become permanent in 1955.
- Arthur C. Clarke publishes the first of his masterpieces, *Childhood's End*.

1954
- Isaac Asimov publishes *The Caves of Steel*.

Late 1950s, early 1960s
- Robert Heinlein, already well-known for his enduring juvenile works, turns to adult science fiction and enjoys a heyday with works such as *Double Star*, *The Door into Summer*, *Starship Troopers*, and *Stranger in a Strange Land*.

1956
- *Forbidden Planet*, a classic of SF cinema, sets Shakespeare's *The Tempest* in space.

Late 1950s, early 1960s
- Ray Harryhausen raises the bar for special effects in film with eye-popping works such as *The Seventh Voyage of Sinbad* and *Jason and the Argonauts*.
- Anthology series such as Rod Serling's *The Twilight Zone* and *Outer Limits* increase the presence of speculative works on television.

1959
- American News Service, the major distribution house for magazines, is declared a monopoly. Many magazines are closed outright by increased costs while circulation for others is greatly reduced. The era of the pulp magazine is on the way out.
- The Soviets launch Sputnik.

1960
- Peter S. Beagle begins his fantasy career with *A Fine and Private Place*.

Early 1960s
- Writers such as Michael Moorcock and Brian Aldiss in Great Britain and Ursula K. Le Guin and Harlan Ellison in the United States popularize New Wave science fiction, downplaying adventure and hard science while increasing consideration of social sciences, gender and sexuality, and literary experimentation.

1961
- Michael Moorcock publishes the first story about Elric of Melniboné. Moorcock builds an influential career based mostly on Elric and other incarnations of his Eternal Champion.
- Harry Harrison begins skewering clichés of heroic science fiction with *The Stainless Steel Rat*. The even more satirical *Bill the Galactic Hero* follows in 1965.

1962
- Marion Zimmer Bradley arrives on the SF scene with *The Planet Savers*. After her long Darkover series, she turns to fantasy with even more success in 1982 with *Mists of Avalon*.
- Anthony Burgess writes *A Clockwork Orange*.

1963
- Andre Norton brings her long-running career to new heights with the first of her Witch World series novels.
- *Dr. Who* begins its long run on British television.

1964
- Lloyd Alexander begins the Chronicles of Prydain, based on tales from the *Mabinogion*. Beginning with *The Book of Three*, these stories are highly influential in children's fantasy.

1965
- SFWA is created by Damon Knight. The organization sponsors the first Nebula Awards, awarding the first award for a novel to Frank Herbert's *Dune*.
- The Ace paperback edition of *The Lord of the Rings* jump-starts the popularity of fantasy fiction in the United States.

1966

- Gene Roddenberry brings his influential *Star Trek* series to television.
- The Society for Creative Anachronism is founded in California with early members including Diana Paxson, Marion Zimmer Bradley, and Poul Anderson. Active groups now spread across the world, including Europe, New Zealand, South Korea, and Panama.

Mid-1960s and early 1970s

- Samuel R. Delany establishes himself with works such as *Babel-17*, *The Einstein Intersection*, *Nova*, and *Dhalgren*. The first prominent African American science fiction writer, his experimental, literary style opens new possibilities for the genre.

1967

- The *Dangerous Visions* anthology, edited by Harlan Ellison, is a major work of the new wave.

1968–1974

- Ursula K. Le Guin is in the heyday of her career, publishing the first three Earthsea fantasies and two science fiction masterpieces, *Left Hand of Darkness* and *The Dispossessed*.

1968

- The film and novelization of Arthur C. Clarke's *2001: A Space Odyssey* are released.
- Charles N. Brown starts *Locus*, an influential magazine of SF & F news and reviews. It institutes the Locus Poll in 1971, giving the top vote-getter the annual Locus Award.
- Anne McCaffrey takes the first of many trips to Pern with *Dragonflight*.

1969

- Neil Armstrong becomes the first human to walk on the moon.
- Kurt Vonnegut, already known in science fiction circles for *Cat's Cradle* and *The Sirens of Titan*, wins major literary accolades for a science fiction work with *Slaughterhouse-Five*.

1969–1974

- Lin Carter's Ballantine Fantasy line returns early fantasists to the limelight and introduces new stars, such as Katherine Kurtz.

1970

- Larry Niven establishes his reputation with *Ringworld*.
- Roger Zelazny begins The Chronicles of Amber.

1971

- Philip Jose Farmer fixes up several stories to create *To Your Scattered Bodies Go*, the first book in his Riverworld series.
- The Mythopoeic Fantasy Awards are established. Mary Stewart's *The Crystal Cave* is the first winner.

1972

- Gary Gygax and Jeff Perrin begin marketing Dungeons & Dragons, launching an era of role-playing games that bring many new fans to fantasy.

- Richard Adams' animal fantasy, *Watership Down*, becomes a sleeper sensation.
- *Foundation*, an academic journal devoted to science fiction, is started in Great Britain. *Science-Fiction Studies* follows the next year in the United States.
- Arthur C. Clarke publishes *Rendezvous with Rama*.
- Robert Silverberg's prolific career reaches what many consider its height with *Dying Inside*.
- The last Apollo mission to the moon ends in December. Eugene Cernan becomes the last astronaut to walk on the moon.

1973

- The John W. Campbell award for best new writer begins. Jerry Pournelle is the first winner.

1974

- The Monty Python troupe skewers Arthurian legends in the film *Monty Python and the Holy Grail*.
- Joe Haldeman publishes *The Forever War*.

1975

- The World Fantasy Awards are established.
- Robert A. Heinlein is named the first Grand Master by SFWA.
- Diana Wynne Jones becomes a young adult literature star with the first <u>Dalemark</u> novel, *Cart & Cwidder*.
- Joanna Russ publishes the feminist science fiction classic, *The Female Man*.

1976

- Octavia Butler arrives on the science fiction scene with *Patternmaster*.
- C. J. Cherryh's career begins quickly with *Gate of Ivrel*, the first book in her <u>Morgaine</u> saga.

1977

- The film *Star Wars* begins a new renaissance for science fiction.
- After a long wait, fans of Tolkien see publication of *The Silmarillion*.

Late 1970s, early 1980s

- Several popular authors, such as Stephen R. Donaldson, Terry Brooks, Patricia McKillip, Piers Anthony, David Eddings, Raymond E. Feist, Guy Gavriel Kay, Gordon R. Dickson, Margaret Weis, and Tracy Hickman, begin publishing fantasy novels, raising the popularity of the genre to new heights.

1978

- SF humor reaches new heights of sublime silliness when Douglas Adams's *The Hitch-Hiker's Guide to the Universe* is broadcast on BBC radio. Several successful books follow.

1979

- *Alien* bursts into cinemas.

Early 1980s

- Talented new writers, such as Robin McKinley, Tamora Pierce, and Brian Jacques, arrive on the scene, invigorating fantasy writing for young adults.

1980–1983

- Gene Wolfe reaches the zenith of his career with publication of the Book of the New Sun.

1981

- John Crowley publishes his literary fantasy *Little, Big*.
- *Columbia* makes the first orbital flight in the space shuttle program. Accidents claim *Challenger* in 1986 and *Columbia* in 2003.

1982

- The film *Blade Runner*, based on *Do Androids Dream of Electric Sheep?*, brings new attention to the iconoclastic work of Philip K. Dick. Unfortunately, Dick dies the same year. His reputation has only increased since his death.

1983

- The first book in Terry Pratchett's popular satirical Discworld fantasy series, *The Colour of Money*, is published.
- The Philip K. Dick award for best paperback original is instituted.
- *The Anubis Gates* is the first major success for author Tim Powers.

1984

- William Gibson launches the cyberpunk craze with publication of *Neuromancer*.
- Urban fantasy finds its first major writer with publication of Charles de Lint's *Moonheart*.
- David Gemmell returns the pulp hero to center stage with his first book, *Legend*.

Mid-1980s

- The so-called "Killer B's," Greg Bear, David Brin, and Gregory Benford, are at the height of their influence, blending hard SF and action in novels such as Bear's *Blood Music* and *Eon*, Brin's Uplift Saga and *The Postman*, and Benford's *Timescape* and Galactic Center novels.

1984

- Gardner Dozois begins his long run editing *The Year's Best Science Fiction*.

1985

- Orson Scott Card bursts on the scene with the expansion of his *Ender's Game* novella.

1986

- Lois McMaster Bujold begins her award-filled career in fantasy and SF with *Shards of Honor*.

1986–1988

- Publication of four works brings graphic novels to new levels of influence and popularity: Art Spiegelman's *Maus*, Alan Moore and Dave Gibbons's *Watchmen*, Frank Miller's *The Dark Knight Returns*, and Neil Gaiman's *Sandman*.

1987

- William Goldman's *The Princess Bride* brings a new level of charm, humor, and romance to fantasy film.

- Iain M. Banks's distinguished career in science fiction begins with *Consider Phlebas*.
- Mercedes Lackey begins her prolific career with publication of *Arrows of the Queen*.
- Harry Turtledove's career writing alternate history begins with *The Misplaced Legion*.

1988

- Terri Windling and Ellen Datlow begin their editorship of *Year's Best Fantasy and Horror*.

Late 1980s, early 1990s

- Writers such as Tad Williams, Robert Jordan, Terry Goodkind, Robin Hobb, George R. R. Martin, R. A. Salvatore, David Farland and L. E. Modesitt Jr. usher in an age of fat, multivolume fantasy epics.
- William Gibson publishes *Neuromancer* in 1984, establishing cyberpunk. Others, such as K. W. Jeter, Bruce Sterling, Neal Stephenson, and Pat Cadigan, further popularize the subgenre.
- Sheri S. Tepper writes important science fiction novels, such as *Grass* and *The Gate to Women's Country*.

1989

- Dan Simmons establishes his reputation with *Hyperion*.

1992

- Kim Stanley Robinson publishes *Red Mars*, the first work in his masterful <u>Mars</u> trilogy.
- Neal Stephenson bursts on the scene with *Snow Crash*.
- Vernor Vinge publishes his best-known book, *A Fire upon the Deep*. It wins the Hugo Award the next year, as does its prequel, *A Deepness in the Sky*, in 2000.

1993

- Three new science fiction television programs, *The X Files*, *Babylon 5*, and *Star Trek: Deep Space Nine*, begin long runs.
- Connie Willis publishes *Doomsday Book*.
- Laurell K. Hamilton publishes the first of her <u>Anita Blake</u> series, *Guilty Pleasures*.

1996

- George R. R. Martin begins his influential epic fantasy series, <u>A Song of Ice and Fire,</u> with *A Game of Thrones*.

1997

- J. K. Rowling arrives on the scene with the British publication of *Harry Potter and the Philosopher's Stone*. The seven-book series breaks every sales record in the book, bringing fantasy fiction its largest audience ever.
- Joss Whedon's *Buffy the Vampire* series begins its seven-year run. The series brings fantasy to a new group of young fans and paves the way for the expansion of urban fantasy.

2000

- Jim Butcher publishes the first of his <u>Dresden Files</u> series, *Storm Front*.

2001–2003

- Peter Jackson's trilogy of <u>*Lord of the Rings*</u> films rule the box office and begin a period of new vigor for fantasy cinema. *The Return of the King* wins the Oscar for Best Picture.

2004

- Susanna Clarke's *Jonathan Strange & Mr Norrell*, an enormous fantasy written in Victorian style, is a surprise smash. Its success, combined with other bestsellers such as Yann Martel's *The Life of Pi*, Elizabeth Kostova's *The Historian*, and Audrey Niffenegger's *The Time Traveler's Wife*, brings new levels of respect and commercial viability to literary fantasy.

2010

- *Discovery* is scheduled to make the last planned flight of the Space Shuttle.

Appendix B
Resources for Further Study

PRINT RESOURCES

Book Groups

The Book Club Companion. Loevy, Diana. 2006. Penguin. ISBN: 042521009X
Good Books Lately: The One-Stop Resource for Book Groups and Other Greedy Readers. Moore, Ellen and Stevens, Kira. 2004. St. Martin's. ISBN 0-312-30961-9.
The New York Public Library Guide to Reading Groups. Saal, Rollene. 1995. Crown Publishers. ISBN: 0517883570.
Read 'Em Their Writes: A Handbook for Mystery and Crime Fiction Book Discussions. Niebuhr, Gary Warren. 2006. Libraries Unlimited. ISBN: 1-59158-303-9.
   A companion volume to this book, aimed at a different genre.

Science Fiction and Fantasy

Anatomy of Wonder, 5th ed. Barron, Neil et al. 2004. Libraries Unlimited. ISBN: 1-59158-171-0.
   The ultimate guide in print reference for science fiction, particularly strong on genre history.
The Cambridge Companion to Science Fiction. James, Edward and Mendlesohn, Farah, eds. 2003. Cambridge University Press. ISBN: 0-521-81626-2.
Encountering Enchantment: A Guide to Speculative Fiction for Teens. Fichtelberg, Susan. 2007. Libraries Unlimited. ISBN: 1-59158-316-0.
Encyclopedia of Fantasy and Horror Fiction. D'Ammassa, Don. 2006. Checkmark Books. ISBN: 978-0816069248.
The Encyclopedia of Science Fiction. Clute, John and Nicholls, Peter, eds. 1995. St. Martin's Griffin. ISBN: 0-312-13486-X.
   In need of an update now, but this is the best one-volume encyclopedia on science fiction.
Fantasy Literature for Children and Young Adults, 5th ed. Lynn, Ruth Nadelman. 2005. Libraries Unlimited. ISBN: 1591580501.
   An excellent bibliography of fantasy literature that is appropriate for children and young adults. It also documents the majority of adult fantasy writers.

Fantasy of the 20th Century: An Illustrated History. Broecker, Randy. 2001. Collectors Press. ISBN: 1-888054-52-2.

Fantasy and Horror. Barron, Neil, ed. 1999. Scarecrow Press. ISBN: 0810835967.
    Not as strong as Barron's science fiction volume, *Anatomy of Wonder*, and in need of a new revision, but still a great starting point for research on the fantasy and horror genres.

Fluent in Fantasy. Herald, Diana Tixier and Kunzel, Bonnie. 2008. Libraries Unlimited. ISBN: 978-1-59158-198-7.

The Greenwood Encyclopedia of Science Fiction and Fantasy: Themes, Works, and Wonders. Westfahl, Gary, ed. 2005. Greenwood. ISBN: 978-0313329500.
    If you can afford it, this three-volume set is the most complete reference on speculative fiction currently available.

The History of Science Fiction. Roberts, Adam. 2007. Palgrave Macmillan. ISBN: 978-0230546912.

Read On . . . Fantasy Fiction. Hollands, Neil. 2007. Libraries Unlimited. ISBN: 1-59158-330-6
    A browsable, readable guide composed of short annotated booklists on many different themes and other appeal factors of fantasy literature.

The Ultimate Encyclopedia of Fantasy. Pringle, David, ed. 1998. Carlton Books Limited. ISBN: 0-87951-937-1.

ONLINE RESOURCES

Book Groups

Book Group Buzz

    http://bookgroupbuzz.booklistonline.com

This blog, hosted by *Booklist* magazine, features advice for book groups. Content is updated almost every day.

Reading Group Guides

    http://www.readinggroupguides.com

An all-purpose support site for book groups with book discussion guides, a variety of advice, and a variety of communication tools to help those who run book groups exchange ideas.

Yahoo Groups

    http://groups.yahoo.com/

Here's a good place to search for science fiction/fantasy book groups in your area or to set up online headquarters for your group. It's free, but does require a Yahoo ID for those who join.

Books in General

Fantastic Fiction

    http://www.fantasticfiction.co.uk/

The best bibliographic resource for genre readers online, this site is particularly good for identifying series order in science fiction and fantasy.

GoodReads

http://www.goodreads.com

A social networking site for readers, where you can create shelves of books that you've read or want to read, write reviews, or exchange views with others. As of this writing, they also host nearly 300 SF/F book groups, some narrowly focused, some broad, some active, some not so active. A list of groups is at http://www.goodreads.com/group/subtopic/25.Science_Fiction_Fantasy. See LibraryThing and Shelfari for similar options.

LibraryThing

http://www.librarything.com

Another good social networking site for readers. See GoodReads and Shelfari for other options.

Shelfari

http://www.shelfari.com

The third social networking hub for readers. See GoodReads and LibraryThing for other options.

Science Fiction and Fantasy

Fantasy Book Critic

http://fantasybookcritic.blogspot.com/

One of the most regularly maintained fantasy blogs, with lots of giveaways and links to all of the major fantasy and science fiction publishers.

FantasyLiterature.net

http://www.fantasyliterature.net

Somewhat slow load times are the only downside of this collection of author information and reviews. It's growing rapidly and is especially good for young adult books.

Feminist Science Fiction and Fantasy

http://feministsf.org/

A compendium of all things in print and online that are related to feminism, gender, or women's issues.

Graeme's Fantasy Book Review

http://www.graemesfantasybookreview.com

Steady fantasy blog, which often features good author interviews.

Green Man Review

http://www.greenmanreview.com

An online review of books and music with special emphasis on genre work. The diverse crew of reviewers here makes for interesting reading.

io9

http://io9.com

The layout may be a bit busy, but this up-and-coming website has a variety of science fiction information on books, movies, comics, and more—all conveyed in a hip, snarky style.

Locus Online

http://www.locusmag.com

The best single resource for science fiction and fantasy book news and reviews, as well as information about Cons, thoughtful obituaries, and diverse interviews. Highlights include an annual Recommended Reading List and the best online index of speculative fiction awards.

New England Science Fiction Association

http://www.nesfa.org

An active club since 1967, their website is particularly notable for reading lists and links to NESFA Press, a wonderful republisher of out-of-print classics that every fan should support.

OF Blog of the Fallen

http://www.ofblog.blogspot.com

A strong blog, with lots of reviews, author interviews, polls, and other goodies.

Pat's Fantasy Hotlist

http://fantasyhotlist.blogspot.com

One of the better fantasy blogs, although with perhaps too much emphasis on book giveaways. Still, there's plenty of good content if you dig.

Peter Sykes: Fantasy 100 and Sci-Fi Lists

http://home.austarnet.com.au/petersykes/fantasy100
http://home.austarnet.com.au/petersykes/topscifi/

An Australian fan maintains this ongoing, poll-based list of the top books, films, and television in fantasy and science fiction. The sites include thematic lists and recommended genre Web links.

Publisher Links

http://www.sfsite.com/depts/press01.htm

Maintained by SF Site, this is a list of links to most of the active publishers of science fiction/fantasy.

Reading Group Guides: Science Fiction/Fantasy

http://www.readinggroupguides.com/findaguide/scifi.asp

A collection of reading group guides—with summary, discussion questions, and blurbs from reviews for 40+ science fiction/fantasy books.

Recommended Fantasy Author List

http://www.sff.net/people/Amy.Sheldon/listcont.htm
An extensive archive of annotated fantasy recommendations.

Science Fiction and Fantasy World

http://www.sffworld.com
A comprehensive site, including reviews and active discussion forums.

SciFan

http://www.scifan.com
An excellent bibliographic site, especially notable for thematic lists of science fiction/fantasy books, lists of upcoming releases, and author bibliographies.

Science Fiction and Fantasy Writers of America (SFWA)

http://www.sfwa.org
Of use to book groups, the SFWA website includes science fiction/fantasy news, the Nebula Awards website, and, under "Resources," recent reviews and lists of recommended reading.

Science Fiction Studies

http://www.depauw.edu/sfs/
One of the original academic journals on science fiction, it's been going strong since 1973. Full content from all but the most recent year is available online, including some excellent bibliographies and chronologies.

SF Signal

http://www.sfsignal.com
An active science fiction blog.

SF Site

http://sfsite.com
This comprehensive webzine covers both fantasy and science fiction and changes content twice monthly. Ongoing reviews and the annual editors' and readers' polls are highlights.

SFRevu

http://www.sfrevu.com
A joint American-British venture, with lots of reviews.

The Ultimate Science Fiction Web Guide

http://www.magicdragon.com/UltimateSF/SF-Index.html
A good site with a great deal of information, including a massive timeline and collection of bibliographies, but it has not been updated since 2004.

Science Fiction/Fantasy Book Group Sites

Denver Science Fiction & Fantasy Book Club

http://www.denversfbookclub.com/

Active since 1994, the Denver club has talked about over 200 books. Their website includes a recap of each book with links to reviews and a fun feature: individual member's numerical ratings of each book read.

FACT

http://www.fact.org

The Fandom Association of Central Texas is celebrating 15 years of reading in Austin. Now two groups, including one that meets biweekly, their site includes reading lists back to 1996, links to the group's many writers, and reports from meetings. Their bylaws are also posted online, a good model for groups who want more formality or are pursuing nonprofit tax status.

KGB Fantastic Fiction

http://www.kgbfantasticfiction.org/

Since 2000, the KGB Bar in New York City has been hosting monthly readings of science fiction and fantasy writers. Their website includes archives listing the many marvelous writers they've hosted.

Lambda Sci-Fi

http://www.lambdasf.org/lsf/

A Washington D.C. area gay-lesbian SF/F group. Their reading list since 1999 is posted online, as is a long annotated list of other good science fiction/fantasy reads.

Los Angeles Science Fantasy Society

http://www.lasfsinc.info

The longest running science fiction/fantasy fan group deserves mention. Their website is a grab bag, with a little bit of everything.

Louisville Science Fiction and Fantasy Reader's Group

http://www.oseland.net/sfreader/

Includes the group's reading selections back to 2003, links to related clubs, regional conventions, and recommended reading.

Science Fiction Association of Bergen County

http://sfabc.org

This active organization has an active calendar of guest speakers, reading groups, viewing groups, topical discussions, and a writer's group, as well as online discussions and publications. Look to their site for inspiration on an integrated program of activities that cross the genre.

Author Index

Title and Series Index

Note: Series titles are underlined; book titles are in italic font.

About the Author

NEIL HOLLANDS is also the author of *Read On . . . Fantasy Fiction* (Libraries Unlimited, 2007). He works at Williamsburg Regional Library in Virginia and is the co-leader of the Williamsburg Science Fiction and Fantasy Book Group. He writes regularly for the blogs *Book Group Buzz* and *Blogging for a Good Book*. He contributed a chapter on the future of readers' advisory to *Research-Based Readers' Advisory* (2009) and a chapter on readers' advisory and reference service to a forthcoming volume. His articles on readers' advisory and fantasy fiction have appeared in *Reference & User Services Quarterly*, and he reviews fiction for *Library Journal* and reference books for *Booklist*. He presents frequently at PLA, ALA, Book Expo America, and many state and regional conferences.

Photo by Sharon Hollands.